Hidden Divinity and Re

MW01255974

This collection of new essays written by an international team of scholars is a ground-breaking examination of the problem of divine hiddenness, one of the most dynamic areas in current philosophy of religion. Together the essays constitute a wide-ranging dialogue on the problem. They balance atheistic and theistic standpoints, and they bring to bear not only the standard philosophical perspectives but also insights from Jewish, Muslim, and Eastern Orthodox traditions. The apophatic and the mystical are well represented too. As a result, the volume throws fresh light on this familiar but important topic in the philosophy of religion. In the process, the volume incorporates contemporary work in epistemology, philosophy of mind, and philosophy of language. For all these reasons, this book will be of great interest to researchers and advanced students in philosophy of religion and theology.

ADAM GREEN is an Assistant Professor of Philosophy at Azusa Pacific University. He has published numerous articles in journals, including *Episteme*, *Synthese*, *American Philosophical Quarterly*, *The Monist*, *Religious Studies*, and *European Journal for Philosophy of Religion*.

ELEONORE STUMP is the Robert J. Henle Professor of Philosophy at Saint Louis University. She has published extensively on philosophy of religion, contemporary metaphysics, and medieval philosophy. Her recent publications include *Aquinas* (2003), *Wandering in Darkness: Narrative and the Problem of Suffering* (2010), and *The Oxford Handbook of Aquinas* (co-edited with Brian Davies, 2012).

Hidden Divinity and Religious Belief

New Perspectives

Edited by

Adam Green and Eleonore Stump

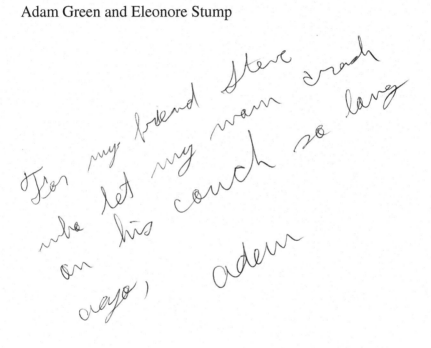

UNIVERSITY PRESS

CAMBRIDGE
UNIVERSITY PRESS

University Printing House, Cambridge CB2 8BS, United Kingdom

One Liberty Plaza, 20th Floor, New York, NY 10006, USA

477 Williamstown Road, Port Melbourne, VIC 3207, Australia

314-321, 3rd Floor, Plot 3, Splendor Forum, Jasola District Centre, New Delhi - 110025, India

79 Anson Road, #06-04/06, Singapore 079906

Cambridge University Press is part of the University of Cambridge.

It furthers the University's mission by disseminating knowledge in the pursuit of
education, learning and research at the highest international levels of excellence.

www.cambridge.org
Information on this title: www.cambridge.org/9781107435032

© Cambridge University Press 2015

First published 2015
First paperback edition 2018

A catalogue record for this publication is available from the British Library

Library of Congress Cataloging in Publication data
Hidden divinity and religious belief : new perspectives / edited
by Adam Green, Eleonore Stump.
    pages   cm
Includes bibliographical references and index.
ISBN 978-1-107-07813-0 (hbk)
1. Theism.   2. Hidden God.   3. God–Knowableness.   4. Knowledge,
Theory of (Religion)   5. Philosophy and religion.   I. Green, Adam, 1981– editor.
BL200.H53   2015
212´.6–dc23   2015028159

ISBN 978-1-107-07813-0 Hardback
ISBN 978-1-107-43503-2 Paperback

For John,
composer, theologian, priest,
and blessing to us both

"What would the world be, once bereft
Of wit and wildness?"
(A slight variation on Poem 33, "Inversnaid,"
by Gerard Manley Hopkins)

Come back to Your servants now, Give back, O Lord, Your light.
The pathways are parting, now we choose.Yet you hide from our sight.
Rupture the heavens, come back to our lives, Come down to your people,
Lord of life.

My Shepherd is the Lord, There is nothing I shall need.
Fresh indeed are the pastures where he'll lead.

Contents

Contributors

SARAH COAKLEY, Norris-Hulse Professor of Divinity, University of Cambridge

HELEN DE CRUZ, Senior Lecturer in Philosophy, Oxford Brookes University

IAN DEWEESE-BOYD, Associate Professor of Philosophy, Gordon College

EVAN FALES, Associate Professor of Philosophy, The University of Iowa

JEROME GELLMAN, Professor of Philosophy, Ben-Gurion University of the Negev, Honorary Affiliate, Australian Catholic University

JOHN GRECO, Leonard and Elizabeth Eslick Chair in Philosophy, Saint Louis University

ADAM GREEN, Assistant Professor of Philosophy, Azusa Pacific University

DANIEL HOWARD-SNYDER, Professor of Philosophy, Western Washington University

JON MCGINNIS, Professor of Philosophy, University of Missouri, St. Louis

PAUL K. MOSER, Professor of Philosophy, Loyola University Chicago

YUJIN NAGASAWA, Professor of Philosophy and Co-Director of the John Hick Centre for Philosophy of Religion at the University of Birmingham

MICHAEL C. REA, Professor of Philosophy, University of Notre Dame

J. L. SCHELLENBERG, Professor of Philosophy, Mount Saint Vincent University

MEGHAN SULLIVAN, Associate Professor of Philosophy, University of Notre Dame

N. N. TRAKAKIS, Senior Lecturer, Australian Catholic University

Acknowledgments

We would like to thank our families and our respective academic communities for their support during the production of this volume. We would like to extend a special thanks to Frank and Sandra Horvath for permission to use their photograph on the cover of this book. We are grateful to Matthew Shea, whose editorial help on this volume was invaluable. We also owe a debt of thanks to Hilary Gaskin and Rosemary Crawley of Cambridge University Press for their excellent help, advice, and patience. And together we are glad to dedicate this volume to Fr. John B. Foley, S.J., composer, theologian, and priest, whose companionship is a blessing to us and to our families.

Introduction

An overview

In 1993, John Schellenberg published *Divine Hiddenness and Human Reason*[1] and thereby stimulated a lively discussion in the philosophical literature on what is now called "the problem of divine hiddenness." Schellenberg assumed three things which at the time seemed relatively uncontroversial: (1) there are many people who don't believe in God but who are not culpable for not believing in God; (2) if there were a God, he would want loving relations with people; and (3) loving relations between God and a human being are at least impeded if the human being does not believe God exists. From these apparently reasonable premises, Schellenberg built an argument for the conclusion that there is no God. There quickly arose an outpouring of philosophical literature on Schellenberg's argument, some of it supportive and some of it critical.[2] In response to this literature, Schellenberg refined his presentation of the argument in a way that made it clear how some of the earlier criticisms of it failed to do justice to the argument.[3] As his revised argument was generally understood, with many of the nuances omitted here for the sake of brevity, it came to something like this:

1. If God exists, then God is perfectly loving, desiring loving relationship with all created persons.
2. If God is perfectly loving, then God would ensure that all persons can participate in relationship with God unless they have excluded themselves through some kind of resistance.
3. There are nonresistant nonbelievers.

   Therefore, God does not exist.

Many philosophers see an analogy between Schellenberg's problem of divine hiddenness and the problem of evil as well as between Schellenberg's argument for the non-existence of God and the argument from evil. The problem

---

[1] Schellenberg (1993).

[2] See, for example, Howard-Snyder and Moser (2002).

[3] Schellenberg (2007).

1

of divine hiddenness has consequently come to be seen as a major problem in current philosophy of religion.

This volume is an attempt to come to grips with this problem in a new, deep way.

The volume begins, reasonably enough, with Schellenberg's explanation of what he sees as the consequences of the problem and his own reflections on it. His essay then sets the stage for the essays that follow.

Part II, "God's Hiddenness: Overlooked Issues," broadens the parameters of the problem of divine hiddenness by bringing to bear on it issues in philosophy of language and additional considerations from the cognitive science of religion. The essays in this section help show additional implications of the problem.

In the next part, "God's Hiddenness: Faith and Skepticism," the essays take account of a great deal of current work on the problem of evil to present the two most basic reactions to the problem of divine hiddenness, the response of faith and the skeptical response that finds the conclusion of the argument from divine hiddenness compelling.

The three subsequent sections attempt to deal with the problem of divine hiddenness by exploring some of its presuppositions and background context.

In Part IV, "Reasons for Hiddenness and Unbelief," the essays avail themselves of recent trends in epistemology, philosophy of mind, philosophical psychology, and philosophy of religion itself to investigate Schellenberg's claim that if God exists, there would be no nonresistant nonbelievers. In one way or another, the essays in this section challenge Schellenberg's claim by suggesting reasons God might have for not being explicitly present to all human beings or by offering explanations of the nonbelief of human beings that do not assign to them either culpability or resistance to God.

In Part V, "God's Hiddenness and God's Nature in the Major Monotheisms," the essays ask whether Islam, Judaism, and some varieties of Christianity, including Eastern Christianity, in fact conceive of God in the way Schellenberg's argument takes for granted. Previous discussions of the problem of divine hiddenness have tended to assume a largely contemporary version of Christian belief. The sophisticated theology philosophically explored in these essays suggests that there are major strands of the major monotheisms that do not accept Schellenberg's characterization of God.

In the final section, "God's Hiddenness: Suffering and Union with God," the essays in effect turn the problem of divine hiddenness upside down. In differing ways, the essays in this section explore the resources of literature and of contemplative or mystical theology for arguing that God's hiddenness is actually a path for human beings to be united with God.

Taken together, all the essays present a deep and powerful reflection on the problem of divine hiddenness and its implications for religious belief.

Background and context

The idea that there is a cognitive gap between human beings and God is not new. One finds within various religions the ready acknowledgment that God's ways are not our ways, that God's ways are higher than our ways. The transcendence of God implies the existence of some sort of gap between creatures and their creator. Far from being something that calls God's existence into question, the unapproachability of God has in fact figured prominently in the worship of God. It is part of what makes God glorious. In particular, the goodness of God is on a scale that human beings simply cannot naturally take in. In Paul's letter to the Romans, for example, Paul extols "the depths of the riches of the knowledge and wisdom of God" as "unsearchable and beyond tracing out" (Rom. 11:33), and the psalmist can glory in a divine mind whose knowledge is "too wonderful for me" (Psalm 139:6).

Yet the psalms also contain haunting refrains like "Why, Lord, do you reject me and hide your face?" (Psalm 88:14) and "How long, oh Lord? Will you forget me forever?" (Psalm 13:1). And Schellenberg has been the most forceful proponent of an argument that the apparent hiddenness of God implies that there is no God.

Schellenberg's original point of departure is the idea that there are honest seekers of the truth who are atheists and agnostics, and there are also individuals who belong to cultures that lack the idea of a personal God altogether. One might think that this apparent fact fits awkwardly with the claim that God exists. A personal God who is unsurpassably great would also be unsurpassably loving since love is something it is better for a personal being to have. An unsurpassably loving God would make sure that anyone who at any time is capable of relating personally to God has it within his or her power to do so. So, if God exists, the only thing that would keep a person out of a personal relationship with God would be some kind of culpable failure to do a good thing which is in that person's power to do. It would appear that one does not have the power to relate to God if one does not yet believe that God exists. Thus, if a loving, personal God existed, God would make sure that no one non-culpably failed to believe in God's existence.

Schellenberg gave a revised formulation of his argument in *The Wisdom to Doubt*[4] where we see several key substitutions in the terms of the argument that draw out themes from Schellenberg's original discussion of the argument and make them explicit within the framing of the argument. He substituted language about resistance for language about culpability and changed talk of something being in one's power to talk of someone's being in a position to participate in a relationship. In this version of his argument, Schellenberg

---

[4] Schellenberg (2007).

put greater emphasis on the claim that if an unsurpassably great God exists, that God would value conscious, interactive relationship. A perfectly loving being would, presumably, value conscious, interactive relationship more than some kind of de re awareness of the existence of God. In his 2007 book, Schellenberg also made sure to focus our attention on various special cases that are especially challenging for the theist. These include people who have lost their faith, people who have sought after the truth their whole lives without coming to believe in God, people who have converted to nontheistic religions, and people who are nontheists because they were always isolated from theistic influence. Even if one could come up with a story that explains some of these cases, Schellenberg thought that it would be hard to come up with an explanation that covers all of them.

In addition to the essays that validate or develop Schellenberg's argument, some of the essays in this volume bring into focus two different critical ways of responding to Schellenberg's line of reasoning. One response focuses on the type of God for whose non-existence Schellenberg is arguing. One can challenge Schellenberg's argument by calling into question either the claim that God's perfection requires relationship or the kind of relationship God would be interested in. For instance, if one stresses the transcendence and ineffability of God, then one must hold lightly any comparison between God's love and human love. This is an important consideration because it is tempting to view God on the model of a loving human parent and then to evaluate God's apparent hiddenness on that model. But it might be that human parallels are inherently misleading. If God is transcendent, then our expectations of the way in which God's love would operate might be very inadequate if they take human love as their model.

A different response to Schellenberg's argument takes the opposite approach. It assumes that God is interested in loving relationships with human beings, but it supposes that closer attention to the nature of relationships undermines Schellenberg's argument. For example, Schellenberg's focus is on human belief that God exists. One might wonder, though, whether the belief that God exists is essential to relationship. If there is a kind of faith that does not require belief, one might think that a relationship can grow in the absence of belief. In fact, it could be a great-making feature of a relationship that it grew in a time of uncertainty.

Furthermore, it may be that greater attention to the nature of relationship reveals relational obstacles that would have to be overcome for desirable divine–human relationships that are not accounted for properly by Schellenberg's discussion. For instance, when someone has a hard time with present relationships because of residual psychological baggage from past relationships, must we say that the problems are culpable ones? Clearly not. A person might be resistant to relationship because of a traumatic experience, but if the resistance is not rooted in one's reflectively endorsed desires and choices, then it may not be the sort of resistance that Schellenberg has in mind when he poses his argument. Another possible complication arises from the nature of love. If love is a matter of two people's enjoying each other just as they are, that is one thing. If love has a level of moral rectitude and self-sacrificial expression built into it, however, then it becomes more plausible that the average person is not entirely receptive to that kind of love.

In addition to these kinds of questions, the problem of divine hiddenness also raises issues about what we value. For example, in trying to identify the sorts of relationships an unsurpassably great God would value, we are in effect reflecting on the kinds of relationships we should value and promote. Is an impersonal benevolence towards others sufficient for human flourishing in relationship, or does human flourishing require something more, such as mutuality and transparency in one's loving relationships?

Finally the problem of hiddenness highlights rival conceptions of epistemic humility. On the one hand, as Schellenberg emphasizes in his essay in this volume, we are limited creatures who may be in the early stages of our history as a species. On this view, the path of epistemic humility seems to require at least entertaining the idea that we will outgrow our current religions as we continue to evolve. On the other hand, the transcendence of God might outstrip our cognitive capacities no matter how long we last as a species, and so the truth about God might have to be revealed to us by God, as the major monotheisms claim God has done. On this view, the path of epistemic humility seems to require learning from and submitting to a tradition or a text. The problem of divine hiddenness therefore also presupposes varying conceptions of the nature and proper expression of epistemic humility.

The essays in detail

In "Divine hiddenness and human philosophy," Schellenberg develops his latest version of the argument from divine hiddenness, taking account of the last twenty years of discussion in his presentation. He also integrates his discussion with reflections on the relevance of evolutionary deep time to religious issues. On his view, a realistic look at human limitations against the backdrop of deep time helps us assess the problem of divine hiddenness with a proper appreciation of what limited human philosophy could be expected to provide. And he concludes with reasons for hope in future progress as regards human comprehension of the truly ultimate in reality.

Meghan Sullivan begins with the fact of religious pluralism. One consequence of the hiddenness of God is that different religions conceive of God in different ways, leading to a pluralism in theology. Her essay investigates the implications of this pluralism for names of God. She asks whether, given pluralism, we have reason to believe that the three Abrahamic faiths all have access to a functioning divine name word; and she considers reasons for supposing that we do not. This is a skeptical argument, of course; and her essay concludes by surveying responses to the skeptical argument and their costs.

Helen De Cruz focuses on work by cognitive scientists who have argued that religion is a cognitively natural phenomenon: religious beliefs arise spontaneously without explicit instruction, and belief in one or more gods is cross-culturally ubiquitous. She argues that more recent work in cognitive science of religion indicates that theism nevertheless requires some informal learning and that there is substantial individual variation in theistic belief, correlating with theory of mind, analytic skills, and other cognitive capacities. She attempts to show that cognitive science of religion can shed light on the question of reasonable, that is, nonresistant, nonbelief, and she examines the plausibility of responses to the problem of divine hiddenness (such as the epistemic distance theodicy) in the light of these findings in cognitive science of religion.

Paul Moser argues that questions about divine hiddenness can benefit from clarification of the nature of God's love. In his view, God's love should be understood as a kind self-sacrifice of a particular redemptive kind, so that God's revelation of himself to human beings needs to occur in a context of self-sacrifice. Consequently, divine revelation can be expected to be absent or hidden in any context where self-sacrifice is absent. For Moser, the implications for conceiving of God's love as self-sacrificial challenges human beings not just to think but also to act in profoundly redemptive ways. The result is, in his view, a new practical alternative to familiar ways of inquiring about God's presence and hiddenness.

By contrast, Evan Fales responds to this argument by Moser, and analogous arguments in the discussions of the problem of evil, by focusing on particular biblical texts, especially the book of Job. Fales argues that proper interpretation of such texts, taken to be revealed by Judaism and Christianity, show that the kind of arguments given to reconcile divine hiddenness and divine love cannot be sustained. For Fales, if there were a God, he would have to be called to account for his injustice, not only with regard to the suffering regularly discussed in connection with the problem of evil but also with regard to the suffering occasioned by divine hiddenness.

John Greco approaches the problem of divine hiddenness by considering explanations for unbelief. A common explanation, both in religious tradition and among contemporary theistic philosophers, is that unbelief signals a cognitive and/or moral flaw in the nonbeliever. In opposition to this line of thought, Greco considers recent advances in the epistemology of religion that should make theists skeptical of that diagnosis. On his view, contemporary religious epistemology tends to ground belief in God in a) religious experience, and b) testimony from the faithful. These recent approaches stress the epistemic importance of social context and especially membership in a community. But then there is a readily available "no-fault" explanation for unbelief. To some extent, in fact, Greco's position makes unbelief expected.

Daniel Howard-Snyder challenges Schellenberg's account of what a loving God would do. By way of objection to Schellenberg's argument, Howard-Snyder argues that we should take the long view of particular relationships between God and individual human beings. It is tempting to think that, for God to be unsurpassably loving, at every time God must be open to being in a positively meaningful and reciprocal relationship with every created person capable of such relationship. Openness to relationship entails that one would never do anything by either commission or omission that would have the result that the other was prevented from participating in that relationship. And so it is tempting to suppose that every human being at every time should be able to participate in relationship with God just by trying. It may be tempting to think this, but Howard-Snyder thinks we should resist the temptation. Ordinary cases help us to see that love does not always demand openness of this sort, and a lack of openness can actually promote a better long-term relationship in certain circumstances.

Like Howard-Snyder, Adam Green draws our attention to diachronic elements of relationship with a special emphasis on the way in which prior states in a relationship help make possible a deeper connection achieved later. Green uses attachment theory and the psychology of shared attention to explore how a closer attention to the way in which we come to know and experience other human persons might help the theist address Schellenberg's argument. Green argues, first, that divine hiddenness is an experiential problem. He then makes the case that our deepest experiences of other persons in the natural realm involve a cultivated attunement to the other person. Acquiring such an attunement can be hindered, however, through our relational histories. Acquiring a bad model from one's prior experiences may not be culpable while nonetheless forming an obstacle to future relationship. An attachment paradigm helps to explain both (i) why it is that God might be more limited than one might initially suppose in the kinds of experiences that God can provide, and (ii) how it could be the case that one could have inculpable, nonresistant nonbelief in a world that contains a loving God desirous of relationship.

In the four essays that follow, the authors mine different traditions within the major monotheisms for insight into the problem of divine hiddenness with a special emphasis on the way in which the transcendence or ineffability of God changes the problem.

Jon McGinnis shows that the contemporary debate over divine hiddenness might be hard to fathom from a medieval Islamic perspective. McGinnis argues that one may go so far as to say that the problem of divine hiddenness would have been hidden from many medieval Muslim intellectuals. For example, the

idea of a personal relation with God would have struck some of these thinkers as ill conceived. God's perfection implies that, though he brings forth and
sustains a good creation, God is not interested in the sort of reciprocal relationship that Schellenberg has in mind. For McGinnis, the perspective of these
Muslim philosophers and theologians exposes certain implicit assumptions in
the debate over divine hiddenness that one might otherwise fail to appreciate
properly.

Jerome Gellman takes a Hasidic perspective on the problem of divine hiddenness. Gellman presents a Hasidic interpretation of the *aqedah*, in which
God's permanent hiddenness is the central theme. According to this interpretation of the story, God tested Abraham in order to teach Abraham God's
unfathomable transcendence. Gellman presents Hegel's attack on Judaism for
having a God who is forever hidden and therefore beyond appeasement. And
he shows that, by contrast, the Hasidic interpretation of the *aqedah* turns the
tables on Hegel's contempt for Judaism by acclaiming God's essential hiddenness. When the angel abruptly stops Abraham from going through with the
sacrifice, Abraham learns the importance of letting go attempts to comprehend
God or to unite with God in this life. Gellman finishes by emphasizing the religious significance of the yearning for God that is at the heart of this approach.

N. N. Trakakis highlights the contribution of Eastern understandings of
the nature of God, with their emphasis on God's ineffability. Trakakis argues
that divine hiddenness underlines the distinctness of God from creatures. As
Trakakis sees it, the hiddenness of God discloses the confused and defective
nature of the anthropomorphic metaphysics of divinity that takes God to be
literally a personal agent.

Finally, in this section, Michael Rea considers the problem of divine hiddenness from the perspective of Western Christian thought in the apophatic
tradition. He argues that in the thought of apophatic theologians, the phenomenon of divine hiddenness seems to be regarded as a perfectly obvious consequence of divine transcendence. He explores the question whether attention to
divine transcendence mitigates the problem of divine hiddenness, or whether
the robust theology of divine transcendence that one commonly finds in the
work of apophatic theologians instead underemphasizes those intuitions about
divine perfection that render the problem acute.

The three essays in the final section of the volume use mystical and literary
elements to bring home the existential dimension of hiddenness while helping
us to think more deeply about the nature of the problem Schellenberg points
to. Sarah Coakley argues that the problem of divine hiddenness represents a
misplaced dilemma which needs to be re-construed. Using John of the Cross's
account of the dark night of the soul, she distinguishes three different meanings of epistemic darkness in play in John's work. She argues that, according
to John, the fear that God is hiding is actually a mistake of spiritual beginners,

as is the correlative desire that God become present in a satisfyingly obvious way. She concludes with a speculative reflection on the conditions under which an atheistic account of divine hiddenness might consider John of the Cross's alternative narrative as probative.

Yujin Nagasawa proposes a new response to the problem of divine hiddenness which utilizes recent work in the philosophy of mind while dialoguing with Shusaku Endo's novel *Silence*. Appealing to Jerry Foder's concept of epistemic boundedness and Colin McGinn's concept of cognitive closure, he argues that the hiddenness of God can be attributed to our significant epistemic or cognitive limitations in relation to the infinite nature of God. On Nagasawa's view, it is not possible for God to be manifested to human beings in such a way that God's existence is evident to all non-culpable or nonresistant people. On the basis of these considerations, Nagasawa tries to sketch an inclusivist or pluralist hypothesis regarding religious belief systems using the spiritual journey of the protagonist in *Silence* as a model.

And, finally, Ian Deweese-Boyd examines the way in which mysticism of a lyric kind can illumine the problem. Throughout his life, the English Jesuit poet Gerard Manley Hopkins struggled with desolation over what he saw as his spiritually, intellectually, and artistically unproductive life; and in these periods, he experienced God's absence in a particularly intense way. What Hopkins faced was the existential problem of suffering and hiddenness, a problem widely recognized to be left relatively untouched by conceptual explanations. Deweese-Boyd argues that Hopkins's poems themselves speak to such existential suffering and create a space in which those who suffer can meet God, even if only to contend with God. Hopkins's poems thus suggest a way to find God in the very experience of God's hiddenness, thereby making God present even in divine absence.

Adam Green
Eleonore Stump

Part I

The Argument from God's Hiddenness against God's Existence

1   Divine hiddenness and human philosophy

J. L. Schellenberg

1   General background to the arguments

Planet Earth has been hosting life for about 3.5 billion years now. Anatomically modern humans arose some 200,000 years ago; behaviorally modern humans practicing something we might recognize as religion probably a good deal later, perhaps as recently as 50,000 years ago. And only a few thousand years ago – in the final tenth of that 50,000 years – did the Earth's current religious traditions and systematic inquiry in philosophy and science come into being.

At 200,000 years of age, *Homo sapiens* is still a fairly young and spry species – its ancestor *Homo erectus* endured more than seven times as long. And the consensus view in science is that Earth will remain habitable for at least another billion years. So especially if we put our much-vaunted inventiveness to work in the right way, our species may just be starting out on its evolutionary journey. Even if our staying power only matches that of *H. erectus*, if religion survives as long as we do we have just completed *one thirtieth* of the total lifespan of human religion. And if we think of that future billion years instead, and allow our imaginations to contemplate intelligent species that may follow us and outdo us in every way, we will see that we *may* have just completed the first and also the least mature *20,000th* of the total history of religion on our planet.

Applying scientific timescales in this way does rather put things in perspective! There is a Great Disparity here between past and potential future that – given our humbly evolved brains and the timescales they can comfortably manage – we ignore all too easily.[1] Suppose we now bring human philosophy into the discussion. Science has produced intellectual wonders, given our inventiveness and despite those limited brains, though often only by resisting what seems natural or intuitive. But philosophy has in its sights even more

For their helpful comments on previous drafts of this paper, I offer my grateful thanks to Eleonore Stump, Adam Green, and Alexander Pruss.

[1] Notice that I speak only of what *may* be the case, and so nothing said here implies what is sometimes called a progressive view of evolution – a view that sees evolutionary processes as inherently such as to lead to improvement over time. Whether we or other intelligent species can help to *make* evolution progressive is another question.

fundamental and much tougher questions, for which nothing analogous to scientific methods has yet been devised. And here our results are, it must be admitted, less spectacular. At least so far. Certainly this is the case if the inability of many minds to achieve anything close to reasoned consensus on answers to these questions is taken as dimming the light of achievement.

Among the questions philosophy has addressed in its extremely short life, even shorter than religion's, are of course questions *about* religion, which offers its own (quite divergent) answers to fundamental questions – usually ones featuring ideas of realities beyond nature and of the special experiences and practices involved in coming to know them. Given the temporal context I have set out, and its own modest track record, philosophy's task could hardly be regarded as complete before it has thoroughly examined a representative set of the distinctive ideas about fundamental questions to be found in religion as we know it today around the world, and sought to determine their intellectual status. This has not yet occurred. And that is not all. For given the (epistemically) possible primitivity of the species, philosophy clearly ought also to be open to important variations on religious themes that haven't been thought of yet – willing to stretch the religious imagination to see what else it may yield.

These parts of philosophy's task clearly fall to what we call *philosophy of religion*. But in the West – and I expect I am writing mainly for Western readers – philosophy of religion has been largely preoccupied with one religious idea, that of theism, and it looks to be moving into a narrower and deeper version of this preoccupation, one focused on specifically Christian ideas, rather than broadening out and coming to grips with its full task.[2] Though distressing, given the temporal context as I have set it out, this is perhaps not surprising. Religion has a powerful hold on many human beings, including human thinkers. And the nascent field of study known as cognitive science of religion (CSR) has already provided striking evidence of the powerful hold that *agential* religious ideas – ideas of personal gods or of a personal God – might be expected to have on our minds, given our evolutionary heritage.[3]

Here the fact of metaphysically naturalistic approaches in philosophy, flushed with the success of natural explanations in science, might seem to push in another direction. But it is interesting to see that it does not. For most naturalists too assume that theistic *God*-centered religion must succeed if any does. Naturalism or theism. These seem to be the only options that many see. The harshest critics of religion, including philosophers such as Daniel Dennett,

---

[2] I take it that the recent rise of 'analytic theology' is symptomatic here – and this primarily because its proponents and practitioners appear to think it doesn't matter whether what they are doing is called theology or philosophy. See, for example, Wolterstorff (2009).

[3] Without properly taking account of our place in time, many theistic thinkers appear to regard these developments as possibly spelling an advantage for their view. See, for example, Barrett (2004).

seem to think *their* job is done when they have, to their own satisfaction, criticized personalistic, *agential* conceptions of a divine reality. Dennett, specifically, tells us that "religion without *God* or *gods* is like a vertebrate without a backbone" (emphasis in the original).[4]

Now it may not be enough here to point Dennett in the direction of nontheistic non-Western religious ideas. Perhaps because of the sorts of cognitive factors emphasized by CSR, even nontheistic traditions like Buddhism and Taoism, *at the popular level*, still involve much urgent worship of and supplication to god-like personal beings. Dennett has a point, and early CSR results may support it. It takes work for human beings to think of the divine as something other than or more than personal. That – or certain special experiences often called mystical. The presence of the latter gives the lie to the notion that our brains must inevitably configure apparent divine revelations personally. Experiences appearing to be of a very different and altogether more mysterious and puzzling divine reality also occur throughout the world, even if their number is relatively small; and those who have them include some of the most profoundly good and wise among us.[5]

Such is the (most general) background I need for the arguments I will make and entertain. Much of this background will be common knowledge for my readers. All of it should be.

2 Ultimate hiddenness

As already suggested, in human philosophy's engagement with religion there have over time – *human* time – arisen certain reasoned defenses of the claim that the ultimate divine reality is a God, a being unsurpassably great who is a person or very much like a person, possessing all power, all knowledge, all goodness and having created every other concrete thing. Arguments against the existence of such a being have of course also emerged and been discussed. Now in the present climate of "theism or naturalism," it will easily be assumed that the latter arguments are implicitly arguments for a *naturalistic* picture of ultimate reality. This fits well with awareness of the bias in favor of a science-oriented picture of the fundamental nature of things that was mentioned earlier. (Some theists may see even the content of section 1 of this paper as expressing such a bias.) And given awareness of this bias, one may reasonably ask: why should we privilege *that* ultimate narrative over others, such as our God-centered one, to which much human experience attests?

---

[4] Dennett (2006, 9).
[5] For some interesting and relevant evidence acquired by a religion journalist, see Gallagher (2002).

I have said that this is a reasonable question. And it is. Indeed, I take it that one of the interesting consequences of a temporalist sensitivity of the sort recommended in section 1 is that we come to notice how *science itself helps us see its reasonableness.* At perhaps a very early stage of evolutionary development, we should – as I have already suggested – remain open to learning that nature isn't all there is. But such temporalism by the same token suggests that any restriction of non-naturalistic alternatives to theism would be an error. It is indeed other, religious pictures of ultimacy *such as* the God-centered one to which we should attend in the philosophy of religion at an early stage of inquiry.

To facilitate my own discussion of such matters (I hope it will also be helpful for others), I have introduced the nontheistic label "ultimism" to stand for the more general religious idea of a reality that is triply ultimate: metaphysically, axiologically, and soteriologically.[6] Theism entails ultimism, but the converse does not hold. This means that ultimism provides breathing room for other conceptions of the divine – both those extant and those we may develop in the future. Of course other general conceptions might also be utilized for this purpose. We might, for example, speak somewhat more modestly of triple transcendence rather than of triple ultimacy. But theism is an ultimistic idea, and so ultimism allows us to expose most clearly the idea of alternatives to theism. And a frame of reference sensitive to temporalist considerations may greatly increase our interest in those alternatives. Philosophers of religion should develop and examine *various* elaborations of ultimism, ready to find one or another of them well supported so as to gain great metaphysical and spiritual illumination but equally ready – given our place in time – to learn that each or any is an early and unsuccessful attempt to say what a religious Ultimate would be, or that the notion of a religious Ultimate is incoherent or for some other reason clearly is *not* instantiated in any way. (This allows us to at least begin to see the difference between philosophy of religion and any form of theology. Theology appropriately assumes that there *is* an ultimate divine reality, and typically will take the parameters of *one* detailed conception of such a reality as its own.)

We are ready now to introduce the basic hiddenness idea. Assuming only a temporalist sensitivity and an ultimistic framework for religious investigation, what might we say about the concept of divine hiddenness? It will, I expect, seem very natural to say that the nature of the ultimate divine reality, should there be one, might very well lie far outside the grasp of evolved humans at an early stage of investigation. Even if there is a divine reality, *that* there is and *what* it is might alike be hidden from us, at least in the sense that many lack the belief that there is such a reality and/or a true belief as to what it is. This should

---

[6] This label was first introduced in my *Prolegomena to a Philosophy of Religion* (Schellenberg, 2005c, ch. 1).

not be at all surprising. And the fact that it should not be surprising, properly understood, adds fuel to the religious quest.

Things may however be very different when we turn our attention to this or that *elaborated* ultimism, such as theism. Perhaps the detailed content added by such an elaboration to the general content of ultimism will suffice to – in some sense – make hiddenness *surprising* rather than something that we might well expect to find. Perhaps we will even see that the general or wide availability for such finite persons as there may be of the relevant form of religious belief is *entailed* by some such claim, and, noting that religious belief as found in the world today is not thus configured, rightly conclude that the claim is false.

Just this is what a certain hiddenness argument I have developed alleges in response to theism's elaboration of ultimism – an elaboration that, as we have seen, employs the concept of a *person*. My central question in the present essay is how philosophy should regard this argument for atheism (i.e., for the denial of personal ultimism). It is important to notice that because of the general background filled in by section 1, if the hiddenness argument is successful in philosophy, the right response will not be to infer that naturalism is true but only that the religious quest continues.

3   Personal love and openness to relationship

Central to the hiddenness argument is an emphasis on the value in persons of a sort of love involving openness to relationship. Before setting out that argument, it will be good to spend some time with the concepts and claims involved here.

First, let's notice what theism's (or personal ultimism's) axiological component entails. The Ultimate, if a person, would have to be an *unsurpassably great* person.[7] The value of power and knowledge as well as benevolence in persons is commonly highlighted by philosophers who spell out the content of theism. But, although neglected, the value of love in persons is certainly no less obvious.[8] So we have to say that an unsurpassably great person could not be other than *unsurpassably loving* toward other persons.

---

[7] I'm assuming we have got our present understanding of a person in view for the purpose of this elaboration of ultimism; otherwise all bets are off. Perhaps the concept of a person will evolve in the future of culture in such a way as to allow for possibilities that our present concept does not allow for, but the theistic elaboration of ultimism I have in mind is built only from materials presently available.

[8] One philosopher who has not neglected love – who, indeed, has had a lot more to say about it than I have – is Eleonore Stump. See especially chs 5 and 6 of her recent book *Wandering in Darkness: Narrative and the Problem of Suffering* (Stump, 2010). Developing a view held by Aquinas, but with subtle reasoning of her own and attention to competing accounts in the recent philosophical literature, Stump argues that love includes two intertwined desires, a desire for the good of the other and a desire for union. This view is broadly in line with my own emphasis on

But what sort of love are we supposing to be a great-making property if we say this? The first thing to note is implicit in the previous paragraph: love of the sort in question is more than just goodness as commonly construed, which is to say more than just benevolence. This "more" involves being in some way aimed at relationship – a conscious and reciprocal relationship that is positively meaningful, allowing for a deep sharing. Call such a relationship a *personal* relationship.[9] Even supreme benevolence may be expressible from a distance. But the one who loves desires to come close to the object of love. The one who loves desires to share *herself* in personal relationship, and is of this disposition so long as love persists.

This is not an unfamiliar phenomenon in human life. Quite the contrary: the disposition involved here is well known, widely regarded as being of great value in a person. The paradigms of love known to us, such as loving parents or siblings or friends, have no trouble maintaining it always. So why have philosophers of religion tended to ignore it when thinking about the properties that a personal Ultimate would have to possess? I will not enter into this issue here, except to say that it may be recent cultural evolution outside theology – including the work of feminists, and all those who have loosened the grip on us of the "strong and solitary male" which even much traditional theology reflects – that we have to thank here. This makes virtually unavoidable for us in the twenty-first century an important insight concerning the great value of relational love, and forces philosophers who have been visited by this insight to apply it when giving content to personal ultimism.

As my reference to sharing already suggests, love does *entail* benevolence even if it also goes beyond it. At least if we are looking for a great-making property that ought to be built into a personal form of ultimism, we will say that love desires to express benevolence within the context of a personal relationship that is valued for its own sake. Obviously God has a great deal to give within the context of such a relationship – more than any other possible lover! – so the component of benevolence will help us see how relational love must be a great-making property in God. But the emphasis on valuing personal relationship "for its own sake" is at least as important, and it arises here for two main reasons.[10]

God being open to personal relationship instead of just exercising benevolence from a distance, discussed below.
[9] Philosophers are very good at distinguishing kinds of things, including kinds of relationships, and it may be tempting for some to ignore the specific content I am giving to 'personal relationship' here and to suppose it sufficient for the relevant sort of love that *some* kind of relationship be made possible. That temptation should be resisted by anyone who can see that love of the sort I have in mind is a great-making property and intends to take seriously the argument to follow.
[10] There is also a third reason, which I shall only mention. We are explicating a sort of love that is necessarily tied to the valuing of personal relationship. But where relationship is valued only instrumentally it will only contingently be connected to one's aims (perhaps in another situation there would be something better I could do for you than seeking to be personally related to you).

First, valuing personal relationship for its own sake belongs to the very nature of such love. Robert Adams puts this well: "The ideal of Christian love includes not only benevolence but also desire for certain kinds of personal relationship, for their own sake. Were that not so, it would be strange to call it 'love.' It is an abuse of the word 'love' to say that one *loves* a person ... if one does not care, except instrumentally, about one's relation to that object."[11]

Second, if God seeks personal relationship with capable finite persons, God must do so for its own sake since God will value the persons involved in the relationship for *their* own sakes. God's valuing for its own sake a relationship with a person, in other words, can be seen as a function of God's valuing each relatum of the relationship for its own sake.

This idea will perhaps be more controversial, so let's spell it out. If God values a finite person for her own sake then God values for its own sake whatever makes her the person she is as distinct from other persons. This will involve valuing for their own sake whatever central dispositions contribute to making her the person she is as distinct from other persons. But then when the behavioral and other dispositions of that person *express* those central dispositions in a positively meaningful way, as will be the case when they relate her personally to God, God will likewise value for its own sake the former dispositions. Hence if they do relate her personally to God, then God must value this side of the relationship for its own sake. From the other side, and at the same time, if God values God's own being for its own sake then this will in a similar way lead to God valuing for its own sake the dispositions involved should God become personally related to the other individual, which must express God's intrinsically valuable nature, and thus to God valuing this side of the relationship for its own sake. But if God values both sides of the relationship for their own sakes, then God must value the relationship as a whole for its own sake. Now God, being perfect, *will* value God's own being and that of *every* other person for its own sake, recognizing their great intrinsic value. It follows that it is a normative fact about God's relation to finite persons, and not just a fact about the nature of love, that when God loves such persons, God values a relationship with them for its own sake.[12]

---

[11] Adams (1987, 187–8).

[12] A few comments on this reasoning. If God values me for my own sake then it must be me as distinct from other persons that is valued. A generic valuing of me as an instance of humanity, for example, would hardly do. For then if another human were instantaneously substituted for me, nothing would change: an instance of humanity would remain available for valuing. But surely if God values me for my own sake and I ceased to exist, something of value *would be* lost. A problem may also seem to arise for the case where a finite person is evil. How could God value for their own sake the central dispositions of such a person? Well, either the person retains a capacity for relationship with God or not. If not, then the case is irrelevant to our discussion, as will be seen in a moment. If so, then there must be something of redeeming value that remains. We should also not neglect to notice that we cannot infer from the fact that some *actual humans* are evil that God would create or allow to come into existence evil beings, without illegitimately

The little phrase "for its own sake" in my earlier statement "love seeks to express benevolence within the context of a personal relationship that is valued for its own sake" is therefore rather important here – much more important than many realize who have discussed the hiddenness argument.[13] The distinctive attitude of love is aimed at personal relationship – *benevolently* aimed, to be sure, but still aimed at personal relationship, and, especially in God, for its own sake too. Without being aimed at personal relationship for its own sake, an attitude cannot count as divine love.

Let us now approach the matter of what the hiddenness argument needs from this account of love by distinguishing certain attitudes toward personal relationship a God might be said to have whose love involved being "aimed at" personal relationship with finite creatures. Notice that if God is unsurpassably loving, then God must always love finite creatures and so the attitude will be one that we should expect God always to display. We might, I suppose, consider a disposition to *force* personal relationship on finite persons – though that can also swiftly be excluded because of its incompatibility with any number of divine attributes, and probably also with the nature of a personal relationship. We might further consider God always *valuing* personal relationship, or *seeking* personal relationship, or *desiring* personal relationship, or *strongly promoting or preserving* personal relationship through such things as signs and wonders or overwhelmingly powerful religious experiences, and also God always *being open* to personal relationship. Seeking presumably would here include both desiring and valuing but could operate subtly and without strong promotion. (Later there will be an emphasis on believing that God exists, but it is very important to distinguish between being in such a state of belief and God being present to one's experience – let alone overwhelmingly present or displayed through signs and wonders.) Such seeking, at a minimum, seems required by any love that is by its very nature aimed at personal relationship, and seeking normally requires openness. (I say "normally" because there are possible and generally unusual circumstances in which a lover may lack the resources to accommodate the possible *consequences* of openness, that is, to make them consistent with the flourishing of all relevant parties and of any relationship that may exist or come to exist between them. But since God is not such a lover, we may ignore this qualification hereafter.[14]) It is this openness to which the hiddenness argument will appeal, so let's have a closer look at it.

assuming that our world is created by God and thus that God exists. As I shall be emphasizing later on, a philosopher must remain open to the possibility that if God would create persons at all, these would be persons very different from those that actually exist.

[13] For a recent example, see Evans (2010, 163–4).

[14] I have given much argument in support of this latter claim elsewhere. Some of it is summarized toward the end of section 4.

If one is always open in the sense I intend then, even if one does not actively seek or promote personal relationship with another person capable of participating in such relationship (i.e., possessing the cognitive and affective properties required to do so[15]), one makes sure that there is nothing one ever does (in a broad sense including omissions) that would have the result of making such relationship *unavailable* to the other, preventing her from being able to relate personally to one when she tries to do so. So for God to always be open to personal relationship with a relevantly capable finite person P in a manner expressing unsurpassable love is for God to ensure that there is never something *God* does that prevents P from being able, should she seek to do so, to participate in personal relationship with God just by trying. Let us say that if P is thus able, at a time, then P is *in a position* to exercise her relevant capacities at that time and to then participate in personal relationship with God. (Notice that none of this implies that participation in personal relationship with God, should P decide in favor of it, would be easy: perhaps it will be hard to relate properly to God.) P may not want relationship or even to be reminded of her religious options, and so may through resistance of God, which would have to involve self-deception, herself produce a situation in which she is unable to relate personally to God, just like that, without first undoing the behavior that led to it. But unless P is resistant in this way at a time, P will find it possible to participate in personal relationship with God should she try, and to do so then. Never will P find the door to such relationship closed. This, at the very minimum, is required if God unsurpassably loves P in a manner aimed at personal relationship with P. It would be, to use Adams's word, an "abuse" of the word "love" to say that God displays unsurpassable love towards finite persons, of the sort distinct from bare benevolence and aimed at personal relationship, if one were to think of God as doing any less.

It may be replied, however, that the word "open" I am using wins its rhetorical power illicitly, by suggesting that not to be "open" means to be "closed" and thus not even *desiring* a personal relationship. There is the possibility of partial openness or quasi-openness – openness need not be an all-or-nothing business. Even if at a certain time I am unable to participate in relationship with God *then*, God may still make it possible for me to do things that will make such a relationship available to me in the future. Wouldn't this count as a sort of openness to personal relationship on the part of God?

But for God's attitude toward personal relationship with you *at the time in question* the word "closed" is perfectly appropriate. It's important not to get distracted from this point. And if it is hard to see why consistent openness should

---

[15] In the case of personal relationship with God, these would involve such things as a capacity at the time in question to feel the presence of God, recognizing it as such; a capacity to exhibit attitudes of trust, gratitude, and obedience to God, and so on.

be built into our idea of God's unsurpassable love, then it may be worthwhile contemplating a bit more the paradigms of loving people in our experience, mentioned earlier. For such people – parents, siblings, friends, teachers – such consistent openness is taken quite for granted: this is where things *start* in the story of their interaction with us. It would be absurd for someone to take as a *goal* someone else's openness to relationship with them while holding that they are already unsurpassably loving toward them.

Notice the fit here between such an emphasis on love and personal ultimism's *soteriological* component. Theism, to count as a religious idea, must have soteriological content: it must be possible for the value of the Ultimate to be in some way communicated to finite persons, if we are working with a religious notion. The concept of ultimism helps us keep this point in focus. And it is natural, when thinking about the soteriological content of theism, to understand it in terms of personal relationship with the person who is divine. Love seeks just such relationship. So there is a match between axiology and soteriology here, as well as a religious and philosophical grounding for the hiddenness argument's emphasis on the openness to personal relationship entailed by God's love.

Some theistic religious traditions – for example, the Christian tradition – have emphasized love in a similar way, but this alone is not a good reason for philosophers, seeking to understand a personal form of ultimism, to include such an emphasis. Nor should philosophers be influenced by the *ambivalence* about love one will quickly note when one looks beneath the surface of the traditions in question. "Yes, God loves us, but an explicit personal relationship with God may not always be possible because of mysterious divine purposes." Or: "Yes, God loves us, but an explicit personal relationship with God is often to be enjoyed in heaven not here on Earth." It is not hard to see why the ambivalence arises: the reason is the very hiddenness problem that this essay is about, combined with theology's prerogative to assume that the way the world is somehow reflects the purposes of God. It cannot be overstated that philosophy has no such prerogative. It has no right to say such a thing as that God's love should be interpreted in a limited way because this is all that is compatible with the actual world, and we know that God exists and has created the actual world! Again, this is not philosophy but theology. Philosophy should take the concept of an ultimate divine reality and think for itself about what a *personal* filling out of such a concept amounts to. When it does, it cannot help recognizing and without ambivalence affirming the importance of unsurpassable love. If that should lead, as the hiddenness argument says it does lead, to the conclusion that no personal Ultimate actually exists, then philosophy must give up that idea and move on to consider others.

4   The hiddenness argument

The form I shall give to the hiddenness argument in a moment reflects what I regard as the importance of starting "far enough back" or reasoning "from above," using necessary truths as premises wherever possible. The strongest hiddenness reasoning will be thus grounded, instead of reasoning "from below," perhaps with the absence of signs and wonders for religious seekers too swiftly read into hiddenness language by the one who wishes to use it in defense of atheism. The sort of approach most likely to yield durable results involves working out what hiddenness-related facts would be absent from the world if an unsurpassably great person were present in it, allowing the problematic phenomenon to *emerge* and receive its shape from reflection on the idea of God of the sort that is found in section 3. This is what I mean by starting "from above." Furthermore, by seeking to have as premises only necessary truths about persons and about love (or else evident empirical facts), the argument can hope to find a hearing even in a climate of evolutionary skepticism of the sort that might be produced by careful reflection on considerations such as those set out in section 1.

As already stated, the hiddenness argument is focused on a requirement of openness to personal relationship. A doxastic consequence of this requirement is exposed by the following general principle about openness and non-openness. I call it *Not Open* because it identifies a condition in which, at a certain time, a person B clearly is not open to personal relationship with a second person A:

Not Open
Necessarily, if a person A, without having brought about this condition through resistance of personal relationship with a person B, is at some time in a state of nonbelief in relation to the proposition that B exists, *where B at that time knows this and could ensure that A's nonbelief is at that time changed to belief*, then it is not the case that B is open at the time in question to having a personal relationship with A then.

After all, a personal relationship is a conscious, reciprocal relationship, and a conscious relationship is a relationship one recognizes oneself to be in. Given these facts, one clearly cannot even get started in a personal relationship without *believing that the other party exists*. Now belief, as most contemporary philosophers would agree, is involuntary in the sense that one cannot choose to believe something at a time just by trying to. So by not revealing his existence B is doing something that makes it impossible for A to participate in personal relationship with B at the relevant time even should she try to do so, and this, according to our definition of openness, is precisely what is involved in B's not being open to having such a relationship with A then.

Perhaps someone will still be inclined to resist at this point by saying that *hope* or even a certain kind of beliefless *faith* could take the place of belief, at least at the start of a meaningful conscious relationship, and so B can be open to such relationship with A even while not enabling the belief in question for A.[16] Applying this to the religious case, if at some later stage belief arose, and at the end of her life the person in question were to be asked when she thinks her personal relationship with God began, would she be *mistaken* if she were to pick the time when her religious hope or faith began, rather than the time when she came to believe?

Well, if she uses the phrase "personal relationship" in the same way we are using it she would be – a conscious relationship is one you recognize yourself to be in as opposed to hoping you're in. (One can't solve the hiddenness problem just by noting that the terms it employs and to which it gives certain senses can be used in different senses.) But to get at the deeper issue here: when belief comes to the person in our thought experiment, who had been under the impression that there might be no God, the change of her perceived relation to God will be a change not just in degree but in *kind*. It is much different than, say, a move from hoping with intensity x that God exists to hoping this with intensity x + 1 or even x + 20. Indeed, in a very real sense now *everything* has changed for her, for what she hoped has (as she sees it) come true! And it is in part because of this difference for the one she loves that the one who loves him will naturally want this to be where things *start* in the story of their interaction, as mentioned before. So from both perspectives, the perspective of the lover and that of the one loved, the relationship made possible by belief is a different relationship than any left to subsist on hope or nonbelieving faith.[17]

Against this background, together with the more general background provided by the previous three sections of this paper, the force of the hiddenness argument for philosophers looking to assess a personal elaboration of ultimism may be apparent:

(1) If God exists, then God is perfectly loving toward such finite persons as there may be. [Premise]

(2) If God is perfectly loving toward such finite persons as there may be, then for any capable finite person S and time t, God is at t open to being in a

---

[16] I am grateful to Daniel Howard-Snyder for pressing me on this point.

[17] For those who disagree, I note that, without losing force, the argument about to be stated could be slightly revised to meet their objection. Just revise (4) in such a way that, instead of referring to nonresistant nonbelief, it refers to *nonresistantly being in a cognitive condition, in relation to the proposition that God exists, that is incompatible with then being able to participate in a personal relationship with God just by trying should one seek to do so*, with this cognitive condition conjunctively construed, cashed out in terms of being nonbelieving *and* without nonbelieving faith *and* without nonbelieving hope. And then also make the appropriate corresponding revisions elsewhere in the argument. I myself think this cognitive condition need not be thus construed, since it clearly is as stated in the text. But even if you disagree, by introducing a conjunctive alternative you will not prevent the hiddenness argument from succeeding, since there are or have been plenty of finite persons, capable of personal relationship with God and nonresistant, who instantiate all of its conjuncts.

positively meaningful and reciprocal conscious relationship (a personal relationship) with S at t. [Premise]

(3) If God exists, then for any capable finite person S and time t, God is at t open to being in a personal relationship with S at t. [1, 2 by Hypothetical Syllogism]

(4) If for any capable finite person S and time t, God is at t open to being in a personal relationship with S at t, then for any capable finite person S and time t, it is not the case that S is at t nonresistantly in a state of nonbelief in relation to the proposition that God exists. [Premise]

(5) If God exists, then for any capable finite person S and time t, it is not the case that S is at t nonresistantly in a state of nonbelief in relation to the proposition that God exists. [3, 4 by Hypothetical Syllogism]

(6) There is at least one capable finite person S and time t such that S is or was at t nonresistantly in a state of nonbelief in relation to the proposition that God exists. [Premise]

(7) It is not the case that God exists. [5, 6 by Modus Tollens]

The argument is evidently deductively valid, so any assessment will restrict itself to considering whether the premises are true or properly accepted as true. The first premise of the argument records an impression as to what it would take for a personal being to be axiologically ultimate that it will be hard for any philosopher today to reject, whatever may have been the case at earlier stages of cultural evolution. The second premise encapsulates the openness requirement that we have seen to represent the very minimum of what might be associated with unsurpassable love. The third premise ((4) in the argument) learns from the principle that I have called *Not Open* and our discussion thereof above. But it may be worth underlining its evident truth by simply asking ourselves: How can anyone express gratitude for what she has experienced as a gift of God's grace or try to find God's will for her life or recognize God's forgiveness and support or know God's encouraging presence or do or experience any of the hundred similar things involved in a conscious, reciprocal relationship with God *if she does not believe that God exists*? It's impossible. To be grateful to someone in the manner of conscious relationship, you have to believe they exist. The same holds for trying to figure out what they favor or recognizing that they've forgiven you, or are offering you moral support and their encouraging presence. So the third premise of the argument, like the others mentioned so far, seems clearly to be a necessary truth. And the last premise of the argument ((6) above), though not a necessary truth, states an evident empirical fact: there are and often have been *nonresistant nonbelievers*.

Those without a true philosophical interest in the argument may look for some way to defeat it instead of considering in a philosophical spirit and for philosophical purposes whether it is on to something, and it may accordingly be hard for them not to misinterpret it in one way or another. (Perhaps this helps to explain at least some of the misinterpretations to which the argument has been subject in its short twenty-five-year history.[18]) It is really a fairly simple and straightforward argument, and it would be ironic if all the efforts I have made to explain its concepts and show how its various moves can be defended should be taken as evidence that it is very complex, or controversial even among nontheists, or that it deals in the obscure: this too would be a misinterpretation! But because the argument has so often been subject to misinterpretation, let me underline some of the main mistakes that might be made here but should scrupulously be avoided.

(i) The argument does not say, in its first premise, that a God would be unsurpassably loving toward *us* or toward *human beings*. Indeed, that premise is compatible with God not creating any finite persons at all. This is as it should be if the argument is a philosophical and not a theological argument. Only the latter sort of argument could assume that God would create at all, or that when God creates, we are going to be among the results. All of this is more important than it may seem, since if the finite persons referred to by the argument are thought to be human beings, then it may mistakenly be supposed that facts about human beings determine whether God has reason to permit nonresistant nonbelief or not.[19]

(ii) Unsurpassable love, as understood in the argument and as discussed above, is not reducible to unsurpassable benevolence but also involves seeking personal relationship for its own sake.

(iii) Not just any sort of relationship that might merit the label "personal" can be substituted for what the argument is talking about: love of the sort that takes us beyond benevolence and is clearly a great-making property seeks for its own sake a conscious, reciprocal relationship with the beloved, as we have seen above.

---

[18] In a two-part discussion in *Religious Studies* in 2005, the entire first part was devoted to explaining misinterpretations of the argument. See Schellenberg (2005a, 201–15).

[19] A helpful example is provided by the previously mentioned discussion of love in Eleonore Stump's *Wandering in Darkness*, which we have already found to be in parts relevant to the hiddenness discussion. This discussion also features Stump's meditations on the negative implications, for easily attained closeness between humans and between humans and God, of what moral psychology reveals about our struggles with psychic integration. But while these meditations may well have important consequences for a *theology* of hiddenness, which can assume that God exists and has created human beings, and also that (as Stump suggests) we human beings are dealing with the consequences of the Fall, they are not easily made relevant here without the dubious assumption that no possible finite persons struggle less with psychic integration than we do. In any case, it is indeed *closeness* between persons with which Stump is concerned, and although closeness may be a goal of personal relationship as here construed, it is not a precondition.

(iv) Being in a position to participate in a personal relationship with God at a time t is not the same as being able at t to do things that might *in the future* bring about a personal relationship with God. For what it *is* to be in such a position, see above.

(v) The argument nowhere states or implies that God should *bring about* a personal relationship between God and finite persons but only that God would make it the case that every capable person is always in a position to participate in such relationship – able to do so just by trying (should she seek to do so) – in so far as he or she is nonresistant.

(vi) The argument nowhere states or implies that God's *presence* would be felt by all, let alone felt overwhelmingly, but only that all who are non-resistant would believe that God exists.

(vii) As suggested above, nothing in the argument gives credence to the idea that what finite persons would be able to do "just by trying" would be *easy* or, more generally, that participating in personal relationship with God would be a joy ride. More generally still, we should note that there can be innumerable *styles* of personal relationship with God and that it is an error to focus on a single troublesome style, suggesting that the hiddenness argument is committed to it. Eleonore Stump provides a nice example of the resources available to the hiddenness argument here. Noting that a friendship between us and God might be problematic because of the danger that either God will dominate us or we will be spoiled by God, she also offers a solution that doesn't require a lack of openness on the part of God to personal relationship or even a lack of friendship: petitionary prayer, which, as she puts it, functions as a kind of "buffer."[20]

(viii) The argument does not claim that God will intervene in the lives of non-resistant believers to give them evidence sufficient for belief, but rather states (at (5)) that if God exists, *there will never be any nonresistant nonbelievers*.

(ix) It will not suffice, to show (6) false, if one can show that reflective *doubters* in the Western world *today* are all resisting belief in God. I think that's clearly false too, but what makes the last premise of the argument clearly true, as claimed earlier, is that the category of nonresistant nonbelievers the argument can work with is so broad, including not just reflective doubters but also those who never have had a real chance to *think* about God; and not just people living today but all finite persons capable of believing in God and responding positively to such belief *who have ever lived* – which of course takes us back very far indeed into evolutionary history.

[20] Stump (1979).

If the argument is approached in a true philosophical spirit, and such inter-pretive errors are avoided, then I think it will be seen to constitute a formidable philosophical challenge to the belief that ultimism is personally exemplified. But are there also formidable challenges *to the argument* that might be raised, when mistaken approaches are avoided? In my view, the best that can be done against the argument is to reason that there are or may be *other* properties of God – properties other than unsurpassable love – that receive due acknowledg-ment in what we say *overall* about the unsurpassable greatness of God only if we moderate what the argument is asking us to accept about love. In particular, it may be argued that there are or may be *great goods* that an unsurpassably great personal Divine would wish to have but cannot have without permitting, at least for someone and for some time, nonresistant nonbelief. In emphasiz-ing this, the critic must either say that the idea of truly unsurpassable love in God has to be given up or is cast into question *or* that we should change our understanding of what unsurpassable love requires in order to accommodate the thought of such goods. Either way, our attention is turned to that idea of a "greater goods" defense against the hiddenness problem.

Here we see one way in which someone might think the hiddenness prob-lem to be very close to the problem of evil.[21] There is no room in this paper for detailed discussion of particular such defenses. But, as it turns out, that may not be needed. A greater goods defense is less impressive in hiddenness terrain than it is in relation to the problem of evil – and this in large part precisely because of what can be done with the emphasis on personal relationship that is central to the hiddenness argument. For example, free will may be a greater good of considerable significance when the question is whether a *supremely benevolent* God might permit *pain and suffering*. But the free will defense is much harder to apply to the hiddenness problem. Free will could be exer-cised in many ways even if everyone believed in God from their first reflective moment. Indeed, free will could be exercised precisely in response to God's loving openness, since one would still have to decide whether to participate in personal relationship with God or not, and also how. And such a choice would be newly available at various points along the way, in one's relation-ship with God, because one would be growing and maturing, and encountering new environments. Here I must issue a reminder that belief in God need not be produced through some brilliant display of celestial pyrotechnics. Religious experience, subtly modulated so as to meet the needs of every moment and the psychological quirks of individuals, is also possible. Thus the free will of those who always believe in God need not be compromised.

---

[21] There are other ways too, but I have elsewhere argued that none is sufficient to show that the hiddenness challenge is not importantly distinct from the challenge presented by the problem of evil. For my most recent work on this topic, see Schellenberg (in press).

This approach can be turned into a general strategy which takes the idea of personal relationship with God and runs with it. Consider an unending, ever-growing personal relationship with God. This would be commodious enough to allow for the realization, *within such relationship*, of the very goods that God is said to be unable to achieve without preventing it from even getting started, or of other goods belonging to the same type. For example, if the idea is that we must be able to make, not just any old free choices, but *seriously wrong* choices in order to be responsible for our characters, and that being thus responsible is a great good for which the permission of nonresistant nonbelief is necessary, it may be observed that character can be molded not only by choosing what is good instead of what is bad but by choosing what is good for its own sake instead of for purely self-interested reasons, and that the moral freedom to make or cultivate the latter sort of choice does not require one to be unable to be in a relationship with God but rather is a sort of freedom that flourishes within it.

Likewise, if the good that we are asked to consider is the good of searching after God, displaying a deep yearning for the Ultimate Good, we can again reply that an instance of the type of goodness to which this good belongs is available within personal relationship with God: given the infinite richness of the divine, such relationship would be multi-dimensional, potentially moving from one level to another everlastingly and continually calling forth a deeper yearning for the Good that is God.[22] This can be seen just by reflection on the concept of God. But if the same goods or goods of the same type as the critic appeals to are in this way available within personal relationship with God, then given that openness to such relationship would have to be compromised for them to be made available otherwise, the hiddenness arguer has a powerful reason to deny that God would choose the latter course. Indeed, since theists will accept that in an important sense every good is in God, it is hard to see how a greater goods defense against the hiddenness problem could succeed: instances of any good to which the critic will or could appeal may be brought within the purview of finite persons experiencing an endless encounter with the richness of the divine person, even if the encounter begins more modestly and with more modest goods.

A special instance of this subversive relationship strategy is also noteworthy. It points us again to the fact that belief in God and experience of God must be distinguished; one might have good reason to believe in the existence of God even when God feels far away. There is therefore the possibility, within a personal relationship with God, of something like what mystics have called "the dark night of the soul" – a kind of *secondary* hiddenness that could make for

---

[22] These arguments are developed more fully, together with several similar arguments, in Schellenberg (2007, 210–16).

whatever goods of testing or courage or difficult choice (and so on) are thought to require God to be hidden in the *primary* way that would involve nonresistant nonbelief. Now it may be that this point, focused on what is available within a personal relationship with God, could also be used by advocates of the argument from evil. But it will be seen that it emerges more "organically" in the context of the hiddenness argument, given the latter's emphasis on relationship with God, and it may leave the hiddenness arguer in a good position in relation to "greater good" arguments, even if the argument from evil should remain vulnerable to them.[23]

5   Belief or acceptance?

There are no easy demonstrations in philosophy, and few swift moves forward. (Seeing ourselves as being at an early stage in the evolution of inquiry helps to make this understandable. It does not make it more pleasant.) All one can do is to develop one's arguments as clearly and forcefully as possible, and then propose them for the acceptance of one's peers in the field. My hiddenness argument, together with all the explicative material surrounding it, is such a proposal.

It is important to see just what is going on here, and what is not. I am not proposing that all theists who become aware of the argument should lose their theistic belief and have it replaced by the belief that there is no God. Indeed, there is a sense in which *belief* – what all of us should believe about God – has very little to do with my proposal. I have come to think, especially in light of the evolutionary considerations sketched in section 1 of this paper, that inquiry in philosophy and perhaps in many other areas too should learn to subsist on acceptance rather than belief. The basic distinction here between acceptance and belief I take over from L. Jonathan Cohen's marvelous little treatise on the subject, though on details I differ with him.[24] The fundamental idea is that acceptance is voluntary while belief is not. To accept that p is to, as a matter of policy, employ that proposition as a premise in relevant reasoning, whereas believing that p is or includes an involuntary disposition to (as one might say) be appeared to p-ly. My proposal is that, however things may be for them at the

---

[23] Opponents of the hiddenness argument sometimes also develop the objection that there might very well be goods *unknown* to us that require hiddenness, for the sake of which God would permit it, but if one has been led to accept the hiddenness argument's premises, then this move fails. That's because from what some of those premises allow us to conclude, namely, that a loving God *would not* permit nonresistant nonbelief, it deductively follows that there are no goods, known or unknown, such that for their sake God *might* do so. So *that* becomes acceptable too – after all, it evidently follows from what one views thus – and the present objection is shown to beg the question.

[24] See Cohen (1992). My understanding of acceptance is in some ways closer to that of Dawes (2013).

level of belief, researchers in *philosophy* should accept that ultimism filled out personalistically (that is to say, theistically) is false because of the case that can be made for the soundness of a hiddenness argument, and move on to consider other ways in which ultimism may be true.

This proposal is still ambiguous, and purposely so, in virtue of how it uses that word "because." One reason to move on would be provided if all of the available evidence suggested that the hiddenness argument we have considered, taken on its own, is sound. But another would be provided if all of the available relevant evidence suggested to a researcher that the hiddenness argument, *taken together with all of the other available support for atheism*, brings us to a tipping point of the sort suggested by my proposal. Either way, the acceptance of atheism (of the falsehood of personal ultimism) would come *because* of the force of the case that can be made for the soundness of a hiddenness argument.

Obviously not everything that should be noted about support for atheism, or even about the case that can be made for the soundness of a hiddenness argument, can be detailed in a paper like this one. To some extent, I count on my readers' understanding of what is in the broader literature. But let us consider some facts that might help to prevent my proposal from appearing unrealistic, at least among philosophers. (1) Inquiry about religion in Western philosophy has been going on for more than two thousand years, and for most of that time has been squarely focused on theistic ideas, giving very little time to nontheistic ones. (2) According to the latest report, 73 percent of contemporary philosophers favor atheism.[25] Now the figure would surely be lower if we consulted philosophers *of religion*, who are predominantly believing theists. But while it might be said that philosophers of religion are the experts on religion in philosophy, we would have to note again the fact that most of these philosophers of religion have not taken their investigations beyond theism, and also that (3) many of them see themselves as working on behalf of their religious communities, and so should perhaps be viewed as doing theology – even if *philosophical* theology – not philosophy. Let me emphasize that I intend no disrespect to theology – I hold many theologians in high regard. But one need not dislike theology to notice that it is different from philosophy. Finally, we need to note that (4) acceptance of atheism does not in any way imply (as those suppose who erroneously accept the "theism or naturalism" disjunction) that we are ruling out the truth of religious claims. Indeed, we are opening the door to religion more widely than has ever been done before!

What should a philosopher qua philosopher say who seeks to be alert to all these facts – while sensitive also to our temporal position and forsaking a focus

[25] See Bourget and Chalmers (2013).

on beliefs – and then notices the forcefulness of the hiddenness argument? I think she should favor the *acceptance* of atheism in philosophy.

Now such judgments are difficult: When do you accept a proposition and when do you say we should wait for more evidence? Many today would say that we are getting ahead of ourselves if we accept that theism is false. I would suggest that we know enough to do so. The details theistic ideas bring to ultimism allow the relevant inference to be made. And it isn't philosophy's task to try to reconcile existing religious beliefs with seemingly inconsistent facts in the world – that, again, belongs to the work of theology. (Of course, it isn't philosophy's task, either, to try to find *in*consistency.) I say we should get on with exploring other fillings for ultimism, leaving open the possibility that *ultimism* is true and so neither believing nor accepting that it is false. Even at an early stage of religious investigation we should draw conclusions where we can, to help keep inquiry moving, while being very careful not to shut off inquiry where we shouldn't. The distinction suggested between the epistemic status of ultimism, which says only that there is a metaphysically, axiologically, and soteriologically ultimate reality of *some* kind, and that of ultimism personally elaborated seems to me to get this balance right and also to respond appropriately to the needs of religious inquiry in philosophy. But if so, then the acceptance of atheism in philosophy is justified. The 73 percent are right.[26]

---

[26] Or at least they have got things basically right. Philosophers today are often not entitled to their religious views or to the confidence with which they hold them. So what I am attributing to them here is little more impressive than a lucky guess!

Part II

God's Hiddenness: Overlooked Issues

2 The semantic problem of hiddenness

Meghan Sullivan

1 Introduction

As a Catholic, I believe that God exists. I also believe a host of other, staggeringly more specific claims about God. Some beliefs are metaphysical – i.e., that it is possible for a person to be resurrected. Some are historical – i.e., that certain events happened in Jerusalem some two millennia ago. Some are ethical – i.e., that we are enjoined to selflessly love one another and God. I have what I have called elsewhere a "thick" religious faith.[1] And when asked what evidence I have for my vast array of beliefs, I will cite a variety of sources.

A few of my beliefs I have reasoned out for myself. For instance, if God exists, he must be highly creative given how complex and surprising the universe is. If God is omnipotent and perfectly good, then there must be some morally appropriate reason why he permits evil. Still, these conclusions are conditional, and as a matter of course, I get very little of my theology directly from my own reasoning. In this, I suspect I am like many others with thick religious faiths.

I also believe there have been times in my life when I have experienced God directly, and these experiences give me some kinds of evidence about what God is like. Religious experiences sometimes happen in prayer or when participating in sacraments. They sometimes happen in more secular venues – taking in a beautiful vista or feeling comfort in the midst of a crisis. Personal experiences fill some of the gaps left by reason. But I suspect that I am like many people of faith in that my religious experiences tend to be both limited in content and susceptible of doubt. The experiences are limited in content because, while I might sometimes have experiences that confirm God's existence or love, I have never had an experience confirming the doctrine of the

This paper benefitted from feedback from audiences at Bogazici University, Niagara University, Hope College, the Purdue Summer Seminar on Perceptual, Moral and Religious Skepticism, and the 2011 BGND Conference. I am particularly grateful to Adam Green, Kevin Hector, Lorraine Keller, Mike Rea, Denis Robichaud, Meg Schmitt, Jeff Speaks, Eleonore Stump, and Tom Senor for useful advice on drafts of this paper at different stages.

[1] Sullivan (2014).

Trinity, or the Atonement or many of the other more specific teachings of my faith. The experiences are susceptible of doubt because I can understand how they might originate from something other than God – perhaps by an intense emotion or by wishful thinking. Moreover, I know of many cases of others seeming to have religious experiences that I doubt were divine in origin, but I cannot point to any epistemically significant difference between these other believers and me. Given that experience is limited in content and susceptible of doubt, God is experientially hidden from me and, I suspect, the vast majority of other religious believers.

So where does my theology come from and what could justify it? Most often, when it comes to my beliefs about God, I am highly dependent on what others tell me. I receive testimony from a wide array of sources. I trust texts like the Bible (under an interpretation). I look to the teachings of the Magisterium and sources from Catholic tradition. I read articles published by my colleagues in philosophy and theology departments. I consider the testimony of friends and loved ones regarding their experiences of God. I consider the testimony of other traditions, adopting theories that seem trustworthy, useful, and consistent with my antecedent understanding of God. This multi-pronged approach is, I suspect, similar to the way that many other modern believers develop and justify their faith.

Indeed, if Saint Augustine is right, there is a deep theological significance to our dependence on the testimony of others. In the preface to *On Christian Teaching*, he writes, "the human condition would be wretched if God appeared unwilling to minister his word to human beings through human agency ... Moreover, there would be no way for love, which ties people together in the bonds of unity, to make souls overflow and as it were intermingle with each other if human beings learned nothing from other humans."[2] If Augustine is right, dependence on testimony is far from a last resort for believers given God's hiddenness – it can be seen as a part of God's plan for knitting us together. We can see Augustine as advancing a kind of "church-making" solution to the problem of hiddenness.[3]

Still, just as there are many ways one might be skeptical about religious experience, there are many ways to be skeptical about religious testimony. How do I know which (if any) texts are authoritative? Why trust the Church? What if my friends, family, and colleagues are simply mistaken? And in this age-old "telephone game" of passing along information about God, how can any of us be confident that accurate content has been preserved? I'll admit that I have suffered all of these doubts. The Church works to relieve these doubts by offering accounts of the nature of revelation, inspiration, authority,

[2] Augustine (1997, 5–6).
[3] Akin to the popular soul-making response to the problem of hiddenness. See Murray (2002).

and reason. I find these accounts compelling, and they go some way toward relieving internal skepticism, even if they only offer partisan solutions to these skeptical problems facing testimony.

But I've also suffered from another kind of doubt about religious testimony, which is the main subject of this essay. How can I be confident that language is able to successfully convey information about God? God's hiddenness makes it difficult to acquire knowledge of him directly or to verify information received indirectly. Does it also make it difficult to refer to God in the first place?[4] Theologians have long struggled with issues of understanding how human minds and human language can grasp a transcendent God. And philosophers have weighed in on the issue, including relatively recent works contending that skepticism about divine names motivates revisionary theology.[5] I hope to add a new wrinkle to this debate by describing a new philosophical challenge facing divine names, one which is peculiar to a causal-historical account of how speakers refer to God.

Here is how the paper will proceed. First, I will review some options for how a particular speaker might manage to refer to God when they use a divine name word in an assertion. I will argue that one account – reference by deference – gives the most plausible theory of how divine names refer (section 2). Then I will introduce some limitations of reference by deference that arise when the community using a particular name word is large and diverse. The connection between a name word and a referent is highly susceptible of disruption in such communities (section 3). I will argue that divine name words are particularly semantically vulnerable, which raises a skeptical problem for religious testimony (section 4). Can we overcome these skeptical problems? I will survey three replies to the challenge which I find implausible (section 5). Finally I will advocate a partisan theological response to the problem based on the doctrine of inspiration. But as we will see, even this response is controversial (section 6). The semantic problem of hiddenness deserves a place among the more widely observed epistemic problems of hiddenness.

2   Ways we might fix reference to God

How is it that a divine name word like "God" might come to refer to God when a speaker uses it in an assertion? To answer this, we must consider different options for how any names acquire referents in the mouths of particular speakers. Let's survey three of the leading options and consider their implications for divine names.

---

[4] A similar question arises for the content of our thoughts, but I won't deal with this here.
[5] See for example Hick (1982) and Johnston (2009).

The first way is a process called "direct baptism." When reference is fixed by direct baptism, a name word "n" refers to an object o in the mouth of a speaker S because S is in a position to perceive o and S performs a speech act to bestow "n" on o. For example, when I was a child, our family adopted a kitten. My parents suggested I choose its name. Holding the animal, I declared, "Her name is 'Punky.'" This speech act associated "Punky" with Punky, and ensured that in my mouth the name word "Punky" picked out that cat and no other.

It is pretty clear that the name word "God" does not refer to God in my mouth by direct baptism. I have never actually performed a speech act where I bestowed that name word on God. And to try to do so seems a risky venture, since he is experientially hidden.[6] More than this, it would be offensive for me to invent a name for the divine and give it to him – it would overstep the boundary between God and man. In general, if you regard someone as an authority, you must be deferential to their preferred ways of being called.

A second way a name word might be associated with a particular referent is by definite description. When reference is fixed by description, a name word "n" refers to object o in the mouth of speaker S because S associates some description (or weighted cluster of descriptions) D with the name word, and o uniquely satisfies D (or satisfies the most of the descriptions in D).[7] For example, I often teach a very large version of Introduction to Philosophy – over two hundred students – with anonymized grading. Looking at my grade book, I might notice that only one student received a perfect score on a recent exam, and I might decide to call that student "Student A." Suppose it turns out that Leslie is the only student to earn a perfect score on the exam. In my mouth, "Student A" refers to Leslie just as long as (i) I associate the description "sole perfect score earner on Intro exam" with "Student A" and (ii) Leslie is the only thing that satisfies the description.

Does "God" get its reference in my mouth by definite description? This theory of divine names seems more promising than reference by baptism. After all, many of God's names seem to be descriptions of his titles and attributes. Christians typically call God "Father," "Lord," or "Most High." Muslims have ninety-nine names for God, all of which describe some attribute he enjoys, that is, "Al Muhyi" (The Lifegiver) and "Al Hakam" (The Judge).

Though many of God's names seem to describe God, there are good reasons to think that description is not the predominant way that divine name words fix reference to God. There may even be good reasons to think divine name words never function as definite descriptions. Here I will describe five.

---

[6] I use the male pronoun in this paper out of deference to tradition and to ease reading but without any presupposition that God has a gender.

[7] The weighted cluster theory is first described in Searle (1958).

First, though many of the honorifics like "The Arbitrator" and "The Life-Giver" seem to be descriptions, they do not *uniquely* describe God, at least not without further background theological assumptions. Judge Judy is both an arbitrator and a life-giver (as a biological mother of two). But Judge Judy is not even a candidate for the meaning of "Al-Hakem" or "Al-Muhyi" in the mouths of observant Muslims. And this is because the honorifics are meant to be taken as referential uses of descriptions of God. Muslims do not mean to pick out any life-giver or other with "Al-Muhyi" but rather *that* particular life-giver which revealed Himself to Muhammad. These name words are *referential* descriptions – phrases that appear to refer by description, but in fact only pick out a single object, regardless of what else might satisfy that description or whether the description is actually an attribute of the referent.[8] For example, "The Queen Mary" is a name word that seems to be a description of a particular female monarch, but in fact refers to a ship in my mouth. It is a referential use of a descriptive phrase. If these divine names are also referential descriptions, then the definite description theory doesn't answer the question of how "God" comes to refer to God, since we still need a theory for how reference is fixed.

Second, I believe that substantive interfaith disagreement is possible. More strongly, I believe that Jews, Christians, and Muslims of both liberal and conservative varieties are able to have substantive debates about one and the same God. This is not just wishful thinking; many variants of Judaism, Christianity, and Islam explicitly teach that practitioners of the other faiths worship the same God. All three faiths overlap with respect to key texts. Shared devotion to God is a central theme of Pope Paul VI's *Nostra Aetate* proclamation to Catholics, one of the most important documents to come out of the Second Vatican Council. And Sura 29:46 of the Quran insists:

And dispute ye not with the People of the Book, except with means better (than mere disputation), unless it be with those of them who inflict wrong (and injury): but say, "We believe in the revelation which has come down to us and in that which came down to you; Our Allah and your Allah is one; and it is to Him we bow (in Islam)."

Can we make sense of substantive interfaith discussion on a descriptive theory of reference? Consider a common theological debate that occurs between Christians and Muslims:

CHRISTIAN: God is three persons and one substance.
MUSLIM: You are wrong. Allah (blessed be His name) is not three persons. Allah cannot be divided in this way.

---

[8] See Donnellan (1966). Kripke (1977) points out that the theory could make sense of distinctions in how speakers might use the name "The Messiah." Thanks to Jeff Speaks for discussion here.

For this debate to be substantive, "God" and "Allah" must refer to the same being. But if "God" and "Allah" are merely abbreviations for descriptions and the most important descriptions of God are contested, then it is not clear the debate is substantive. If there is no agreement about the definite description, there is no reason to believe the terms co-refer.

We could solve this problem by insisting that reference-fixing descriptions are only descriptions that are uncontested. For example, what if we assume "God," "Allah," etc. are just shorthand for *whatever is the causal origin of the universe*? Jews, Christians, and Muslims can agree that God satisfies that description. But such an assumption would save the substantivity of interfaith disputes only at the cost of explaining the substantivity of common theist/atheist debates. Here is one such debate:

THEIST: God is the causal origin of the universe.
ATHEIST: You are wrong. The Big Bang is the causal origin of the universe.

How can the atheist claim the theist is wrong if "God" in the theist's mouth just means *whatever is the causal origin of the universe*? We might soup up the description to *whatever is the personal causal origin of the universe.* But what exactly God's personhood consists in will be a matter of further controversy within the faiths, again raising the fear that religious disputants are talking past one another rather than co-referring.

Could disputants insist on some shared historical description – for example, perhaps "God" refers to *whoever made a covenant with Abraham*? Jews, Christians, and Muslims share the Pentateuch as a common text. And atheists will presumably deny that anything made a covenant with Abraham. So this would solve the earlier problems. But only at the cost of preventing substantive religious dialogue with theists who deny the historical veracity of the Pentateuch. More generally, it is difficult to find a reference-fixing description of God that (i) enjoys wide enough agreement to do justice to the assumption that many different faiths co-refer and (ii) is not so permissive as to make it impossible for theists to disagree with atheists about whether "God" refers at all.

Third, the descriptivist theory of divine names fails to explain how children and those who are incapable of grasping any theologically rich reference-fixing descriptions of God can nonetheless refer to Him. I know many two-year-olds who appear to know the name "God" but know nothing of the divine attributes or God's work in history. I should like to think that when these children offer simple prayers, they are directed to God, even if their theology is highly limited. William Alston raises this point in favor of a causal theory of divine names.[9] In general, the descriptive theory places too much emphasis on the speakers having prior knowledge of God. This is a more common problem for

---

[9] Alston (1989).

reference by description – there are many name words we seem to be able to use to refer without having much background knowledge of our subject.[10]

Fourth, and again borrowing from Alston, the descriptive theory does a poor job of explaining our judgments about cases of deception. Suppose that Jim knows nothing of God. And suppose that Satan sets out to deceive him. Satan reveals himself to Jim, performs some pyrotechnics, calls himself "God," and convinces Jim that he is the all-powerful ruler of the universe. Satan then commands Jim to pray to him. It is natural to think that he is in fact praying to Satan when he uses the name word "God."[11] But on a descriptive theory, if *all-powerful creator of the universe* is the primary description Jim associates with "God," then he *is* referring to God.[12] More generally, descriptive theories fail to account for the phenomenon that we seem to be able to use a name to refer even if we are radically mistaken about the referent. And again, this is an example of a more general problem for reference by description.[13]

Finally, the descriptivist theory cannot accommodate certain forms of thoroughgoing apophaticism. Some strands of the Abrahamic traditions deny that we have access to any true, unique description of God. If descriptions are needed to fix reference to God, then such apophatics are forced to conclude that we cannot refer to God. This may seem like a further reason to reject extreme forms of apophaticism. More mild forms of apophaticism admit we can have some true descriptions of God, but no true description that expresses God's essential nature. Such moderate apophaticism is in principle compatible with a descriptive theory of divine names as long as those names are nonessential descriptions of God. For instance "God" might be an abbreviation for the description "whatever being created and sustains me." Still such a theory does a poor job of accommodating common Jewish, Christian, and Muslim teachings about the holiness of divine names. In each of these traditions, the divine names enjoy a protected moral status because they are revelations from God. But by the lights of the descriptive theory, any true definite description is as good as any other for the purposes of naming. "The Almighty Lord" is just as much a reference-fixing name for God as "The divine being that created and sustains Ozzie Osbourne." And moderate apophatics must rely on more contingent descriptions, like the latter, to name God. But descriptions like the latter seem far less worthy of the title *divine name* than descriptions like the

---

[10] See Lecture II of Kripke (1980).

[11] See Alston (1989, 110–11).

[12] Descriptivists might insist that Jim is primarily deferring to some other description when he worships – for instance *whatever is the source of the pyrotechnics*. This highlights a puzzle for understanding how descriptions are weighted in the "weighted cluster" version of descriptivism. In this case, we assume Jim does not primarily intend to refer to this other description.

[13] See again Lecture II of Kripke (1980).

former. And names like the latter are certainly not the ones we've received in revelation.

As I mentioned in the introduction, I have a host of very specific beliefs about God, many of which I take to be literally true claims. So I am no apophatic. Even still, I acknowledge the possibility that I am radically mistaken about God's true nature or that all of our knowledge of God is only analogical. I admit it is possible that on the day of judgment I will realize I was mistaken in most of the historical facts and I did not understand God's real nature. If this is revealed to me, I would not conclude that I prayed to and worshipped something other than God all along. Rather, I would realize that I had worshipped God but very imperfectly and with radically mistaken assumptions. The descriptive theory has no resources to account for this.

All of these considerations lead me to hope that there is a way of referring to God that is less cognitively demanding, explains the substantivity of interfaith dialogue, can make sense of mistaken worship, and reflects a proper theological humility. Happily there is yet another way that a name word might become associated with its referent that seems flexible enough to give an account for all of these desiderata.

The third way a name word might be associated with a referent is a way that I will call "reference by deference." The theory comes from Saul Kripke's hugely influential causal-historical account of reference.[14] We refer deferentially when we learn a new name word and form the intention to refer in exactly the same way as the name word refers for our teacher. More precisely, on the reference by deference strategy, a name word "n" refers to an object o in the mouth of speaker S because (i) S intends to defer to whatever the referent of the word is for some other speaker (or speakers) and (ii) S stands in a causal chain of reference by deference that terminates with either a direct baptism of o or a successful definite description of o. The upshot of reference by deference is a speaker need not know anything significant about the object they are naming in order to refer to it. They may even have radically mistaken beliefs. For example, suppose you tell me about a folk singer named "Neil Young." I don't know anything about the singer, but intend to use "Neil Young" to refer to whoever you are referring to. Later I come to the (mistaken) belief that Neil Young is the person who wrote "Sweet Home Alabama," and this is all the information that I associate with the name. If I was attempting to refer by description, "Neil Young" would not refer to Neil Young; indeed, it wouldn't refer to anyone at all since there is no unique individual who wrote "Sweet Home Alabama."[15] But as long as I intend to refer deferentially, and as long as you are part of a causal

[14] Kripke (1980).
[15] Ronnie Van Zant, Ed King, and Gary Rossington are jointly credited with the lyrics. See the liner notes for *Second Helping* (1974).

chain that terminates with someone or other successfully associating "Neil Young" with Neil Young, then the name does refer to Young in my mouth.

Reference by deference can avoid many of the problems that faced the definite description theory of divine names. Speakers do not need a unique description of God, nor do they need even an accurate description of God in order to use a divine name to refer to him. Children and anyone else who finds themselves theologically impoverished can refer merely by deferring to others who are in a position to refer. Likewise, different traditions can co-refer as long as they defer to chains that originate with the same God. So reference by deference makes it substantially easier for divine names to refer. To allay skeptical worries, we just need to be confident that there is a chain of reference that terminates with someone successfully naming God and to which we can defer. Can we be confident that there is such a chain of reference?

3   Ways reference can be destroyed

There are two conditions that must be fulfilled for an agent to succeed in referring deferentially to something. First there must be a successful *start* to a causal chain – there must be some point in the history of the name where someone either directly perceived the referent or uniquely described it. In the case of God's names, we might think that there were several occasions where a causal chain might have started. Most directly, in the Abrahamic traditions it seems God initially knows his name (or names himself) and then shares the name with a prophet, as in the story of God sharing the names "YHWH" and "The Lord" with Moses in Exodus 3:13–15.[16] In other cases, a divine name might be bestowed by a speech act – for example with Joseph following the directives of the Angel and naming his son "Jesus" in Matthew 1:20. The more removed an initial naming event is, the more we might doubt whether it ever occurred. But let's set aside such worries about divine names for present purposes and focus instead on the second condition.

For an agent to succeed in referring deferentially, there must also be a proper chain of reference connecting the speaker back to that initial naming event. Reference by deference means the intentions of other speakers in one's community strongly influence the meanings of one's own name words. And as causal connections might change or break, so might reference change over time. There are at least three ways a causal chain might be disrupted, thereby destroying a name–referent relation. The first I will call *semantic break*:

---

[16] There is perhaps some case to be made for the view that certain of God's names (like God Himself) have no starting point – they have always existed. They "start" in human language, when they are revealed.

SEMANTIC BREAK: A semantic break occurs when speakers in a future generation cease to use a name word. If there is a long enough gap, the link between the name word and the original referent will be broken.

An example illustrates the mechanism:

GEOFFREY: In the sixth century a peasant boy was born in an isolated village on the English coast. His parents named him "Geoffrey." A few years later, Vikings invaded, killing everyone and wiping out all of the records of the village. Given that there is no current practice causally associating use of "Geoffrey" with the original baptism, Geoffrey's original name is lost to history. If a contemporary historian stumbles upon the fossilized remains of Geoffrey and coincidentally dubs the remains "Geoffrey," then she has a coined a new name rather than revived the old one.

The easiest way for a name to be destroyed is to fall out of use in a community.

The second way a name might be disrupted I will call *semantic shift*:

SEMANTIC SHIFT: A semantic shift occurs when a competing chain of reference by deference enters the linguistic community, and speakers eventually defer primarily to this new chain.

Gareth Evans proposes cases like this as a challenge to some formulations of the causal-historical account of reference.[17] But the most famous description of this phenomenon comes directly from Kripke. Here is the case, paraphrased:

MADAGASCAR: While sailing in the Indian Ocean, Marco Polo dubbed a region of mainland East Africa "Madagascar." He shared the name with other sailors who also began to call an island off the coast "Madagascar." Eventually everyone deferred to other sailors in the use of the name. Since the island is now the object at the source of the primary causal chain associated with "Madagascar," the island is now the referent of "Madagascar."

A name–referent relation can be broken if the name word is causally assumed by a new chain of deference with a different referent as its source. And this shift may happen without any speakers even noticing that they have begun deferring to a new causal chain.

Finally a name can be disrupted by what I will call *semantic pollution*:

SEMANTIC POLLUTION: Semantic pollution occurs when many competing chains of reference by deference enter the linguistic community, and speakers defer indiscriminately to the different chains.

Another example illustrates the phenomenon:

ARTHUR: In the sixth century, a boy was born and his parents named him "Arthur." His exploits in the Anglo-Saxon wars made him famous throughout Britain. Initially

---

[17] See Evans (1973) and Addendum (e) in Kripke (1980, 163).

those close to Arthur successfully used the name to refer back to him. Over time an oral tradition celebrating Arthurian victories developed, with bards often merging the tales of his exploits with those of other soldiers, both real and mythical. Centuries later, these Arthurian legends were edited, embellished, and preserved in histories and Romantic poetry. Many real and mythical soldiers are the causal source of these different practices. And all contemporary speakers defer to this family of traditions when they use the name "King Arthur." Even though the name phrase "King Arthur" has remained in continuous use over intervening centuries, it no longer refers to the sixth-century soldier. It does not refer to any person whatsoever.

A name–referent relation may become so swamped by competitors over time that there ceases to be a determinate connection between the name word and its original referent. In these cases, the name–referent relation is broken, and the name word ceases to determinately refer to anything. And as with semantic shift, semantic pollution can destroy a name–referent relation without speakers even being aware of the change.

If initial naming events are temporally remote and linguistic communities are significantly large and diverse, it increases the chance that semantic disruptions will occur. Remoteness means there are more links in the causal chain susceptible to change. Size and diversity mean there are more potential sources for competing causal chains to enter the community. A name word is *semantically vulnerable* if (i) speakers primarily use the name word to refer deferentially, (ii) the event establishing it as a name is remote, and (iii) the linguistic community is large and diverse.

The phenomenon of semantic vulnerability leads us back to the main theological question of this essay. If the arguments from section 2 are persuasive, then the primary way that we refer to God is deferentially. It is also clear that initial divine naming events are very remote. And our current linguistic community is very large and very diverse, with many different forms of religious discourse. So divine name words meet the criteria for semantic vulnerability. How troubling is this? It depends on how likely it is that divine name words have undergone shift or pollution. And this pushes us to think about the history and theology of shared religious language.

4   Hiddenness and semantic vulnerability

At this stage in the argument a bit of vertigo sets in. I've been using "God" throughout this essay as though it were referring to something. Now I am questioning whether it does. Doesn't that make the earlier arguments incoherent? To reduce the vertigo, we can pose the skeptical question as a challenge. Suppose (like me), you believe that God exists. And suppose you concede that most of your evidence about God comes from testimony. And suppose you acknowledge that divine name words are semantically vulnerable. Trusting testimony requires trusting that your various sources are all conveying information about God. And to convey information about God, these sources need a divine name word that refers to God. So to trust religious testimony, you must have reason to believe that even though divine names are vulnerable, they still refer to God. In particular, there hasn't been any shift or pollution. What grounds might you (or I) have for thinking this?

First, you might think that there aren't any competing causal chains for divine names that you might defer to, so there is no chance of shift or pollution for a divine name. We can call this the *no actual competition* response.

The no actual competition response seems wildly implausible as a social and historical posit. For one, we live in a religiously diverse, multicultural, and increasingly connected world. Contemporary English is a language with many tributaries issuing from these different traditions.

Moreover, there are explicit examples of cultural and linguistic mergers in the history of many religious traditions. To choose a case study close to home, the contemporary Catholic Church is the product of two thousand years of theological mergers and linguistic acquisitions. Recall the changes the Church underwent in the fifth and sixth centuries, when Neoplatonic metaphysics was taken up by the Christian tradition. In the work of Pseudo-Dionysius, many Neoplatonic descriptions of "The One" were taken as a basis for theories about the God of Christianity. "The One" and "God" clearly have different causal histories; the former was initially fixed by definite description and a priori speculation while the latter (if the tradition is believed) was revealed. Indeed, early Church history is full of events where distinct cultures puzzled over how to combine their metaphysical theories with the growing church and made tricky decisions about common reference. And Catholics are not alone in this; nearly every major contemporary religion can find syncretistic events in their formative years. Of course, syncretistic events alone do not give sufficient reason to doubt that a particular faith is revealed by God. But they do give reason to suppose that there are different strands of traditions within major faiths that have distinct histories.

Competing causal chains can also arise within mature traditions. In a sufficiently large linguistic community there are bound to be speakers who use divine name words improperly. Idolators, blasphemers – any individuals who baptize the non-divine with a divine name word – are sources of new causal practices, which we might defer to without even recognizing the chains as new.[18]

Perhaps you concede that there are many competing causal chains, but you think God is the origin of all of them. We can imagine cases where the mere

---

[18] See Sullivan (2012).

fact that there is a diversity of beliefs about an object does not entail any kind of semantic problem. For example:

JAMES BOND: James Bond is an international man of mystery. He has caused some people to believe he is a top MI6 spy. He has duped others into believing that he is an affluent London business man. And he has fooled still others to believe he is a skilled thief. There are three different camps with respect to Bond theory. If the thief camp encounters the businessman camp or the spy camp, the thief camp is likely to think the others are wildly misguided. They may even deny they are speaking of the same person, given how divergent their beliefs are. Nonetheless "James Bond" refers to James Bond in all of their mouths, because he is the source of all of their different referential chains.

Might God be like James Bond – the causal source of all of the different belief systems in a diverse community? If so, competing causal chains do not pose any threat of semantic shift or pollution. Call this the *common source* response to the problem of semantic hiddenness.

The Bond–God analogy is problematic insofar as Bond intentionally deceives some groups as to his true identity, but presumably God is never deceptive. So the common source response requires an accompanying theological view about the pluralistic nature of divine revelation. John Hick offers a theory along these lines in his work attempting to reconcile religious pluralism and theistic belief. Hick proposes that every established world religion (not just the Abrahamic) is worshipping the same divine reality, but practitioners are worshipping under radically different modes of presentation. As Hick puts it,

our human religious experience, variously shaped as it is by our sets of religious concepts, is a cognitive response to the universal presence of the ultimate divine Reality that, in itself, exceeds human conceptuality. This Reality is however manifested to us in ways formed by a variety of human concepts, as the range of divine personae and metaphysical impersonae witnessed to in the history of religions.[19]

Hick's theology requires an extreme form of apophaticism. A Christian cannot truly claim that "Jesus was the Son of God simpliciter," she can only truly claim that "Jesus was the Son of God relative to our cognitive response to the divine reality." This common source response will not be acceptable for any theist who thinks some of their claims about God are absolutely true – true without respect to how different communities cognize the divine. Likewise, it is difficult for a Muslim to have a substantive disagreement with a Christian about core theological tenets, since it is not in doubt that *Christians believe* Jesus to be the Son of God. So this version of the common source response also fails one of our qualifications for a theory of divine names – that it explain substantivity of interfaith disagreement. Another major difficulty for the common source response comes in squaring it with the particular theologies whose

[19] Hick (2009, 64).

testimony it is meant to justify. Judaism, Christianity, and Islam all have teachings about the exclusivity of God's revelation that are straightforwardly incompatible with Hick's theology. So this kind of common source response is no solution for adherents of these faiths.

We could supplement the common source response with a more exclusive theology than Hick offers. We might suppose that God reveals himself (non-deceptively) to many different traditions, but only one tradition – presumably one's own – accurately preserves the full content of revelation. Such an approach will preserve substantive interfaith debate. But it won't solve the problems of shift and pollution induced by blasphemy. And proponents of this kind of common source response still face the tricky issue of deciding which traditions to assume are revealed (in this attenuated sense) and which are not.

I've given reasons for thinking there are many competing causal chains of reference in our language and reasons to doubt the assumption that God is the source of all of these chains. Still, could we avoid the problem of semantic shift or pollution by resolving to only defer very selectively when we use divine names? Suppose my community thinks only Moses was a trustworthy source of divine names. Suppose further that we resolve to defer to whatever Moses meant by "YHWH" and to defer to no other. "YHWH" in my mouth will refer to God just so long as Moses successfully established reference to God and so long as I do not slip back into deferring to the broader community's use of divine name words. And because I am using an unpolluted name word, I can still say true and false things about God. So religious testimony is secured, at least for me and my small community. We can call this the *quarantined deference* response to the semantic problem of hiddenness.

This kind of long-term selective deference is very difficult for speakers in a large pluralistic society to accomplish. Certainly believers (like me) who consult a wide variety of sources and traditions are not making any effort to quarantine their language. For proponents of quarantined deference, traditions outside of one's very local chain of deference cannot provide any testimonial evidence about God. But perhaps very insular religious sects are capable of these kinds of extended deferential uses. Still, even if each community reverts to selective deference to their favored prophet, it is not at all clear that interfaith testimony is substantive. Consider an analogous case. I do not know Mary, but when I speak of her, I resolve to refer to whoever my friend Rob means by the name. You do not know Mary either, but you resolve to refer to whoever your friend Amy means by the name. If I tell you "Mary just finished her thesis," do you have any reason to believe I am talking about your Mary? It seems not. On the causal-historical theory, we only have reason to think name words have the same referent if we have reason to suppose they have the same causal-historical source. Jews, Christians, and Muslims who each insist on deferring to their particular favored historical prophet have no reason to believe there is a shared historical source. So there is no reason to believe that interfaith dialogue is substantive. At best, we have to relax the "shared reference" assumption as a precondition for substantive interfaith dialogue. I think these are serious costs for the quarantined deference proposal.

5   Reference and inspiration

The solutions I have considered thus far ignore any agency that God might exercise in securing the reference of divine names. And this points to a different kind of solution to the problem of semantic hiddenness – the one I prefer, but admittedly it also comes with costs.

There are theological precedents for thinking that God exercises corrective semantic power within linguistic communities. For example, the Christian doctrine of inspiration holds that the Bible is God's revelation because God actively worked through the individual authors and editors of the different books of scripture to preserve a content across translations and over time. Ordinarily if a narrative were recorded by many different authors, in many different languages, and frequently retranslated, the content would change over time. But the Christian solution to this threat is a supposition that even though fallible human agents are involved at every step in transmitting the revelation, the Holy Spirit works in faith communities to prevent the distortion. The work is miraculous since it defies all of the causal and historical pressures that would ordinarily shift meaning.

If God has the power to ensure that entire contents are preserved across time and translation, it is not so strange to think God also has the power to ensure that some building block of content – names – also preserve their reference across time and translation. Indeed, it seems that God could not preserve the content of revelation without preserving the reference of divine names. Call this the *semantic inspiration* response to the problem of semantic hiddenness. According to the semantic inspiration view, we can be confident that divine name words have not suffered semantic drift or pollution because God wills through the Holy Spirit that they be preserved. Versions of this response could also be formulated for other theistic traditions that subscribe to a theory for how their holy books persist as revelations across time and translation.[20]

There are at least four kinds of objection one might raise to the inspiration response. I'll discuss them in order of the ones I find least troubling to most troubling.

The first is that the inspiration strategy is objectionably circular. The semantic problem of hiddenness is a problem for understanding how religious

---

[20] In a similar vein, Kevin Hector (2011) offers an account of how the Spirit of Christ fixes the meaning of our concepts pertaining to God.

testimony could be a source of evidence for religious belief. Theological doctrines concerning the nature of revelation and the work of the Holy Spirit come to us via testimony. So these beliefs are subject to the very doubts that they are meant to assuage. To make use of the semantic inspiration response one must be already committed to the view that testimony justifies religious beliefs.

I don't find this objection particularly troubling, since the same kind of objection can be raised against secular testimony – and really any other source of knowledge. Suppose I became skeptical about whether historical writings were a good source of evidence about ancient Egypt. I discover an ancient text outlining the record-keeping practices of Egyptian scholars, and that text presents the scholars as having very exacting standards. Discovering the text will boost my confidence about the historical writings more generally, and this boost is an epistemically appropriate response to the discovery. But my confidence is based on circular reasoning – testimony in this case seems to "bootstrap" its own justification. This is a central problem in epistemology. But defenders of semantic inspiration are under no obligation to provide a full-scale solution to the problem of epistemic circularity, and the kinds of bootstrapping used to defend religious testimony are no worse than the kinds of bootstrapping used to defend other means of knowledge.

One might also think the semantic inspiration solution is too partisan – it relies on highly specific claims from one theistic tradition to answer a more general philosophical problem. To be clear, most of the major religions we have considered thus far have some theory for how revelation is preserved over time. But for each of these religions, there are different and incompatible theories of the mechanism of this preservation. Any sufficiently developed version of the inspiration response will thus appeal to theological beliefs that will not be shared among faiths and that will not be endorsed by agnostics or atheists. How bad is this?

It depends on what one wants out of response to the problems of hiddenness (or out of philosophical theology more generally). For instance, one might want a theory that would persuade what Peter van Inwagen calls "ideal agnostics" of a given position.[21] The ideal agnostic is someone without pre-existing theological (or atheological) commitments who is willing to devote sufficient time and reasoning powers to evaluate the relevant philosophical arguments. The semantic inspiration response will not move any ideal agnostic to greater confidence in the justification of religious testimony. But the philosophical theologian's job is not merely to serve the ideal agnostics. As van Inwagen himself concedes, they are a difficult audience to please! There is also a respectable task of demonstrating that particular belief systems are coherent, and that those who subscribe to the system have the resources for answering skeptical objections from within their systems. In this project, the goal of

---

[21] van Inwagen (2006).

philosophical theology is to explain particular theological doctrines in a way that makes them relevant to philosophical problems and still plausible enough to be endorsed by a practitioner of this faith. And in this project, the semantic inspiration response seems well founded.

One might also object that the solution is too mysterious. It leaves us no more enlightened as to the mechanism by which divine names work. This objection gives me a bit more pause; I am not typically very comfortable invoking the work of the Holy Spirit to solve my philosophical problems. And the semantic inspiration response seems miraculous, in the sense that it would require a deviation from ordinary and well-understood causal processes that determine meaning. Is it a strike against a semantic theory if it relies on a primitive, non-causal mechanism to settle reference?

There is some precedent in secular philosophy of language for thinking that some referents "attract" terms in a primitive, non-causal way. The process is called "reference magnetism," and it is typically deployed as a solution to skeptical challenges stemming from indeterminacy in the denotations of predicates. The idea is easiest to grasp by considering a common thought experiment. Suppose you think that causal processes determine the denotations of predicates. For instance, the meaning of the word "green" is just the set of objects that we've been disposed over time to classify as green. Then we are asked to give a definition of "green." We consider two options:

> Option 1: "Green" denotes the set of objects always disposed to reflect light in such a way as to appear greenish to normal human perceivers.
>
> Option 2: "Green" denotes the set of objects disposed to reflect light in such a way as to appear greenish to normal human perceivers before the year 2050 and to appear bluish to normal human viewers after 2050.

Presumably our use of the predicate "green" up until now hasn't been sensitive to how objects will appear after 2050 – it is indeterminate between the two options. But Option 1 is a better candidate for the denotation of "green" than Option 2. In virtue of what is it a better denotation? There is no solution to be found in just our patterns of use. The best we can do is appeal to some primitive feature of Option 1 that makes it more eligible as a referent. Without such an assumption, it seems that denotations of predicates would be radically underdetermined.[22]

If it is acceptable to appeal to primitive, non-causal features to explain how predicates get their determinate denotations, then it should likewise be acceptable to appeal to primitive, non-causal processes to explain how indeterminacy in name words is resolved. In fact, the semantic inspiration response is

---

[22] See Lewis (1984), Lewis (1999), and Sider (2011) for discussions of reference magnetism.

less mysterious than the reference magnetism posit. The primary evidence for reference magnetism comes from a form of inference to the best explanation – something must resolve indeterminacy, it cannot be patterns of use, so we should infer there are primitive eligibility constraints. But semantic inspiration has outside theological support, and Christians have a detailed theory of how and why the Holy Spirit acts in the world more generally. There is little we can say about how reference magnetism works. There is a lot we can say about the Holy Spirit.

Finally one might object that the semantic inspiration solution carries with it a kind of objectionable semantic exclusivity. To my mind, this is the biggest challenge facing the inspiration response. Scriptural inspiration is typically held to occur for a single community and its accepted revelations. And so Christians believe that the collected books of the Bible are inspired by the Holy Spirit, but the Quran is not. Muslims believe the Quran was given to Allah directly from angels of God, while other faiths' scriptures are lesser revelations. But if the semantic inspiration response is to preserve coreference of divine names across different faiths, then it must be an *inclusive* mechanism: God must inspire the meaning of divine names across the faiths. The theology of scriptural inspiration gives us no clear analogy for how and why God might do this. Presumably we'd need to augment our response with an account of how the Holy Spirit works in individuals outside of one's faith community. But developing such a theory will require confronting some of the most controversial issues in pneumatology – issues which, I fear, are beyond the scope of this essay.

6   Conclusion

In the introduction, I expressed sympathy for an Augustine-inspired "church-making" defense of our reliance on testimony (rather than religious experience). According to the church-making defense, our reliance on testimony is beneficial insofar as it encourages the formation of a religious community and promotes bonds of love and dependence between believers. The desire to make a church offers a potential reason for God's remaining experientially hidden. To the extent that it is the task of the Holy Spirit to make the church, I think the inspiration response is particularly theologically fitting and of a piece with how we should approach other problems of hiddenness. But like other problems of hiddenness, the semantic problem resists a tidy and theologically neutral solution.

3   Divine hiddenness and the cognitive science of religion

Helen De Cruz

1   Divine hiddenness and natural belief in God

Theism is cross-culturally widespread. Approximately 55 percent of the world's population believes in the God of the Abrahamic religions.[1] An estimated 85 percent of the world's population is theist in a broader sense, which includes, among others, polytheism and theism in those without religious affiliation (Zuckerman, 2007). Yet few people would hold that God's existence is an obvious fact. If God exists, he is to some extent hidden. Theism is not universal; several world religions, such as Buddhism, Jainism, and Hinduism, do not require belief in a personal god, and a large part of Western Europe is secular.[2] Moreover, monotheism correlates with large group sizes, sedentarism, and literacy, making it unlikely that belief in a personal God arose before the invention of agriculture about 10,000–12,000 years ago, a brief timespan given that our species is about 200,000 years old (Roes and Raymond, 2003; Sanderson and Roberts, 2008).

Those who do believe in God frequently experience doubts; prayer and other spiritual practices feel unrewarding; and God seems absent or non-responsive. This spiritual dryness can take many forms, for instance, believers may feel as if they are just going through the motions, or they may get an acute sense of loss of earlier religious experiences, like Mother Teresa who felt spiritual dryness for most of her adult life. In this paper, I take spiritual dryness to mean a lack of religious experiences in people who desire a relationship with God.

Atheism and spiritual dryness are features of a broader phenomenon, the problem of divine hiddenness or divine silence. There are two ways in which

This research was funded by a postdoctoral fellowship grant from the British Academy. I would like to thank John Schellenberg, Michael Rea, Eleonore Stump, Adam Green, Johan De Smedt, and an anonymous referee for comments on an earlier version of this paper, and members of the audience of the Hiddenness panel at the American Academy of Religion, San Diego, November 22–25, 2014, for their remarks.

[1] This estimate is based on surveys conducted by the Pew Forum's Global religious landscape published in 2012, http://www.pewforum.org/2012/12/18/global-religious-landscape-exec/.

[2] In this paper, I will not elaborate on the uneven distribution of nontheism across cultures. For a discussion on this, see Maitzen (2006).

this problem is treated in the philosophy of religion literature. From an atheist perspective, inconclusive evidence for God can be taken as a potential source of evidence against God's existence. A simple form of this argument from divine hiddenness, as developed by Schellenberg (2006, 83), goes as follows:[3]

1. If there is a God, he is perfectly loving.
2. If a perfectly loving God exists, there are no nonresistant nonbelievers.
3. There are and often have been nonresistant nonbelievers.
4. No perfectly loving God exists.
5. There is no God.

Schellenberg assumes premise 2 is true because God would want to have a loving relationship with his creatures. As he observes (chapter 1, p. 23, this volume): "one clearly cannot even get started in a personal relationship without *believing that the other party exists.*" We can expect therefore that God would see to it that creatures capable of such a relationship would believe he exists. However, there are people who nonresistantly do not believe in God (premise 3). Therefore, there is no perfectly loving God, and thus no God. Notice that the argument from divine hiddenness critically relies on empirical facts about nonbelief and doubt. If a full 100 percent of the world's population believed in God with rock-bottom certainty, the problem would not arise. An exploration of the cognitive underpinnings of divine hiddenness could shed light on debates on this topic. From a theistic perspective, divine hiddenness (or, as it is also called, divine silence) is a puzzling phenomenon in need of explanation. If God exists, why does he not make his presence more unambiguously known? This question is the topic of a rich body of religious literature, for instance, Psalms 22, 42, and 43.

In this chapter, I consider the problem of divine hiddenness from a cognitive perspective, distinguishing between the atheistic argument from divine hiddenness and the theistic problem of divine silence. I explore the psychological mechanisms underlying nonbelief and the sense of a relationship with God, using cognitive science of religion and attachment theory. I begin with a treatment of the atheistic argument by a review of theories on the cognitive origins of theism (section 2). Section 3 examines the conditions under which nonbelief arises, focusing on individual cognitive variations. Section 4 considers the epistemic distance reply in the light of the cognitive science of religion. The remainder of the paper focuses on the theistic problem of divine silence. Section 5 examines the relationship that religious believers feel with God as

[3] There are several versions of the argument of divine hiddenness; see also Drange (1993) and Schellenberg (2007, and chapter 1, this volume). For the purposes of this paper, a simple version of the argument suffices. I have replaced the term "reasonable nonbelief" in the original formulation with Schellenberg's more recently preferred "nonresistant nonbelief."

an attachment relationship. Section 6 explores the cognitive mechanisms that underlie spiritual dryness. Section 7 considers how, in spite of a lack of direct religious experiences, humans can feel an indirect experience of God through scripture and liturgy.

2   The cognitive origins of theism

To understand why nonbelief occurs, it is useful to first consider the conditions under which religious belief emerges. Since antiquity, scholars have attempted to provide naturalistic explanations for religious belief. For instance, Euhemerus (fourth century BCE)[4] claimed that gods were deified renowned ancestors and rulers; myths recount their historical deeds that, through retelling, were exaggerated over time. Hume (1757 [2007]) argued that polytheism, which he took to be the earliest form of religious belief, is motivated by fear and insecurity of the future. Over the past twenty-five years, investigations on the cognitive origins of religion have crystalized in a distinct scientific domain, the cognitive science of religion (CSR). CSR is an interdisciplinary field of study that aims to understand religious beliefs and behaviors. Its practitioners rely on empirical observations from a wide and not clearly delineated range of disciplines, including anthropology, developmental psychology, cognitive psychology, and neuroscience (see e.g., Barrett, 2004; Bloom, 2007).

CSR authors have identified stable and recurring features of religious beliefs and practices, some of which emerge in young children, prior to the time when extensive cultural learning can take place. They argue that religion is cognitively natural, which means that it is easy to acquire. Robert McCauley (2011, 197), for instance, likens the acquisition of religious beliefs and practices to acquiring other "maturationally natural" skills, such as walking or learning one's mother tongue. While there is some cultural input involved, children typically do not need systematic education and practice to learn about religious beliefs.

Some CSR authors hold that humans are born believers, equipped with innate capacities that robustly lead to religious belief (e.g., Kelemen, 2004; Barrett, 2012). Others defend the weaker claim that religious belief is not innate, but rather, arises as a byproduct of several evolved cognitive capacities, including our ability to detect agents (Guthrie, 1993) and theory of mind (Bering, 2006). Stewart Guthrie (1993) hypothesizes that humans have a tendency to overattribute agency to features in their environment, such as mistaking the wind, rustling in the bushes, for a predator or another human being. This hypersensitivity to agency cues makes sense from an evolutionary point of view (it is

---

[4] The original work by Euhemerus is lost, but it is mentioned in Diodorus Siculus (first century BCE [1939], book 6, 333, 335, 337).

better to be safe than sorry), and makes humans prone to imagine supernatural beings.

Mind reading is an important element of religious belief, particularly of practices in which believers imagine interactions with supernatural beings. Mind reading is our ability to explain and understand other people's behaviors by attributing to them invisible mental states, such as beliefs and desires. In one fMRI experiment (Schjoedt, Stødkilde-Jørgensen, Geertz, and Roepstorff, 2009), Christian participants prayed spontaneously, said the Lord's Prayer, recited a nursery rhyme, or expressed wishes to Santa Claus. Compared to the other conditions, spontaneous prayer elicited activation in the temporo-parietal junction, the temporopolar region, and the anterior medial prefrontal cortex. These areas are the same as those elicited in everyday social interactions. So spontaneously praying to God is cognitively similar to ordinary social interactions with other people.

In many cultures, theism is intimately connected to moral norms and values. Some CSR authors (e.g., Shariff, Norenzayan, and Henrich, 2010) argue that belief in morally concerned, powerful gods arose because of its effects on human cooperation and altruism. All human groups face the problem of cooperation: it is beneficial to live in a group of cooperators, but even more advantageous if one can reap the benefits bestowed by group members without doing anything in return. If many people within the group adopt this strategy, the group falls apart, and the benefits of cooperation are lost – now everyone is worse off than they were before. One way to prevent this from happening is to police and punish freeriders, a strategy that becomes difficult to maintain with increasing group size (see Nowak, 2006, for review), which necessitates other strategies. All things being equal, someone who believes she is being watched behaves more altruistically than if she thought herself unobserved. For example, simply placing pictures of staring eyes and the message "Cycle thieves, we are watching you" at bicycle parking stalls at Oxford University resulted in a significant drop in bike thefts (Nettle, Nott, and Bateson, 2012). Belief in watchful, morally concerned invisible beings motivates people to behave more altruistically. If many group members share such beliefs, the overall benefits of altruism are distributed, and the group will fare better than competing groups without belief in God or gods. Ara Norenzayan (2013) hypothesizes that widespread theism is the result of a cultural selective process: groups whose members sincerely believe in punishing and rewarding deities became larger and more cooperative than groups without belief in such beings, and enjoyed greater success in competition for resources and habitats.

Our minds are receptive to many religious ideas, a diversity that is reflected in CSR research on topics such as belief in local spirits (Purzycki, 2013), spirit possession (Cohen, 2007), and fire-walking rituals (Konvalinka et al., 2011). This attention in CSR on a broad spectrum of religious beliefs and practices stands in sharp contrast with the rather narrow focus on a generic form of monotheism in contemporary analytic philosophy of religion (see also Schellenberg, chapter 1, this volume). Theory of mind and agency detection also support belief in ancestors, fairies, ghosts, and spirits. Belief in moralizing, powerful deities correlates with large groups, meaning that members of small groups with good social control are less likely to believe in moralizing gods (Roes and Raymond, 2003). So while CSR holds that belief in supernatural beings is natural, it does not privilege belief in the God of the Abrahamic monotheisms.

3   Nonresistant nonbelief and the cognitive origins of atheism

Given that religious belief emerges so easily, what can explain nonbelief? Cognitive scientists of religion have only recently begun to work on the cognitive origins of atheism (e.g., Norenzayan and Gervais, 2013). This work suggests that both cultural and individual psychological factors can give rise to nonbelief. For instance, when one is not exposed to religious displays in one's cultural milieu while growing up, the probability of becoming a theist decreases markedly. Another cultural factor is the rise of secular institutions, such as modern nation states, which are effective enforcers of cooperation through policing mechanisms and the redistribution of wealth. Such institutions may come to displace religion, which fulfills a similar functional role. For instance, Scandinavian states, which provide an effective social safety net, have the lowest levels of religiosity worldwide (Zuckerman, 2012). Some authors (e.g., Norenzayan and Gervais, 2013) have hypothesized that better secular provisions such as healthcare and social security lower feelings of insecurity and lower the motivation to be part of cooperative religious groups.

Next to these cultural factors, nonbelief also results from individual cognitive variations. I will focus on the autistic spectrum as a causal factor of nonresistant nonbelief. As we have seen, mind reading supports the representation of supernatural agents by imagining their mental states. People who are high on the autistic spectrum typically score lower on theory of mind tasks: they are less able to understand that others hold false beliefs. Norenzayan, Gervais, and Trzesniewski (2012) show a positive correlation between atheism and autism. They found that adolescents on the autistic spectrum were only 11 percent as likely to strongly endorse God's existence as neurotypical teenagers. Increasing severity of autism was associated with further decreases in belief in God: each standard deviation of decrease in mentalizing was associated with a further 20 percent lower likelihood of belief in God. To examine whether diminished theory of mind was causally responsible, Norenzayan et al. (2012) used a standardized empathizing/systemizing questionnaire[5] and correlated

---

[5] This questionnaire is used to detect natural variations in mentalizing in the normal population. A lower empathizing score and a higher systemizing score are associated with the autistic spectrum.

scores with belief in God. They found correlations between lower empathizing scores and a reduced belief in God. Although correlation does not automatically mean causation, it seems plausible that a reduced ability to think about others in terms of their mental states is responsible for the higher incidence of atheism in people with autism. They may be nonresistant nonbelievers because it is hard for them to represent supernatural beings (especially their mental states).

Traditionally, autism has been (and often still is) regarded as a cognitive disability. However, given the relatively high prevalence of autism in the population, some authors have explored the view that high-functioning forms of autism are part of normal cognitive variation (Jaarsma and Welin, 2012). People with autism tend to have cognitive strengths that are less developed in neurotypical individuals, such as a heightened attention to details, patterns, and regularities, and improved insights into mechanical systems and numbers (e.g., Iuculano et al., 2014). Autistic spectrum is more prevalent in engineers, physicists, and mathematicians (Baron-Cohen et al., 1998). According to the archaeologist Penny Spikins (2009), the relative high prevalence of autism came about through natural selection. Cultural innovations may require a collaboration of different kinds of minds. Already since the Pleistocene, we can see technological innovations such as calendrical notation systems (e.g., the Abri Blanchard plaque, 30,000 years old), which require sustained attention to details and recurrent patterns of phases and positions of the moon. Autistic individuals, who are good at noting such cyclical patterns, may have contributed to the development of such artifacts, which may have given them an adaptive advantage and increased their prevalence in the gene pool. Some people may be less likely to believe in God (i.e., be nonresistant nonbelievers) because of the way their minds function, and this is not necessarily a cognitive malfunction. Autism and its relation to atheism thus provides support for premise 3 of the argument from divine hiddenness: due to natural cognitive variations, there are today, and have been in the past, nonresistant nonbelievers.

4   The epistemic distance reply

Theists offer several responses to the argument from divine hiddenness. Some (e.g., Calvin, 1559 [1960]) have denied premise 3, that is, they deny that nonbelief is nonresistant. According to the Reformed tradition, people have an innate sense of the divine, in which case the denial of theism always amounts to resistant nonbelief. However, as we have seen, cognitive and cultural factors underdetermine belief in God, and can easily give rise to other religious beliefs or no religious beliefs at all. In the picture that CSR offers nonbelief isn't a noetic effect of sin, but a result of our evolutionary history[6].

---

[6] De Cruz and De Smedt (2013b) develop this point in detail, arguing that CSR is more compatible with an Irenaean than with an Augustinian picture of noetic effects of sin.

Most responses to the problem of divine hiddenness focus on premise 2. Is it plausible that a loving God allows for nonresistant nonbelief? God may have reasons to make his existence less obviously known. In John Hick's (1966) terminology, God creates an epistemic distance between his creatures and himself to allow us to make morally significant choices. As Michael Murray puts it:

> At least one of the reasons that God must remain hidden is that failing to do so would lead to a loss of morally significant freedom on the part of creatures. The reason, in brief, is that making us powerfully aware of the truth of God's existence would suffice to coerce (at least many of) us into behaving in accordance with God's moral commands. Such awareness can lead to this simply because God's presence would provide us with overpowering incentives which would make choosing the good ineluctable for us. (Murray, 2002, 63)

Murray, following Hick, regards libertarian moral freedom as an instrumental good. In our earthly life, when God's existence is veiled from us to some extent, we can develop morally significant characters (soul-making). If God revealed himself in a way that would eliminate all nonresistant nonbelief, "Our fear of punishment, or at least our fear of the prospect of missing out on a very great good, would compel us to believe the things that God has revealed and to act in accordance with them" (Murray, 2002, 68).

Although this hypothetical situation cannot be directly tested through experiments, CSR provides some indirect support. Making God more salient, for instance, by priming participants with religious words like "spirit" and "divine," makes them more altruistic and less likely to cheat. In one experiment, participants received 10 dollars, which they could choose to split any way they liked between themselves and another participant. Recipient and donor were anonymous to each other. People who were religiously primed donated on average 4.22 dollars, those who received a neutral prime only offered 1.84 dollars (Shariff and Norenzayan, 2007). Similarly, participants who received a religious prime were less likely to cheat on a test than those who received a secular prime (Randolph-Seng and Nielsen, 2007). Several psychological studies also found a "Sunday effect," an increase in prosocial behavior in religious believers on Sundays, such as an increased response to appeals for charity. Sunday effects are more pronounced in regular churchgoers, indicating it may be the increased salience of God that induces prosociality (Malhotra, 2010). These findings provide some support for the epistemic distance reply, as they indicate that priming God concepts makes people more likely to behave morally.

The epistemic distance reply holds that it is not knowledge of God's existence simpliciter that would be morally coercive, but specifically knowledge of God as someone who is capable of punishing or rewarding us through eternal punishment in hell or eternal bliss in heaven. If God's existence becomes more obviously known, he would have "to make the corresponding facts about human fulfillment (or misery) based on a relationship with God more hidden"

(Murray, 2002, 76). CSR evidence is in line with this claim, indicating that belief in a vengeful God of justice deters people from doing bad things, not belief in God in general. To test the effect of different God concepts on moral behavior, Shariff and Norenzayan (2011) let participants perform tedious mathematical tasks. They were told that due to some computer glitch the correct answers would sometimes appear on the screen. If this happened, they should press the space bar so that the answer disappeared. Not hitting the space bar was coded as cheating. The experimenters found that the extent to which participants cheated could be predicted by their image of God: those who conceived of a God of justice and anger cheated significantly less than those who conceived of a God of love and mercy. A large cross-cultural study (Shariff and Rhemtulla, 2012) found that belief in hell, all things considered, lowered crime rates, whereas societies with a prevalent belief in heaven (but not hell) actually had elevated crime rates. It is difficult to extrapolate from these findings what would happen if God were to reveal himself to all. It seems plausible that this would increase prosocial behavior, but it would be disruptive in other ways. It would cause serious problems for any religion that held incompatible beliefs. The extent to which people would feel morally coerced would also depend on what aspects God would reveal about himself. A God who is regarded as forgiving and loving, as we have seen, can even decrease prosocial behavior. Thus, it would be consistent with findings from CSR that God could reveal some aspects of himself (e.g., being loving) while keeping other elements hidden, without compromising our ability to make moral choices.

5   CSR and spiritual attachment

We have seen how CSR provides some support for the argument from divine hiddenness: it explains how nonresistant nonbelief can occur (premise 3), and it explains this phenomenon as a result of normal human cognitive variability. However, CSR offers some support for the epistemic distance reply against premise 2 (i.e., priming God influences people to behave more morally). Not all the literature on divine hiddenness argues from hiddenness to atheism. The problem of divine silence asks why, if theism is true, people who desire a relationship with God sometimes lack religious experiences. In the remainder of the paper, I will look at the theistic problem of divine silence, using relational theories in CSR, in particular those drawing on attachment theory. The attachment literature is crucial in explaining how humans can sense any emotional attachment to the divine. Without the psychological features of the attachment system, including the feelings of anger and loss when the attachment figure is absent or unresponsive, the problem of divine hiddenness would simply not arise, because nobody would care about God's hiddenness.

Relational theories conceptualize religious beliefs and practices as a relationship between a religious believer and a supernatural being. Given that CSR is methodologically naturalistic, such theories may seem incoherent: how can one speak about relationships with the divine, if one cannot assume God exists? However, relational theories are compatible with naturalism: even if these relationships are illusory, their psychological consequences are real, for instance, they affect a believer's relationships with other human beings. In this way, the theistic problem of divine silence can be addressed with the resources of CSR if CSR remains agnostic about these relationships.

In scripture, God is frequently depicted as a father or mother, for example, "How often have I desired to gather your children together as a hen gathers her brood under her wings, and you were not willing!" (Luke 13:34). Sigmund Freud (1927) used the similarity between the relationships of humans to God and young children to parents as a starting point to debunk religious beliefs: religion is an illusion, a childlike longing for a father figure caused by feelings of helplessness. More recently, Lee Kirkpatrick (1999) and Matt Rossano (2010) have used attachment theory as a theoretical model to explain religious practice without Freud's debunking agenda (see also Green, chapter 8, this volume, for a discussion on the relationship between attachment and divine hiddenness).

Attachment theory (developed by John Bowlby, 1969 and expanded by Mary Ainsworth, 1979) seeks to understand the relationship between children and their caregivers, and the impact on children's mental health and well-being. Attachments are strong and enduring bonds of affection between a child and a parent or alloparent. They first emerge when an infant establishes a relationship with one or more caregivers, such as the mother, father, or a foster parent. In a secure attachment, they provide a haven of safety where the infant can turn to when she feels distressed, and a secure basis from which to explore the environment. When distressed, an infant turns to her caregiver by crying or seeking physical proximity. When she feels secure, she ventures away, periodically checking if her caregiver is still present. There are also insecure attachments: in an ambivalent attachment, the infant is uncertain about whether her caregiver is responsive, leading her to be anxious, clingy, less willing to explore the environment. Caregivers in these relationships tend to be erratic in their responsiveness to the infant. In an avoidant attachment, the caregiver does not appear to be a secure haven. They tend to push the infant away and avoid physical contact.

Although other primates also have attachment relationships with their mothers, some features of the human attachment system are unique. The primatologist Tetsuro Matsuzawa (2009) argues that the relative helplessness and supine position (lying on the back) of human infants facilitate eye contact and other social interactions with caregivers. When humans hold their babies, they face them. Chimpanzee mothers, by contrast, don't regularly face their infants, which cling to their backs. Human infants need to actively solicit their caregiver's attention due to their lack of mobility, whereas the more mobile chimpanzee infants do not. In a longitudinal study that observed infant chimpanzees and their mothers, Mizuno, Takeshita, and Matsuzawa (2006) did not observe a single instance of crying in the chimpanzee infants, presumably because "They had no need to cry or scream like human infants, who in fact need to capture their mother's attention to be embraced or to suckle" (Mizuno et al., 2006, 227–8). Human infants need to actively solicit and solidify the attachment relationship with their caregivers, by crying out to them. In a secure attachment, such cries are answered by the caregiver. A state of emotional attunement, facilitated by mutual gazing, is a core element of a secure attachment relationship. From birth, infants are sensitive to gaze directed toward them (Farroni et al., 2005). For a neonate, mutual gazing is the primary means of becoming emotionally attuned with one's primary caregiver. From about two months onward, infants show clear emotional reactions, such as increased smiling when a caregiver looks directly at them. From about four months, they attempt to re-engage when the caregiver looks away by making vocalizations. Starting six to nine months, they also initiate games like peek-a-boo, which involve gazing and looking away. These forms of dyadic interaction form the basis of more complex social interactions, such as joint attention, whereby both parties engage in mutual attention to objects and situations (Reddy, 2003). Two-month-old chimpanzees also engage in dyadic smiling and gazing with their mothers, but these episodes are much less frequent than between human infants and mothers. Unlike human infants, chimpanzee babies never spontaneously share attention with others (Tomonaga et al., 2004).

Kirkpatrick (2005) proposes that the connections believers experience between themselves and God meet the criteria of an attachment relationship. Theists actively work to be closer to God (e.g., in ritual and prayer), and turn to God in times of distress (the safe haven). They ground their exploration of the world in a secure sense of God's presence. Kirkpatrick and Shaver (1990) empirically tested the attachment theory of religion by surveying respondents' relationships to their mothers, God concepts, and factors precipitating religious conversion. They found that participants with secure attachments during childhood were more likely to conceptualize God as loving than those who had avoidant or ambivalent attachments. Moreover, people with insecure attachments were more likely to experience sudden religious conversions than those securely attached. Spiritual attachment is made possible by human-specific cognitive adaptations for secure attachment between humans and caregivers. Rossano (2010) builds on this framework, arguing that the attachment relationship with the gods/God that prehistoric religious believers experienced helped to strengthen relationships between the worshippers as well, fostering strong cooperative bonds of social support.

6   Spiritual dryness as insecure attachment

The relationship with God that religious believers experience (or believe they experience) is not always a secure one. In the ambivalent attachment pattern, infants are not certain about the caregiver's availability. This results in displays of anger and helplessness directed at the (allo)parent. They simultaneously seek contact and preemptively seem to resist it. The desparate and angry cries of the insecurely attached child and the person who experiences divine silence share an analogous phenomenology. Mother Teresa, a devout Roman Catholic nun, expressed acute pain, abandonment, and desolation at the continued lack of religious experiences later in life, which contrasted sharply with the religious experiences in her early life. In a letter dated 1959, she wrote:

Lord, my God, who am I that You should forsake me? The Child of your Love – and now become as the most hated one – the one You have thrown away as unwanted – unloved. I call, I cling, I want – and there is no One to answer – no One on Whom I can cling – no, No One. – Alone. The darkness is so dark – and I am alone. – Unwanted, forsaken. The loneliness of the heart that wants love is unbearable. – Where is my Faith – even deep down right in there is nothing, but emptiness & darkness – My God – how painful is this unknown pain. It pains without ceasing. – I have no Faith – I dare not utter the words & thoughts that crowd in my heart – & make me suffer untold agony. (Mother Teresa, 2007, 186–7)

What goes wrong in insecure attachment relationships? Most studies on attachment agree that the reactions of the child (clinginess, anger) are responses to the parent's erratic availability or lack of reaction. As Jude Cassidy (1994, 232) summarizes in a review of the literature, "Several studies converge to suggest that infants whose mothers respond sensitively to their signals are more likely to be securely attached." By contrast, mothers who respond erratically to their children or neglect them are more likely to have an avoidant or ambivalent attachment relationship (Cassidy, 1994, 241).

Given the phenomenological similarities between carer/infant attachments, and human/God attachments, the theist seems inevitably led to the conclusion that God's silence is causally responsible for Mother Teresa's and other believers' sense of spiritual dryness. Would a parent treat her children in this way? Across cultures, 65 percent of infants exhibit the secure, 21 percent the avoidant, and 14 percent the ambivalent pattern (Van IJzendoorn and Kroonenberg, 1988). The description of different attachment patterns has a normative flavor, being colored by Western ideas about how a parent – especially a mother – should always be available for her children. The secure attachment with a responsive, sensitive mother is put forward as the golden standard, and the other attachment patterns are regarded as suboptimal. It is important to realize that this ideal of parenthood described in terms of duties toward one's child is a relatively recent, Western concept. For instance, the Beng, a West African rain forest culture where alloparenting is the norm, find a strong loving attachment between mother and infant rather regrettable, as the mother cannot rely on allocare and is thus prevented from doing her other work (Gottlieb, 2014). Should our recent Western idiosyncratic ideals of parenthood color our ideas about divine love? Michael Rea (chapter 12, this volume) argues that traditional Christian theology has not done so, and that the holiness and transcendence of God have precedence over the parent analogy. Even if spiritual dryness is uncomfortable, it is not something to be laid at God's doorstep.

Another response comes from mystics such as Teresa of Ávila and John of the Cross, both of whom experienced long bouts of spiritual dryness. Both suggested that God's apparent lack of response allows for a more mature relationship. Humans are so filled with their own plans and desires that there is often no room for God. In order to become fully united with God, John of the Cross (see Garcia, 2002) proposed that people of faith need to pass through three stages of purification (dark nights), including a prolonged inability to feel God's presence, the dark night of the soul. In their view, spiritual dryness is a phase that one needs to go through in order to be weaned from the simple attachment to God as to a nursing mother (to use a different parental analogy), so that one can engage in a more mature relationship. Psalm 131:2 hints at this with powerful maternal imagery of a weaned child, who is still with his mother but who no longer receives the milk he craved so much before:

> But I have calmed and quieted my soul,
> like a weaned child with its mother;
> my soul is like the weaned child that is with me.

The author of this psalm lived in a culture where mother-led weaning (i.e., weaning initiated by the mother, rather than the infant) was the norm.[7] Just as mother-led weaning is a psychologically difficult time for the child, God's withholding his felt presence is hard on the religious believer. Combining the observations of mystics that spiritual dryness is common with the attachment theory on ambivalent attachment, the theist can explain spiritual dryness as a temporary state where God seeks to take the relationship to the next level, a state that elicits great discomfort, and that for some may take a long time. These considerations not only provide a response to the theistic problem of divine silence, but also cast doubt on some assumptions about divine love that underlie Schellenberg's argument from divine hiddenness: the attachment literature reveals that there is cross-cultural variability in the way infant–parent attachments are evaluated. The Western ideal of the responsive and sensitive

---

[7] Mothers living in areas where infant formula is not routinely available tend to wean their infants at about 2.5 years. For an explicit reference to mother-led weaning in the Bible, see 1 Samuel 1:23. When children are allowed to self-wean, they tend to do this between four and five years of age (Kennedy, 2005).

parent, on which Schellenberg relies, predicts that God would always want a two-way responsive relationship with creatures who are capable of such a relationship. However, even if parental analogies hold, the theist may argue that there is no reason to expect God to conform to a recent Western model of attachment, and God might desire a different kind of relationship with some of his creatures.

7   Mediate religious experience

Most theistic replies to the problem of divine hiddenness have focused on the atheist argument from divine hiddenness, attacking the key premises on which this argument is founded. However, even if the argument from divine hiddenness can be successfully addressed, the problem of divine silence remains a challenge for the theist. One response to the problem of divine silence has been to note that absence of religious experience can be mitigated by other, cultural means: God may provide some "widely and readily accessible way of finding him and experiencing his presence despite his silence" (Rea, 2009, 88). This experience is not direct (as in mystical perception), but rather, is mediated by cultural practices such as reading scriptural narratives, attending liturgy, and contemplating religious art.[8] Poignant narratives of the Bible give readers an insight into who God is. Liturgical actions, such as the ritual breaking of bread and pouring of wine in the Eucharist, also provide mediate knowledge of God: "the saving events of God which are commemorated in the liturgy are made present, or actualized, by way of the performance of the liturgy. The acts of God commemorated are not just acknowledged as having present significance; in some way the commemoration makes them actually present" (Rea, 2009, 92).

Such practices do not immediately and ineluctably afford a mediate sense of God's presence. The atheist who wanders into Christ Church Cathedral, Oxford, during Evensong may only hear beautiful music and see atmospheric candlelight, without experiencing God. However, for the religious believer who frequently visits the cathedral, the music can afford a sense of God's presence. In her autobiographical account, *Surprised by Oxford*, Carolyn Weber describes how, as an undergraduate, she gradually transitioned from an atheist skeptic into a Christian, by reading the Bible and attending Evensong across Oxford colleges:

---

[8] Rea does not discuss interactions with religious art specifically (only indirectly in the context of liturgy). Cross-culturally (e.g., western Africa, Oceania, Australia), art is an important feature of religious life; often, the majority of artworks in societies with little material culture have religious meaning.

Atheist, believer, and everywhere in between, we would often go to Evensong, or the Anglican liturgy of prayer that is sung in the evening. Bound by a common liturgy, each college offers a different experience of the service. A motley crew, we would travel together, dropping into services first on a whim, then eventually as a custom of common enjoyment. With its candlelit and melodic beauty, the evening ritual brings peace at the close of day. (Weber, 2011, 91)

According to Sarah Coakley (2013), liturgy can be thought of as a set of doxastic practices in an Alstonian sense (see Alston, 1991), involving memory, introspection, and associative thoughts. Drawing on Lorraine Code's (1991) feminist epistemology, Coakley argues that our physical surroundings, our embeddedness in a community, and our position in society matter to what we can know. Liturgical practices, scripture reading, and religious art situate believers, including those who do not enjoy direct religious experiences, within a rich, sensory, and affective environment in which they can acquire religious beliefs they would not easily acquire under other circumstances.

Theories in embodied and extended cognition can explain how liturgies and other doxastic practices can accomplish this. Philosophers of mind increasingly recognize that human cognition is embodied and materially embedded. We are not disembodied Cartesian souls that impassively survey the world around us; rather, we probe the world through physical interaction. External media can enhance cognitive processes. Material culture helps to make elusive, hard-to-grasp concepts more concrete. For example, mathematical symbols like i (introduced to denote square roots of negative numbers) help mathematicians to work with ideas that otherwise would be intractable, and have played a crucial role in the evolution of new mathematical ideas, such as complex numbers (De Cruz and De Smedt, 2013a).

Similarly, liturgical practices vividly bring events described in the Bible to life. They not only illustrate the Last Supper, but also allow one to take part in it. In this way, and through frequent repetition of Gospel stories, believers are brought closer to the historical Jesus, who would otherwise be quite distant and unfamiliar. Through familiarization with liturgy and scripture reading, Christians tend to forget that Jesus was Jewish, and are routinely unaware that the culture he was born in is quite unlike ours, with, for instance, people reclining to eat and keeping slaves as common practices.

Material objects, such as representations of the Trinity in painting or sculpture, can make God's presence more concretely felt. Two distinct religious traditions, Hinduism and Eastern Orthodox Christianity, have converged upon a similar practice in gazing upon the faces of representations of the gods, God, and saints. When Hindu worshippers visit a temple, they gaze upon (*darśan*) the sculpture or image of the deity that is worshipped there. This is not a one-way direction: the worshipper also wants to be seen by the deity. Even very crude, hasty representations of Hindu gods have eyes, and their faces are always directed at the worshipper. This mutual gazing establishes a sense of intimacy, and also allows the believer to acquire some of the power and insights of the god or goddess (Babb, 1981). Mutual gazing keys into our evolved capacity for joint attention and our great sensitivity to the gaze of others. A similar cognitive affordance is offered by icon gazing; the large eyes are directed at the person who venerates the image. Intimate interactions like kissing the image further help to establish a sense of attachment. Both Hindu and Eastern Orthodox believers are well aware that the material objects they venerate aren't the actual deities or saints. Rather, they assume that the sculptures and icons provide a mediate experience of God. This experience can be explained by the fact that interacting with representations of human faces and bodies homes in on our evolved sensitivity to faces in social interactions.

Communal practices may also overcome individual cognitive difficulties for belief in God, for instance, in people with autism and other nonresistant nonbelievers. The problem of divine silence focuses on direct religious experiences. Even if one's mind is not well attuned to acquiring religious beliefs, cultural practices can facilitate this process. Because the liturgy makes connecting to God structured and repetitive (features that people with autism respond well to), it can help them overcome difficulties in imagining an invisible person with internal mental states. From his personal experiences as a practicing Roman Catholic with autism, Christopher Barber recounts:

A lack of imagination often makes certain forms of prayer such as meditation and contemplation difficult for me in that I often feel the need to hang onto something concrete that I can connect with. Thus, I find prayer that has a concrete structure such as the Divine Office and the Rosary easier to connect with than extemporary or contemplative prayer ... Ritualized prayer can also be helpful because for people with autism there is a need for predictability and order in almost all aspects of our lives. Prayer as connection to God is no different ... In my own tradition, the Mass follows a reasonably set and predictable format of the liturgy of approach, confession, the word then of the Eucharist. Indeed, the Eucharist is the beginning, middle and end of all prayer and is the single act or manifestation of God from which all prayer springs ... These combined elements provide a framework onto which the autistic brain can latch, with which someone can be at ease. (Barber, 2011, 206–7)

For now, we lack a systematic study of how structured practices of the liturgy may help overcome the extra difficulties people with autism face when seeking a relationship with God. This personal account tentatively suggests that liturgical practices can provide mediate religious experiences through their predictability and making things concrete. CSR provides support for the claim that lack of direct religious experience can be mitigated by cultural practices.

8   Concluding remarks

This essay has focused on two philosophical puzzles on divine hiddenness: the atheistic argument from divine hiddenness, which takes the presence of non-resistant nonbelief as evidence against God's existence, and the theistic problem of divine silence, which attempts to understand why God does not seem to communicate with those who actively seek a relationship with him. CSR indicates that belief in God emerges as a result of several cognitive factors, including our ability to attribute mental states and our need to cooperate with others in large social groups. Nonresistant nonbelief can arise as a result of cultural factors or individual cognitive variations. In the light of CSR, the main assumption of the epistemic distance reply, i.e., incontrovertible evidence for God's existence would hamper our ability to make significant moral choices, is plausible, although it is hard to predict the consequences of a God who would reveal himself unambiguously.

Religious believers experience an attachment relationship with God, which capitalizes on features of human psychology, such as actively soliciting and maintaining contact with caregivers. Such factors foster religious beliefs, but they are not inevitable. In human parent–child attachment relationships the main initiators of insecure attachments are the parents, indicating that, for theists, God does not seem to respond all the time to some who wish a relationship with him. One reply to the theistic problem of divine silence is that doxastic practices like participating in the liturgy, reading scripture, and contemplating religious art allow for mediate religious experiences. CSR studies on the role of liturgy and interactions with material culture support this view.

Part III

God's Hiddenness: Faith and Skepticism

4   Divine hiddenness and self-sacrifice

Paul K. Moser

If God is inherently *agapē*, as parts of the Christian tradition suggest, and *agapē* is self-sacrifice of a redemptive kind, then God is self-sacrifice of that redemptive kind. This widely neglected lesson has significant implications for the topic of divine presence and hiddenness and the topic of human knowledge of God. This paper draws out some of those implications, thereby clarifying how the question of God's existence challenges humans not just to think but also to exist and to act in profoundly redemptive ways. The result offers a new practical alternative to familiar ways of inquiring about God's presence and hiddenness. It also prompts us to think of God as inherently *curative* toward humans, owing to the divine effort to heal people of their tendencies to self-destruction and moral failure by God's standards. In this perspective, our problems regarding divine hiddenness are not purely intellectual or cognitive, but are profoundly moral and existential.

1   An imagined scenario

Let's imagine the following *possible* scenario, even if not endorsing its actuality. This scenario overlaps with some Christian ways of conceiving of God, but we need not embrace the latter ways now. We do need, however, a rather definite conception of God before we can turn to the topic of divine hiding. Being self-sufficiently morally perfect, God is worthy of (and hence merits) worship as adoration and full love, trust, and obedience. Accordingly, God seeks what is morally and spiritually best for all humans, even for the resolute enemies of God. In doing so, God does not opt for the immediate extermination or the coercion of humans. Instead, God makes a divine self-offering to humans that invites them freely to cooperate with God's purpose of redemption as reconciliation in mutual companionship. We might think of this as God's "peace offering" to humans that offers forgiveness as a release from divine condemnation and as an entryway to a reconciled relationship. The desired reconciliation is no *mere* agreement among persons, of the kind had by partners in crime,

I thank Eleonore Stump and Adam Green for comments.

for instance. Instead, it conforms to God's perfectly good moral character and hence is robustly normative and righteous.

In an ancient Jewish tradition, the divine offering emerges in God's "bending low" in various ways to sustain and to rescue Israel, despite Israel's frequent resistance to God (see, e.g., Hosea 11:1–4). God's sacrificial offering is anticipated in Abraham's remark to Isaac that "God himself will provide the lamb for a burnt offering" (Gen. 22:8). In the canonical Christian tradition, the divine offering culminates in God's sending Jesus as the Son of God to offer himself for humans on God's behalf (see Rom. 3:24–6; cf. 1 Cor. 5:7, Heb. 9:11–15, John 3:14–17). This self-sacrifice emerges in the enacted parables of the Last Supper in the synoptic Gospels (see Mk 14:22–5) and the foot washing by Jesus in John's Gospel (see John 13:3–15).

It is striking that, in Paul's message, the death of Jesus Christ is where *God* proves his holy love (*agapē*) for humans (Rom. 5:8; cf. Rom. 8:39). This divine self-offering aims for what is best for humans, all things considered. In particular, it aims to prompt their reciprocating toward God, that is, their offering themselves to God in obedient cooperation with God's perfect will. The latter, reciprocating self-offering to God forms the center of human faith in God, because it is the means of intentionally receiving and manifesting God's redemptive self-offering to humans. This key component of faith in God is, however, widely neglected among theologians and philosophers of religion. God's self-offering aims to be freely received and *re-manifested* by humans as personal agents who intentionally image God's moral character of *agapē*. In sum, then, God seeks a world of mutual self-sacrifice for the moral and spiritual good, including the reconciliation, of all concerned. This fits with God's perfect moral character, but nothing humans have done obligates God to provide their redemption; nor was God required to create humans.

We can imagine the following background for our scenario. Contrary to the exaggerations of some people, humans lack the power to live self-sufficiently or independently of a stronger intentional power. In particular, they lack the resources of their own to extend their lives for the indefinite future, and their impending deaths confirm this, loud and clear. More to the point, they lack the power of their own to flourish lastingly in a morally good community of humans. Left to themselves, humans face a bleak future indeed, as Bertrand Russell candidly acknowledges in "A Free Man's Worship" (1903). Accordingly, in our scenario, God has a vital educational and curative project aimed at personal reconciliation: in particular, a project to lead people non-coercively to recognize and to value their needed cooperation with the divine power that aims to sustain them in a flourishing community. People need to be healed of their contrary tendencies on this front.

The needed divine power contrasts with the kind of power that dominates power exchanges in cases of exclusive competition. It centers instead on the kind of redemptive self-sacrifice that seeks reconciliation and fits with a divine standard of worthiness of worship, moral perfection, and perfect love. The divine project therefore faces the difficulty of going against typical human selfishness in order to promote the moral and spiritual good of all concerned. It calls for, and offers to empower, the replacement of human selfishness with redemptive self-sacrifice that promotes reconciliation with God and humans. Cooperation with this ongoing project of human renewal is the way to enter and to abide in the kingdom of God. Indeed, this challenging kingdom stems from the power of redemptive self-sacrifice, and such power goes beyond talk and even sophisticated philosophical talk (the occupational hazards of the life of the mind). This kingdom thus offers distinctive power that opposes one's living mainly for oneself or for one's clan.

The redemptive self-sacrifice in question includes, as its motivation, what various New Testament writers call *agapē*, and it figures in the striking claim that "God is *agapē*" (1 John 4:8, 16). In fact, we plausibly can translate the latter claim as: "God is self-sacrifice" (of the redemptive kind just sketched). This translation is preferable to the familiar translation, "God is love," given the merely sentimental uses of "love" that are widespread in contemporary English. A God worthy of worship, being morally perfect, would be anything but merely sentimental. As a result, the writer of 1 John characterizes *agapē* in terms of active self-sacrifice for the good of others. One pertinent statement from 1 John is: "We know love by this, that he [Jesus] laid down his life for us – and we ought to lay down our lives for one another" (1 John 3:16, NRSV, here and in subsequent biblical translations; see 1 John 2:1–5, 4:9, and, for the writer of John's Gospel, see John 15:12–14).

Paul closely relates *agapē* with self-sacrifice in his remark about Jesus: "The life I now live in the flesh I live by faith in the Son of God, who loved me and gave himself for me" (Gal. 2:20). The key self-sacrificial language is: "gave himself for me." Paul also relates grace (*charis*) closely with self-sacrifice, as follows: "You know the generous act (*charis*) of our Lord Jesus Christ, that though he was rich, yet for your sakes he became poor, so that by his poverty you might become rich" (2 Cor. 8:9). This self-giving of Jesus is inherently sacrificial for the good of others, and it occupies the center of Paul's thought and message (see Phil. 2:5–8, Rom. 3:24–6). The relevant love, then, does not reduce to anything merely sentimental, but is, instead, action-oriented with self-giving for the good of others.

In the imagined scenario, which may or may not be actual, God offers a self-sacrifice to humans for their good, in particular, for their being invited to a reconciled life of companionship with God. This offer prompts some simple but formative questions. What, if anything, would we humans do in response? Would we just think and talk about the offer, and avoid conforming to it? Would we demand some kind of "proof" of its veracity, and, if so, what kind of proof?

Would we follow the rich young ruler of Mark 10:17–22 in turning away with some regret? (See Thielicke, 1962, 55–7.) Would we turn away, instead, without any regret? Alternatively, would we let the offer grip us in a manner that redefines us, in thought, attitude, and action? Would we let the author of the offer make us new in God's image, come what may? Clearly, one answer does not fit all humans, given the wide variation in human motives and goals. The present lesson is that our scenario would leave us humans with a crucial decision, one which bears on the basis and direction of their lives.

Seeking full human redemption for each human, God as curative would want people to decide to enter in fully to the life of divine self-sacrifice. Accordingly, God would want people to experience, welcome, and manifest this life rather than just to think, talk, or even know about it. This divine want would fit with God's desiring the willing redemption of the whole person, not just a single human aspect, such as the human intellect. In particular, God would want to engage the human will, in order to encourage free human compliance with God's perfect will. This compliance would include a primary self-commitment to, and a consistent practice of, redemptive self-sacrifice of the kind manifested by God, even if people making this commitment fall short at times. The divine challenge for humans, then, would call for an internal and an external manner of existing and living, in terms of internal commitments and outward practices suited to God's character of holy love. Anything short of this manner would be redemptively inadequate by a divine standard of moral perfection.

Let's use the word "God" as an honorific title that connotes the kind of morally perfect agent just imagined, a self-sacrificial being who is worthy of worship. Our use of this title allows for the non-existence of God, and hence does not beg important questions against atheists and agnostics. Even so, this title gives determinate semantic meaning to our questions about God's existence, and thereby saves us from a predicament akin to Lewis Carroll's hunting of the snark. In addition, this title sets the bar suitably high for candidates for the title "God," because without worthiness of worship and the corresponding moral perfection, a candidate will fail to be God. This is how things should be, if we are to retain the perfectionist strain in traditional monotheism as represented in parts of Judaism, Christianity, and Islam. We need to clarify how self-sacrifice figures in this unique role and how it bears on divine hiddenness. If we lack an adequate understanding of God's character, we will be unable to make needed sense of divine hiddenness. (I do not expect, however, that humans will reach a full explanation of divine hiddenness on their own.)

2   Two sides of sacrifice: divine and human

The English term "sacrifice" derives from the Latin *sacrificium*, which stems from the terms *sacer* ("sacred") and *faciō* ("do, make"). The idea of "making something sacred," by an offering in relation to God, looms large in the ety-mology of "sacrifice." Perhaps the most common notion suggests something consecrated, or solemnly offered, by humans *to* a divinity. It would be a mis-take, however, to regard this notion as having a monopoly or even the priority relative to its alternatives. Our imagined scenario, in keeping with some promi-nent strands of the Jewish and Christian traditions, portrays *God* as taking the initiative in self-sacrifice in order to reconcile humans to God. Just as various biblical writers suggest that God first loved us humans, they also suggest that God first offered self-sacrifice on our behalf, and that our self-sacrifice (to God and others) is to be a fitting, imaging *response* to the divine initiative (see 1 John 4:10, 19; cf. Rom. 3:24–6). Our imagined scenario likewise suggests that we put first things first, relative to *God's* initiative in sacrifice as a sacred offering. In this context, we would seek an understanding not of sacrifice or self-sacrifice in the abstract, but rather of sacrifice or self-sacrifice as exem-plified or commanded by God. (On some of the various understandings, see Daly, 2009.)

Human self-sacrifice, like human love, is not intrinsically good, because we can sacrifice to bad things, just as we can love bad things. For instance, we can sacrifice to destructive idols of greed, hate, and death rather than to the God worthy of worship. Human history illustrates this serious problem with seemingly endless examples. The history in the Old Testament, for instance, abundantly confirms this lesson, even in the presence of divine challenges to avoid idolatry and other destructive sacrifices. Bad sacrifice, however, need not be obviously destructive from the perspective of all observers. When sacrifice is altogether morally superficial, such as in the case of empty religious ritual-ism, it can be bad, even when some people fail to recognize this. Some of the Old Testament prophets had genuine concerns in this regard (see, for instance, Micah 6:6–8), and such concerns should persist in the face of empty ritualism in religion, which lacks redemptive self-sacrifice. Good sacrifice is intention-ally redemptive in conforming to the divine project to reconcile humans to God and to each other. So, we have a definite contrast between good and bad sacrifice, including good and bad self-sacrifice.

If God is inherently self-sacrificial for the redemptive good of all concerned, some important consequences emerge for divine presence and hiddenness. In particular, if God is inherently self-sacrificial in moral character, then divine presence to humans is likewise self-sacrificial, given that it would represent God's moral character. That is, divine presence would include the essential motive of being self-sacrificial for the redemptive good of all concerned. In that regard, at least, divine presence would be morally robust in what it includes, and may call for human sensitivity to its moral robustness. This perspective stands in sharp contrast to any image of God's presence as merely aesthetic, without moral significance.

If God's power alone, rather than human power, is the ultimate source of redemptive self-sacrifice, then certain results are noteworthy. Wherever redemptive self-sacrifice occurs, the power of God is present too, as is divine presence, even if humans overlook or ignore it. Sacrificial divine presence, in this case, does not owe its reality to our embracing or even acknowledging it. In fact, if God first self-sacrificed for us, just as God first loved us, then divine self-sacrificial presence does not delay in waiting for our invitation, acknowledgment, or approval. Instead, it comes first, aiming to prompt our response in kind, by our chosen reliance on the divine power of self-sacrifice on offer. Correspondingly, our opposing or even ignoring the reality or the importance of redemptive self-sacrifice can obscure divine reality, leaving it hidden from us. For instance, if I hold that God would never stoop to redemptive self-sacrifice, I will not recognize or acknowledge God in such sacrifice.

The human sacrificial response will characteristically fall short of divine perfection, given human frailties. Accordingly, Vincent Taylor remarks:

No Hebrew could think of offering himself as he was, frail and sinful, to a holy and righteous God (cf. Isa. 6:5–8), while the idea of a purely spiritual offering would have seemed to him abstract and meaningless. The life offered must be that of another, innocent and pure, free from all impurity and sin, and yet withal the symbol of an ideal life to which he aspired and with which he could identify himself ... (Taylor, 1937, 60)

This perfectionist standard suits the moral character of a God worthy of worship, but it raises a serious problem for morally imperfect humans (cf. Heb. 7:11). The problem concerns how humans can supply the needed redemptive perfection in their sacrifices.

Left to our merely human resources, we lack a sacrifice that accurately images or reciprocates God's perfect self-sacrifice for us. Our own resources fall short of willingly offering a morally perfect self-sacrifice for the sake of redemption as reconciliation. Vincent Taylor identifies a key part of the problem as follows: "The main obstacle to a healthy development [of the idea of self-sacrifice in the Old Testament] was the passive character of the Levitical offering; the worshipper faced the demand of identifying himself with that which could neither will nor experience the glory of vicarious sacrifice" (1937, 60). Despite human alienation from God, the ideal sacrifice is an intentional self-sacrifice that draws from and manifests the moral perfection of God in order to offer redemption as reconciliation to God.

From the standpoint of available resources, only God would be able to deliver the ideal, perfect sacrifice. Mere humans, lacking the power of perfect love, will fall short of any perfectionist standard for self-sacrifice. In addition, if the perfect sacrifice is to be a *human* sacrifice to God, only God would be able to supply the human who can serve this redemptive purpose with perfection. That is, the needed human mediator for redemptive self-sacrifice must come from God in order to supply redemptive perfection. Accordingly, the Good News of the Christian message is that God has done just this in Jesus Christ as God's perfect Son, Mediator, and Priest (see Mark 14:22–24, Heb. 7:14–28, 9:14, 1 Cor. 5:7). This divine offering through Jesus aims to meet the perfectionist standard that was only approximated in the Levitical system of sacrifices and could not be met by humans alienated from God. The divine offering in question includes redemptive suffering that can transform human sin into divine grace aimed at the redemption of humans, as seen in the crucifixion of Jesus (see Robinson, 1942, ch. 13).

A twofold theme of the Christian message is that, courtesy of God, Jesus supplies the representative human self-sacrifice on behalf of humans, and other humans can, and should, share in this offering by "faith" in God and Jesus. Such faith is no mere assent to information, even theological information about redemption. Instead, to be redemptive, it must provide human union with the self-sacrifice of Jesus, whereby we humans willingly share in the perfect self-sacrifice offered on our behalf. It is thus active, obedient trust in God that goes beyond belief that something is true. It includes endeavoring with God for God's redemptive purposes, and this includes endeavoring with God in self-sacrifice (see Jas. 2:17–20; cf. Matt. 7:21). The key role of self-sacrifice in human faith in God is widely neglected in theology and the philosophy of religion, and therefore we need to introduce an important correction here.

The New Testament evidence for the needed sharing in redemptive self-sacrifice is extensive and clear. For instance, the Gospels portray Jesus as saying: "If any want to become my followers, let them deny themselves and take up their cross and follow me" (Mark 8:34; cf. Luke 9:23, Matt. 16:24). Even more strongly: "Whoever does not carry the cross and follow me cannot be my disciple" (Luke 14:27). His talk of the cross here suggests that his disciples must image him in self-sacrificial commitment and action, in redemptive obedience to God. This lesson is confirmed by Paul's remarks that he is to "complete what is lacking in Christ's afflictions for the sake of his body, that is, the church" (Col. 1:24), and that the Roman Christians are "by the mercies of God, to present [their] bodies as a living sacrifice, holy and acceptable to God, which is [their] spiritual worship" (Rom. 12:1). Similar confirmation comes from the author of 1 Peter: "Let yourselves be built into a spiritual house, to be a holy priesthood, to offer spiritual sacrifices acceptable to God through Jesus Christ" (2:5; cf. 2:21). The latter sacrifices are "through Jesus Christ" at least in that they follow his self-giving redemptive path in obedience to God. (For related discussion, see Richardson, 1958, ch. 13; Bradley, 1995, ch. 4; John Taylor, 1992, 202–5.)

What Paul calls "the obedience of faith" (Rom. 1:5, 16:26; cf. 10:15–17) is best understood as the self-sacrifice characteristic of faith in God, after the pattern of Jesus. In this obedience, people offer themselves, if imperfectly, to God for the sake of redemption as reconciliation to God. Such self-sacrifice to God includes one's receiving God's power of self-sacrifice and thereby giving oneself to God in similar self-sacrifice. This kind of self-sacrifice does not include any human earning or meriting of redemption, and therefore it does not qualify as what Paul calls "works" in contrast with faith, in some contexts (see Rom. 4:4). As a result, this self-sacrificial component of faith is compatible with Paul's understanding of faith in God that excludes one's earning redemption. There is no Pelagian idea of earning redemption here, even if people have the ability to receive or to reject God's gifts. (For a detailed treatment of Paul on faith and works, see Moser, 2013, ch. 4.)

If redemptive self-sacrifice is the locus of divine presence, where humans can meet and commune with God, a simple question arises. Why does God offer redemptive self-sacrifice to humans and then demand similar sacrifice from them? A straightforward answer now arises. As morally perfect God would seek what is best (all things considered) for all concerned, and hence would seek the reconciliation of humans to God's character of redemptive *agapē*, or holy love. If genuinely good relationships and communities among intentional agents require self-sacrificial *agapē*, then a morally perfect God would need to offer such relationships and communities on the basis of such *agapē*. Accordingly, a genuinely redemptive God would put self-sacrifice front and center on the stage of personal life, both for God and for humans, in order to reconcile all agents under God's perfect moral character. This redemptive mission would encompass the ultimate meaning of human life for God and for humans, even if some humans ignore or resist it and thereby ignore or resist God. Accordingly, this mission also would include the path to human self-fulfillment: self-fulfillment as redemptive self-sacrifice with God. Selfishness, by contrast, would fall short of lasting self-fulfillment, because it would run afoul of God's moral character and the corresponding redemptive mission and sustenance.

3   Self-sacrifice in evidence for God

Is the previous scenario pure fiction, just a wishful fairy tale? Obviously, it *could* be, but our answer should depend on the actual evidence available to us. The word "available" is crucial to the previous claim, because our coming to have the needed evidence of God's reality may require our seeking it in a particular way (see Moser, 2013b). In that case, we should not settle for the evidence we happen to have, apart from our seeking (and perhaps acquiring) relevant evidence in a suitable way. We need to explore this matter in order to be in a position to comment on the reasonableness of the previous scenario.

Questions about the evidence for God can benefit from reflection on the kind of moral character God must have to be worthy of worship. Such reflection can calibrate our expectations regarding the evidence for God. To be morally perfect, and not just morally tolerable, God would have to be inherently self-sacrificial toward a redemptive end for everyone. Here we have an indicator of where we may expect to find God's presence: in redemptive self-sacrifice as we ourselves participate in it. In this vein, the writer of 1 John states: "Whoever does not love does not know God, for God is love" (4:8). A corresponding, more suitable translation is: "Whoever does not self-sacrifice, redemptively, does not know God, for God is redemptive self-sacrifice." Accordingly, coming to know God in acquaintance with God's presence is not a spectator sport or an armchair pastime. Instead, it requires one's joining, by one's own free decision, in what is inherent to God's moral character: redemptive self-sacrifice. Such knowing is foreign to certain modern conceptions of disengaged knowledge, but it fits with the expectations of a redemptive God, who would seek human cooperation in redemption for the good of all concerned. Knowing God, then, is morally robust and challenging.

If we are not expecting God to self-manifest in self-sacrifice, we may overlook salient evidence for God, even when it is close at hand. For instance, in that case, the self-sacrificial death of Jesus on the cross may appear to be a place just of human suffering, and not God's aiming to reconcile the world via divine self-manifestation in self-sacrifice. Paul's theological epistemology suggests that a person needs to rely on "spiritual discernment" to apprehend things revealed by God (see 1 Cor. 2:14), and that this reliance includes one's having the "mind of Christ" (1 Cor. 2:16). Paul does not elucidate his notions of spiritual discernment and the mind of Christ in the ways a contemporary philosopher or theologian might, but he does leave readers with some helpful clues. He introduces these notions in a context that is explicitly concerned with redemptive self-sacrifice, both from God and to God.

Paul suggests that having spiritual discernment and the mind of Christ includes being (in) "God's temple" (1 Cor. 3:16–17), which is a place of redemptive self-sacrifice from and to God. In addition, Paul likens Christian life to the Passover sacrifice (cf. Exod. 12:21, 27), as follows: "Clean out the old yeast so that you may be a new batch, as you really are unleavened. For our paschal lamb, Christ, has been sacrificed" (1 Cor. 5:7). The Passover shows both sides of redemptive self-sacrifice: God's self-sacrifice (now in Christ) for humans and the response of human self-sacrifice to God (in the obedience of faith in God). The omission of either side undermines human redemption by God. In addition, "the mind of Christ," being that of a willing Passover lamb for God, is now seen to be inherently redemptive and self-sacrificial, in willing obedience to God. Accordingly, we now see that the mind of Christ is the mind of Gethsemane (Mark 14:36), where a human will offers itself in redemptive obedience to God. Perhaps Paul's clearest linking of knowing God's Son and one's sharing in his redemptive suffering is: "I want to know Christ and the power of his resurrection and the sharing of his sufferings by becoming like him in his death, if somehow I may attain the resurrection from the dead" (Phil. 3:10–11; cf. 1 Cor. 2:2).

We should expect God to reveal God's self-sacrificial character directly, by self-manifestation of the divine moral character. This is confirmed by the suggestion of some New Testament writers that God self-authenticates divine reality by direct "self-manifestation" (see Rom. 10:20, 1 Cor. 2:4, 10; cf. John 14:23). It is doubtful that there is any better way to reveal who God truly is, because other, indirect means seem to fall short of the needed moral character and to be easily distorted by humans (see 1 Cor. 1:21, 2:5). If God works by such self-manifestation, however, there are definite consequences for knowing God, which cannot be reduced to knowing that God exists. Although God's perfect self-manifestation is in Jesus Christ, we should not limit this manifestation to the historical Jesus. The manifestation can continue in the risen Christ and his Spirit (see Mackintosh, 1912, 310–20). Indeed, God would be a cognitive failure if the divine self-manifestation ceased some two thousand years ago.

For redemptive purposes, God would want people to know God directly, as a personal agent in an "I–Thou" acquaintance relationship, without the dilution or the distraction of philosophical arguments. God would want people to depend directly on *God* in this connection, because God alone is the Lord, the redeeming giver and sustainer of lasting life (see 1 Cor. 2:4–5). Accordingly, God would want the self-commitment of a human agent *to God*, in the spirit of Gethsemane, not ultimately to an inference or a conclusion of an argument. God would want to be one's evidential foundation for believing in God and for believing that God exists, and hence would not want an argument to assume this role. This would serve God's redemptive purpose to be one's ultimate rock and stronghold of security, even in the area of knowing God.

Strictly speaking, the evidential foundation would be *God in God's self-manifesting interventions* in one's life, including in one's conscience. This would maintain God's vital cognitive and existential significance for human inquirers, but God would have the final decision in when to self-manifest to humans. Even so, we can put ourselves in an improved position to apprehend divine self-manifestation, particularly by being sincerely and willingly open to receive and to participate in redemptive self-sacrifice, the hallmark of God's perfect moral character. Human indifference or resistance to such self-sacrifice can interfere with the reception of foundational evidence for God. (We shall return to the importance of deciding to participate in self-sacrifice.)

God would be self-authenticating regarding divine reality in a way that arguments are not and cannot be, given that arguments are not a causally interactive personal agent. By self-manifesting God's moral character to a receptive human, God could self-authenticate divine reality. This would be roughly akin to one human's self-manifesting her reality as a person (and not just a body) to another human. In addition, a redemptive God would sustain a flourishing human life in a way that arguments cannot, for the same reason: arguments are not a causal personal agent. Accordingly, God would supply the needed foundational evidence of God's reality by divine self-manifestation, and God would want this manifestation to provide the ultimate reason for human hope in God. So, directly knowing God in mutual fellowship would be central to eternal life for humans (see John 17:3). Such knowing would include foundational evidence and knowledge that God is real, but it would not need to wait for an argument that God exists. A commitment to this kind of position on direct knowledge of God accounts for the absence of the traditional arguments of natural theology in the Old and New Testaments.

An argument can obscure the importance of directly knowing God, and many arguments by advocates of theism actually do this, particularly when they serve as blunt instruments for intellectual warfare. In addition, when familiar theistic arguments (for instance, ontological, cosmological, or teleological arguments) come under plausible critical challenge, many critics mistakenly take this challenge to underwrite agnosticism or atheism. This kind of argumentative process is dangerously misleading when it neglects the relevant foundational evidence for God. Even if we can represent foundational evidence for God in a sound argument from a first-person perspective, such an argument cannot exhaust or replace the underlying experiential evidence arising from divine self-manifestation; nor will it generalize to a sound argument from a third-person perspective. (On this matter, see Moser, 2008, ch. 2, and Moser, 2010, chs. 3–4.)

In keeping with an experience of divine self-manifestation, one's foundational reasons or evidence for God need not be discursive or assertive in the way a statement or an argument is. Instead, the relevant evidence can be nonpropositional character traits supplied by God's Spirit in self-manifestation: love, joy, peace, patience, gentleness, and so on (see Gal. 5:22–3; cf. Rom. 5:5). Accordingly, John's Gospel portrays Jesus as announcing that his disciples will be known by their *agapē* for others (John 13:35). Jesus did not mention, allude to, or use any philosophical arguments in this connection, or in any other connection, for that matter. The same is true of his followers represented in the New Testament, although some of them were quite capable intellectually of wielding philosophical arguments. This noteworthy fact, moreover, does not qualify as a deficiency in their actual reasons, evidence, or mode of engagement. Talk is cheap, especially regarding God, and therefore many inquirers will wonder whether a theological statement or conclusion has support from a corresponding nondiscursive witness, which can have power and cogency irreducible to statements and arguments (see 1 Cor. 2:5). The idea of *personifying evidence* in humans, particularly in their moral character, for God's reality seeks to incorporate such a nondiscursive witness (see Moser, 2010).

4   Sacrificial discernment and decision

Having outlined the kind of evidence to be expected of a God worthy of worship, we need to clarify the human contribution in its appropriation. We have noted the relevance of "spiritual discernment," which calls for a larger personal undertaking with regard to God. The apostle Paul points us in the right direction, as follows: "Do not be conformed to this world, but be transformed by the renewing of your minds, so that you may discern what is the will of God – what is good and acceptable and perfect" (Rom. 12:2). I have referred to the needed transformation as an "undertaking," because it includes intentional action on the part of humans. Accordingly, the discernment in question is not passive, and it arguably calls for an ongoing struggle, even against some of one's own tendencies.

As indicated previously, Paul identifies the relevant intentional action in terms of a kind of redemptive self-sacrifice: "I appeal to you therefore, brothers and sisters, by the mercies of God, to present your bodies as a living sacrifice, holy and acceptable to God, which is your spiritual worship" (Rom. 12:1; cf. Col. 1:24). A role for such sacrifice rarely emerges in contemporary writing on knowing God, spiritual transformation, or discernment of God's will. An excessive focus on relevant intellectual content may account for this deficiency, but, in any case, a correction in emphasis is needed.

In order to discern God's will adequately, according to Paul's epistemology, humans need a spiritual transformation that requires their self-sacrifice to God. The latter self-sacrifice is a way of sharing in Christ's perfect sacrifice by the obedience of faith in God. This includes dying to one's selfishness and pride in order to flourish in life with God, who seeks to kill human selfishness and pride (see Rom. 8:13). We may understand this transformation in terms of the need to undergo the crisis of Gethsemane, yielding one's will to God's perfect will, in order to be in a position to discern further aspects of God's will. This Gethsemane experience is the core of the needed redemptive self-sacrifice to God, as one shares in the exemplary sacrifice by Christ to God for all humans.

Paul's ideas of spiritual discernment and sacrifice may seem too messy for some theorists who clamor for cut-and-dried definitions, principles, arguments, and algorithms. Such a worry should subside, however, when we consider that our ultimate audience is not a logical principle, an argument, or an algorithm, but is a personal divine Spirit who is inherently self-sacrificial and can self-manifest. Relative to this God, the cardinal human failing is alienation whereby we fail to commune with God in a manner that shows and empowers us how to love God and others as God does. From this perspective, we should not identify the cardinal human failing with a human's not having or accepting a conclusive argument for God's existence. The challenge for humans is much deeper, instead, relative to a purposive, interactive God who seeks to be curative toward humans needing redemption.

Human decision, but not blind decision, plays a key role in overcoming the alienation in question. Christian hyper-intellectualism implies that humans should be able to settle or resolve matters regarding Christian commitment with the giving of pro-Christian arguments. This view is naive at best, in assuming that the conclusion of a sound argument would settle or resolve the matter of Christian commitment. The matter instead is irreducibly agent- and decision-oriented, because it involves a volitional, decisional response of one intentional agent to the expressed will and offer of another intentional agent. Such interactive, decisional agency requires the free self-commitment of a human will to another agent, and hence is not reducible to or settled by logical proof or any argument. Logical proofs and arguments do not entail human decisions to self-commit to another agent; nor do the latter decisions need to rely on such proofs or arguments for their reasonableness or evidential support. Even if an argument concludes with a recommendation, an agent still must decide on the recommendation: to endorse it, to reject it, or to withhold judgment regarding it. An argument cannot make this decision for an agent. In any case, the needed foundational evidence of divine self-manifestation for an agent is much more profound, existentially and experientially, than an argument.

The decisional interaction in question can begin with God's self-authenticating of divine reality by the intentional self-manifestation of God's perfect moral character, including divine love, to a person (perhaps in conscience). This self-authenticating fits with the biblical theme of *God* as the one who confirms God's reality for humans, given that God inherently has a morally perfect character and cannot find anyone or anything else to serve this confirming purpose (see, for instance, Gen. 22:16–17, Isa. 45:22–3, Heb. 6:13–14). The alternatives fall short of the needed perfection. This self-authenticating also fits with the recurring biblical theme that God alone is our foundation, rock, and anchor, including our cognitive or evidential foundation, regarding God's reality (see, for example, Ps. 18:2, 31, 28:1, 31:3, Isa. 44:8; cf. 1 Cor. 2:9–13). The decisional interaction can develop with a cooperative human response of intentional self-commitment to the divine manifestation, on the basis of one's experiencing its perfect goodness. Such interaction is central to a redemptive I–Thou relationship between God and humans. A person can have pre-receptive evidence from God's intervention, but this evidence would deepen and expand upon being received cooperatively.

An influential biblical injunction recommends that humans "taste and see that the Lord is good" (Ps. 34:8). This advises a first-hand acquaintance with

God, particularly with God's goodness, as a way of confirming God's reality and goodness. It would be odd to suggest that we should confirm God's reality first and then seek to confirm God's goodness. Being inherently good and redemptive, God would seek to keep the two together, and we should too. If, however, people need first-hand acquaintance with God's perfect goodness, then one cannot experience God by proxy. For instance, you cannot experience God for me, even if you can witness to me regarding God (discursively or nondiscursively) on the basis of your experience of God. God would want each person to be redeemed directly into a life of communion with God, in order to remove wavering from lesser intermediates.

We sometimes talk of human experience of God, but we can refine such talk as human experience of what God experiences (see Moltmann, 1981, 3–5). Given this refinement, we face the following existentially important questions. Are we willing to experience what God experiences? In particular, are we willing to experience God's self-sacrificial love for others, God's redemptive suffering, and God's joy in redemption? In addition, are we willing to go where God goes to experience such things? Are we willing to leave our sheltered experience to share in God's self-giving experience? The latter issue includes the question of whether we are willing to risk sharing in God's redemptive experience, which is challenged by human rejection. In this perspective, our cooperating with God requires our co-experiencing with God. It therefore requires our being willing to experience self-sacrifice with God. We may think of such willingness as central to sharing "the mind of Christ" (1 Cor. 2:16). This would include learning not just to think like Jesus Christ, but also to experience *with him*, to experience what he experiences in ongoing redemption for all humans.

5   Whither hiddenness?

We cannot solve "the" problem of divine hiddenness, if this requires our having the means to explain or to remove all such hiddenness for all people. Given our obvious human limitations in matters cognitive, that kind of solution would ask too much of us. If, however, God is at work, elusively and subtly, in the world's episodes of redemptive self-sacrifice, we have an option for drawing near to God: the option of voluntary participation in and cooperation with redemptive self-sacrifice. This option would include drawing near to God, because it would include drawing near to God's distinctive power and presence, even if many people are unaware of God's role here.

W. R. Matthews has identified a common human problem, as follows:

There are, I suppose, many in these days who long for the assurance that God is a reality and not a fiction, and the lover of men, but who are looking for that spiritual assurance in the wrong place. They turn over the arguments for and against the Christian belief in God, "and find no end in wandering mazes lost"; or they seek for some overwhelming religious experience which will sweep doubt away, only to be haunted by the suspicion that this experience when it comes is nothing but a drama played on the stage of their own minds. (Matthews, 1936, 182)

Clearly, then, we need an alternative to being lost or haunted in those familiar ways of seeking God, and, fortunately, we have such an alternative.

Matthews explains as follows, taking the lead from the author of 1 John:

The guidance which comes from the earliest days of our religion would not indeed lead us to despise intellectual enquiry and mystical vision, but it would not lead us to begin with them. It would tell us to start loving our fellows, to cultivate the settled and resolute will for their good. So by coming to know what "love" means we shall come to know what "God" means, and by realizing [love's] power, its reality as a human force, we shall be in contact with a power which is more than human, with the creative energy of the world. "Beloved, let us love one another, for love is of God and everyone that loveth is born of God and knoweth God. He that loveth not knoweth not God, for God is love" [1 John 4:7–8]. (Matthews, 1936, 182)

This is no recipe to make God self-manifest to all people whenever and however we wish; such a recipe would be simply presumptuous of humans relative to God. If, however, self-sacrificial love, when redemptive, is indeed "of God" and self-manifesting of God's powerful presence, we can have some hope regarding divine revelation on God's terms.

Matthews notes that Christian belief in God as inherently loving does not stem from speculative philosophical reflection or a theoretical assessment of probabilities. Instead, this belief emerges from the self-manifesting of God in Christ, although it is anticipated in parts of the Hebrew Bible (see Hos. 11:1–9; cf. Heschel, 1962, 39–60, 289–98). As Matthews remarks: "Because we find God in Christ, we discover that God is love" (1939, 223). As a result, we are well advised not to try to establish that God is love on the basis of speculative philosophy; we would do better to look to the prospect of ongoing experience of God's love in redemptive, self-sacrificial action. In addition, the love in question is no mere emotion, but originates in the will of God for what is best, all things considered, for all concerned. Such love can manifest the stability of a divine will that is morally perfect and hence redemptive toward humans.

Our experiencing and cooperating with redemptive love, in the perspective on offer, will entail our experiencing and cooperating with the redemptive power and self-manifesting of God. The perfect human exemplar of this love, according to Christian theology, is Jesus Christ, now risen to sustain and proliferate God's redemptive love, even toward God's enemies. One can cooperate with his power *de re*, without awareness of his role in the power of redemptive love from God. So, one's experiencing and cooperating with redemptive love does not require one's acceptance of a Christian account of such love. This lesson is important, because it enables people unfamiliar with a Christian account to experience and cooperate with God (see Moser, 2010, ch. 5).

We may desire pyrotechnics and other diversions from heaven, but, being perfectly redemptive, God would be more profound and more subtle than any such desire. God's redemptive character would be inherently curative in seeking to heal people from everything alienating them from God, their sustainer of lastingly good life. Jesus put forth this neglected message as follows: "Jesus ... said to them, 'Those who are well have no need of a physician, but those who are sick; I have come to call not the righteous but sinners.'" (Mark 2:17; cf. Matt. 9:12, Luke 5:31–2). We may think of "sinners" as people alienated from God, and we may think of "sickness" as spiritual or physical deficiency. Jesus portrays his mission from God to include himself as a "physician" devoted to curing people of their sickness. In addition, he thought of spiritual sickness as a problem harder to cure than physical sickness (see Mark 2:9–11). God freely can offer forgiveness as part of a cure for spiritually sick people, but this offer by itself would not yield a cure. Humans would need to receive or appropriate the offer in a manner suitable to what it seeks: the reconciliation of humans to God.

We can expand the point about forgiveness in terms of redemptive love, given that the relevant offer of forgiveness would include such love. Merely experiencing redemptive love will fall short of not only an I–Thou acquaintance with God but also a suitable appropriation of such love in one's endeavoring with God. Something more is needed, and this "more" would stem from *God's call* to a human to cooperate with redemptive love. We may think of this as the *call of Gethsemane* where God calls for the yielding of a human will to God's will, after the model of Jesus in Gethsemane. This call would be relationally curative in intent and arguably the basis of all lasting spiritual healing of humans.

We should expect God to call humans at the opportune time for redemption, by *God's* timing. We therefore should not assume that everyone has already received God's call or self-revelation, or that people lacking faith in God are automatically culpable of this. Even so, humans would do well to be ready for God's call; otherwise, they may miss it, owing to a less important focus that obstructs a suitable response. A human's response of cooperation is crucial, because it would enable God's call to be redemptive for *oneself*, in virtue of being appropriated by being internalized and thus becoming motivational for oneself. This cooperative response would be the means of appropriating by "faith" God's gracious call to redemption and thereby endeavoring with God. So, faith in God is not a leap in the dark; it is a response to something on offer from God. In a cooperative human response of faith and hope, Paul suggests, "God's love has been poured into our hearts through the Holy Spirit" (Rom. 5:5). Redemption thereby begins to be realized in a human life, and it has a cognitive anchor in God's power of love when cooperatively received.

The person who truly desires to overcome divine hiddenness should seek to experience and to cooperate with the self-sacrificial love on offer. In failing to do so, one may exhibit a misplaced desire for divine hiddenness, perhaps in the interest of deadly human autonomy, self-sufficiency, or some other kind of waywardness from God. For the sake of honesty in inquiry, one should sincerely entertain the prospect of the priority of a question from God to oneself: "Where are you?" (Gen. 3:9). Specifically, are you in a place of hiding that seeks to avoid the aforementioned call of Gethsemane? Perhaps hiddenness is ultimately more characteristic of humans than of God. At least one philosopher, Thomas Nagel, has expressed with candor his desire that God not exist, as follows: "I want atheism to be true ... I hope there is no God! I don't want there to be a God. I don't want the universe to be like that" (Nagel, 1997, 130). Perhaps Nagel is motivated by a desire for moral independence of God. If so, it would be natural for him to suppose that God raises an intolerable problem of moral authority for humans. God, in any case, would put at risk ultimate moral authority by humans. So, a Gethsemane call to volitional submission to God would be intolerable from a perspective of human moral autonomy.

God's question, "Where are you?" can reveal in a human an oppositional attitude toward God. It thus can reveal the following about a human, as indicated by Helmut Thielicke: "You do not really want the kingdom of God and in spite of your moral life and serious questions, you have no interest in fellowship with God. What you really seek is yourself" (1962, 55–6). If this is true of a person, two considerations arise. First, this person is not in the best position to comment on the availability of evidence for God, because a motivational bias is present and easily can distort an examination of relevant evidence. Second, as curative, God can rightly withhold evidence, and thereby hide, from such a person, in order to avoid increasing that person's opposition to God. In short, the person in question is not ready to handle evidence from God aright, with suitable care, interest, seriousness, and willingness to endeavor with God in redemptive self-sacrifice. We may plausibly suppose that some divine hiding stems from such absence of human readiness. God hides, however, for various good purposes, and we should not seek a reduction to just one divine purpose (see Moser, 2008, 109–13).

6   Conclusion

Finally, we face a question that is simple but vital. What do we actually desire: divine hiddenness or divine presence? Only an individual can answer for himself or herself. Our answers must be honest and responsible, as we patiently look for God's call in the midst of a noisy and distracting world. This call alone, coupled with a suitable human response, will begin to remove the divine hiddenness we all face at times. Our search for an answer, however, must entertain an option noted by Thielicke: "God never comes through the door that I hold open for him, but always knocks at the one place which I have walled up with concrete, because I want it for myself alone. But if I do not let him in there, he turns away altogether" (1961, 134). If we fail to see God's presence, we should ask why some other responsible people testify to their having evidence from God. We then should ask which places of our lives we have walled up with concrete. Our inquiry about God's hiddenness will then become honest and suitable to God, and not just an intellectual game.

We lack a full explanation of God's purposes in hiding from some people at times, and this is appropriate given human cognitive limitations regarding God's purposes. Even so, one still could cooperate with the redemptive purposes suitable to a God worthy of worship, and the chapter recommends this for evidential purposes. In particular, one could acquire evidence of unique divine power in such cooperation, and this result could lead to further evidence of God's reality. In this respect, the "proof," or at least the evidence, may be in the practice conformed to God's character. If a divine self-manifesting call to renewal is also there, we have the beginning of a new evidential situation, and perhaps a new life too. In any case, the matter is worthy of an individual's careful exploration, for the sake of truth that matters. A religious epistemology, therefore, should leave adequate room for such exploration of the available evidence.

5   Journeying in perplexity

Evan Fales

A man said to the universe:
"Sir, I exist!"
"However," replied the universe,
"The fact has not created in me
"A sense of obligation."
Stephen Crane, *War is Kind*

William James (1896) observed that, just as getting to know someone often requires that we make some initial overture of friendship, so getting to know God may require some overture on our part towards Him. This may be met with a response, not otherwise forthcoming, that can afford knowledge of God's existence and character to which access might otherwise be unavailable. James's thought has lately been rehabilitated, particularly in work on the hiddenness of God by Paul Moser and, a bit less directly, by Eleonore Stump. Moser (2002, 2008) argues that God remains hidden to skeptics because they want what Moser calls "spectator evidence," rather than a personal relationship with God on God's terms, requiring acknowledgment of God's supreme authority and a voluntary life commitment to God's lordship. Stump's (2010) discussion is directed more generally at several dimensions of the problem of evil. Divine hiddenness is problematic because it seems to represent one type of gratuitous evil; several of the biblical stories that Stump uses to illustrate her understanding of how God turns innocent suffering to good purpose are ones in which divine silence or absence plays a prominent role in that suffering – notably, in the book of Job and the story of Mary, Lazarus' sister (John 11 and passim). It's worth remarking that both Moser and Stump, although they flesh out James's idea quite differently, share commitment to the view that Christians shouldn't argue, along these lines, for "bare theism," but should use the rich resources contained in the specifically Christian understanding of God.

I aim to engage the suggestion that divine hiding – in particular, divine hiding from those whose personal formation makes them unprepared for loving union with God (including skeptics) – is consistent with divine love. This thesis offers a claim that is as worthy as any of serious consideration by those who deny God's existence or are agnostics at least in part because they cannot find (or haven't found) sufficient evidence for theism. First, however, I want to clear the decks by mentioning and setting aside two replies to the argument from divine hiddenness, the loss-of-freedom and wrong-relationship objections. The former claims that God's making His presence clearly evident would be coercive, intruding upon human autonomy; the second that divine grandstanding might induce submission through intimidation, but not freely given love. Moser raises and dismisses these replies, but his reasons differ from mine. It's evident, first, that human autonomy is enhanced, not diminished, by greater knowledge; thus we require informed consent, especially concerning life-changing decisions. Regarding the "wrong-relationship" reply, I rest my case with the observation that the testimony of both the Bible and the behavior of modern believers confirms that human rebellion against God remains obdurate even in the face of firm conviction and divine fireworks.[1]

A   Cognitive idolatry or epistemic necessity?

Still, I want to explore the possibility that God hides himself from many non-believers because their hearts aren't in a condition properly to receive Him. Perhaps, out of respect for each person and the aim of achieving salvific union, God bides His time, awaiting an opportune moment when self-revelation stands a realistic chance of reordering the affective and conative structures of the nonbeliever's character. Perhaps, bringing about such an opportune moment requires the nonbeliever's taking certain initial steps in recognition of God's character (if He exists). If so, it'll behoove nonbelievers to reflect upon what such steps might be.

According to Moser, it's God who calls the shots here; and it's cognitive idolatry for a nonbeliever to set prior epistemic conditions upon evidentiary revelation. Moser rejects *spectator evidence*, where the nonbeliever (like any good Missourian) has preconceived standards of evidence for rational belief. The nonbeliever withholds commitment to the belief that God exists, and *commitment to God*, pending justified belief that God indeed exists. (*After* arriving at conviction that God exists, the enlightened nonbeliever may, naturally, well want to undertake personal reformation of an appropriate sort.) Moser, against this, makes three claims: (1) It's up not to us, but to God, to set the terms for His self-revelation; (2) God's revelation is *available* to everyone, but only on condition of a *prior* moral orientation to God that involves seeking Him out as LORD over one's life, and making a lifelong commitment to serve and obey

---

[1] There are nuanced attempts to formulate and defend these objections, for example, those of Murray (2002) and Swinburne (1979, 202–14; 1998, 203–12), which I have no space to discuss here but believe do not succeed.

Him; and (3) that such commitment engenders a personal relationship with God involving a self-revelation certifying God's existence and character in a uniquely apodictic way – one that outdistances standard appeals to natural theology, miracles, and mystical experiences. (To be sure, such self-revelation occurs in God's own good time: one can no more set a temporal constraint upon God's response than other epistemic conditions.)

Considerably amplified, this echoes William James's suggestion that faith itself may make available evidence not otherwise acquirable. What are we to make of Moser's three claims? The first two appear, in a way, humdrum. Just as a teacher might refuse to give piano lessons to an aspiring student who refuses to pay tuition, so God may refuse to impart knowledge of Himself to those who don't meet certain requirements. One might suppose that *others*, to whom God *has* vouchsafed this knowledge, can pass it on, though they may not be believed. But the *kind* of knowledge Moser takes God to impart to the faithful appears, in its full richness at least, not to be the sort of thing that can be communicated purely in propositional form.[2]

It appears, moreover, that there's something deeper at stake in Moser's first claim. It is cognitive idolatry, according to Moser, to demand that God provide spectator evidence. But this is nothing more than the sort of evidence we require *generally* for justified belief. It is, as Locke put it, the evidence of sense and reason. The better to see this, consider the evidence available to those who seek God with a properly contrite heart, convicted of sin and committed to a moral transformation oriented toward the divine. Moser (2008, 10) calls this *perfectly authoritative evidence*. It is *conclusive* evidence, not only for the existence of God, but of His loving nature and moral authority – though, since Moser allows that the evidence could be defeated (2008, 139), it's hard to see what "conclusive" amounts to.[3] What's more, since God's transformative

---

[2] Moser (2008, 127).

[3] What is defeasible, strictly speaking (see Moser, 2008, 134–5), is the *proposition* "I have been offered, and have willingly unselfishly received, the transformative gift." The *transformative gift* is the gift of one's sins having been authoritatively forgiven, of having been led into volitional fellowship with God (which includes perfect love and proper worship), and being transformed from a condition of selfishness and despair into one whose "default position" is unselfish love, forgiveness of all, and hope of ultimate triumph of good over evil. It's unclear, unfortunately, what's meant by love being a "default position." Evidently, it doesn't mean that one gets to hate under the proper circumstances, as Moser takes a strong position on the duty to love and forgive (see pp. 171–80). In any event, it appears that the *evidence* one has for this proposition is not conclusive: it might be defeated – for example, one might have been hallucinating the offer of divine grace. Moser claims one can know that the gift *hasn't* been defeated, and that's all that matters. But 'conclusive' carries modal force: it suggests the evidence *couldn't* be defeated. What's worse, how does one know, for example, that one *hasn't* hallucinated the divine gift? Can Moser suggest how to acquire conclusive evidence for *that*? (In an appendix, Moser addresses the skeptical challenge more generally. He opens by denying that we can be mistaken about our semantic intentions – in particular in what we mean by epistemic terms such as 'evidence.' Then comes the key move (p. 275):

response to a sincere seeker will be offered "at God's appointed time,"[4] and may take place slowly *over* time, it's not easy to specify conditions under which Moser's prediction could fail. Nor is it easy to specify the conditions under which it's been shown to *succeed*. That's because, although divine grace is supposed to confer upon the believer superhuman powers to overcome sin and strive toward moral perfection (2008, 155–7), it's apparently hard to tell when this power has been conferred, at least if we judge by observed behavior. Perhaps because he has in mind studies that show that societies whose religious culture is strongly oriented toward evangelical Christianity score lower than many other societies on standard measures of moral conduct,[5] Moser allows that "Given the difficulty of this aim [loving God and others unselfishly], we shouldn't be surprised that communities of unselfish people are few and far between. In fact, one has to wonder if any such community has existed for any length of time." That suggests that remarkably few people – even remarkably few self-identified Christians – have actually met God's conditions for reception of the gift of grace (or that the gift is less powerful than Moser wants to claim). But then, are we to infer that God's fellowship remains withdrawn from a large number of devout Christians, even Christians certain of His presence? And making things worse, it appears that one can experience the divine gift of love without understanding that it comes from God.[6] So reception of the gift can come, evidently, in a guise that doesn't confer conclusive (or perhaps any) identifiable evidence for God's existence.

Still, what can be said about the paradigm cases – cases in which someone seeks God in the right way, and comes to have transformative experiences of a sort that involve conviction of sin, sincere repentance, humble submission to God, whose presence is felt as loving and authoritative, and the requisite changes in behavior as part of a lifelong commitment to worshipful fellowship with God? What sort of evidence will such a person have of God's existence

---

Suppose we form the ... intention to use "truth-indicator" and "epistemic reason" in such a way that a visual experience of an apparent X in a situation with no accessible defeaters is a (possibly defeasible) truth-indicator, and thus an epistemic reason, for a visual proposition or belief that X exists. This intention, given its meaning-conferring role for us, could then serve as a directly accessible semantic truth-maker for our ascription of an epistemic reason for a visual belief that X exists. It would be *part of what we mean* by "epistemic reason" that *such* an ascription captures an epistemic reason for a visual belief that X exists.

Shades of Peter Strawson's defense of induction in his (1952). If we can simply *define* truth-indication in this way, then defeating the skeptic becomes easy indeed. (Or, as Bertrand Russell would have said, it has all the advantages of theft over honest toil.) So far from conclusive, Moser's evidence is wide open to skeptical challenge.

[4] Moser (2008, 131 and passim).   [5] See, for example, Zuckerman (2009).
[6] Moser (2008, 136).

and nature? Unfortunately, Moser has surprisingly little to say about the *phenomenology* of this engagement with the divine. It's central to Moser's account that God is experienced as a loving and authoritative *person*; the interaction is, broadly speaking, the sort of interaction one has with other agents. Moreover, God is seen as the source of a kind of superhuman power to overcome natural tendencies toward selfishness and hatred of enemies. Beyond this, things are left largely to our imagination – except that, clearly, whatever their quality, these experiences generate a kind of certainty of the loving presence of God.

Is this certainty epistemic certainty? It's hard to see how it could be, even though Moser thinks it strong enough to trump the problem of evil.[7] We are told that it comes from an authoritatively conferred self-revelation of God that's a subjectively given experience, non-propositional though evidence-providing (2008, 131). But how are we to understand this? The agent is the Holy Spirit, who, as part of the divine self, has first-hand knowledge of God; this Spirit imparts that knowledge to the seeker by means of an "intervention" (2008, 149–50). Moser speaks of the resulting experience as self-authenticating, but what he says on this score is unhelpful:

As an agent, I myself can be self-authenticating of firsthand veridical evidence of *my being a genuine agent*, because I can act in ways that *create* and *sustain* firsthand veridical evidence of my being an agent for a person by actually intervening as an agent ... in that person's experience. God's Spirit would have, of course, the same capability...[8]

Usually, self-authentication is understood as a quality of mystical experiences, which makes their veridicality "clear and distinct." But Moser expressly denies that he is speaking of mystical experiences (along with miracles and natural theology, he devalues them as evidence for God) – which can be hallucinatory. But in the quoted passage, self-authentication isn't a quality of an experience, but means that *I* can authenticate *my* existence and agency *for another* simply by giving her (veridical) evidence of that. That's no doubt true – but quite ordinary. It's quite another thing for that evidence to be *conclusive* for the *other*. Even ordinary human action admits of fallible judgment – of the possibility of zombies, hallucination, dreaming, and the other usual suspects. When it comes to judging that one's in *God's* presence, things become still chancier – as I'll now show.

Ontologically speaking, the self-revelation of the Holy Spirit isn't fundamentally different from human self-revelation: in both cases, an agent A causes another agent B to have experiences that provide B with evidence of A's presence. Although Moser denies that such interventions by the Holy Spirit are

---

[7] A loving God exists; ergo there's a morally sufficient reason for any evil that God allows (Moser, 2008, 124).

[8] Moser (2008, 149–50).

mystical experiences, it's hard to see how they differ at this level.[9] What's fundamental, so far as knowledge of God is concerned, is the existence of a causal relation (and not one somehow more intimate) between God and the evidential human experiences. Epistemologically, assessment of the veridicality of such experiences of the divine in fact raises multiple difficulties.[10] Obvious worries arise from the non-public nature of the perceptual experiences of divine presence.[11] But here I'll just note another familiar difficulty: the many-contenders objection. That's the objection that others who aren't Christians, and who don't, for that matter, worship Yahweh, can and do claim similar certitude on the basis of *their* experiences of another divine presence (or of Nirvana or some other transcendent reality). But then, how can the Christian's evidence be conclusive? Here's a question-begging answer to this objection: "We will properly apprehend this Spirit's reality ... only if we are *willing* to have 'eyes to see and ears to hear' this Spirit in keeping with God's redemptive purposes."[12] Other than that, Moser's only advice is that we "test the spirits" in the way Jesus suggests: "You shall know them by their fruits." But, as I have mentioned, Christians don't fare very well, as a group, on that criterion. The objection stands.

Even setting this consideration aside, one ought to be especially skeptical of the epistemic bona fides of the conditions under which, according to Moser, God selectively allows self-revelation to occur. For those conditions require a frame of mind all too conducive to both the triggering of religious experience and to its uncritical evaluation. This is well known, and can be observed across societies in religious contexts in which communion with the supernatural is a cultural expectation.[13] Moser's response to this worry is that "Willingness to submit to God's will doesn't entail willingness, or any other

---

[9] Moser uses a narrow definition of mysticism as involving the indwelling of a divine spirit in a human being – that is, a possession state. But both anthropologists and philosophers of religion usually cast the net much wider than this, to include any experienced presence of a divine being, and more besides (see, e.g., Alston, 1991).

[10] There's a large literature; Alston's work has played a prominent role. Here I'll just mention in addition 1991, chs. 7–9 and the relevant bibliography in Fales (2010). Moser seems to concede the complexities of epistemic evaluation here by appeal to abduction from the "whole range" of relevant experiences at 2008, 138–9.

[11] Alston (1991, ch. 1) defends the characterization of these experiences as perceptual; see pp. 209–22 for his effort to deflect the charge that the content of particular mystical experiences can't be confirmed by others.

[12] Moser (2008, 157).

[13] I offer here just one personal experience (for another, see Fales, 2005). Hitching across Illinois, I was offered a ride by a nice gentleman in his thirties who turned out to be a Pentecostal. This was his conversion experience: Having been raised in another denomination, he married a Pentecostal woman. His wife's church and religious community were of deep importance to her. For her sake, he attended the Sunday services and was welcomed, but always felt himself to be an outsider, because he had not been saved. Indeed, it was clear that his soteriological status deeply pained his wife, and this, in turn, was deeply troubling to him. And then one day, he suddenly found himself standing up in church involuntarily as there burst forth from him a

tendency, to *fabricate evidence* of God's reality in the absence of any such evidence ... Religious frauds are typically *unwilling* to submit to a perfectly loving God's will."[14] But of course, the objector's concern isn't *at all* aimed at religious fraud. It is that certain religious attitudes make one susceptible of *being deceived by others* or by experiences generated by those very attitudes. Moser's reply, then, simply misses the mark.

B   The real deal

Although I judge Moser's defenses of divine hiddenness and the epistemic bona fides of divine revelation when God comes out of hiding unsuccessful, his work is nevertheless extremely valuable for having brought attention to a matter that atheists – and not just those who have pointed to divine hiddenness as an argument for atheism – need seriously to consider. Perhaps it's true, after all, that God reveals Himself to some, for good and loving reasons, and remains hidden from others, either through some fault of theirs or because God has reasons, also good and loving, for a cryptic strategy. And even if God's self-revelations aren't somehow self-authenticating, they may nevertheless both be evidential and have profound pastoral effects upon those who are their suitable recipients. Moreover, such an understanding of divine hiddenness need not be predicated upon a single, one-size-fits-all diagnosis of what's wrong with the human condition. It can be sensitive to there being many varieties of human brokenness, and many different individualized ways in which God can speak to human spiritual needs.

That brings us to Stump's work on human suffering and God's redemptive engagement with humanity, with its emphasis upon the power of narrative to achieve understanding of the particular. It's not that Stump denies the significance of certain universal truths that inform soteriology – specifically, she adopts the Thomist view that the true telos of every human being, the true condition of *eudaimonia*, consists in achievement of loving communion with God and a community of saints. I shall find occasion to dispute this, but – given a certain conception of God – it's hard to resist the claim that enduring enjoyment of a relationship of the best kind of love between oneself and God would be a superlative good. This would be the more true if that love wouldn't be simply a *generic* love (though it would have certain general features), but a love that pays attention as well to satisfaction of the particular passions and heart's

verbal stream that everyone recognized as speaking in tongues – whereupon he was promptly welcomed into full fellowship. Now, he would certainly describe his glossolalia as a baptism by the Holy Spirit (as would his fellow Pentecostals). But the social-psychological conditions that prepared him for this might cause one to wonder where the primary agency lay. For further evidence on this score, see Sargant (1974, 183–4).

[14] Moser (2008, 80).

desires[15] that contribute to the deepest sources of individuality that make us each a distinctive human being, so long as these are in harmony with the universal good of union with God.

In helping human beings achieve this end, God faces a variety of impediments often distinct from – sometimes more complex than – human sinfulness and resistance to divine authority. One sort of stumbling block is a will that's oriented toward what God despises, a will that's therefore in disharmony with itself; but there are other conditions that can destroy the search for spiritual wholeness, such as deep shame, or despair over the loss of what one most deeply cared about.[16] Someone who complains about the hiddenness of God needn't be (or needn't recognize themselves to be) laboring under the heavy burden of some such condition. Despite these obstacles, God tries to bring it about that each person's undeserved sufferings can eventually be compensated for. God provides each person with opportunities that, responded to in the right sort of way, will ultimately lead to their greatest good: union with God and satisfaction of their (ultimate) heart's desires. In this condition, a person will treasure the suffering they had to endure, in recognition of its essential role in the path to salvation. God's maximally loving providence therefore involves offering each of us an optimal path to salvation – an OPTS. We can freely OPT-in or (like Satan) reject the offer by, inter alia, not making good use of our involuntary suffering.

Stump's emphasis on narrative is supported by Bible stories she engages to illustrate a wide range of causes of human alienation from God and threats to trust and union. She aims to show *how* alienation can threaten, and how it can be thwarted or overcome, sometimes in ways requiring divine absence for a time. Here I'll examine just one such case, the story of Job. That may seem an odd choice: the most dramatic scene in the story, after all, is God's confronting Job; God is anything *but* silent. But God is silent for a long time. He remains silent through all of Job's afflictions (essential, however, to the narrative's plot), then through the lengthy speeches by Job's companions. Job finally complains: "Even when I cry out, 'Violence!' I am not answered [by God]; I call aloud, but there is no justice." "If I go forward, he is not there; or backward, I cannot perceive him; on the left he hides, and I cannot behold him; I turn to the right, but I cannot see him" (Job 19:7, 23:8–9).[17] When God does eventually speak, what's most striking is His silence – He doesn't answer Job's question. So in the story, God hides Himself from Job in important ways.

I face here an important quandary. Stump's acute reading of the book of Job – indeed, her whole hermeneutical approach to biblical narratives – is quite

---

[15] The term is Stump's. For discussion, see especially Stump (2010, chs. 11, 14, and 15).
[16] See Stump's discussion of the difference between guilt and shame in her (2010, 140–9).
[17] All Bible quotations are from the NRSV translation unless otherwise indicated.

different from mine. But because my aim is to grapple with her defense against the problem of (certain kinds of) evil – here that of divine silence – it's her interpretation that deserves pride of place. Yet I want to draw from my own reading as well. My plan, therefore, is first to briefly present and discuss what can be learned about divine hiddenness from the book of Job, as Stump reads it. Then I'll sketch, as briefly as possible, my own reading of Job, and show how that reading encourages a rather different response. By drawing upon both interpretations and reflecting upon the lessons they teach us (which aren't entirely incompatible), I hope to articulate my own thinking about the problem.

C   Stump's Job

Stump (2010, ch. 9) focuses attention first upon God's reply to Job, the final segment of the story but for a brief coda. She then turns to God's opening interaction with Satan, who has nothing further to say after obtaining permission to afflict Job with boils. Stump offers two arguments to show that God's reply to Job isn't, as first appearances might suggest, unloving or dismissive. Her first, and main, aim is to find in the language of God's description of His creation of the cosmos and His relations to its creatures a revelation of divine love and caring. Even in the somewhat curious passage about the nesting behavior of the ostrich, in which God admits to having made the bird "forget wisdom" (Job 39:17), Stump sees an expression of divine care. More difficult are the final chapter and a half that God devotes to his creation of Behemoth and Leviathan.[18] Noting God's teasing words about human inability to engage in jest with Leviathan, Stump finds even here an intimation of God's close and friendly relationship with these great beasts.

What's significant is that this explains Job's recanting when faced with the divine presence. Although Job had declared his readiness to stand his ground and insist upon an explanation for his suffering, now he suddenly retreats, even though no explanation has been offered. What's been offered, rather, are two precious things: insight into God's deep care for the world, and an I–thou direct encounter with God. In this face-to-face encounter, as well as God's description of His works, there's been impressed upon Job the indelible knowledge of God's love – even if Job doesn't know, and perhaps couldn't understand, the specific reason for his suffering.

But what about God's tone of voice? That seems anything but loving. It's more than stern; God seems roused to anger. This is misleading: Stump deploys analogies to human relationships in which someone properly objects vigorously to an accusation she knows to be false, while nevertheless all the while

---

[18] Stump cites the conjecture that 'Behemoth' may denote the hippopotamus. This creature is not elsewhere attested in the Bible.

approving the accuser's pluck. For the accused might recognize that from the accuser's point of view, the accusation justifiably appears to have merit; the accused may approve of the moral courage of her accuser. And she may know that her reaction of apparent anger will itself have a salutary effect upon the accuser. If all that's true of God's situation vis-à-vis Job, then perhaps God's impatient tone with Job is itself a manifestation of His love for Job.

But God doesn't aim, through both His silence and His speaking, only to achieve a newly flourishing union between Himself and Job. He also desires to do what He can (though He knows failure is likely) to reunite Satan with Himself. Stump points to features of the encounters between them that signal alienation: Satan is invited to the heavenly council of the gods (or angels), but he's been off afar; God implies a spiritual distance by asking where he's been. Satan, apparently, is alienated, not only from God, but therefore also from himself. He restlessly wanders the earth; he cannot find a spiritual home there – to say nothing of one in heaven. Moreover, his business on earth directly opposes God's. But he can't attack Job, because of God's protection. On Stump's view, God accedes to Satan's challenge respecting Job in order that, by witnessing the exemplary goodness of Job, Satan will become the more acutely aware of the division within himself, of the shallowness of his cynical way of interpreting the good behavior of others, and of the need to repair the rift with God. So, in the end, God is not silent in the face of Job's questions; nor is He prepared to turn His back even upon Satan.[19] Stump provides a compelling portrait of Satan and of how God's responses to him align with His desire to offer Satan a loving relationship, while seeking equally Job's own highest good.

D   Another Job

Attractive as Stump's picture is, I want first to suggest that there's a historically more plausible way to read the story, and second, to draw from that alternative some thoughts about how a nonbeliever might sensibly react to the absence of divine presence in his or her life, and the lives of many others. Stump herself is modest about her project. She doesn't claim to have *the* right interpretation – or even, given the redactional complexities of many biblical texts – that there's one determinate correct interpretation.[20] Stump's appreciation of the Bible's stories as literary masterpieces is reflected in her approach to them.

---

[19] Contrast Rom. 1:24–5.

[20] That's not to say that Stump is (or that I am) a relativist about interpretation. We would agree that, roughly, authorial intent is the paramount consideration in fixing interpretation. But authors' intentions can be complex, often multi-leveled, and sometimes vague or not fully conscious. Redactional layers add obvious complications. If one subscribes to a particularly narrow view of divine inspiration on which human authors of scripture are mere transcribers of divine dictation, many complications (at the metaphysical, but not the epistemological level) can in theory be avoided; but neither Stump nor I find such a view plausible.

She meditates with great care on what they imply about the psychology of their protagonists. Her hermeneutical method, therefore, is to reconstruct the mental lives of these figures in ways that provide deep insight into the human condition and the wide range of human (and angelic) relationships with God, so as to teach us something about ourselves. Although God withholds Himself from his children in many of these stories, the stories themselves are striking in their compression, in how much silence they greet their reader with. Those silences provide Stump ample opportunity to offer a richly detailed filling in of the inner lives of the biblical figures.

I approach the stories quite differently. Any human story, certainly any humane story, requires an implied or explicit psychological dimension. That doesn't mean, however, that the primary intention is to convey the thoughts and emotions of the characters, and silence on such matters may indicate that the inner state of a character is not where the emphasis lies. In any case, we do well to be on alert for the use biblical authors make of symbolic motifs that their cultural traditions make available to them as a powerful way to convey meaning, often functioning at a level independent of the (inferred) private thoughts or feelings of the protagonists. While the characters in Job give extensive expression to their thoughts, I'd insist upon careful attention to symbolic dimensions as well.

Let's begin with the satan. Stump discovers in his conversation with God a malicious being who's frustrated by God's protection of Job. But it is generally understood that the satan, or adversary, as he's presented in Job, is not the malignant character he came to be in later Jewish and Christian demonology, but rather God's district attorney (or attorney general). He's a police detective/prosecutor, whose job is to root out wrongdoing. So when God asks where he's been, his reply is that he's been patrolling his beat – that is, he's been doing his job. He does display a certain cynicism concerning the motivation for Job's piety, but there's little to show that he harbors malice toward either Job or God. If not – if he's not God's enemy – then Stump's understanding of why God allows Job to suffer (as an overture to the satan) lacks much support.

But even if Stump's right that what God seeks in acceding to the satan's request concerning Job is a reintegration of the satan's divided self, it's hard to understand God's rationale. He perceives the satan's enmity toward Him (and toward Job), and He perceives that the success of His overture to the satan is, given the satan's hardened nature, a very long shot. Nevertheless, Stump argues, the satan has been benefitted by having been given an *opportunity* to achieve restoration, even if he rejects it; at the same time, Job has an opportunity to achieve glorification, even if at the cost of ten children, his wife's good graces, many servants, and much else. Is that a fair trade? Well, perhaps. Suppose the story implies that the satan causes untold misery and suffering in the world; but restored to a loving relationship with God, he would cease his evil ways. Stump doesn't mention this consideration; she seems to judge, even in its absence, that God is justified in allowing the satan to torture Job. But we should consider both cases.

An analogy: Suppose you were a friend of Hitler's, who encountered circumstances in which your acting toward him in a certain way stood some small chance of transforming him from a murderous madman into a humble, virtuous person. You know him well enough to know it's a long shot, and you know that if you fail, he'll turn against you and murder your three children. Since you know that an *un*reformed Hitler will also almost certainly go on to murder thousands upon thousands of innocents, you'll understand that a case could be made for the action in question. Case two: Suppose your friend is not Hitler but an evil-minded schlub with very limited ability to cause others serious harm. If your action succeeds (a long shot), your friend will be a new man. If it fails, he'll murder two of your children. Even if it fails, however, one consequence will (somehow) be the glorification of someone you love – say, your third child. Fair trade?

E   God speaks; Job sees

We need, then, to consider Job. Here, like Stump, I'll focus on Job's audience with God. Job understands the formal futility of his demand for a hearing before God, for God is both the defendant and the judge; moreover, there's no question of God's recusing Himself from the case.[21] Nevertheless, Job wants to confront God and argue his case. He wants to know what he's done to provoke God's enmity.[22] All he asks is that God not appear in so intimidating a guise as to render Job unable to keep his faculties and speak. God finally grants this request – but only minimally. For, rather than hearing Job out, God launches directly into a long discourse whose topic is Job's ignorance and impotence, in comparison to God. In the end, Job is reduced to admitting his ignorance – reduced, effectively, to silence. He never presents his case. If this is a conversation, it is an entirely lopsided one. But Job does receive the honor of seeing God, to which I'll return.

There is a noteworthy irony. At the end of his discourse, God rebukes Job's advisors, saying that unlike Job, they didn't speak the truth about Him. Yet God's own self-description mirrors, at numerous points, the very language used by the advisors (and by Job himself). Thus Job compares his day of birth to a

---

[21] "If it is a matter of justice, who can summon him [God]? ... For he is not mortal, as I am, that I might answer him, that we should come to trial together. There is no umpire between us, who might lay his hands on us both" (Job 9:20, 32–3).

[22] "I will say to God, Do not condemn me; let me know why you contend against me" (Job 10:2; cf. also 23:1–7, 31:35). Job fully agrees that if he's guilty of transgression, he should be punished (Job 31:5–33).

night dark like the chaos waters, inhabited by Leviathan whom only God can control (Job 3:1–8), and asks God whether, like God's enemies the Sea (*yam*) or the Dragon (*tannin*), God should place a guard over him (Job 7:12). Zophar, like God, mocks Job's ignorance of the cosmos (Job 11:7–9). Similarly, Bildad extols God's cosmic powers, especially His control over the waters of the firmament and the Sea and its dragon inhabitant Rahab (Job 26:6–14); similarly Job (Job 28:20–7). And Elihu speaks expansively of God's powers and Job's ignorance in similar terms (Job 36:26–37:24). But these are the same terms God uses to describe himself, sometimes with verbal identity (cf., e.g., Job 9:8//38:8; 9:9//38:31; 28:26//38:25). There is one exception: although Job's advisors (and Job himself) speak incessantly of God's justice and goodness, and human sinfulness (e.g., Bildad at Job 8:3, and passim), God Himself does not once describe Himself as just or morally good. On the very issue between them, God maintains a profound silence before Job.

On Stump's reading, God's pride in his power over even Behemoth and Leviathan, who willingly submit only to him, suggests that He has a loving, perhaps almost playful, relationship with them (2010, 189–90). Now Behemoth and Leviathan were mythical denizens of the wilderness and the deep – the chaos waters – which symbolized the forces of social disorder and disintegration.[23] They, rather than the satan, were the demonic forces in Job's thought world. God's ironically playful tone here reflects a boast that He, and He alone, has the power to subdue (even with ease) the forces of social chaos, but that hardly entails loving friendship.

At the center of God's response to Job is a fantastically impossible challenge to match God's power and command over the universe. Job's right to question God's justice and ask for, and receive, an explanation or vindication is permissible only if Job himself can exercise the prerogatives of divinity, including the sheer power to judge and punish all who are proud and wicked (Job 40:10–14). But why should Job have to do anything like *that* to receive fair treatment or an honest hearing from God? How can this be seen as anything other than divine insistence upon the prerogatives of power – the mark of a tyrant rather than a just ruler? This conclusion seems inescapable, *even if*, during the course of His peroration, God displays to Job his loving concern for His creation and its creatures, because, for all that, He has treated Job unfairly. This can hardly be disputed; indeed, we have a confession (to the satan) from the LORD's own

---

[23] See, for example, Ps. 74 and 2 Sam. 22. It's not unlikely that these "dragons" or monsters were borrowed by Israel from the Canaanites, who in turn were likely to have gotten them from Egyptian religious traditions. Read in this way, the book of Job proves to be a profound meditation upon the question of what claims the individual legitimately has upon the state to care for his or her well-being in the face of misfortune: is the primary responsibility of the state (or of God) to insure general social order, at the expense of individual well-being if necessary, or is there some balance to be struck? Expanding on this suggestion would take me too far afield here.

lips: "There is no one like [Job] on the earth, a blameless and upright man who fears God and turns away from evil, although you incited me against him, to destroy him for no reason" (Job 2:3). For no reason. But God does not confess this to Job.

What Stump sees in this interaction between God and Job, besides God's honoring Job with the longest divine speech in the Bible, is a display of God's deep loving care for His creation and for Job, something Job comes to understand when he sees God, and recognizes, in the context of a second-person, I–thou relationship, God's true beneficence.[24] Yet the tone of Job's brief responses to God's questions can more naturally be read as expressing shame, the shame of one so overwhelmed by the very fearful aspect of the deity that he had begged to be spared from, that he can no longer plead his case.

Clearly Stump and I have very different readings of the book of Job. Does it matter which reading is correct, or nearer to the author's intentions? Perhaps not. Stump uses the story of Job (and others) to give narrative depth to her conception of how divine care for us, including divine silence, works. Even if she happens to misread Job, she may be right about God. But it surely does matter whether the Ruler of the Universe is Stump's sort of God or the sort of sovereign I see in the mirror of Job.[25] Nevertheless, Stump's reading of Job is compelling; it may well be correct, and even if it's not, one might wish it were. Suppose it *is* correct. What lesson, then, ought it teach the skeptic? What light might it shed on the problem of God's silence toward *him* or *her?* What might it suggest the skeptic do in response to an admission of this possibility?

Well, the skeptic can't (or at least doesn't) *know* that Stump's God is the Ruler of the Universe, and shouldn't claim to know even that Stump's interpretation of Job is correct. There are, after all, other plausible interpretations. So the rational skeptic will be wary. A rational skeptic ought to admit that God might have good reason to maintain silence, toward him or her and toward many others. But God might also *not* have such reasons, for all the skeptic knows – or there might not be any God. Still, suppose God definitively breaks His silence, a possibility such a skeptic ought to be open to. What's the right response *then?* For clearly, if Stump is right about God, then the skeptic ought not only to confess that God exists, but ought to seek closeness to God. Would Job's response (as Stump interprets it) therefore be the correct response? I think not. Moral union with God requires knowledge that God is indeed good and no tyrant; and this cannot be achieved but by the occurrence of two things,

---

[24] Stump, as I noted, takes God in fact to have two reasons for allowing Job's suffering: to provide Job with an opportunity for glorification, and to provide the satan with an opportunity for reintegration.

[25] Some will say that *that* sort of sovereign of the universe would not qualify as God. I don't wish to quarrel over names or definitions. The question is: To what sort of relationship with the sovereign of the universe, if there is one, should we aspire?

one intellectual and the other affective. One must *understand* why God has permitted the world's sufferings, including God's apparently harmful silences, and one must *see and feel* the love and goodness of God. If Stump is correct, God did convey the latter to Job. But not the former. Neither mystery nor mystification are what the case requires. Nor is the excuse that Job will not be able to understand. If Stump has been able to explain to *us* why God acted as He did in response to the satan's challenge, then certainly God could have explained it to Job.

If, on the other hand, the moral order of the universe is beyond our comprehension, if it must in the very nature of things remain a mystery, then we are indeed tragic beings, and full unification with the Maker is beyond what's possible for us. That itself, to the extent that such an understanding is our very heart's desire, is an evil that removes us from full communion with God. (On Aquinas's own view, God hasn't created the best possible world because there is no best possible world. I think that isn't true, but supposing it is, it seems to me that a minimal condition on the goodness of any possible world God *does* actualize is that creatures in it who are called to communion with God be granted the ability to achieve this kind of understanding. I see no reason to think that *that's* not possible, even if it's not possible for human creatures.)

Is Job in any case guilty of the sin of pride in pressing his demands? His companions certainly level the charge. But Job is steadfast: "Far be it from me to say that you are right; until I die I will not put away my integrity from me. I hold fast to my righteousness, and will not let it go; my heart does not reproach me for any of my days" (Job 27:5–6). Good for Job. The accusation utterly misses the point – and would do so even if Job were not righteous. For what is at stake is justice, not pride, and if divine justice is so far removed from human understanding that it is incomprehensible to us, then one of our deepest reasons for caring about God is removed.

F   Denouement?

In the end, Job's courage apparently fails him and he allows God to remain silent. Perhaps he's come to understand that God *has* a good explanation for his suffering, but he appears to have lost interest in what it might be. It's not that he comes to believe that the explanation passes human understanding; nor should we think that Job's pressing for an answer to his question would somehow be a betrayal of a new-found affirmation of God's love, rather than faith seeking understanding. We can understand why God would not have told Job the reason for his suffering *before* Job's trial of pain; that would have reduced the ordeal to something quite different. But we don't thereby understand why God withholds explanation afterwards. It's not as if Job would have been incapable of understanding the explanation, one that (as Stump sees it), we can understand and so, too, could Job. Of course, all that would have intruded upon the literary quality of the narrative, as a story. Perhaps Job figured these things out for himself. But that would be eisegesis.

Stump recognizes that among the hardest cases in which God faces the challenge to offer each of us our heart's desires are those cases in which fulfillment of this promise requires the freely willed cooperation of another person. If that's not forthcoming, then the best God can hope to achieve is what Stump calls the refolding of one's heart's desire: a recognition of God's perfect love and an ability, from within that love, also to love unrequitedly another.[26] But what about Job? What if – as the text surely suggests – *his* heart's desire was to have an explanation from God for his suffering, an explanation that would affirm God's justice? What, then, if the person upon whose free decision the satisfaction of our heart's desire depends is *God*, and God doesn't come through?[27]

If an understanding of God's moral order is at the very center of Job's heart's desire, how can we understand his reaction to his audience before God? How can we understand his own silence? Was he indeed so awestruck as to be dumbfounded? There are other possibilities. Elie Weisel has proposed one such: Job dissembled.

Therefore we know that in spite of or perhaps because of appearances, Job continued to interrogate God. By repenting sins he did not commit, by justifying a sorrow he did not deserve, he communicates to us that he did not believe in his own confessions; they were nothing but decoys. Job personified man's eternal quest for justice and truth – he did not choose resignation. Thus he did not suffer in vain; thanks to him, we know that it is given to man to transform divine injustice into human justice and compassion.[28]

Wiesel, therefore, affirms our universal moral understanding in his defense of Job's integrity. Wiesel, indeed, can write a play in which Jews under immanent threat from a pogrom put God on trial; a similar theme provides the plot for the televised movie *God on Trial*, set in Auschwitz.[29] On this understanding of the

---

[26] See Stump (2010, 473–6).

[27] Stump will surely want to reply that what the book of Job teaches is that Job's heart's desires, if they included the desire for such an understanding of God's justice, became refolded, in the context of his seeing God's love for him, so as to achieve unification of his greatest desire – union with God – with all his other heart's desires, as these emerged from his encounter with God. I'm unsure what this refolding would involve. (Stump mentions as Job's heart's desires only his desire for his family, and being known for his piety and prosperity – to which God restores him.) It's not at all obvious to me that the story teaches this. At best, we have silence on this essential matter.

[28] Wiesel (1976, 235).

[29] It turns out that the similarity between Wiesel's play and the movie may not be a coincidence, although the former is set in Ukraine in the mid-seventeenth century as a *Purimspiel*, and the latter in the Nazi concentration camp. Wiesel has related that he was present at an actual trial of God staged by the inmates of Auschwitz – the trial upon whose legend the movie script

book of Job, God never does grant Job his heart's desire, though it was in His power to do so.

G   Eschaton

To many nonbelievers, the cosmos doesn't seem, even prior to any philosophical reflection, to be God-inhabited. In those moments when the heart cries out, it is greeted by an empty echo chamber; there is no Thou there. Such seemings may not count for much in the arena of reasoned arguments, but they do count for more than we tend to allow in the narratives of our lives. In the light of reflection upon the ambiguities of the book of Job (and much else in ancient scripture), a nonbeliever is constrained by caution. Perhaps divine silence has a reason; and perhaps that reason is love. One might somehow discover this, even when it is least expected. But, puzzled by ongoing silence, one will not be sanguine.

Yet even if one were brought into God's presence, one ought (and let me now speak in the first person) to have reservations. If, to my great surprise, I should reawaken after my demise, and find myself escorted into the presence of the Divine Being, there would indeed be a reckoning. It will be an accounting on both sides. I shall have to answer for my sins – no small task. And from God, I shall demand an explanation for the suffering of the innocents, an accounting that meets the standard of justice, without mystery or mystification. Let God explain why Job suffered; let him explain the suffering of the Midianite maidens,[30] and of the small "tortured child who beat itself on the breast with its little fist and prayed in its stinking outhouse, with its unexpiated tears to 'dear, kind God.' "[31] Such explanations are in order – not from theologians or philosophers, but from God.[32] If that standard is not or cannot be met, then there's nothing for it but respectfully to decline – if (to my even greater surprise) it were offered – an invitation to the heavenly banquet.

was based. See http://www.youtube.com/watch?v=5caAug5n8Zk for the movie; http://www.fpp.co.uk/online/08/09/JChron_190908_Wiesel.html for Wiesel's testimony. (As this website belongs to David Irving, caution is in order. But the claim is corroborated at http://www.jewishvirtuallibrary.org/jsource/biography/Wiesel.html.)

[30] Num. 31:17–18. If, as is very likely, the story is not historical, we have not far to seek to find equivalent ones that are.

[31] Dostoyevsky (1950, 290) – Ivan's conversation with Alyosha in ch. 4, "Rebellion." I take it that Ivan's stories are non-fictional ones Dostoyevsky gleaned from news media.

[32] Though it would have, I think, to be not dissimilar to Stump's defense, turned into a convincing theodicy.

Part IV

Reasons for Hiddenness and Unbelief

6 No-fault atheism

John Greco

The Problem of Divine Hiddenness is to explain why a loving God is not clearly present to all of creation. Put differently, it is the problem of explaining nonbelief. A common response, both in the tradition and among contemporary theistic philosophers, is that nonbelief signals a cognitive and/or moral flaw in the nonbeliever.[1] In this paper I will argue that the "flawed atheist" response to the Problem of Divine Hiddenness is unsupported by an adequate epistemology of religious belief, insofar as that response looks for the explanation of nonbelief only in the atheist.[2] On the contrary, explanations of nonbelief might also be found in a) believers themselves and b) the social environment. In particular, we can find explanations of nonbelief in the nature and quality of our interpersonal relations, informal communities, and formal institutions, in both their moral and practical aspects.[3]

A second claim of the paper is that a shift of focus to social epistemology enriches religious epistemology. In this regard, a "social religious epistemology" turns our attention to personal relationships, communities, and institutions, and shows how the moral and practical dimensions of these can have epistemological significance. Finally, by turning attention away from atheists and on to themselves, theists might better understand how aspects of their personal relationships, communities, and institutions can undermine the transmission of religious knowledge and faith and thus promote nonbelief. In this regard, a "social turn" in religious epistemology might have practical as well as theoretical benefits.

Thanks to Donald Bungum, Adam Green, Roger Pouivet, John Schellenberg, Daniel Smith, Eleonore Stump and Tedla Woldeyohannes for comments on earlier drafts and discussion. Thanks also to participants at *The Epistemology of Atheism* conference, Université de Lorraine/LHSP-Archives Poincaré, France.

[1] For example, see Moser (2008); Plantinga (2000); Moser (2010). See also the passage from Romans below.

[2] In fact, the terms "flawed atheist response" and "no-fault atheism" are too restrictive for the positions I mean them to label, in that nonbelievers can include agnostics as well as atheists. Nevertheless, I will continue to use these labels, since "flawed nonbeliever response" and "no-fault nonbelief" are not nearly as catchy.

[3] In this respect, the present paper develops a position that I defended in Greco (2008).

Part 1 of the paper briefly explores the Problem of Divine Hiddenness, partly by comparing it to the Problem of Suffering. Part 2 defends a framework for thinking about testimonial knowledge and evidence, and for how knowledge is transmitted within an epistemic community.[4] Part 3 considers the implications of this framework for epistemology in general and for the Problem of Divine Hiddenness in particular.

Part 1:   The problem of divine hiddenness and the problem of suffering

The Problem of Divine Hiddenness, we noted, is to explain nonbelief. Given God's nature as all loving and all-powerful, why should there be nonbelief? Why does God not clearly reveal Himself to all?[5] These questions can (and do) turn into doubts, and then into an argument *against* God's existence.

1   The argument from hiddenness

Here is one reconstruction of the present line of reasoning.[6]

1. If God exists, then He is all-loving, and so desires to be in a loving relationship with all created persons.[7]
2. If God exists, then He is all-powerful, and so does what is necessary to achieve what He desires.[8]
3. To be in a loving relationship with another person, one must reveal oneself to that person in the following sense: one must allow that person to know him/her. Put differently, one cannot remain hidden from the person.

---

[4] I call the position defended in Part 2 a "framework" because it is not a full-blown theory of testimonial knowledge or knowledge transmission. Rather, it is consistent with a variety of approaches to knowledge and justification and thus might be wedded to any of these.

[5] See, for example, the Introduction to Howard-Snyder and Moser (2002); Schellenberg (1993).

[6] Here I consider a relatively straightforward formulation of the argument. For more careful formulations, see Schellenberg (chapter 1, this volume) and Schellenberg (1993).

[7] Here is a more careful formulation from Schellenberg: "If God is perfectly loving toward such finite persons as there may be, then for any capable finite person S and time t, God is at t open to being in a positively meaningful and reciprocal conscious relationship (a personal relationship) with S at t" (chapter 1, this volume). As Schellenberg's formulation makes explicit, the premise makes a claim about created beings at a time, and about God's desire for a relationship with them at any such time that they exist. The remainder of the argument should be read accordingly.

[8] Again, a more careful formulation of the argument would have to include qualifications regarding the nature and scope of God's omnipotence. Since my treatment of the argument will not exploit any such qualification (or lack thereof), I will use this more straightforward formulation.

Therefore,

4. If God exists, then He allows Himself to be known by all. He does not remain hidden from anyone.   (1, 2, 3)
5. But some people do not believe in God.
6. If some people do not believe in God, then God does not reveal himself to all persons in the relevant sense: He does not allow Himself to be known by all.

Therefore,

7. God does not allow Himself to be known by all.   (5, 6)

Therefore,

8. God does not exist.   (4, 7)

Here we may note a structural analogy to the Problem of Suffering.[9] In each case, we begin with assumptions about the nature of God, which in turn make the existence of suffering (nonbelief) problematic. In effect, suffering (nonbelief) demands an explanation: How is God's existence compatible with the thing at issue? And in each case, the question can turn into an argument against God's existence. The line of thought is that God's existence is *not* compatible with the existence of suffering (nonbelief), but since the existence of suffering (nonbelief) is undeniable, we should conclude that God does not exist.[10]

2   The flawed atheist response

Responses to the Problem of Divine Hiddenness continue the analogy. Thus, responses to the Problem of Suffering generally follow one of two strategies. The first is to explain the existence of suffering in terms of God's own intentions, for example to make possible some greater good, or prevent some greater evil.[11] The second is to find the explanation for suffering in something external to God, for example the exercise of human free will.[12] The "flawed atheist" response to the Problem of Divine Hiddenness takes this latter route: Nonbelief

---

[9] For example, see Mackie (1955); Plantinga (1974).

[10] Here is a contemporary update of the argument from suffering: The "data" of suffering does not entail that God does not exist, but it makes the existence of God improbable. That is, the probability of God's existence on the data is low. An explanation e would, depending on one's strategy, allow the theist to deny that $P(G/d)$ is low, or affirm that $P(G/d\&e)$ is not low. Clearly, the Problem of Divine Hiddenness can be understood along probabilistic lines as well. See Howard-Snyder (1996b); Rowe (1979).

[11] Hick's "soul-making" strategy falls into this category. See, for example, Hick (1966).

[12] The traditional "free will defense" includes this strategy as well as the "greater good" strategy. That is, free will is considered to be itself a great good, and the use of free will leads to unnecessary evil besides. For example, see Plantinga (1974).

is to be explained in terms of a moral and/or cognitive flaw on the part of the nonbeliever. As we saw, the response is as follows: The fact that some people do not know God, and do not even believe in God, can be traced to a flaw *in them*. That is, God does reveal himself to all, but some people resist.

Here are some examples of this kind of response – the first from the apostle Paul, the next two from more contemporary authors.

Ever since the creation of the world his eternal and divine nature, invisible though they are, have been understood and seen through the things he made. So they are without excuse: for though they knew God, they did not honor him as God or give thanks to him, but they became futile in their thinking, and their senseless minds were darkened.[13]

... according to the A/C [Aquinas/Calvin] model this natural knowledge of God has been compromised, weakened, reduced, smothered, overlaid, or impeded by sin and its consequences ... here the A/C model stands Freud and Marx on their heads ... according to the model, it is really the *unbeliever* who displays epistemic malfunction; failing to believe in God is a result of some kind of dysfunction...[14]

Some people have a psychological attitude-set closed or even opposed to a divine redemptive program ... Their attitude-set, in guiding what they attend to and how they interpret what they attend to, obscures or even blocks for them the purposely available evidence of the reality of God. The volitionally sensitive evidence of God's reality is, I contend, actually available ... People need, however, appropriate, God-sensitive "ears to hear and eyes to see" the available evidence aright ...[15]

It is hard to deny that there is something awkward about explaining nonbelief in terms of some moral or intellectual flaw in the nonbeliever. Of course, there are ways to soften the blow. We can quickly add that we are all sinners. Or we can make a distinction between original and personal sin, or distinguish between culpable and non-culpable flaws.[16] But even with these additions, it seems to me, the flawed atheist response remains awkward. One of my goals in this paper is to argue that it is also unnecessary. Here I am making two claims. The first is that the flawed atheist response is not required, or even supported, by good epistemology. The second is that there is a better strategy available.

3   No-fault atheism

By way of diagnosing the problem, we may notice a common structure in two lines of thinking. Once again, we see an analogy to the Problem of Suffering. Thus, the atheist thinks:

---

[13] Romans 1:20–1.   [14] Plantinga (2000, 184).   [15] Moser (2008, 112).

[16] Plantinga emphasizes the former: Original sin "carries with it a sort of blindness, a sort of imperceptiveness, dullness, stupidity. This is a cognitive limitation that first of all prevents its victim from proper knowledge of God and his beauty, glory, and love" (Plantinga, 2000, 207). Stump emphasizes the latter possibility (2010).

1. The evidence against God is overwhelming.
2. The same evidence is available to all, including the theist.

Therefore,

3. The theist must be either ignoring or misevaluating the available evidence.[17]

Analogous thinking is behind the flawed atheist strategy:

1. Theists have ample evidence for God's presence.
2. The same evidence is available to all, including the atheist.

Therefore,

3. The atheist must be resisting the available evidence.

The approach that I want to defend rejects the common premise – the assumption that theists and atheists have the same evidence available to them. Motivating this approach is the thought that knowledge of God falls into the category of knowledge of persons, and so we should adopt our best epistemology of persons as our epistemology of God. But knowledge of persons is typically via interpersonal perception and testimony – we typically learn about people from our experience of them, and from what they tell us about themselves and others.[18] And that kind of evidence is typically *not* shared or public, not available to all.

For example, persons typically self-disclose in a selective manner. There are many and obvious examples of this from both interpersonal perception and testimony. But this simple point does much to explain how theists and atheists can both be rational in their respective epistemic positions. That is, if God is like other persons in that God chooses to self-disclose in a selective manner, then that would explain how two persons could have different evidence regarding God's existence, and without tracing the difference in epistemic position to any flaw in the persons themselves. By way of illustration, consider the following case.[19]

Uncle Joe
It has been long taken for granted in your family that Uncle Joe is dead. Everyone knows the story of how his plane went down in the Atlantic, no survivors were ever found, etc. But one day you are on a business trip in Chicago and you clearly see Uncle Joe crossing the street. The two of you make eye contact, there is a look of recognition on his face, and then he gives you the slip in the crowd. The next day you go back home

---

[17] Cf. Rowe (1979).
[18] By "interpersonal perception" I mean the perception of persons as persons. See Greco (2008); Green (2009); and Stump (2010, esp. ch. 4).
[19] Taken from Greco (2008). A similar example is provided by Rowe himself.

and report to your family that Uncle Joe is alive – that you saw him in Chicago. You are certain of what you saw, but your family reacts with skepticism.

Good Friend
You have a very good friend that you have trusted for years and who has always been honest and truthful. While you are talking with a colleague, your friend comes up to you and tells you something that is hard to believe – that he was just outside minding his own business, and a perfect stranger walked up and handed him a twenty-dollar bill.

In the Uncle Joe case, it is perfectly reasonable for your family to think that you are somehow mistaken, while it is perfectly reasonable for you to believe that you are not. Depending on the quality of your perception and their contrary evidence, it might very well be that you *know* that Uncle Joe is alive, and yet unreasonable for your family to believe that he is. Likewise, in the Good Friend case it might be perfectly reasonable for you to believe your friend, while it is perfectly reasonable for your colleague to disbelieve him. Depending on the quality of your relationship, it might very well be that you *know* that that your friend is telling the truth, and yet unreasonable for your colleague to believe that he is.

And now the important point is this: there is no need to attribute a cognitive flaw to anyone in the two cases. Put differently, there is a readily available "no-fault" explanation for nonbelief. To some extent, in fact, the present point of view makes nonbelief expected. This is because variability in epistemic position is typical in cases of interpersonal knowledge.

More needs to be said, however. This is because at least one author who embraces the flawed atheist response also endorses the idea that our knowledge of God is through interpersonal experience. Thus Paul Moser has emphasized that our evidence for God is "volitionally sensitive" and therefore precisely not a kind of public or shared evidence that is available to all persons in the same way.[20] Likewise, Eleonore Stump has emphasized the "second-personal" nature of our experience of God.[21] Stump has not addressed the Problem of Divine Hiddenness directly, but what she says about interpersonal experience of God might be used to fuel the "flawed atheist" response. For example,

Given divine omnipresence, the only thing that makes a difference to the kind of personal presence ... that God has to a human person is the condition of the human person herself ... If Paula wants God to be significantly present to her, what is needed to bring about what she wants depends only on her, on her being able and willing to share attention with God.[22]

---

[20] For example, see Moser (2008, 2010).
[21] Stump (2010).
[22] On Stump's view (2010), someone might fail to be "able and willing" to enjoy a second-personal experience of God, but through no fault of her own. For example, such failing might be due to non-culpable psychological brokenness.

On the current line of thinking, God's self-disclosure is not selective in the way that human self-disclosure can be, and therefore the analogy to human-to-human interpersonal relations breaks down at a crucial point. Since God's self-disclosing experience is not selective, the explanation for "deafness" or "blindness" to God's self-disclosure must remain with the nonbeliever.[23]

On the present view, then, the traditional response to divine hiddenness remains essentially in place:

1. Theists have ample evidence for God's presence in terms of interpersonal experience.
2. That evidence is available in the relevant sense, that is, it is equally available to all who are open to it.

Therefore,

3. If atheists do not have the experience of God that theists do, then they must not be open to it.

So is the traditional response right after all? Again, it is helpful in this context to emphasize the nature of interpersonal evidence. One thing about interpersonal evidence, whether through interpersonal perception or testimony, is that self-disclosure is not only selective, but also *intentional*. In other words, people often *choose* or *decide*, sometimes for good reason, to self-disclose some things but not others, at some times but not others, to some people but not others. But the intentional nature of self-disclosure allows us to deny that experiential evidence of God must be available in the relevant sense – at all times available to all persons who are open to it. It is consistent with God's nature that, as other persons typically do, God has *good reasons* for selective self-disclosure.[24]

In response, one might agree that God is indeed free to restrict His self-disclosure, but argue that He would not choose to do so. Human beings do so choose, but God's goodness and love for us is such that He would not.

---

[23] Again, proponents of the "flawed atheist" response can avoid attributing personal blame to the nonbeliever. The cause of the flaw might be original sin rather than personal sin, or the flaw might have some other non-culpable cause. The present point is that a "no-fault" response need not attribute any flaw to the nonbeliever, whether culpable or non-culpable. Better, a no-fault response need not *explain* nonbelief in terms of some flaw in the nonbeliever. Presumably, we are all flawed in some ways or others. The present point is that flaws in the nonbeliever need not be cited in the explanation of nonbelief; they need not be, in that sense, explanatory "difference makers."

[24] In effect, the present response denies premise 1 of The Argument from Hiddenness above, at least when that premise is read this way: If God exists, then He desires to be in a loving relationship with all created persons at every time that they exist. Recall Schellenberg's formulation of the relevant premise: If God is perfectly loving toward such finite persons as there may be, then for any capable finite person S and time t, God is at t open to being in a positively meaningful and reciprocal conscious relationship (a personal relationship) with S at t. Alternatively,

But now we are back in a familiar dialectic – one that we know well from the Problem of Suffering. Thus we can a) posit possible greater goods to explain God's selective disclosure, or b) plead skepticism about God's intentions, what God would choose, etc. That is, we can adopt either the "greater goods" response or the "skeptical theism" response, or some combination thereof, exactly as is available regarding the Problem of Suffering.[25] And of course, the usual responses to these responses are also available. Plausibly, this will play out, for better or worse, just as it does in the Problem of Suffering.[26] I like the chances here. That is, it seems to me that the usual responses to the Problem of Suffering are good ones, and that they work equally well in the present context.

4   Interim conclusion

I do not mean to argue, of course, that no atheist is correctly diagnosed by the "flawed atheist" response. That would require insight into the deep psychology of particular nonbelievers, and I make no claim to competence there. The present point, rather, is that good epistemology does not *require* the traditional explanation of nonbelief. It makes other explanations available, and even expected.

That is in itself a substantial conclusion, in that many philosophers would seem to disagree, and many epistemologies of religious belief would not allow for it. But there are further benefits of the present response to divine hiddenness. First, it raises interesting issues for religious epistemology, by interacting with more general questions regarding our knowledge of persons, the epistemology of interpersonal perception, and social epistemology. Second, from the point of view of theists, the present position takes our focus off the atheist and puts it on ourselves. For theists, it helps to turn our attention away from "the speck in our brother's eye" and "notice the log in our own."

The remainder of the paper proceeds accordingly. Part 2 develops a general model for thinking about testimonial knowledge, thereby engaging relevant issues in social epistemology. Part 3 draws some further implications for general epistemology, and applies these to the Problem of Divine Hiddenness in particular.

---

the present response denies premise 3, now read this way: To be in a loving relationship with another person, God must allow that person to know Him at every moment that the person exists. The present response claims that, consistent with God's all loving nature, God might for good reasons choose to self-disclose in a more restricted way.

[25] For example, see Bergmann (2001); Dougherty (2012).

[26] It is important to note that Schellenberg argues otherwise. See Schellenberg (2010). Clearly, it is beyond the scope of this paper (not to mention my abilities) to resolve all the relevant issues here.

Part 2: A model for testimonial knowledge

1   A problem in the epistemology of testimony

Here is a deep and persistent problem in the epistemology of testimony: Different cases of testimonial knowledge seem to require very different things on the part of the hearer. In particular, some cases seem to require that the hearer do a lot of work to earn her knowledge. Other cases seem to make testimonial knowledge very easy, requiring little or no work at all on the part of the hearer.

By way of illustration, consider the following cases.

> **Case 1.** A police investigator questions a potentially uncooperative witness.
> **Case 2.** A lawyer tells you that his client has no money.
> **Case 3.** A job applicant tells a personnel director that he has no criminal record.
> **Case 4.** You ask a stranger for directions to the train station, and she confidently tells you where it is.
> **Case 5.** You ask a stranger whether the city has a subway system, and he says yes, it does.
> **Case 6.** Your own lawyer tells you how to hide some money.
> **Case 7.** You ask your friend whether she has been to the United States, and she says that yes, she has.
> **Case 8.** A third-grade teacher in the United States tells his students that France is in Europe.
> **Case 9.** A mother tells her child that there is milk in the refrigerator.
> **Case 10.** A father tells his child that she was born in the U.S.

Clearly enough, the investigator in Case 1 can't simply believe what the witness says. Nor can the personnel director just believe the job applicant. As the cases progress, however, it becomes more and more plausible that the hearer can believe straightaway what he or she is told, and that he or she thereby knows. It also becomes more plausible that something epistemically special is going on – for example, that the speaker and hearer enjoy some special relationship, and that this is making an epistemic difference.

So here is the problem to solve: Why does testimonial knowledge seem easy to get in some cases, but hard to get in others? Put differently, Why do the epistemic burdens on the hearer seem so different in the different cases? Really there are two puzzles here. First, why do (at least some) cases of testimonial knowledge seem so different from cases of non-testimonial knowledge with regard to epistemic burdens on the knower? That is, why does testimonial knowledge (in at least some cases) seem easier to get than non-testimonial knowledge? Second, why do different cases of testimonial knowledge seem so different from each other?

2   The "information economy" model

A number of philosophers have argued that a central purpose of our concept of knowledge is to flag quality information and quality sources of information for use in practical reasoning and decision making.[27] The general idea can be summed up like this: The concept of knowledge serves to govern the production and flow of actionable information, or information that can be used in action and practical reasoning, within a community of information sharers.[28]

Now consider some elaborations on that general idea. First, if our general idea is even broadly correct, then we should expect there to be at least two kinds of activity governed by the concept of knowledge. On the one hand, there will be activities concerned with *acquiring* or *gathering* information, or getting information into the community of knowers in the first place. For example, empirical observation serves to produce information about physical objects in our environment, introspection serves to produce information about accessible mental states. On the other hand, there will be activities concerned with *distributing* information throughout the community of knowers; that is, there will be mechanisms for distributing information that is already in the social system. For example, teaching in the classroom, testifying in court, and reporting in the boardroom all serve this distributing function. In sum, there will be activities that input information into the system in the first place, and activities that keep the information flowing.

Let's call the first *acquisition activities* and the second *distribution activities*. The norms governing acquisition activities play a "gatekeeping" function – they exert quality control so as to admit only high-quality information into the social system. The norms governing distribution activities, on the other hand, answer to a distributing function – they allow high-quality information already in the system to be distributed as needed throughout the community of knowers. Insofar as testimony plays this distributing function, it serves to make information already in the system available to those who need it.

Here now is a second elaboration that will be important for our purposes: It is reasonable to suppose that the norms governing the acquisition of information will be different from the norms governing the distribution of information. Suppose we were writing the norms, or setting the standards, for these two

---

[27] I present this model, and argue for it in more detail, in Greco (2015).
[28] For example, see Craig (1990); Fantl and McGrath (2009); Greco (2015); Hawthorne (2004); Stanley (2005); Williamson (2000).

kinds of activity. We should make it harder to get information into the system than we make it to distribute that information, once in. This is because, again, the dominant concern governing the acquisition function is quality control – we want a strong gatekeeping mechanism here. But the dominant concern governing the distribution function will be easy access – we want information that has already passed the quality control test to be easily and efficiently available to those who need it. Different norms or standards are appropriate to these distinct functions.

Scientific knowledge provides a good illustration of this general picture. Any item of scientific knowledge must have its original source in scientific methods of investigation, including those of gathering evidence, testing theories, etc. But eventually that knowledge spreads through a shared system by means of various kinds of testimony. Through record keeping, formal and informal teaching, journal articles, public lectures, media reports, and the like, what begins as knowledge for few becomes knowledge for many. Moreover, the norms and standards governing the first kind of activity are different from the norms and standards governing the second. Quality control is exercised over both kinds of activity, of course, but in different ways. Hence the norms governing the exchange of information through journals, seminars, etc., are distinct from those governing experiment design, statistical analysis, theory choice, etc.

In the case of scientific knowledge, then, various institutional and social practices are in place so as to bring high-quality information into the system, and also to distribute it thoughout the system. Different norms govern these different practices, each according to its distinctive purpose or function. What holds for scientific knowledge in this regard plausibly holds for knowledge in general.

Here now is a third suggestion for elaborating the model: It is plausible that testimonial knowledge *itself* comes in two kinds. That is, it is plausible that testimonial knowledge sometimes serves the distribution function of the concept of knowledge, and sometimes the acquisition function. The distribution function gives us what might be considered paradigmatic cases of testimonial knowledge; for example, the attorney/client, student/teacher, and parent/child cases above. But testimony sometimes serves an acquisition function, bringing information into a community of knowledge for the first time. Plausibly, this is what is going on in the investigator case and the job applicant case above. Hence the present model explains why a student or a child can believe straight away what a teacher or a parent tells her, and also explains why an investigator or interviewer cannot (see Figure 6.1).

To be clear, the idea is not that, in the distribution role, testimonial knowledge involves no burdens on the hearer at all. In most or all of our cases, it would be implausible that the hearer can "just believe" what she is told, with

Information acquisition

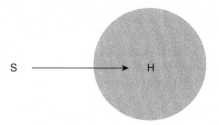

Information distribution

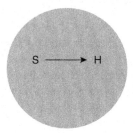

Figure 6.1

no engagement of her own critical faculties whatsoever.[29] Rather, the idea is that the burdens on the hearer are different in the distribution role than in the acquisition role, insofar as the norms governing the two activities are at the service of different purposes. This is enough to explain the differential burdens on hearers in cases of testimonial knowledge, as well as the difference in burdens associated with (some cases of) testimonial knowledge and non-testimonial knowledge.

3   Three modes of testimonial exchange: interpersonal, social, and institutional

On the present view, testimonial exchanges are governed by two sets of norms: those pertaining to the acquisition of quality information and those pertaining to its distribution. Moreover, the norms governing testimonial exchanges in the distribution role are themselves various, depending on additional factors regarding the social location of speaker and hearer. Here we may distinguish at least three kinds of relation that structure our social environment,

---

[29]   Although it is consistent with the model that there might be limit cases, where there are no epistemic burdens on the hearer at all. Perhaps this is true in the case of very small children being taught by their caregivers.

and that enable successful testimonial exchanges in the distribution role. For lack of better labels, we may call them "interpersonal," "informal social," and "formal institutional."

Interpersonal relations depend primarily on interpersonal experience and "mind reading" that is more or less independent of particular social or institutional roles. Rather, there is a person-to-person connection that underwrites personal trust to one degree or another. This kind of interaction can take place between parents and children, siblings or friends, but also between strangers meeting for the first time. For example, one might trust one stranger to tell the truth but not another, based on quite limited interactions with the two persons. This is because, at times, even limited interaction can be sufficient to mind-read for sincerity and competence, especially in restricted circumstances and for a particular domain.

In contrast to "bare" interpersonal relations, *informal social* relations depend more on well-defined social roles, for example parent–child, sibling–sibling, neighbor–neighbor, and various kinds of friendship. Interactions in these roles will be governed by interpersonal skills, as above, but also by the social norms governing these specific relationships.[30] For example, it is necessary to mind-read in order to cooperate with one's neighbors in some neighborhood task, but how one cooperates (what expectations one has, what one is willing to sacrifice, etc.) will also be influenced by the social norms structuring the neighbor–neighbor relationship.

Here is one example of how the norms structuring social relations might enable the reliable distribution of quality information. We may suppose that in many cultures it is considered a matter of love and respect to go to one's parents for advice regarding childcare. Norms structuring the relationship thereby create a channel of communication from experienced parent to new parent. The information carried by that channel will likely be of high quality, given that the parent of a parent has had some success in the childcare domain. The channel itself will likely be of high quality as well, given the norms governing the communication of this kind of information between parent and child. Thus the experienced parent will be highly disposed to provide sincere and competent advice, the new parent will be highly disposed to take that advice seriously, and both parties will be motivated to take care against misinformation and/or misunderstanding.

And now an interesting point is this: The interpersonal skills and social norms underwriting this successful exchange need not have an epistemic motivation or goal. That is, neither the speaker nor the hearer need be motivated (at least not directly) by considerations about truth, knowledge, etc. On the contrary, the entire exchange might be explained in terms of the demands of the

---

[30] For more on the epistemic significance of social norms, see Graham (2015).

relationship, such as love and respect, or even guilt. Likewise, good neighbors might ask and give reliable information about bus routes, or other neighborhood practicalities, primarily motivated by the values of civility, helpfulness, and mutual cooperation that structure the neighbor–neighbor relationship.

Both interpersonal relations and social relations, then, have the effect of structuring exchanges of information between speaker and hearer. Moreover, both kinds of relation can contribute to the epistemic quality of such exchanges. In most testimonial exchanges, perhaps, both kinds of relations work together. For example, there are two reasons that one might trust a friend, one based on interpersonal interaction, and one based on the social relation. Thus one might trust that a friend is telling the truth because "I know *her*." Alternatively, one might trust a friend because "That is how *friends* treat each other." And of course, one might trust for both reasons. Similarly for parent–child trust, neighbor–neighbor trust, etc.

Finally, some relations are defined by more *formal institutional* roles. For example, teacher–student, doctor–patient, lawyer–client, and employer–employee relationships are largely governed by relevant institutional rules. Here again, the rules in question function in addition to or "on top of" the interpersonal skills and informal social norms discussed above. And here again, institutional rules can contribute to the quality of testimonial exchanges, thereby creating additional reasons to trust. For example, the doctor–patient relationship is underwritten by institutional rules that are designed to guarantee competency and honesty in practitioners. Likewise for the lawyer–client and the employer–employee relationships. Such rules might take the form of government regulations, legal contracts, professional standards, or professional ethics. Together they provide additional structure to the social environment, often in ways that contribute to the epistemic quality of testimonial exchanges. Finally, as in the case of interpersonal skills and informal social norms, institutional rules need not have epistemic goals as their direct or primary motivation. For example, a particular lawyer might have little regard for the truth as such, a particular doctor might place little value on knowledge for its own sake. But in each case there are institutional mechanisms in place to insure honesty and competence in the relevant domains, thereby creating quality channels of information that can be exploited by patients and clients.

Here we may note an analogy to the flow of information in perceptual uptake. In cases of perception, a stable *physical* environment allows perception to exploit information-carrying signals. For example, a particular profile reliably signals *dog*, whereas a different profile reliably signals *cat*. This is not necessarily the case – the environment must be well suited to visual perception; that is, it must be enabling of the perceptual skills in play. A stable *social* environment plays the same role regarding the flow of information in testimonial exchanges. Just as natural laws construct a (more or less) stable physical environment, giving it the contours that it has, social norms construct a (more or less) stable social environment, giving it the contours that it has. Natural laws thereby underwrite regularities that can be exploited by perception. Social norms thereby underwrite regularities that can be exploited by testimony.

The case of small children is interesting here. Plausibly, small children have only limited skills for determining the sincerity and competence of speakers. That is, small children, left to themselves, can be somewhat gullible.[31] So how do children manage to learn from testimony as well as they do? The answer is that children are rarely left to themselves. On the contrary, we construct and monitor their social environments so as to keep them safe from insincere and incompetent speakers.[32] Put differently, we engineer environments that enable the transmission of knowledge that their informal education requires. Later in life, we engineer environments that enable their more formal education.

Part 3: Implications for epistemology in general, problem of divine hiddenness in particular

In this final part of the paper I will draw some implication of our model for epistemology in general and the Problem of Divine Hiddenness in particular. But first an observation: all three modes of testimonial exchange reviewed above (interpersonal, informal social, and formal institutional) seem relevant for religious epistemology. That is, at times religious testimony occurs in the context of a personal relationship between hearer and trusted speaker. At other times, testimony occurs in the context of more well-defined social roles, as when parents talk to their children about their shared faith. And of course, religious institutions are organized so as to produce religious testimony in various contexts, including formal education, preaching, ritual, and many other religious and cultural practices.

Clearly then, our model has application in the domain of religious belief in particular. In what follows, we may consider some more general implications of the model.

1   Social location is epistemically important

Let us say that one's "social location" is determined by one's personal relationships and by one's membership, participation, and roles in a community, including a community's formal institutions. On the present model, one's social location is epistemically important in a number of ways. First, one's

---

[31] The picture presented by empirical studies is mixed. For an overview of some relevant literature, see Harris and Koenig (2007).
[32] Cf. Goldberg (2007).

location in a community allows one to receive an important kind of testimonial evidence in the first place. Specifically, it allows one to receive testimony in its distribution function, as opposed to its acquisition function. (Cf. Figure 6.1.)

Second, social location affects the epistemic quality of that evidence, including whether testimonial knowledge is thereby transmitted. Specifically, one's social location will be constituted by personal, social, and institutional relations that are more or less enabling or undermining of the reliable distribution of information and hence the successful transmission of knowledge. In these ways, social location very much determines epistemic position. Put differently, one's epistemic position is partly constituted by one's social location.

2   Moral and practical aspects of the social environment have epistemic consequences

The reliable distribution of information, and hence the effective transmission of testimonial knowledge, depends on moral and practical aspects of interpersonal relations, informal communities, and formal institutions. This is true for a number of reasons. First, testimony in the distribution role depends on phenomena such as trust, authority, expertise, and social position, all of which clearly have practical and/or moral dimensions. Second, the very existence of personal relations, informal communities, and institutions, as well as one's participation in them, depends largely on their moral and practical value. For example, one goes to a school, or attends a church, largely because of its moral and practical benefits, real or perceived. Or from a different angle: There is pressure to leave a social environment, or not enter into it in the first place, if it fails to serve practical and/or moral purposes.

Third, the epistemic efficacy of a social environment is often parasitic on its practical/moral efficacy. For example, there is a reliable channel of communication between mother and child largely because the mother loves the child and is motivated by that (and other moral and practical considerations) to care for her. There is a reliable channel of communication between lawyer and client largely because the lawyer is paid by the client, and is motivated by that (and other moral and practical considerations) to act in her interest. All this implies that the epistemic value of our relationships is often parasitic on their moral and practical value. The epistemic efficacy of our relationships often rides on their moral and practical efficacy.

3   Obstacles to transmission might be found in a) the hearer, but also b) the speaker, and c) the social environment

A third implication of our model is that failures of transmission can be varied. That is, when things don't go well in a testimonial exchange, the explanation can lie in a number of places. We may use the case of religious belief as an example.

First, the problem might lie in the personal character of the speaker (for example, a believer), who lacks the moral virtue, or the motivation, or the practical talent, or the intellectual competence, to cultivate trust in the hearer. Second, the problem might lie in the informal community (for example, a family), which lacks the motivation or resources to adequately teach its children about their own religious tradition. Third, the problem might lie in the formal institution (for example, a church), which lacks the moral integrity or practical competence to attract new members and keep old ones.

Here is a more specific example. A combination of institutional arrogance and incompetence undermined the ability of the Catholic Church to address various sexual abuse scandals.[33] This in turn undermined the moral authority of the Church for many of its members, which in turn undermined its teaching authority. This is an effective illustration of how the transmission of knowledge can be adversely affected by practical and moral considerations. To be clear, the idea is *not* that members of the Church argued from premises about practical and moral failure to conclusions about epistemic authority. Rather, effective channels of testimony were eroded or destroyed, because members of the Church became less trusting of the institution and its authorities, or simply opted out altogether.

Conclusions

I have argued that the "flawed atheist" response to the Problem of Divine Hiddenness is unsupported by an adequate epistemology of religious belief, insofar as that response looks for the explanation of nonbelief only in the atheist. On the present view, explanations of nonbelief might also be found in believers and in the social environment, where the latter includes the nature and quality of interpersonal relations, informal communities, and formal institutions, in both their moral and practical aspects.

A second conclusion is that a shift of focus to social epistemology and the epistemology of testimony has the effect of enriching religious epistemology. The present approach turns our attention to personal relationships, communities, and institutions, and shows how the moral and practical dimensions of these can have epistemological significance.

Finally, by turning attention away from atheists and on to themselves, theists might better understand how aspects of their personal relationships, communities, and institutions can undermine the transmission of religious knowledge and faith and thus promote nonbelief. In this regard, a "social turn" in religious epistemology might have practical as well as theoretical benefits.

---

[33] As documented, for example, in Rezendes, Caroll, and Pfeiffer (2002).

7   Divine openness and creaturely nonresistant nonbelief

Daniel Howard-Snyder

We can view divine hiddenness in at least two very different ways. On the one hand, we can view it as evidence against the existence of God and, on the other hand, we can view it as partly constitutive of our relationship with God, insofar as we assume that we are in a relationship with God. There are connections between viewing divine hiddenness in these two ways, connections we might systematically map. My aim here is much more modest. I aim to assess a version of the argument from divine hiddenness for atheism, as it is sometimes called. I hope, however, that what I have to say might provide some idea as to how at least some of us might understand and be at peace with the hiddenness of God, insofar as we assume that we are in a relationship with God. Before I turn to my task, some preliminary remarks are in order.

First, "divine hiddenness" misnames that to which the argument by that name appeals. It sounds as though it moves from the premise that there is a God who is hidden to the conclusion that there is no God. Nobody argues like that. Rather, the idea is that if there is a God, there are no reasonable nonbelievers, or inculpable nonbelievers, or nonresistant nonbelievers (all of these terms have been used); but there are, and so there's no God.

Second, perfect being theologians agree that God, whatever the details, is an unsurpassably good personal being. I am a perfect being theologian. However, unlike many of my kind, I posit unsurpassable love as the most central feature of an unsurpassably good personal being, a feature that constrains all other features that an unsurpassably good personal being must have. Thus, for example, *if* God unsurpassably loves such created persons as there may be only if God is unable to do certain things, and *if* God is omnipotent only if God is able to do those things, I infer that God is not omnipotent. Does it follow that, on my view, God might be a bit of a wimp? No, it only follows that omnipotence might not be the best way to understand the power of God. Perhaps almightiness is a

Thanks to Adam Green and Eleonore Stump for their insightful comments and objections, none of which I have addressed properly. This paper was supported by a grant from Templeton Religion Trust. The opinions expressed in it are those of the author and do not necessarily reflect the views of the Templeton Religion Trust.

better way, where at a first approximation, what it is for a person to be unsurpassably almighty is for her to be the source of every power of every possible being other than herself. Fortunately, nothing in what follows hangs on my idiosyncratic theology. I mention it only to stress from the outset that, as will soon be evident, the argument I will discuss targets the heart of my view.

Third, I bring three assumptions to my task. (i) The argument from divine hiddenness is independent of other arguments for atheism, notably the argument from evil and the argument from suboptimality. If an adequate defense of the argument from divine hiddenness must appeal to the conclusion that God would not allow bad things of a certain sort, or if it must appeal to the conclusion that God would never do less than the best God could do, then the success of the argument from divine hiddenness depends on the success of the arguments for these other conclusions, arguments that are failures, to my mind. I'm interested in an argument from divine hiddenness that isn't, by my lights, a failure from the outset. (ii) If there is a God, then each created person will live forever. This implies that, for human creatures, and perhaps others too, their "earthly life," as we sometimes call it, is just an infinitesimal portion of their existence. (iii) Each created person will at some time enter into, and from that time onwards maintain, a positively meaningful, reciprocal conscious relationship with God that will be evident to all concerned.

With these remarks in mind, let's turn to the argument from divine hiddenness.

I will focus on a version of the argument recently put forward by J. L. Schellenberg, one that features nonresistant nonbelief and a certain sort of openness to a certain sort of relationship. He puts it like this:

The argument from nonresistant nonbelief

(1) Necessarily, if God exists, then God unsurpassably loves such created persons as there may be.
(2) Necessarily, if God unsurpassably loves such created persons as there may be, then for any capable created person S and time t, God is at t open to being in a positively meaningful and reciprocal conscious relationship with S at t.
(3) Necessarily, if for any capable created person S and time t, God is at t open to being in a positively meaningful and reciprocal conscious relationship with S at t, then for any capable created person S and time t, it is not the case that S is at t in a state of nonresistant nonbelief vis-à-vis the proposition that God exists.
(4) There is at least one capable created person S and time t such that S is or was at t in a state of nonresistant nonbelief vis-à-vis the proposition that God exists.

(5)   Therefore, God does not exist.[1]

What should we make of this argument?

The conclusion formally follows from the premises and, as I have already said, I think premise (1) is true. I will also grant premise (4). Before we can assess whether the remaining premises are true, we must understand them. Since I mean to engage Schellenberg, I will tend to what he has to say about its central concepts and I will do so as I summarize his reasons for believing premises 2 and 3.

So then: suppose God unsurpassably loves a created person, call her *Anna*. How might we characterize that love? At a minimum, it must involve *benevolence*, says Schellenberg, caring for Anna's well-being. But it involves much more. God unsurpassably loves Anna, says Schellenberg, only if God aims "at relationship – a conscious and reciprocal relationship that is positively meaningful, allowing for a deep sharing" between them. Moreover, if God unsurpassably loves Anna, God will value that relationship *for its own sake*, and not merely for the sake of something else. Furthermore, if God unsurpassably loves Anna, then God must *always* love her, and so God must always value, seek, desire, promote, or preserve personal relationship with her, although God will not force himself on her. At the very least, all this requires that God will always be *open* to personal relationship with her.[2]

This notion of openness to personal relationship with those who are *capable* of it – that is, with those who possess "the cognitive and affective properties required to [participate in such relationship]," which, in the case of God, "would involve such things as a capacity to feel the presence of God, recognizing it as such; a capacity to exhibit attitudes of trust, gratitude, and obedience to God, and so on" – is crucial. Here's what Schellenberg says about it:

If one is always open in the sense I intend then, even if one does not actively seek or promote personal relationship with another person capable of participating in such relationship…, one makes sure that there is nothing one ever does (in a broad sense including omissions) that would have the result of making such relationship *unavailable* to the other, preventing her from being able to relate personally to one, even should she then try. So for God to always be open to personal relationship with a capable created person such as Anna in a manner expressing unsurpassable love is for God to ensure

[1] Schellenberg (chapter 1, this volume). I have deviated in one respect from Schellenberg's statement of his argument. Where I have used "created persons" Schellenberg uses "finite persons." Since I don't understand "finite" as a predicate applied to persons, I don't understand any premise that uses "finite persons," which means I don't understand any of Schellenberg's actual premises. But I do understand "created" as a predicate applied to persons; at least I understand it much better than "finite." So I have substituted the former for the latter. Also, where he uses "personal relationship," I substitute his more informative "positively meaningful and reciprocal conscious relationship."
[2] Schellenberg (chapter 1, this volume).

that there is never something *God* does that prevents her from being able, just by try-ing, to participate in personal relationship with God.... *She* may not want relationship or even to be reminded of her religious options, and so may through resistance of God, which would have to involve self-deception, herself produce a situation in which she is unable to relate personally to God just by trying. But unless she is resistant in this way at a time, she will find it possible to participate in personal relationship with God, and to do so then. Never will she find the door to such relationship closed. This, at the very minimum, is required if God unsurpassably loves Anna in a manner aimed at personal relationship with her.[3]

As for premise 3, Schellenberg says that Anna could not be in a positively meaningful and reciprocal conscious relationship with God unless she believed that God exists. He writes:

a personal relationship is a conscious, reciprocal relationship, and a conscious relation-ship is a relationship one recognizes oneself to be in. Given these facts, one clearly cannot even get started in a personal relationship without *believing that the other party exists*. Now belief, as most contemporary philosophers would agree, is involuntary in the sense that one cannot choose to believe something at a time just by trying to. So by God's not revealing God's existence, God is doing something that makes it impossible for Anna to participate in personal relationship with God at the relevant time just by trying, and this, according to our definition of openness, is precisely what is involved in God's not being open to having such a relationship with Anna then.

Upshot: if God is open to being in a positively meaningful and reciprocal con-scious relationship with Anna, then, if she is capable of such a relationship and she does not render herself unable to participate in it, God will reveal himself in such a way that Anna believes that God exists.

I have four things to say about this argument.

First, although we might question Schellenberg's understanding of what it is to be open to relationship, I will grant his meaning. Specifically, I will grant that one is open to relationship with another only if one never does anything (by commission or omission) that would have the result that the other was prevented from being able, just by trying, to participate in that relationship.

In that case, and this is the second thing I want to say, it is not clear to me that unsurpassable love requires openness, so understood; and so it is not clear to me that premise (2) is true. Let me explain.

I begin with a more general question. Why couldn't preventing one whom we love from being able, just by trying, to participate in relationship with us sometimes be the loving thing for us to do? Why couldn't making ourselves unavailable be what love requires, or at least allows? If that's possible, then, presumably, we would have to have some good reason to make ourselves

---

unavailable. Gratuitous unavailability is not consonant with love aimed at personal relationship. Can we make sense of this suggestion?

Maybe.[4] Let's approach it by first thinking about it in the context of a positively meaningful, reciprocal, conscious relationship that is already evident to all. Sometimes our attachments to others in such relationships can be hurtful to ourselves, as when we depend on them, intentionally or not, to sustain bad habits we've acquired. In such a case, the loving thing for them to do might be to make themselves unavailable to us, and perhaps even to shun our efforts to participate in the relationship. In this connection, think of the advice sometimes given to those who unwittingly enable self-destructive behavioral tendencies on the part of the addicts who are their spouses, children, or friends, by preventing those whom they love from experiencing the natural consequences of their addiction. Moreover, sometimes our attachments to others in such relationships have their source in motivations that, in effect at least, involve viewing them as instruments to our own ends, whether consciously or unconsciously. Once again, in such a case, the loving thing for them to do might be to make themselves unavailable to us, and perhaps even to shun our efforts to participate in the relationship. In this connection, think of the advice that you might well give to a woman who discovers that her partner was motivated, whether consciously or unconsciously, to enter into their relationship, and now stays in it, largely for the sake of the gratification of his own domestic and other needs, especially when he refuses to own these sources of his attachment to her when he is repeatedly confronted with the truth.

Of course, even if we can make sense of making ourselves unavailable in the context of such relationships, it does not follow that we can make sense of making ourselves unavailable *before* any such relationship begins, at least not when our love aims at such a personal relationship and the person whom we love is capable of such a relationship and is in no way resisting it. Our question, then, is whether such unavailability in such circumstances can make sense *before* any such relationship even begins.

Notice that when we make ourselves unavailable within the context of personal relationship, and when our doing so is no strike against our love or even flows from our love, we typically aim to reform the one we love, or at least make it more likely that he will be reformed, and we aim to do so not only for his sake but for our sake, and for the sake of the relationship itself, that it might be better than it otherwise would be. Might something like this guide us, in a loving way, *before* we even initiate personal relationship with those whom we love? More to the point, might something like this guide God, in a loving way, *before* God initiates personal relationship with such created persons as there may be?

---

[4] In what follows, I develop lines of thought in Howard-Snyder (1996a).

To begin to look into this question, notice that some created persons, at the dawn of their capacity to relate personally to God, might already be ill-disposed toward such a relationship.[5] Through no fault of their own, they might have become ill-disposed toward anything having to do with God. Perhaps they were raised to be hostile or indifferent toward religion, whether by family members or the social groups in which they grew up. Religion is for the servile and spineless, the stupid and the unscientific, they were taught, day in and day out. God is a crutch, worse yet, a stretcher, for the weak and cowardly. And the teaching stuck; they are now ill-disposed. Or perhaps they had instilled in them an extreme self-centeredness or disrespect for proper authority. Or perhaps they were raised in abusively strict religious surroundings. Or perhaps there was some other cause. But, whatever the cause might be, they now find themselves, through no fault of their own, *ill-disposed nonbelievers*. That is to say, if God were to reveal himself to them in such a way that they came to believe that God exists, they would or would very likely respond inappropriately; they would or would very likely either reject God's self-revelation or believe with anything from indifference to hostility.

How might an unsurpassably loving God respond to people like this, as their capacity to relate personally with him emerges? Well, first off, God might think that there is no point in revealing himself to them. For, even if such a revelation does result in their believing God exists, God doesn't care about mere belief; he cares about an appropriate response. But such a response would be at least very unlikely. Second, if God were to reveal himself in such a way that they came to believe, he would at the very least stand a good chance of contributing to their ill-disposition being confirmed in them by their actually rejecting his self-disclosure or their actually believing with indifference or hostility. That would be counter-productive to his purposes since he wants their ill-disposition toward him to be weakened, not strengthened. So God waits for a time, waits to reveal himself in such a way that they believe that he exists, giving them the opportunity to become more receptive to him and so more apt to respond appropriately to his self-disclosure, and he influences them in subtle but respectful and loving ways toward this end, for example, by placing religiously serious people in their lives who are neither stupid nor unscientific, neither servile nor spineless, and so on.

One might object. After all, we must remember the variety of ways in which God could reveal himself to ill-disposed nonbelievers; and "if we consider that this could occur... through a direct encounter with an omnipotent love capable of softening even the most self-centered or embittered soul, then it seems that this class of individuals must be empty."[6] By way of reply, three

---

[5] I emphasize that here and below I am not describing nonbelievers "in the midst of life" (Schellenberg, 2005a, 205–6).

[6] Schellenberg (1996, 460).

points need mentioning. First, this class of individuals could be empty in the envisioned circumstances only if the direct encounter with God at the dawn of their capacity to relate personally with him wipes out the dispositions toward him that are definitive of their being ill-disposed. That God would not do. For the actions, attitudes, and affections that would result from such a miraculous disposition-adjustment would arise from something over which ill-disposed nonbelievers had no say, in which case those actions, etc. would be a farce, a sham, and God would know it. Second, unsurpassable love does not force itself on created persons in the way envisioned; at least not when they have yet to be given an opportunity to contribute to the desired changes and to own them. Third, for nonbelievers to be ill-disposed toward God *just is* for them not to be capable of being "softened" by a direct experience of his love, or at the very least for them to be very unlikely to be "softened" by it, in which case we cannot infer that "this class of individuals must be empty."

One might object again. For, on the suggestion put forward here, God aims in various ways to facilitate a better disposition in ill-disposed nonbelievers through subtle, respectful, and loving ways that are compatible with nonbelief. But "it is hard to see how God's task here would not be more effectively prosecuted by means of the many influences presupposing belief," especially in light of the fact that they are resistant through no fault of their own.[7] By way of reply, that all depends on what God's task is. If God's task is (i) to facilitate a better disposition in ill-disposed nonbelievers, one that they are in no small part responsible for, and (ii) to do so without running the risk that their ill-dispositions will become more deeply entrenched in them by their responding inappropriately to God's revealing himself to them in such a way that they believe that he exists, then it is false that God's task would be more effectively prosecuted by means that presuppose belief.

Of course, even if we can make sense of what has just been said about ill-disposed nonbelievers, it is irrelevant to the argument at hand. That's because the argument at hand appeals to *nonresistant* nonbelievers, and no ill-disposed nonbeliever is a nonresistant nonbeliever. Still, seeing what might be said about ill-disposed nonbelievers prepares us for what might be said about well-disposed nonbelievers, or as Schellenberg calls them, nonresistant nonbelievers. So let's consider nonresistant nonbelievers, nonbelievers who are well-disposed toward God as their capacity to relate to him personally emerges, those who would welcome entering into a personal relationship with God of the sort Schellenberg describes if God were to reveal himself at that time in such a way that they came to believe that he exists. And let's distinguish two cases: (i) well-disposed nonbelievers who are not responsible for

---

[7] Schellenberg (1996, 460).

being well-disposed and (ii) well-disposed nonbelievers who are responsible for being well-disposed.

As for the first sort of case – those who are *not* responsible for being well-disposed – examples might include created persons who have been virtually determined, say, by parental or other social training, to be well-disposed but who for one reason or another do not yet believe that God exists. In that case, as they become capable of relating personally to God, they are disposed to enter into such a relationship with him, alright; but they had no say in becoming so well-disposed. This is unfortunate because, all else being equal, a state of affairs in which one enters into a personal relationship with God but one had little if any say in being disposed to do so in the first place is not nearly as good as a state of affairs in which one enters into such a relationship with God and one had a significant say about becoming disposed to do so. Suppose God prefers the better state of affairs. In that case, God might well not reveal himself in such a way that well-disposed nonbelievers who are not responsible for being so well-disposed believe that God exists. For, again, they are not responsible for being disposed to enter into such a relationship, and God prefers them to confirm their good disposition toward him, on their own, in the face of contrary desires and competing allegiances, before he reveals himself to them in such a way that they come to believe that he exists. In that way, God allows them to make their involuntarily acquired good dispositions toward him and relating to him personally genuinely their own.

Now consider the second sort of case – those well-disposed nonbelievers who were responsible for becoming so disposed. They constitute the most difficult case for the suggestion I'm exploring. Nevertheless, it seems to me that we can say something plausible about them.

But let me first register a worry, a significant worry, to my mind. There are no such created persons. Character formation is not under the voluntary control of a child. Thus, by the time a nonbeliever becomes capable of a relationship with God, she won't be responsible for being well-disposed toward God, assuming she is well-disposed. If that's right, then what I've said about the first sort of case will suffice since there will be no instances of the second sort of case.

I've put this worry rather starkly. Why should I suppose that there are no such created persons, no created persons who, at the dawn of their capacity to relate personally with God, are both well-disposed toward God and responsible for being so well-disposed?

That's a good question. A more measured claim is that it's pretty likely that there are no such persons. We know enough about the sources of character formation in children to say that's it's not likely that, on the assumption that a child is well-disposed toward God at the dawn of her capacity to relate personally to God, she is responsible for being so well-disposed. Still, the point of the question stands. Why couldn't there be exceptions? And my answer is that there can be – for all I can tell. So I should not categorically state that there are no such created persons. Nevertheless, it strikes me as a pretty unlikely.

Those who think that there are some created persons who, at the dawn of their capacity to relate personally with God, are well-disposed toward God and were responsible for becoming so well-disposed need to tell us why they think this. Do they know of a particular person who satisfies this description? Who is it? And why do they think that this person, at the time in question, is or was well-disposed and responsible for being well-disposed? What's their evidence? To the extent that we are really in the dark about whether there are such persons, we should be reticent to affirm that there are nonresistant nonbelievers of this sort.

Still, what if there are? What might be said about created persons who, at the dawn of their capacity to relate personally to God, are well-disposed nonbelievers and responsible for being well-disposed? Well, as is well-known, one's motivations for entering into a personal relationship can be significantly less fitting than they otherwise might be, and one might not even be aware of it. For example, sometimes what motivates one to enter into a personal relationship is a desire to extend one's power or influence, to increase one's pleasure, or to satisfy one's curiosity. Other times its source is insecurity or fear, for example, fear of being alone or unprotected. Or a desire to please one's peers, parents, or social group. And there are other unfitting sources of motivation as well.

Likewise in the sort of case we are currently considering. Well-disposed nonbelievers may well be disposed to welcome a personal relationship with God upon on coming to believe that he exists, but they might be so disposed for reasons that are unfitting. For example, it is arguably most fitting to want to relate to God personally mainly for God's moral beauty, his holiness. Relatedly, perhaps no disposition to enter into a personal relationship with God is properly motivated unless its source is a strong desire to surrender to God's will, to unite one's own will with God's will. In that case, the possibility arises that if God were to reveal himself in such a way that such people believed that he exists, they would welcome entering into a personal relationship with him, alright; but their *initial* welcome would not be properly motivated.

This is unfortunate. For, all else being equal, a state of affairs in which one enters into a personal relationship with God as a result of a good disposition grounded in unfitting motivations is not nearly as good as a state of affairs in which one enters into such a relationship with God as a result of a good disposition grounded in fitting motivations. Suppose God prefers the better state of affairs. In that case, God might well not reveal himself in such a way that well-disposed nonresistant nonbelievers who are responsible for being so well-disposed believe that God exists. For, again, although they are responsible for being disposed to enter into a personal relationship with God, God prefers

that, right from the start of their relationship, the sources of their good dispositions toward being in a relationship with him are better than they in fact are.
And why shouldn't God want this for people such as this, people he loves?
After all, what's the hurry? There's an eternity of love ahead of them. So why
shouldn't God want those whom he loves to have a shot at the better state of
affairs? Consequently, before God reveals himself to them in such a way that
they come to believe that he exists, he allows them to change the source of their
good dispositions toward him and to confirm that change over time before he
reveals himself to them in such a way that they come to believe that he exists.
Indeed, it may well be *im*perfectly loving of God to *not* to want this for them.

One might object. After all, can't God's reasons as I have described them for
not revealing himself be "accommodated" in the context of a positively meaningful, reciprocal, conscious relationship that is accompanied by self-revelation
that produces belief? Well, in a word, no; for what God prefers as I have just
described it can only be realized *before* any such relationship gets started. In
the case of well-disposed nonbelievers who were not responsible for being
well-disposed, God prefers this state of affairs:

- that they make their good disposition toward entering into a relationship with
  God their own, and confirm it as such, before God reveals himself to them
  in such a way that they come to belief and begin a personal relationship with
  him.

And, in the case of well-disposed nonbelievers who were responsible for being
well-disposed, God prefers this state of affairs:

- that they modify, or at least aim to modify, the unfitting sources of their good
  disposition toward entering into a relationship with God, and confirm this
  modification or aim, before God reveals himself to them in such a way that
  they come to belief and begin a personal relationship with him.

It's absolutely impossible for either of these states of affairs to obtain after the
persons in question come to belief. So the "accommodationist strategy," as
Schellenberg calls it, won't work with respect to the suggestion I'm exploring.[8]
Of course, God's preferences might go unsatisfied, in which case he'll have to
adopt another strategy if he aims to bring about relationship with such people.
But the suggestion on offer is that it is no strike against God's love if God holds
out – for a time, not for an eternity – for the preferable state of affairs.

One might object again. Have I really described a preferable state of affairs?
After all, consider the alternatives. In the case of well-disposed nonbelievers
who were *not* responsible for being well-disposed, the alternative is this:

---

[8] Schellenberg (2005b).

- that God reveals himself to them in such a way that they believe, they begin a personal relationship with him, and then they make their good disposition toward God their own and confirm it.

And, in the case of well-disposed nonbelievers who were responsible for being well-disposed, the alternative is this:

- that God reveals himself to them in such a way that they believe, they begin a personal relationship with him, and then they modify the unfitting sources of their good disposition toward God and confirm this modification.

Surely, the objection goes, this latter pair of state of affairs is better than the former, and so God would prefer them.[9]

I'm not so sure about that. Consider an analogy. Suppose that over several months Nancy describes her friend Joe to Mary, in glittering detail. He is intelligent, kind-hearted, witty, athletic, responsible, and just plain fun to hang out with; moreover, as the photos reveal, he's handsome as heck. To make a long story short, Mary finds herself attracted to Joe. She wants to meet him. Then she learns that Nancy has been talking her up to Joe as well, and he's attracted to her and wants to meet her too. Excellent! She has those first pangs of love for Joe, to get to know him, and him her. And the same goes for Joe. Now suppose that Mary (somehow!) learns that some trait of character that makes for a long-term relationship has never been tested in Joe, for example, faithfulness through difficulty. Or suppose that she (somehow!) learns that Joe's budding love of her is in no small part motivated by an unconscious desire to benefit from her connections to people that can advance his interests.

Would we count it against Mary's budding love if she were to pause, mull it over, give it some time, *before* she connected with Joe? I wouldn't. After all, his capacity for faithfulness is untested; the source of his budding love isn't what it should be, or at least it could be significantly better. Is it a strike against her love if she prefers a state of affairs in which Joe's faithfulness in relationships is tested before she connects with him, if she prefers a state of affairs in which there is a more admirable source of his attraction to her before she connects with him? Again, I wouldn't. What would be the point of waiting? Well, it would be better for both of them if, right from the start, his faithfulness had some mettle and his love of her had a more admirable source; and it would be a better relationship as well, right at the start. And in the waiting she might discover something else about Joe: that he's the sort of guy who does have some mettle, or at least a tendency in that direction, and that he's the sort of guy who is willing to let others close enough to help him to become a better person.

---

[9] Schellenberg (1996, 461).

On the suggestion that I'm exploring, that's what it's like with God and the well-disposed nonbeliever. He's giving it a couple days or weeks, so to speak, to see whether they can get the relationship off to a better start. That's a preferable state of affairs, by my lights.

Perhaps there are other goods we know of for the sake of which God, by virtue of being unsurpassably loving, might be temporarily unavailable to people at the dawn of their capacity to relate personally to God. And, of course – and this is the third point I want to make – there is always the possibility that there are goods we do not know of for the sake of which God might temporarily refrain from making himself available to such people. Regarding this suggestion, Schellenberg writes:

> Opponents of the hiddenness argument sometimes also develop the objection that there might very well be goods *unknown* to us that require hiddenness, for the sake of which God would permit it, but if one has been led to accept the hiddenness argument's premises, then this move fails. That's because from what some of those premises allow us to conclude, namely, that a loving God *would not* permit nonresistant nonbelief, it deductively follows that there are no goods, known or unknown, such that for their sake God *might* do so. So *that* becomes acceptable too – after all, it evidently follows from what one views thus – and the present objection is shown to beg the question.[10]

I find these words perplexing. For, although it is true that, *if* a loving God would not permit nonresistant nonbelief, then there are no goods such that for their sake a loving God would permit nonresistant nonbelief, any open-minded inquirer with a modicum of intellectual humility will refuse to accept that a loving God would not permit nonresistant nonbelief until she had first satisfied her natural curiosity about whether there are any goods, known or unknown, such that for their sake a loving God would permit nonresistant nonbelief. To satisfy such curiosity requires two things. First, it requires that she consider known goods such as, in my opinion, those I have mentioned, and others mentioned in the literature as well. Second, it requires that she consider whether she is in a position to tell whether there are any goods unknown to her that might figure in a loving God's purposes in permitting nonresistant nonbelief. This second requirement is crucial. For suppose that she were to discover that, even if there is no good basis for thinking there is a God, and even if she does not know of any good that might figure in a loving God's purposes in permitting nonresistant nonbelief, she should be in doubt about whether she is in a position to tell whether there are any unknown goods of the sort in question. In that case, I would think, we would expect her open-mindedness and intellectual humility to lead her to refrain from accepting that a loving God would not permit nonresistant nonbelief. And in refraining from accepting that proposition, she would

[10] Schellenberg (chapter 1, this volume).

refrain from accepting Schellenberg's premise (2). Would she thereby deserve to be derided as an "opponent of the hiddenness argument"? Would she thereby deserve the charge of "begging the question"? I don't see why. Perhaps she is simply attentive to, and owns, her intellectual limitations; and perhaps she does so out of a love for truth, knowledge, and understanding. In that case, any such derision and accusation would be wholly out of place.

A fourth, and final, point has to do with premise (3). As Schellenberg makes clear, the thought that is driving this premise is that one cannot even "get started" in a personal relationship – a conscious, reciprocal, positively meaningful relationship – without *believing that the other party exists*. And that's because, as Schellenberg puts it, one can "get started" in such a relationship only if one is consciously aware of the other party, and one is consciously aware of the other party only if one "recognizes" oneself to be in such a relationship, and one recognizes oneself to be in such a relationship only if one believes that the other party exists.

Let's look into this line of thought briefly.

First, we need to distinguish *de re* awareness from *de dicto* awareness. You can be aware *of* something without being aware *that* it, under a certain description, is what you are aware of. You can be aware of Jimmy Carter without being aware that Jimmy Carter is the person you are looking at. And Anna can be aware of God without being aware that God is the one whom she is aware of. Second, one can be in a reciprocal, positively meaningful relationship with another person without believing that the other person exists, as when, unbeknownst to you, a benefactor has been looking after your interests in various ways. So a lot seems to be riding on the qualification that an unsurpassably loving person would seek a relationship with the beloved in which he was *consciously* aware of her. But is it *de re* or *de dicto* conscious awareness that is required, or both?

I'm not really sure. But if only *de re* conscious awareness is required, then it seems much more plausible that we can at least "get started" in a conscious, reciprocal, personal relationship with God even if we lack belief that God exists, perhaps even if we believe that God does not exist. Would that be ideal? Well, no. But hopefully we've gotten past identifying the real with the ideal. That is, presumably we can have a real conscious, reciprocal, personal relationship with God that is not ideal, and perhaps that relationship can commence with *de re* conscious awareness of God instead of *de dicto* conscious awareness.

Adam Green

In the eighth chapter of the Gospel of Luke, Jesus tells the parable of the sower. Seeds are sown on many different kinds of ground but with very different results. The seeds themselves are the same in each case. What is different is the ground. It is against this backdrop that we get the following quotation.

> For there is nothing hidden that will not be disclosed, and nothing concealed that will not be known or brought out into the open. Therefore consider carefully how you listen. Whoever has will be given more; whoever does not have, even what he thinks he has will be taken from him. (Luke 8:17–18)

In this context, the metaphorical image paired with "whoever has will be given more" is that of the maturing of a seed. What is hidden is the seeds and how they are received. Ground that has seeds growing in it is initially indistinguishable from ground that has had its seeds eaten by birds or ground that has accepted bad seed as well as good. In time, however, the difference will be obvious.

According to a prominent strain of argument within the hiddenness literature, the model of divine–human relations figured in the parable could not be the case. It could not be the case that God relates to each human being the same way and that the bearing of fruit is a simple function of the receptiveness of the human being in question. Instead, very many people lack belief in God through no fault of their own, and, amongst those who do believe in God, many experience a very painful absence of God in their lives (cf. Schellenberg, 1993, 2007). Thus, we are invited to suppose that what explains the curiously uneven harvest of theistic belief and experience we find in the actual world may be that there is no sower.

I   Divine hiddenness as an experiential problem

I find it plausible to suppose that the issue of hiddenness only really arises when we posit the existence of a personal God who is interested in us. That is

I would like to thank John Schellenberg and Eleonore Stump for helpful comments on earlier versions of this paper.

the kind of being we would expect *not* to be hidden and, indeed, that is the kind of being that John Schellenberg focuses on in posing his atheistic arguments from hiddenness. The fact that some people do not believe in an impersonal divine force is not necessarily a reason to believe there isn't any such thing, and the fact that people do not experience the God of deism is no reason to think that deism is false. There are, it turns out, many conceptions of the divine on which it is not "visible."[1]

If a problem of hiddenness only arises for a God that is both personal and interested in us, however, then not all evidence for the existence of God is equally central to the problem. Compare, for instance, two worlds. In the first one, God gives every single person continuous religious experiences. It is as if God walks beside the person throughout her entire life. Outside of these experiences, however, no one is aware of any evidence for God's existence. They are unaware of any good arguments for theism. They fail to notice any features of their world that indicate that it was designed. Perhaps they don't even talk much to each other about these experiences they're having. Each person just quietly walks through life with God. I submit that there is nothing worth calling a problem of hiddenness here even though the people in this world lack access to any kind of evidence other than experience.

In contrast, consider a world in which everyone is aware of powerful conceptual arguments for the existence of a personal God of love. No one thinks that suffering is problematic for this hypothesis. Everyone knows what the state of play is as far as the arguments for and against God's existence. In this second world, however, no one has any religious experiences whatsoever. I would think that in this world the problem of hiddenness is quite acute. In this second world, everyone may even believe that God exists based on the available arguments. If no one experiences the world in a way that resonates with belief in God, however, we have a problem of hiddenness.[2]

There is a related consideration that speaks in favor of the primacy of experience. It would be desirable for one's account of divine hiddenness to honor what is similar in the atheistic versions of the problem and the attempts within particular faith traditions to make sense of God's hiddenness. What unifies things like the dark night of the soul and atheistic arguments from hiddenness is not the absence of belief. It is not the absence of evidence that God exists per se. It's the absence of him. That is, it is the absence in experience of a personal entity identifiable with God relating to us in any way that we can recognize.

---

[1] See N. N. Trakakis, John McGinnis, and Jerome Gellman (chs. 11, 9, and 10, respectively, this volume) for interesting essays that fit this theme.

[2] These worlds make for a nice contrast with Peter van Inwagen's secular utopia thought experiment (van Inwagen, 2002).

Instead of comparing two worlds, this time compare two persons, Russell and Søren. They both think that the evidence for God's existence is mixed. Thus, neither thinks that the evidence compels one to believe in God and neither thinks it compels one to disbelieve in God. It is perfectly consistent with their shared evidential situation that Russell adopt a posture of agnosticism and Søren an attitude of faith. Russell sees the mixed evidence as canceling out,[3] while Søren decides to trust in the face of grounds for doubt. Despite the fact that they think very differently about their respective situations, their awareness of what they lack might be equally moving for both of them. Either might ask God in the afterlife, "Why was the evidence so mixed?" Since it is not disbelief that unites them, their common problem needs to be posed in different terms, and I find it plausible that what it should be posed in terms of is experience. Is it or is it not the case that the course of one's experience testifies to the presence of a divine being? Why do we have so many experiences that seem to lack God's presence if God actually exists and is interested in us? Thus, the problem of divine hiddenness is first and foremost a problem of experiential absence.

Although the absence of God in experience has certainly been discussed in the literature (e.g., Schellenberg (1993) has a fair bit to say about it), it is worth highlighting that, by claiming that hiddenness is first and foremost an experiential problem, I am also claiming that the problem of divine hiddenness is only indirectly related to belief. "Victims" of hiddenness are those who do not experience God, not those who do not believe in God. We will revisit the matter of posing the problem in terms of belief at the end of the paper. For now, let us suppose that I am right and that hiddenness is an experiential problem.

II   Shared attention and religious experience

In order to understand the absence of God, we need a model of what it would mean for God to be present. The model I wish to use can be usefully contrasted with William Alston's well-known perceptual model of religious experience (Alston, 1993; cf. Green, 2009).

In *Perceiving God*, Alston argues that experiences of God, "mystical experiences," are like the perception of material objects. In both mystical experiences and sense perception one is aware of something that one takes to be "given" to one's consciousness. On Alston's account of sense perception, one perceives some object iff that object appears to one in a mode appropriate to a sense modality, where "appropriateness" is a phenomenal requirement (Alston, 1993, 55–6). One sees a tree iff one is appeared to treely. One smells hibiscus iff one is appeared to in a hibiscus-like manner and so on. The qualia that allow

[3] For a model of how this might go, see Draper (2002).

one to be appeared to by different objects can vary radically (e.g., the *look* of a tree versus the *smell* of hibiscus), but, despite the apparent differences, perception always involves the object itself appearing to one through some kind of distinctive phenomenology.

For Alston, one perceives God iff God appears to one in a mode appropriate to the perception of the kind of thing God is. Whatever else is true of the perception of God on Alston's view, it is supposed to be non-sensory in nature. One may have sensory images along with one's perception of God (Alston, 1993, 51–4) but these images are not of epistemic significance because the perception of God is the perception of a spiritual entity. Moreover, paradigmatic mystical experiences will lack sensory imagery since they add epistemically unnecessary clutter to the experience (pp. 19–20). For the same reason, Alston favors "focal" mystical experiences in which "the awareness of God occupies one's attention to the exclusion of all else" (p. 32). Alston's paradigmatic experience, then, is one in which no sensory imagery occurs to distract one from distinctive divine qualia and in which one's awareness of God is the exclusive focus of attention.

Within Alston's framework, to experience God is to have distinctive kinds of qualia that belong to God much like the scent of hibiscus is naturally apt for conveying the presence of hibiscus. God's experiential absence would be the absence from one's experience of this distinctive range of qualia. Consequently, the problem of divine hiddenness takes the following form. Why is it the case that some people only experience normal, everyday material reality while some people some of the time have a very different and distinctive kind of religious experience? If the realm of ordinary experience contains the wrong kinds of things for conveying the presence of God, then what matters is only whether one happens to have an extra-normal element added on top of all the normal kinds of experiences we all share.

Alston defends the credentials of mystical experiences through appeals to the respectability of sense perception. There is something curious about Alston's strategy. On the one hand, it is important that mystical experiences and sense perception be similar. On the other hand, Alston is very clear that sensory imagery has no substantive role to play in conveying God's presence. What, however, gets reported in mystical experiences? Three kinds of things do – sensory imagery (e.g., a bright light), personal characteristics (e.g., experiencing God as loving), and the ineffability of the experience. If Alston sets aside sensory imagery as so much window dressing, then what justifies him in making the claim that mystical experiences involve a process like perception? There is nothing about an experience being ineffable that suggests that it must be akin to sense perception. One can imagine a drug trip inducing an experience that defies description without thinking that the experience must have been of something that was really out there. That leaves us with the personal characteristics – loving, forgiving, and the like. In that case, however, we have been looking at the wrong analog. Religious experience is not like seeing an apple so much as it is like experiencing a person. As it turns out, getting clear on how we come to experience persons will allow us to retain a substantive role for sensory imagery in religious experience.

Luckily, there is a way of thinking about what it is to experience another person that is both realist and at least quasi-perceptual. In the natural order, we infer some of the states of others, but we also engage in a kind of pattern perception. The pattern in the movements of another person conveys to us something of their mental states. Pattern perception is not an especially mysterious phenomenon. One can recognize a melody line non-inferentially and perceptually without that melody line being identifiable with any one note. One hears the melody in the structured flow of the notes. Similarly, the synchronic pattern in someone's face or the diachronic pattern of how someone moves can convey a sense of what another person is doing and feeling (cf. Green, 2012).

How much information is conveyed to one through pattern perception is a function of a number of factors. Expert perception in general is facilitated by relevant background knowledge, specialized training, and past experience. Within the context of person perception, however, an important factor in what one can perceive concerns whether one is interacting with the other person and at what depth. Person perception is at its best when it is interactive. In that sense, it is perhaps more like the way one knows music by playing than it is simply recognizing a melody line one hears. I will illustrate what I have in mind through the development of what is called "shared attention" or "joint attention."[4]

Shared attention occurs when one is engaged in an act of attending to something and in doing so one is coordinating with another on what both are attending to. In dyadic shared attention, the "something" to which the parties attend is each other, as when lovers stare into each other's eyes. In triadic shared attention, the center of attention is something other than each other but the feel of the experience includes its jointness, such as when two people watch a sunset together. The dyadic element gets taken up into the triadic experience, coloring the background of the experience and transforming what could otherwise be a private activity into a relational one.

Dyadic shared attention develops very early. By two months of age, an infant engages in the giving and receiving of facial and vocal signals in patterns of interaction. The infant has gone past picking agents out as interesting objects in the environment and has begun engaging other people. For instance, by this age, infants typically exhibit clowning and coy behavior.

---

[4] For discussion of the relevant science and some philosophical appropriations of it, see Reddy (2008), Eilan et al. (2005), and Seemann (2011).

The mother is not simply calming and familiar. The infant *plays* with the mother at this point. In fact, if one disrupts the timing of a parent's reactions to an infant, then the child will grow distressed (Murray and Trevarthan, 1985) despite the fact that the mother is cooing and smiling. Over the first year of life, dyadic shared attention becomes more and more involved until triadic shared attention emerges between nine and twelve months. Proto versions of triadic shared attention occur early as infant and caregiver share attention on things like hands or toys in the space between the persons. When triadic shared attention has arrived in full, however, infant and caregiver engage in pointing and directed looking toward distal objects. The process is one of making a connection with another person and then having the aperture of that connection widen more and more until one is able to experience the wider world together.

With the phenomenon of shared attention in mind, one can distinguish different depths of interpersonal interaction. Consider the case of two people. Oscar first sees Rebecca across the room at a party arranged by a mutual friend. Rebecca looks like a warm, pleasant person. He catches her eye from across the room, and he feels her warmth as directed at him. He gets more from the shared glance than he did by merely observing her. Rebecca introduces herself, and Oscar gains a still richer first-hand experience of Rebecca than he got from across the room. Meeting Rebecca in this way doesn't give Oscar a window into her soul, but it does provide a platform upon which more substantive interactions can be built. The pattern of relational gambits and responses they exchange gradually allows Oscar to acquire a better sense of what kind of person Rebecca is.

Suppose that the meeting at the party grows into a romance, and fast forward to a time when they have been married for forty years. When Oscar experiences that same look he originally saw from across the room at the party, that look for him is transformed into an encounter with who Rebecca is that Oscar could not have gotten forty some odd years before. The very same pattern is experienced at a much deeper level. Insofar as there is some distinctive qualia in Oscar's mature experience, something special it is like to experience Rebecca as loving, it does not float free from the relatively normal experience of seeing someone at a party.

What then of the case of God? Recall that the problem of hiddenness only arises for a divine being that is personal and interested in us. Schellenberg is even willing to make it more specific and claim that love is necessary to the idea of the God he argues does not exist (cf. Schellenberg, 2007, 199ff.). Thus, I will help myself to the idea that God, if he exists, is a personal being that can be said to interact with us. One should expect, then, that we can use the levels of interaction we see in the case of the infant and mother or the case of Oscar and Rebecca to make sense of different levels of divine–human interaction.

A first-level religious experience would correspond to identifying the divine as a something much like the newborn might pick out persons as a special kind of object in the environment. A second-level religious experience would involve gaining some sense of how to think about what this thing one experiences is doing. This level would correspond to the infant who has gained a little bit of facility with observing people. It has gone from thinking of the caregiver as a something to thinking of it as a doer. The third level would be a basic dyadic encounter with God akin to when Oscar meets Rebecca at the party. In this kind of experience, the pattern of the experience communicates the presence and attention of God but the experience is diachronically shallow. Much like Oscar can only have limited confidence in how representative his experience of Rebecca is at the party, so this level of dyadic interaction is open to reinterpretation and second-guessing in a way that higher levels of experience will typically not be.

Once shallow dyadic interaction is secured, progress in understanding God will track a history of interaction. One might imagine that, as the infant first moves from dyadic attention to shared attention on objects like its hands or toys that are brought into its body space, so it is that the fourth level of religious experience would involve sharing attention on objects of local interest to the human person. A fifth level would involve moving beyond a focus on only objects tied to the narrow interests of the human person to encompass shared attention to items of wider concern to oneself and God and to common projects that involve both kinds of objects. This level would correspond to the triadic shared attention that a typically developing infant comes into at nine to twelve months. Finally, the highest level of religious experience would correspond to Oscar and Rebecca's communion with each other after many years of marriage. The deeper kind of dyadic shared attention present at this level takes up a history of interaction into the meaning and affect conveyed between oneself and the other person. Special qualitative features of the experience at this level are not independent from the everyday patterns present at the very first level. Rather, a history of interaction has built toward this level of interpersonal resonance.

Adopting the shared attention model allows us to shift how we think about the experiential absence of God. What Alston identifies as the marker of divine presence, a strange and unique range of qualia, is conspicuously absent from the experience of almost everyone almost all of the time. Arguing that these strange experiences are widely available but that we somehow miss out on them is an awkward dialectical position to be in. If God doesn't make the experiences that matter available to almost all people almost all of the time, then one has to ask how a just and loving God could act in this manner. By contrast, if we suppose that something like the shared attention model is correct, then there is no a priori reason to suppose that the realm of ordinary experience and that of ecstatic experience are as widely separated as all that. It becomes an open question whether it might be that experiential absence is often a matter of failing to pick up on something that is in fact present within the pattern of one's experience or of failing to be aware of what exactly one has picked up on.

III   A story about attachment

It is a truism in counseling that one's past relationships and the attachment patterns that one forms in those relationships impact one's future relationships. This is true both cross-culturally and across the lifespan (cf. Erdman and Ng, 2010; Mikulincer and Shaver, 2007). Furthermore, it is a truism within pastoral counseling that the same holds when it comes to God (cf. Noffke and Hall, 2007). If, for instance, one has a troubled relationship with one's father, then one should expect the damage and pain of that relationship to carry over when it comes to a being one is told is one's "heavenly father." I think of this phenomenon as an instance of the way in which past experience in general can create schemata that help guide future interactions. The schemata we use to navigate the world can, of course, both help and hinder us.

Return to the example of Oscar and Rebecca, and suppose that Oscar brings into the relationship a conviction based on past experience that at heart everyone is really out for themselves. Due to his own measure of human brokenness, Oscar has learned to look for people to act selfishly, and he holds lightly all indications of a more expansive and selfless kind of love. In this version of their tale, Rebecca starts off more hidden from Oscar than a new acquaintance should be because Oscar has relational tendencies that create further epistemic distance between them *even before they begin to get to know each other.* In fact, it may be that interacting with Rebecca could easily lead to an *increase* in that distance as Oscar discovers opportunities to play out his own personal neuroses by foisting them upon her. Ironically perhaps, the best way for Oscar to make progress in his relationship with Rebecca is to adopt a posture of relational openness and good faith that empowers Rebecca to surprise him. The catch, of course, is that adopting such a posture is exactly what Oscar finds hard given his relational problem. The disease involves difficulty appropriating the cure.

When it comes to the case of God, the situation is more complicated. For one thing, there is reason to think that God would be hidden from us in some sense no matter what. God is always strange even when he ceases to be a stranger. One does not need to believe that God is *actus purus* to believe this to be true. A being possessed of the usual list of omni-properties will always outstrip our ability to take that being in. The familiar dialectic of relational brokenness and attachment nevertheless adds an additional layer of dysfunction on top of the challenge of having dealings with a transcendent and infinite being. Thus, there is a kind of hiddenness that we should expect that comes with the nature of God and another that tracks our dysfunctional or less developed ways of relating to God.

It should be emphasized here that dysfunctional ways of relating to someone else don't need to be rooted in anything that reflects poorly on the person with the problem. It makes little sense to say that the daughter of an abusive father is culpable for the way in which this relationship has tainted her outlook on the world. Vices for which one is obviously responsible such as selfishness and pride can impede the development of relationship but so too can baggage for which one is not responsible. There is a vulnerability and an openness to disappointment that comes with adopting a relational posture toward God in the pursuit of an intimate sharing of oneself with the divine. Without the unguardedness of trust, we may be unable to experience God at the level that is available to us.

Without the requisite trust, one should expect that shared attention with God will not naturally progress to deeper and deeper levels. If I do not trust you, shared attention between us will be fragile both because I will have a hard time fully entering into the jointness of the experience and because I am not building the history of trustful interactions necessary to achieving a higher level of dyadic shared attention. I will be less inclined to enter into common projects with you. I will need a special reason to be interested in what you value and to want it for us simply because you want it. Each stage of shared attention is hobbled when trust is damaged. Put another way, we are all hidden from each other until we are received with open hands.

IV   The case of the atheist

What should one say, however, about the atheist? What about someone who takes herself to lack an experience of the divine entirely? It is one thing to experience another person through the lens of one's past relationships but quite another to fail to acknowledge someone else's existence.

The model of religious experience I have presented doesn't require that God's making his presence available tracks the occurrence of an extraordinary qualitative experience, although it is certainly the case that some atheists report out of the ordinary, quasi-spiritual experiences. Rather, God's presence can be manifest in the pattern of otherwise ordinary experiences. It could be that God is available to be experienced for the atheist, but that the experience of God is left undeveloped in no small part because that development is blocked by the atheist's background beliefs. The experience of seeing flesh does not automatically convey happiness or sadness. It is seeing purpose in the pattern of a smile or a frown that does that job, and we are all familiar with autistic persons who have genuine difficulty seeing and interpreting the pattern, much less engaging with other people. One could suppose that the historical anomaly of atheism concerns an analogous inability to pick up on patterns that have to most people at most times been interpreted as revealing the existence of the supernatural.

The absence of belief does not preclude telling a story about attachment and social modes of reasoning in the case of the atheist, though it will be a special sort of story. One can disbelieve in something while still having a set of expectations concerning how it would be experienced if it did exist. One can know what it would be like to spot a large, aquatic, reptilian beast without having seen the Loch Ness monster.

Suppose, however, that the schema one brings to bear to show that something doesn't exist is inaccurate. In that case, one's experience of the entity in question might be thwarted at even the first level of the shared attention model. Suppose for instance that the Loch Ness monster, Nessie, is similar to a chameleon. One's expectation is that if Nessie really existed then one would spot a distinctive form sticking out from the backdrop of the lake that could only be a large aquatic beastie but that anything that falls short of this standard is no evidence at all. Since, however, Nessie the chameleon is only likely to manifest herself through a pattern that stands behind otherwise normal visual experiences, one fails to give the Nessie hypothesis a fair shake without realizing it.

If experiences of God are, pace Alston, intimately intertwined with everyday experiences, often supervening on the pattern of everyday qualia, then bringing a deflationary or overly particular schema to bear on one's experiences will risk throwing out a lot of evidence. As we've seen with the shared attention model, throwing out the evidence available at the most basic level of development impedes gaining further kinds of evidence that are conveyed to one through the course of a relationship. Furthermore, if, as I have supposed, the kinds of ecstatic experiences Alston has in mind should be associated with the deepest forms of shared attention, then the consequence of employing a deflationary schema to one's experiences that discounts anything but an ecstatic experience is that one won't ever start down the path that one would have to travel to get to such experiences. The reason that one misses the presence in the pattern can vary. It need not be as simple as shutting one's eyes to readily available evidence. It can be as subtle as being shaped by a cultural and personal context in such a way that one is not easily moved to pick up on the way that God's presence tends to be manifested in the day-to-day business of life.

At this point, a special case cries out for explanation. What about the case of atheists who long for religious experiences? What about the atheist who wishes that God existed but who simply believes he doesn't? To my mind, this is the truly challenging case. It is not the dutiful cataloger of evidence that should give the theist pause. It is, instead, the case of someone who finds the world a cold place for its lacking a God. Surely, one wants to say, if God existed, God would embrace such a person and never let her come to such straits.

Return once again to the case of Oscar and to a time in Oscar's life before he met Rebecca. Oscar believes that everyone is out for themselves, but he is willing and indeed eager to be proven wrong on this score. Oscar could sincerely want to believe the best of people and yet not be able to do so. There is a certain kind of person that he wants to believe exists, and he does not believe there are any. We could specify that there are people in Oscar's life who are altruistic and look out for others. Perhaps his neighbor does, but Oscar does not experience his neighbor that way. It is only when he meets Rebecca that the presence of a better sort of person is registered by him in a way that makes him aware of the opportunity to either open himself up to her in trust or not. Although I do not have anything approaching a complete answer when it comes to the atheist who desires God's existence, it is surely relevant that we are aware of familiar cases like Oscar's. It is possible for a desire for relationship to be present simultaneously with someone who could fill that desire and yet there be problems that need to be worked through in connecting the two.

One of the cases that Schellenberg draws attention to is that of the former theist (Schellenberg, 2007, 228ff.). One might think that this case is an especially problematic one for the proposal of this essay. I have been talking about the need for progress to be made over time in a relationship, but the former believer's life has the opposite trajectory. Suppose Harriet used to be a Christian, but then became convinced as an adult that atheism is true. This was not a happy or a freeing event in Harriet's life. She feels haunted by her upbringing and finds little joy in her mature way of seeing the world. She even on occasion prays, "God, if you really are out there, show yourself to me!" In answer, she hears nothing. Aren't cases like that of Harriet inconsistent with the existence of a good and loving God?

Harriet's case is a troubling one, and there surely are some people out there who are in her position. One piece of critical information that is missing from the scenario as described so far, however, is what her relationship with God was supposed to have been like prior to her losing her faith. For all that's been said so far, Harriet's story could involve no shared attention with God at all, a high level of shared attention, or something in between.

Different experiences on the continuum of shared attention should be handled in distinct ways. If we are on the side of the continuum where Harriet has had no religious experiences to speak of, then one does have to ask why God didn't give these experiences to her. If Harriet has had little by way of shared attention with God, then the key question is whether the fact that, earlier in her life, Harriet believed that God exists makes Harriet's case any harder to explain than the case of an atheist who never believed in God. I do not see how belief by itself makes things too much harder. Not believing that someone exists makes it hard to share attention with them, but believing that someone exists does not guarantee that obstacles to sharing attention are all removed.

I can believe that Barrack Obama exists but think him too important and busy to be available to me. Likewise, I might believe that someone exists and is worth knowing but sabotage my chances to interact with her for any number of reasons. Thus, I do not think this version of the case is different enough from other cases to be a cause for special concern.

If, on the other hand, we travel to the other side of the continuum and posit that Harriet had developed an advanced level of intimate shared attention with God, it becomes completely mysterious how she could lose her faith. If you've never met Michael Jordan, then you may or may not believe hearsay about what he's really like. If Michael Jordan is your father and you've spent your whole life with him, then your personal experience trumps hearsay, especially if you have hitherto had an intimate relationship with him. You may develop a more nuanced understanding of who he is as you realize how other people have experienced him, but, fundamentally, you shouldn't easily give up what you know about your dad from first-hand experience. Likewise, it is not at all clear how one could make rational sense of losing one's faith if one had previously possessed an advanced level of dyadic shared attention with God. If the universe went to the trouble of concocting an illusory history of interaction with a divine being of such a sort, then one should tip one's hat to the universe and pay it the compliment of belief.

However we fill out Harriet's story, there is a familiar way in which shared attention can be undone after the fact. Othello loves Desdemona when Iago begins to poison his mind, but their love is still fairly new. Iago provides Othello an alternative schema for organizing Othello's experiences on which Desdemona is not a trustworthy spouse. The schema is not neutral. Adopting it is already a way of moving from trust to distrust, and it is hard to use a method of distrust to vindicate a relationship. With Iago's help, Othello comes to reorganize and reinterpret the narrative of his relationship with Desdemona. The deflationary schema that Iago offers Othello in this case doesn't just keep him from discovering the truth about Desdemona. Rather, it remakes Othello's memories in a way that robs him of the truth he already had. It is important, though, that Othello and Desdemona have a shallow history with each other. Iago's work would have been much more difficult if Othello's regard for Desdemona was founded on a long history. The longer and more rehearsed the narrative, the harder it is to recast.

V   Objections and disclaimers

In this essay, I have focused on hiddenness as an experiential problem. I have tried to make sense of the general phenomena while showing how the framework I develop here could be applied to the case of the atheist and the former believer. At this point, it is worth drawing the reader's attention to what I have not tried to explain and to a couple versions of an objection to my project.

First, there is a way of developing the argument from hiddenness that focuses on religious pluralism (Maitzen, 2006). Instead of the non-culpable atheist, the focus of this argument is the influence of socio-cultural and historical position on belief and experience. A hiddenness argument developed along these lines can strengthen concerns about religious disagreement in a cumulative case against theism. Such an argument is worth taking seriously, and I think the shared attention model has a few points of application for such a problem. I have left it unaddressed here however.[5]

Second, as his essay in this volume nicely illustrates, Schellenberg wants to help us gain perspective on the phenomenon of hiddenness in at least two ways, the first of which I do not address and the second of which can be parlayed into an objection to what I have said. It is important to Schellenberg that we discuss the hiddenness of God with a sense of our place in history. The story one tells about divine hiddenness, according to Schellenberg, should not just fit the experience of a few people at this particular juncture of recorded history. Religion has existed for a very long time on this planet. From the perspective of deep evolutionary time, however, religious beings have been a blip on the screen, and, if one considers how long our planet might remain habitable, then everything we know about religion may be a preface to what lies ahead. I cannot but gesture at what might be said in response. I only note in passing that it is not obvious to me that the story arch of where we have been and where we are going as a species cannot be told in terms of a developing relationship with a personal God who is interested in us as a species. A panoramic view of human history surely induces epistemic humility, though, and that is undoubtedly helpful.

Another way in which Schellenberg tries to ensure that the discussion proceeds with appropriate perspective is to stress that there is a difference between philosophy and theology. Insofar as I follow the point, I take it to be a caution against religious philosophers who attempt to square our experience of the world with religious background beliefs without fully or fairly considering just how unexpected or improbable our experience is on those background beliefs. One can imagine God creating any number of worlds that differ from this one in which divine hiddenness is either absent or ameliorated. Even if we suppose that God could exist and be hidden, why think that he would? Let's look at two ways of developing this objection, first in terms of belief and then in terms of shared attention.[6]

---

[5] As tempting as it is to apply the shared attention model to the dark night of the soul, that task is also beyond the scope of this paper. See, however, Sarah Coakley's essay (chapter 13, this volume).

[6] I would like to thank John Schellenberg for sensitizing me to these objections and how they enter the discussion.

One way to develop the objection is to reject the argument from the first section of this paper. One cannot, according to the objector, simply set aside belief. It may be that there is an experiential and a doxastic version of the problem of hiddenness. Doesn't God have the power to ensure that everyone believes in God? If God can ensure theistic belief but does not do so, then perhaps that's a reason to think God doesn't exist. After all, even if there is a way to make sense of how God would be hidden in worlds where theistic belief is not assured, that does not tell us why we are in such a world to begin with.

A full response to this objection would require an explication of what the human condition consists in and how our being in that condition is consistent with the goodness of God. In this space, I cannot give such a story. What can be said, however, is that belief in God is not necessary to start down the path of shared attention. An infant does not have to believe that other people exist in order to begin to experience other people. Moreover, an infant can be aware of another person without being aware of what they are aware of. Not being aware of what it is that one has a *de re* awareness of is not a death sentence for the relationship, however. Infants grow into greater awareness of the other person over the course of development. Given that belief is not necessary to start down the path of shared attention and that belief does not by itself pick out a relationally interesting state anyway, I conclude that God's ability to ensure belief in some possible worlds does not obviously defeat my proposal.

There is a way of developing a similar objection from within my framework, however. Schellenberg (personal communication) notes that there is an interesting tension between the case of Oscar and Rebecca and the case of a mother with its child. Oscar brings baggage to his relationship with Rebecca that the infant does not have. It is unsurprising, then, that we can predict that the mother and infant's relationship will have a predictable developmental timetable and that it will eventuate in a healthy relational state, but that we do not have the same when it comes to Oscar. On the objection in play, we should not take for granted Oscar's relational brokenness and whatever analogs to it there may be when it comes to relating to God. We have to ask why God would allow people to be in the position of Oscar in relation to the divine rather than the position of the infant. It is all well and good if relationship with God has to develop, but surely a good and loving God would not let it be handicapped.

Notice that the modal intuitions that Schellenberg needs for this version of the objection are much more subtle and less plausible than in the case of the parallel objection put in terms of theistic belief. I think it fairly obvious that God could create creatures who start life already possessing the belief that roses are red or that Africa is a continent. If there's no reason to believe that God couldn't create beings with all sorts of beliefs already formed, then it's plainly possible for God to create beings that all have theistic beliefs. Moreover, if we are thinking that whatever relational good we posit God as being interested in requires belief in God's existence as a prerequisite, then it is plausible that God would do exactly what we have said he could do, namely, create a world in which nonbelief is absent.

In contrast, consider the following claims:

(a) If God existed and wanted to create creatures like us, God would ensure that we have shared attention with God at every moment of our lives.
(b) If God created a world in which creatures developed relationships through the stages of shared attention, God could and would ensure that human beings never had relational baggage that would get in the way of relationship with God (unless the human being was culpable for that baggage).

I think both (a) and (b) are not obviously true and are probably false. Concerning (a), what is the analog of forced shared attention in the natural world? Is it forcing a child to look at you, forcing a child to do things with you? Forced shared attention doesn't seem like the sort of thing that we should expect a perfectly loving being to engage in very often. One might protest that it needn't be forced in the sense of creatures receiving something they don't want. God could just create beings that are determined to want shared attention with God and enjoy it perpetually. One can plug in familiar concerns about the value of freely chosen relationship into this scenario. Whereas there is more of a conceptual gap between belief and freely chosen relationship, it is plausible to me that a high degree of shared attention and freely chosen relationship go together organically. I find it plausible then that a perfect being either couldn't or wouldn't create beings like us who had no alternative to sharing attention with God.

Concerning (b), ensuring that human beings did not accumulate relational baggage across their life would require much more stringent constraints than ensuring belief in God would. One can easily imagine God setting up a world in which people believe in God without God's having to intervene to make sure that people maintain that belief. God could simply create people with a very strong encapsulated module devoted to theism, a super-duper *sensus divinitatis*. If God gives people the capacity to relate to each other freely, however, then a natural consequence of such freedom is its misuse or non-optimal use. The natural consequences of the misuse of a connection with another person would touch both oneself and the other person. God might have to intervene quite a lot to ensure that any relational baggage accrued in the natural order is quarantined in such a way that it does not color relationship with God. If God wants human beings to relate to God as integrated social beings, if he wants relationship with God to be an expression of identity, then there is no way to bracket potential negative effects that come from relating to other people without intervening artificially in a way that introduces psychic division into the person. If love of God and love of neighbor are connected as is taught in the Christian tradition, one can imagine that the relation between the two works in both directions. Poisons that disrupt the fraternal harmony of humankind should have a like effect on relating to the divine.

In conclusion, I have presented a model for thinking about God's presence, the shared attention model, on which God can be available to be experienced ubiquitously. Not all experiences are equal, however, and deeper experiences of God are built toward through a history of interaction. Intimate relationship cannot be created by fiat. It must be grown into. The obstacles to such growth are various, but the seed from which relationship grows need not be either belief or a powerful experience. It can simply be a patient presence waiting to be received.

Part V

God's Hiddenness and God's Nature in the Major Monotheisms

9   The hiddenness of "divine hiddenness": divine love in medieval Islamic lands

Jon McGinnis

Introduction

The issue of divine hiddenness has come to the forefront of philosophy of religion as one of the more pressing arguments against theism. J. L. Schellenberg first formulated the contemporary version of the problem in his 1993 book *Divine Hiddenness and Human Reason*; again more succinctly in dialogue form in "What the Hiddenness of God Reveals: A Collaborative Discussion"; and most recently in part III of *The Wisdom to Doubt*. The simple version of that argument is frequently framed in terms of an unsurpassably loving God who seeks to have a personal relation with His creation and the apparently obvious fact that, through no fault of their own, many never experience such a personal relation. Seemingly, then, if an omnibenevolent God existed, there should be no inculpable nonbelievers, yet there are inculpable nonbelievers, and so, the argument concludes, an omnibenevolent God does not exist.

Schellenberg's argument purportedly applies to all forms of theism, and particularly to the monotheism of the three great Abrahamic traditions, Judaism, Christianity, and Islam. Thus, it is worth noting that most discussions of the divine hiddenness argument are framed within the context of Christianity and Judaism.[1] Correspondingly, then, most versions of the argument assume a number of tenets more proper to modern Christianity and Judaism than to Islam, to say nothing of medieval interpretations of Islam. Given the limits of the current discussion, I propose to survey how certain medieval Muslim philosophers and theologians (and even certain medieval Jewish philosophers influenced by these Muslim thinkers) may have viewed divine hiddenness.

Before beginning, I should make one personal confession and a caveat. I am neither a Muslim theologian nor even an expert on Islam itself; rather, I study Arabic philosophy as it was practiced in the Neoplatonizing Aristotelian tradition of the classical period of Islam (*c*.850–1200), a tradition known as *falsafa*. Thus the readers should be forewarned that I am not making claims about what

---

[1] See, for example, Howard-Snyder and Moser (2002, "Introduction: The Hiddenness of God," esp. 1–3). One exception is Azadegan (2013).

Muslims today (nor even the average medieval Muslim) might say (or have said) about divine love and other related topics. Despite this study's limited purview, the *falsafa* tradition was formative in the development of Islamic philosophical theology as seen in its influence on such major (orthodox) Sunni and Shia theologians, as, for example, al-Ghazālī (d. 1111), Fakhr al-Dīn al-Rāzī (d. 1209), and Naṣīr al-Dīn al-Ṭūsī (d. 1274), and thus its impact can still be felt today. Hence there is some merit in seeing how a certain relatively small but historically significant group of Muslim intellectuals interpreted their religion, and in light of that interpretation what they may have said in response to Schellenberg's argument.

I believe that we can learn no less than two things from our medieval predecessors, points which are still of interest to us today. First, many of the assumptions of the argument from divine hiddenness, so these thinkers would suggest, are at odds with other deeply held theistic beliefs that one might have about God. These beliefs include: God is perfect; God is simple; God is unchanging. The second point of interest to be drawn from this study is that many of the assumptions of the argument from divine hiddenness are (not to put too fine a point on it) unique to Christianity rather than to theism or even the Abrahamic religions more generally. In the end, I hope to reveal a number of elements in need of further philosophical and theological examination hidden within the argument from divine hiddenness.

To this end, I consider in particular Schellenberg's claim, "if a perfectly loving God exists, all human beings capable of personal relation with himself are, at all times at which they are so capable, in a position to believe that he exists."[2] Schellenberg goes on to explicate the notion of divine love thus:

> In claiming that this proposition ["God seeks to be personally related to us"] is essential to any adequate explication of "God loves human beings," I am claiming that God, if loving, seeks *explicit, reciprocal* relation with us ... So understood, this proposition seems obviously required. For only the best human love could serve as an analogy of Divine love, and human love at its best clearly involves reciprocity and mutuality. [emphasis in original][3]

In *The Wisdom to Doubt*, Schellenberg prefers the expression *"relational-personal* love" for *"explicit, reciprocal* relation."[4] Whatever expression one prefers, are such presumptions about God, the analogy with human love, and the possibility of a personal relation with God truly theological desiderata, particularly as conceived within the broader Abrahamic tradition so as to include not merely (modern) Christians but (medieval) Jews and Muslims as well? In the following, I suggest that many of Schellenberg's assumptions

[2] Schellenberg (1993, 18).   [3] Schellenberg (1993, 18).
[4] Schellenberg (2007, 198–206).

would have sounded odd, ill conceived, and even perhaps blasphemous to certain thinkers within the *falsafa* tradition – particularly al-Fārābī, Avicenna, and Moses Maimonides (the last of whom, while obviously not Muslim, was working within the same philosophical framework).

Preliminaries: the vocabulary of love in medieval Arabic

Let me begin to approach the subject of divine love within the medieval *falsafa* tradition indirectly by considering certain references to divine love, first, from Christian scriptures as those scriptures appear in Arabic translation and, second, from the Qur'ān. These observations help provide the mise en scène for medieval Muslim philosophers' accounts of divine love and the possibility of having a personal relation with God. To this end, consider the following claims about divine love as they are found in the oldest known Arabic translation of Christian scriptures:[5]

> John 3:16: "For God so loved (*aḥabba*) the world that he gave his only begotten son ...";
> 1 John 3:1: "See how great a love (*maḥabba*) the Father has bestowed upon us, that we should be called children of God";
> 1 John 4:8: "Whoever does not love (*lā yuḥibbu*) does not know God, because God is love (*maḥabba*)."

In all cases the language for love comes from the Arabic root Ḥ-B-B. This root refers to a general notion of love, ranging from an inclination of the soul for a thing to, quite literally, being lovesick – which medieval Muslim physicians identified in certain cases with a form of melancholy – to simply being overpowered by or mad with love.[6] Medieval philosophers writing in Muslim lands seemed to understand this root as the love between humans. For example, in *On the Virtuous City*, Abū Naṣr al-Fārābī (*c*.870–950/1), when speaking about connections among creatures, describes the term *maḥabba* (love) thus: "*maḥabba* is that by which humans are connected, for it is a state in them."[7] Similarly, Avicenna (980–1037) suggests that *maḥabba* is simply the more general notion of love as opposed to the more specific form of deep love (*'ishq*), while in his *Metaphysics* he uses *maḥabba* for the proper relation between husband and wife if children are to be successfully reared.[8]

The Qur'ān too uses expressions of love derived from this root (e.g., Q 2:195, 9:108, 49:9), but when said in the context of God those Qur'ānic uses

---

[5] This is the language of the Mt. Sinai Arabic Codex 151 [II, vol. 42], which is the earliest known Arabic translation of the New Testament. This same language still appears in three more recent Arabic translations – Smith and Van Dyck (the preferred Bible of the Coptic Church), *Arabic Life Application Bible*, and *Book of Life*. Also see Griffith (2013).

[6] See Lane (1985, s.v. *ḥubb*); also see Avicenna (1963, § 10).

[7] Al-Fārābī (1985, 96–7).

[8] Avicenna (1963, § 10) and (2005, X.4, [6]).

most frequently refer to what God prefers. For example, God loves a good doer or one who is pure or one who is just. In this respect, the Qur'ānic use of *maḥabba*, or love, and other etymologically related expressions appears different from the Johannine use of those terms noted earlier, for in the Qur'ān these expressions are used to tell us what behavior God wants or expects from us, whereas in John's Gospel and epistle those terms indicate God's desire for a relation with us and how that relation should affect our relations with others.

The Qur'ānic vocabulary for divine love is hardly limited to terms derived from the Ḥ-B-B root. Indeed, and perhaps more importantly, one of the ninety-nine beautiful names of God within Islam is "the loving one" (*al-wadūd*). Examples include, "Ask forgiveness of your Lord and then repent to Him. Indeed, my Lord is Merciful and *Loving*" (Q 11:90) and in the same vein, "He is the Forgiving, the *Loving*" (Q 85:14). In these *āyāt*, or verses, the reference to God's being loving is much akin to God's forgiveness and the fact that we are indebted to God. This point is one that al-Ghazālī notes in his commentary on the ninety-nine beautiful names of God.[9] Al-Ghazālī adds, however, that God's loving is different from His mercy and forgiveness in that in loving, the object of that love has not necessarily committed some fault, and so there is no clear indication of need or poverty on the part of the recipient. Thus the action of the loving one, according to al-Ghazālī, is to favor or to bestow goods on the beloved. Similarly, the great Muslim mystic Ibn 'Arabī (1165–1240) in his treatment of the divine names understands *al-wadūd* as God's conferring existence on and sustaining moment by moment the created order.[10] In other words, the notion of *al-wadūd*, for these thinkers, indicates God's generosity and munificence, that is, God's love is another way of speaking of creation and divine providence.

Of course, such a conception of divine love is also replete in Jewish and Christian scriptures. Hence, none of what I have said should be viewed as diminishing the Muslim conception of divine love; rather, it is just to note that certain Christian scriptures describe divine love in terms of a personal relation, which is not the explicit language for God's love in the Qur'ān (even though it might be implicit). I mention this point simply because Schellenberg takes relational-personal love to be essential to any form of theism, whereas certain medieval Muslim philosophers happily interpreted their religion without such a notion. Before turning to "personal relation," let me look at some of the historical players and consider their various philosophical views about divine love.

---

[9] See al-Ghazālī (1992, s.v. *al-Wadūd*, pp. 118–19).

[10] See, for example, Ibn 'Arabī's chapter on the divine names from the *Futūḥāt*; an online English translation is available at The Muhyiddin Ibn 'Arabi Society, "The Servant of the Loving One: On the Adoption of the Character Traits of al-Wadūd," http://www.ibnarabisociety.org/articles/alwadud.html#ref26.

Divine love within the *falsafa* tradition

According to Schellenberg, if there were an unsurpassably great or ultimately perfect entity, it also necessarily would be an unsurpassably or perfectly loving one.[11] Consequently, Schellenberg's claim requires that love be a perfection. I certainly concede that many of us, at least in the West today, do view love as a perfection, but it is not clear that everyone would so agree nor that these dissenters are simply wrong if they do not accept this characterization of love. What is needed is an analysis of divine love.

Certainly one of the more important philosophers during the classical period of Islamic philosophy is Abū Naṣr al-Fārābī. In *On the Perfect State*, he has this to say of divine love: "As for [the First, that is, God], the one showing deep-love and the object of that deep-love (*'āshiq/ma'shūq*) and the lover and the beloved (*muḥibb/maḥbūb*) are the same, and so [God] is the first beloved and first object of deep-love."[12] This claim, which is virtually repeated verbatim in other works of al-Fārābī, such as *On the Principles of Existing Things*,[13] is part of a long chain of arguments all motivated by al-Fārābī's insistence that the divinity is completely perfect and so deficient in nothing. So, for example, speaking of divine knowledge, al-Fārābī notes:

In order to know, [God] needs no other entity outside of Himself, which by knowing it He would acquire excellence, nor in order to be an object of knowledge does [God need] some other entity that knows Him. Instead, He is sufficient in His substance in order to know and be known. His knowledge of Himself is nothing other than His substance, for His knowing, being known and knowing Himself as one are one substance.[14]

The philosophical basis of al-Fārābī's claim here is that since God is absolutely perfect, He must also be self-sufficient and so is in need of nothing external to the divine essence. Moreover, philosophical and theological issues associated with a doctrine of divine simplicity (*tawḥīd*) motivate al-Fārābī's claim.[15] More specifically, according to al-Fārābī and others in the *falsafa* tradition, within an absolutely simple being, there cannot be the distinction between what is *potentially* known and what *actually* knows, for there would be potentiality in God. Arguably even more damning is that whatever has parts – such as a part that

---

[11] See Schellenberg (1993, ch. 1); (2002, §II); and (2007, 195, 198–206).

[12] Al-Fārābī (1985, 88–9).

[13] Al-Fārābī, *On the Principles of Existing Things*, 47 (in McGinnis and Reisman, 2007, §30).

[14] Al-Fārābī (1985, 72–3).

[15] Here and throughout the notion of divine simplicity drives much of the thought of the various thinkers I consider. It thus should be noted that the notion of simplicity that these Muslim and Jewish thinkers require of God is arguably more demanding than that found among certain Christian philosophers. For a summary of (primarily Christian) conceptions of divine simplicity as well as pertinent secondary literature, see Vallicella (2006). For more specific discussions on the differences between Maimonides and Aquinas over divine simplicity see Stump (2011a, 2012).

is in potentiality and a part that is in actuality – needs a cause to explain the unification of those parts, and God as the Cause of causes cannot stand to anything else as an effect to a cause.[16] Armed with this schema, again exemplified in God's being both knower and object known, al-Fārābī applies it to a host of other divine attributes, lover and beloved being among them.

In addition to these explicit philosophical reasons for identifying subject and object in God, readers of Aristotle will immediately recognize al-Fārābī's claims about divine knowledge as just those of Aristotle's *Metaphysics* (Lambda, 9). In that text, Aristotle famously describes the unmoved mover as thought thinking itself. Thus it is perhaps worth noting that one of Aristotle's pressing reasons for identifying the unmoved mover with thought thinking itself was to address the issue of what object of thought is worthy of the divinity. According to Aristotle, for God to ponder anything other than himself is analogous to our contemplating foul and obscene things; some material simply should not be thought. While al-Fārābī does not mention this point, certainly the idea would not have been lost on many of his readers. Read in this light, then, al-Fārābī's insistence that God is both lover and beloved suggests that anything other than God would not be worthy of God's loving it. Put bluntly, God not only does not need us in order to love, but has no will nor desire to love us or even to know us.

It was perhaps because of such unfriendly implications (and I am not suggesting that al-Fārābī actually held them, although they were certainly ascribed to Aristotle) that the great Muslim philosopher and scientist Avicenna, while adopting much of al-Fārābī's philosophical theology, nonetheless altered it to allow for God's knowing and loving us as part of the order of the good at least in some "accidental" sense. Thus in the *Metaphysics* of his monumental philosophical encyclopedia, the *Cure*, Avicenna has this to say of divine love:

[The First, that is, God] is a lover (*'āshiq*) of Himself, who is the principle of all order and good insofar as [He Himself] is such. Hence the order of the good is for him an accidental object of love; however, He is not moved toward that as a result of desire (*shawq*). That is because there simply is no passivity within Him: He neither desires anything nor seeks after it, for this will of His is devoid of [any] deficiency that would bring about a desire and arouse an intention toward some end.[17]

One quick terminological point before turning to an analysis of Avicenna's account of divine love: Avicenna's preferred term for divine love comes from the root '-SH-Q, not Ḥ-B-B. This point is to be contrasted with al-Fārābī, who used both roots in describing divine love. The '-SH-Q root among philosophers

[16] See al-Fārābī (1985, ch. 1) and *On the Principles of Existing Things*, 42–53 (McGinnis and Reisman, 2007, §§21–37). Avicenna also adopts this same position; see Avicenna, *Metaphysics* (2005, VIII.3–4) and *Najāt*, 551–2 (McGinnis and Reisman, 2007, 214).
[17] Avicenna, *Metaphysics* (2005, VIII.7 [3]).

and physicians frequently indicates the highest degree of deep-love prior to the love's becoming pathological.[18] Indeed Avicenna dedicated an entire treatise to ʿishq (deep-love), a text to which I return shortly.[19]

As for the current passage, Avicenna starts with the very Farabian claim that God loves Himself. Moreover, Avicenna does so for the same reasons that al-Fārābī had held this claim: There is no passivity or potentiality in God. Avicenna's God is absolutely perfect and so deficient in nothing, which in the present case means that Avicenna's God, like al-Fārābī's, does not need some external object of love in order for God to be possessed of unsurpassable, perfect love, for He wholly and perfectly loves Himself. Despite these core similarities, there are also two notable differences. Avicenna emphasizes in his account of divine love, one, that God is the principle of the order of the good, and, two, as such there is some sense that God loves, albeit accidentally, that order too. Avicenna explains the significance of these points immediately after introducing them, which he does by presenting his own understanding of divine self-knowledge.[20]

Again, like Aristotle and al-Fārābī before him, Avicenna's deity is thought thinking itself. Avicenna also agrees with them that the divinity must be free of any potentiality or deficiency and so is completely perfect. Avicenna further adds, however, that inasmuch as the deity is completely perfect He must know Himself completely and perfectly. Avicenna then continues that God is the cause of all that is, and so for God to know Himself completely and perfectly, He must know Himself as cause. Avicenna continues that if one is to know a cause completely and perfectly, one must also know the effects of that cause. Consequently, according to Avicenna, since God completely and perfectly knows Himself, He, by that very fact, also completely and perfectly knows His effect, which is the created order. This last point is the reason for Avicenna's emphasis in his account of divine love that God is the cause of order and good, or jointly "the order of the good," which includes the created order.

Consequently, according to Avicenna, while what God essentially knows and loves is Himself, in that very act of knowing and loving Himself there is an accidental (bi-l-ʿaraḍ) sense in which God knows and loves the created order. The issue of Avicenna's theory of God's knowledge of particulars is well traveled, even if tortuous, and so I shall not pick it up here, other than to note the following.[21] The notion of "accidental" employed here should not be understood to indicate that there is anything accidental in God when He knows created things. Instead it simply means that there is a concomitant or residual effect that follows upon God's knowing Himself, and that concomitant or residual effect is nothing less than the creation of the cosmos.

This last point, about the created order's being a concomitant that follows upon God's self-knowledge and love, throws light on what Avicenna means by saying that the created order is an *accidental* object of God's love. In his *Ta'līqāt*, or *Notes*, Avicenna observes that when one wholly and completely loves another, one not only loves the individual but whatever the individual does inasmuch as what proceeds from the beloved are concomitants or actions of the beloved itself.[22] To provide a somewhat earthy example, as any first-time parent knows, we not only love the little newborn bundle of joy but also its little messes (at least for a while). Of course nobody loves poop for itself but one can love it in an accidental sense as the byproduct of the child who is loved essentially and in itself.[23] Analogously, God essentially loves Himself perfectly and completely, and inasmuch as the created order is the byproduct or concomitant of God's love for Himself, there is a sense that God loves the created order too, not in itself but accidentally.

Now one might complain that this conception of divine *accidental* love, rather than reciprocal and personal love, makes Avicenna's brand of divine love fairly anemic. Such an objection seems rooted in our own biases that love is a kind of perfection rather than a defect. Even before Avicenna, however, Plato had suggested that love is defective in some sense, since it is a desire for beauty and so entails that the lover is lacking some good, namely, some beauty, which it desires to possess.[24] In both Avicenna's account of divine love from the *Cure* and his "Treatise on Love (*'ishq*)," he, either implicitly or explicitly, endorses this Platonic sentiment about love. Indeed in the treatise on love, Avicenna explains love in terms of an intense attraction to the beautiful and fitting (*istiḥsān al-ḥusn wa-l-mulā'im jiddan*).[25] Consequently, virtually the whole of that treatise is an account of how all creatures, from the simplest of elements to the greatest of angels, love God and so are directed toward God as their natural perfection. Moreover, this Platonic–Avicennan analysis of love in terms of a deficiency or lack rather than as a perfection is not unique to the *falsafa* tradition; indeed the great Muslim mystic Ibn 'Arabī (1165–1240) embraces it wholeheartedly in his account of love.[26] In fact, Ibn 'Arabī goes so far as to say that love can only

---

[22] Avicenna, *Ta'līqāt* (2013, 11 and 15).

[23] While the example is a bit graphic, the imagery is not wholly my own, but part of the *falsafa* tradition. For example, Ibn Ṭufayl in his philosophical novel *Ḥayy Ibn Yaqẓān* likens the terrestrial sphere to the chyme and chyle in the stomach and intestines of an animal; see McGinnis and Reisman (2007, 290 [19]).

[24] Cf. *Symposium*, 199D–20C.   [25] Avicenna, "Risāla fī l-'išq" (1894, 4).

[26] For a discussion of Ibn 'Arabī's discussion of love, see Chittick (2005, ch. 3).

exist when there is the complete absence of any perfection, including (paradoxically) existence.[27]

As for God's love, Avicenna again repeats that since God is absolutely perfect, His "natural desire" can only be for Himself. For Avicenna, then, it is only the divine being itself that God finds fitting and beautiful, and so something essentially worthy of His love.[28]

This point is directly relevant to Schellenberg's characterization of divine love in terms of God's *seeking* personal relation with us. In the *Metaphysics of the Cure* Avicenna explicitly explains that God does not seek (*ṭalab*) anything; for what is sought is some imagined, opined, or intellectual good that the agent recognizes as such and yet does not possess.[29] In other words, for Avicenna only an agent deficient in some perfection *desires* or *seeks* something. Since God is perfect in all respects, Avicenna's divinity would not seek a personal relation with us, if by that one imagines that it provides God with some good that He otherwise would not possess. In short, at least one conception of "seeking," namely, one involving the acquisition of some absent good, is abhorrent to Avicenna's conception of an unsurpassably great or perfect God, a point that many theists share.

In fairness to Schellenberg, he does not take "seeking" as an unanalyzed notion. That God seeks personal relation with us, according to Schellenberg, is that:

God ... will see to it that the only thing that can prevent us from interacting with God is our own free choice (whether it is the free choice to ignore a God we are aware of, or to take steps to remove that awareness, and so to remove ourselves from that place where we are in a position to relate personally to God). This is what I should be taken to mean when I speak of a loving God *seeking* personal relationship with us. [emphasis in original][30]

Here again there are some implicit assumptions. First, it is not evident from this formulation whether Schellenberg understands God as seeking so as to perfect Himself. I suspect not, but if so, then his position is subject to the previous criticism, namely, God, a purportedly all-perfect being, would lack some perfection that He seeks to obtain, a blatant contradiction.

Second, Schellenberg's conception of God's seeking personal relation with us presumes that humans have free choice, or alternatively, if there is to be a reciprocal loving and personal relation, there must be free will. This assumption

---

[27] Thus, Ibn ʿArabī writes, "As long as there is love, one cannot conceive of the existence of the created things along with it, so the created thing never comes into existence" (cited in Chittick, 2005, 42; unfortunately, I did not have access to the same edition of the *futūḥāt* as Chittick, so I could not track down the reference to check the translation).

[28] Avicenna, "Risāla fī l-ʿišq" (1894, 4).

[29] Avicenna, *Metaphysics* (2005, IX.2 [12]); also see Avicenna, *Taʿlīqāt* (2013, 12).

[30] Schellenberg (2002, 42–3).

is not one that all Muslims (or even all Christians) would share. Indeed, on the standard interpretation of Avicenna and his philosophical system, he is a strict determinist, who denies free will and yet, as seen, believes that God loves (even if not in the way Schellenberg would have it).[31] Similarly, it was (and still remains) a common position within Ash'arite theology – a decidedly orthodox Muslim position – that literally all power is reserved for God and God alone.[32] For these orthodox Muslims God literally creates within us at every moment our desires, wills, and actions, leaving little room for at least certain conceptions of free will. This last point about Schellenberg's association of love and free will has taken me afield, and I only mention it as a possible area for further enquiry.

To sum up the most salient points of this section, for al-Fārābī and Avicenna, inasmuch as divine love is a perfection God must essentially be both lover and the object of that love. As for creatures, divine love does not involve seeking some reciprocal personal relation with creatures; rather, divine love is the source and end of all of creaturely goods and perfections, a love that is expressed most fully in God's providential care for us, which raises its own distinct set of issues.[33] What is notable about al-Fārābī and Avicenna's accounts of divine love is that neither man seemed to think that God's seeking a personal relation with us is at all essential to either divine love, specifically, or one's theism, more generally. While such a conception need not be identified with the Qur'ānic or Islamic view of divine love, it does represent one way that monotheism can be understood when issues of divine perfection and simplicity are pressed.

Understanding "personal relation" in medieval Islam: persons

So a question that theologians and philosophers of religion need to ask is whether having a personal relation with God should be a desideratum of one's

---

[31] For critical discussions of Avicenna's view of free will and determinism with a survey of the literature see Belo (2007) and Rufus and McGinnis (2015).

[32] For a discussion of Ash'arite theology see Gimaret (1990).

[33] I have not spoken of the theory of providence (*'ināya*) in Islam or the *falsafa* tradition and its relation to divine love, for a number of reasons. Concerning traditional Islam, a prevalent Islamic understanding of providence is that our world is "providentially unambiguous." In other words, according to a standard reading of the Qur'ān, God has provided abundant and unambiguous signs all around us indicating the exclusive truth of Islam, such that anyone who is not a Muslim is culpably so. In short, Muslims who accept this line of interpretation would simply deny that there is some phenomenon, "divine hiddenness," that needs to be explained. For a discussion of the traditional belief about providence in Islam, which at the same time attempts to address the issue of divine hiddenness, see Aijaz (2008). As for *falsafa*, there were multiple conceptions of providence, varying from those that allowed for only general providence to various interpretations of special providence, and so a full discussion would take me well beyond the scope of the present paper. Moreover, the issue of providence is historically associated with the classic problem of evil – how does one reconcile God's purported providential care with the existence of evil – which is a different argument against theism from that based upon divine hiddenness.

philosophical theology. In the next two sections, I consider the notion of "personal relation" and what thinkers in the *falsafa* tradition might say about such a notion when applied to creatures and Creator. To this end, I first look at the concept of person, particularly its historical origins, and suggest that it is not a clearly demarcated notion within the medieval Islamic world. Second, I consider the idea of relation, particularly as it applies to God and creatures. What one sees is that within the framework of *falsafa* there are deep philosophical problems associated with God's seeking a *personal relation* with us.

To begin, I take it as obvious that in order for a personal relation to exist between God and creatures, there must be persons. Already red flags should pop up, for the doctrine of God's personhood was forged in the heat of debates about the triune nature of God, a doctrine unique to Christianity among the Abrahamic religions. According to the standard Trinitarian formulation, God is one in substance or being (Gk. *homoousios*; Lat. *consubstantialis*) but three in persons (Gk. *hypostasis* or *prosōpon*; Lat. *persona*). It is perhaps, then, of more than passing interest to consider the language of "person" but now as it occurs in Arabic.

The fact is that the term "person" has no immediately apparent Arabic translation. Indeed, medieval Arabic discussions of the Trinitarian formulation frequently used specialized vocabulary, which is rarely seen outside of this limited purview. For example, the Christian apologist Abū Rā'ita (*c.*775–*c.* 835) and the Christian Bishop of Ḥarrān, Abū Qurra (755–830), both prefer *uqnūm* when discussing the three persons of the Trinity.[34] Even outside of Christian circles *uqnūm* seemed to be the preferred philosophical translation for "person" (that is, *hypostasis*), and so one sees the Baghdad Peripatetic Abū Sulaymān al-Sijistānī (*c.*912–985), in his treatise "On the Proper Perfection of the Human Species," uses this term for Christ and the divine nature.[35] *Uqnūm*, however, is not an Arabic term but is a transliteration of the Syriac *qnome*, and at least within Arabic appears to be reserved solely to express the Greek term *hypostasis* within the context of Christian theology. Abū Rā'ita on a limited number of occasions uses the native Arabic term *shakhṣ* to speak of the individuals of the Trinity, but *shakhṣ* means literally that, "individual," and as such applies to any denotable, singular object. Thus the scope of *shakhṣ* is much broader than that of our notion of person. Additionally, Abū Qurra uses the Arabic *wajh* for "person" as applied to God the Father, Son, and Holy Spirit as well as to humans. *Wajh*, however, means "face" or "facade," and so is simply a literal translation of the Greek *prosōpon*, "face." Outside of discussions of the Trinity, the Arabic *wajh* no more indicates a person as we now understand that

---

[34] For Abū Rā'ita, see Keating (2006, 351); for Abū Qurra see Markov (2012, esp. III.2, "Person und Hypostase").
[35] Sijistānī (1974).

term than do words in English like "face" and "way" in English (another, and indeed the primary, sense of *wajh*).

One might press here and say, "Certainly there is some non-technical Arabic term used to describe the notion of person." If so, it is not obviously so. For example, possible Arabic translations of "person" might be *mawjūd, shay', dhāt, 'ayn*, or, as already noted, *shakhṣ*. These terms translate into English respectively as "existent," "thing," "entity," "concrete particular," and again "individual." All of these, however, are much broader than our notion of person, in that they apply to inanimate and animate things alike, whereas I take as a minimum that a person must be alive.

Nafs, or soul – and so a term that applies exclusively to living things – can equally be excluded, since within the medieval Islamic world, at least within the *falsafa* tradition, a soul is that which animates a suitable body, and so is inapplicable to immaterial entities such as God.[36] Moreover, the notion of soul applies to all living material things, and again I take the notion of person to be narrower than merely a living material thing.

Perhaps the closest possibility is *'aql*, or intellect; for at least such a term has the same scope as "person," for God, angels, and humans are all intellects. Still, for many of the thinkers under consideration "intellect" is an equivocal term, which applies to God in an active sense, while it applies to created intellects only in a passive sense.[37]

To clarify this last point, again consider Avicenna's account of divine knowledge noted earlier. When God intellectually knows Himself and thereby knows some other element in the order of the good, that known thing comes to be as a result of God's knowledge. While such an account of knowledge may seem counterintuitive to some, and indeed no less than al-Ghazālī thought so,[38] for most of those in the *falsafa* tradition it is a consequence of viewing God as wholly perfect and simple: God's knowing something must be identical with God's causing that thing, otherwise divine knowledge and divine causation would be distinct in God, and so God would not be conceptually simple. In stark contrast to the active divine sense of knowing, all created intellects require that the thing known already exist, and then that already existing thing – call it x – acts on the intellect of creatures so as to bring them to a state of intellecting x. In other words, God's intellectually knowing x is a necessary (and perhaps sufficient) condition for x's existence,[39] whereas for created

---

[36] On this point, most medieval Muslim philosophers accept Aristotle's definition of soul (*psyche*) in term of the first actuality of a natural organic body (*De anima*, 1.2, 412b5–6).

[37] See Avicenna, *Metaphysics* (2005, VIII 6 [13]); and Averroes, *Decisive Treatise* (2001, 13–14 [17]).

[38] See al-Ghazālī, *The Incoherence of the Philosophers* (2000, Discussion 1 [24]).

[39] The more astute reader might note that this claim is stated broadly enough that x might include God, in which case God's knowing Himself is the cause of His existence. Interestingly, Avicenna

intellects the existence of *x* is a necessary condition of our intellectually know-ing *x*. In short, "intellect" in the case of God refers to a cause, whereas "intel-lect" in the case of creatures refers to a recipient, that is, something that is affected. Consequently, according to many thinkers in the *falsafa* tradition, God qua intellect and creatures qua intellect are not the same kinds of intellect such that they could stand in a common relation to one another.

My main point of this section is merely that the notion of person historically is aligned more closely with Christianity than other Abrahamic religions. Of course just because one does not have the term or concept of person, it need not follow that God is not a person in one's theology, particularly, if by "per-son" one means merely something with an intellect and will – all attributes that medieval Muslim philosophers ascribed to God. Still the inference might be too quick, since, as seen above, for these thinkers the notion of intellect as applied to God and to humans is an equivocal term, and the same holds for will. Thus even if it is true that Avicenna and others would concede that God is a person, "person" would be said only equivocally of God and humans. Obviously without a univocal or at least analogical notion of person, the idea of a *personal* relationship limps, as does any notion of divine love in terms of a relation between persons. At least from an historical point of view, a concep-tion of person does not immediately appear to be a necessary requirement of divine love or theism more generally.

Understanding "personal relation" in medieval Islam: relations

Let me now consider the idea of relation in personal relation, at least as that notion appears in the *falsafa* tradition. Unlike person, which finds no imme-diately obvious parallel in medieval Arabic, the notion of relation is replete in medieval Arabic. Standard Arabic terms that denote relations include *iḍāfa* ([the Aristotelian category of] relation), *taʿalluq* ([dependence]-relation), and *nisba* (kinship or proportion), as well as the more psychological and theologic-ally robust terms *ittiṣāl* (conjunction) and *ittiḥād* (union). It is not clear, at least within the *falsafa* tradition, whether God stands in any of these relations to us.

Let me begin with what I called the psychological or theological notions of relation, namely, conjunction and union. I first consider the notion of union or *ittiḥād*, since we do speak of union with God, although within Christianity this notion most frequently takes the form of union with Christ. Avicenna deals with the idea of union in his *Book of Definitions*:

(and others in the *falsafa* tradition) would not necessarily shirk away from this implication. Avicenna's strong commitment to divine unity requires that he identify God's self-knowledge with the divine existence, and as such God is a self-necessitating existence (*wājib al-wujūd bi-dhātihi*).

"Union" (*ittiḥād*) is an equivocal term. "Union" is said of [(1)] things participating in one and the same essential or accidental predicate ... "Union" is [(2)] said of [multiple] predicates participating in one and the same subject ... "Union" is [(3)] said of the composition of subject and predicate in one and the same entity ... And [finally (4)] "union" is said of the composition of multiple bodies either through succession ... contiguity ... or continuity.[40]

Of these senses, only (1) and (2) might describe what we consider a personal relation, and yet both imply that the unified thing is the product of two distinct entities. Now while it is true that certain Sufis thought that through spiritual exercises one can obtain union with God, such a view was more frequently viewed as a heresy by philosophers and orthodox Muslims alike, precisely because it undermines divine simplicity, the doctrine that God is absolutely one and unified in Himself. Thus both philosophers of the *falsafa* tradition and orthodox Muslim theologians were leery, if not outright hostile, to the suggestion that creatures could be related to God by union.

By far the most common medieval Arabic term used to describe the ultimate goal, end, and perfection of human life (and spiritual practice) is conjunction (*ittiṣāl*). While for some medieval Muslim theologians and mystics, the aim is indeed to conjoin with God, such a conception of conjunction is not how al-Fārābī, Avicenna, Maimonides, and most others in the *falsafa* tradition understood conjunction.[41] For these thinkers, conjunction in its most basic sense is part of a psychological process by which humans acquire concepts, initially of sensible things in the world around us but ultimately of the insensible higher intellectual realm, which includes coming to know the existence of angels and God. It is true that for these thinkers conjunction is only fully and completely achieved in the afterlife, nonetheless, this ultimate conjunction is not with God. Instead the human intellect conjoins with an angelic intellect, named the Active (or Agent) Intellect (*'aql fa''āl*), which in fact corresponds with the very lowest of the separate intellects in an entire angelic hierarchy of increasingly more perfect intellects between the Active (or Agent) Intellect and God. It is then through the intermediacy of the Active (or Agent) Intellect that the conjoined human intellect intellectually and eternally "sees" and contemplates God as the cause of the universe. All of this is to say that, at least according to one philosophical interpretation of Islam, the goal of human spirituality is not personal relation with God, but an understanding of God as cause of all that is.

A more common and general Arabic term for relation is *iḍāfa*. An *iḍāfa*-relation refers to the logical Aristotelian category of relation (*pros ti*), and even Aquinas in the Christian tradition denies that relation in this sense

---

[40] Avicenna, *Book of Definitions* (1963, §§ 97–8).
[41] For a discussion of conjunction within the *falsafa* tradition, see Davidson (1992).

is predicated of God.[42] Moreover, on Avicenna's analysis of an *idāfa*-relation, he sees it as involving (1) some account (*maʿnā*) that inheres in a thing and (2) that account requires some second thing to be understood.[43] For instance, for Avicenna fatherhood really is some account that exists in me but that account can only be understood by reference to my children. So understood, were an *idāfa*-relation predicated of God, divine simplicity and perfection would be lost – there would exist in God some distinct thing or account and that thing would depend upon another for its intelligibility – a conclusion that an ardent monotheist like Avicenna rejects.

As for *taʿalluq*, Avicenna frequently used it to describe a sort of dependence relation between two things. Thus in his *Physics*, he defines it thus: "the meaning of the *taʿalluq*-relation is that the existence of [the relation] is proper to that of which it is said to be dependent as something requiring it."[44] In his *Psychology*, he identifies three ways such a dependence relation might be understood between A and B: (1) A and B stand to one another as coexistents, like concave and convex; (2) A stands to B as one (or more) of the four causes, namely, like either matter, form, agent, or end; (3) A stands to B as one of B's necessary or essential effects, like heat stands to fire.[45] While it is true that for Avicenna God stands to us as efficient and final cause, and indeed on a common interpretation of Avicenna's metaphysics creation stands to God as God's necessary effect, such relations indicate a causal relation between God and us rather than a personal relation with us.

Let me now return to the Arabic term *nisba*, which of all the relation terms canvassed thus far perhaps comes closest to capturing the notion of relation in "personal relation," and yet as the great Jewish philosopher and rabbi Moses Maimonides notes, even a *nisba*-relation cannot be predicated of God. The root N-S-B takes as its primary meaning "relationship," in the sense of (family) lineage, from which is derived its further sense of "attribution."[46] A *nisba*-relation in turn refers to a relation, proportion, or comparison. Consequently to the extent that any comparison or analogy between human love and divine love could be made it would involve a *nisba*-relation. Thus the *nisba*-relation, with its basic sense of lineage and comparison, seems most suited to capture the notion of a personal *relation* as well as generate the analogy between divine love and human love.

Despite this happy beginning, there are also reasons from within the *falsafa* tradition for *not* ascribing any such *nisba*-relation to God. Maimonides lays

[42] Aquinas, *Summa contra Gentiles*, II.12.
[43] Avicenna, *Metaphysics* (2005, III.10); also see Marmura (1975).
[44] Avicenna, *Physics*, I.8 [3].
[45] Avicenna, *De Anima* (1959, V.4, p. 227).
[46] See Lane (1985, s.v. N-S-B).

them out for us.[47] In his classic work of philosophical theology, *The Guide for the Perplexed*, Maimonides famously expounds his apophatic theology in which he claims that we can only ever know what God is *not*. On pain of denigrating God, we simply cannot say anything positive about the deity, or so Maimonides argues. While Maimonides's negative theology is arguably part of the natural progression of certain strands within *falsafa*, it also is in keeping with sentiments found among earlier Jewish *mutakallimūn* like Saadia Gaon (882–942).[48] For example, Saadia maintains that none of the categories that apply to created things apply to God, and so God is wholly dissimilar to anything in the created order. Indeed, he dismisses such biblical passages as "God created man in his own image" (Gen. 1:27) as merely a literary trope intended to confer honor on humans. Unlike Maimonides, however, Saadia acknowledges the need to speak of God, albeit such language is restricted solely to metaphor (*istiʿāra*) and simile (*tamaththul*). For, he continues, if scripture limited itself solely to expressions that are literally true of God, it could only say that God is, since expressions like God hears, sees, is merciful, and wills all involve some figurative extension of the language.[49]

Returning to Maimonides's negative theology, he needed to show that no attributes (*sifāt*) can positively be predicated of God, which he did by classifying all attributes into five kinds, and then showing what is problematic about predicating each kind of God.[50] For my purpose the most important kind of predicative attribute from Maimonides's list is relational attributes (*bi-nisba*). On a positive note, Maimonides observes that attributes of this kind neither imply multiplicity nor change, that is, passivity, potentiality, or deficiency, in the thing itself to which the attribute is predicated. Thus, it appears that the earlier concerns of al-Fārābī and Avicenna should not arise in the case of applying to the deity relational attributes, like being in a personal relation.

Despite this fact, Maimonides sees other, equally damning, problems with predicating relational attributes of God. His critique begins with a general comment about relations. In any relation between two things, the two relata must in some respect be of the same kind. So, for example, there is no relation between green and sweet save inasmuch as they are both qualities. There is

---

[47] For an excellent study of another medieval Jewish thinker responding to the *falsafa* tradition see Lobel (2000, esp. part 1, "The Language of Relationship").

[48] For a medieval Jewish rejection of at least the more striking features of Maimonides's negative theology, see Gersonides's discussion of divine attributes in book III of *Wars of the Lord*; also see Eisen (1995, esp. 157–67), who suggests that Gersonides was willing to think of God as having a personal relation with the Jewish people.

[49] For Saadia's complete account of God's dissimilarity with all creatures, see Saadia Gaon (1880, treatise II.9–10); a complete English translation is available in Saadia Gaon (1948).

[50] The five sorts of predicative attributes that Maimonides identifies are: (1) definitions, (2) individual parts of the definitions, for example, genus and difference, (3) accidents, (4) relations, and (5) attributes of action. See Maimonides (1980, I 52, pp. 114–19).

even less so a relation between human and color, that is, between something in the category of substance and in another in that of quality. Maimonides generalizes his point thus:

Necessarily, relation is only ever found between two things falling under one and the same proximate species, whereas when the two fall under only a genus, there is no relation between them.[51]

Clearly in the case of God and anything within the created order, they do not share a common species.

In fact, Maimonides goes even further and claims that there is absolutely *nothing* in common between God and creatures, not even existence. That is because for Maimonides, who is himself following Avicenna, God is essentially the *Necessary* existent in itself, whereas all other things are merely *possible* existents in themselves.[52] These are two fundamentally different kinds of existence, and so "existence" is said of them equivocally.

While one might think that existence functions like a genus with two subspecies – necessary existence and possible existence – one must resist this urge. First, as Aristotle had already argued, being, or existence, is not a genus or kind, since the only thing that could function as its difference would be non-being or non-existence, which is nothing, but if there is no difference there are no sub-species.[53] Second, and more immediately, Maimonides had claimed earlier in the same chapter of the *Guide* that a genus could not be predicated of God, since then the divinity would be composed of genus and difference, namely, of existence in general and that by which God's existence differs from the existence of creatures.[54] Genus and difference, however, stand to that of which they are predicated as causes to an effect, but God is not caused in any way. In short, concludes Maimonides, God simply cannot stand in any relation to anything in the created order. This conclusion applies equally to God's being in a personal relation with us.

To sum up the conclusions of this final section and indeed the paper as a whole: the notion of a personal relation presupposes two things: first, an account of person, and, second, the possibility of a relation's holding between two persons. Certain medieval Muslim philosophers (and some Jewish ones too) would have found both elements doubtful if not damnable when applied to the purported relation between God and creatures. First, it is not clear that these thinkers even have the requisite notion of person, and so, accordingly, talk of a

---

[51] Maimonides (1980, I 52, 118 [the translation is my own from vol. 1, p. 121]).
[52] Maimonides, *The Guide for the Perplexed* (1980, I 52, p. 117); and Avicenna, *Metaphysics* (2005, VIII.3).
[53] See Aristotle, *Posterior Analytics*, B.7, 92b14, *Metaphysics*, B.3, 998b22.
[54] Maimonides, *The Guide for the Perplexed* (1980, I 52, p. 115), where he discusses why part of a definition cannot be ascribed to God.

relation between *persons* would have been equally unclear. Second, even supposing that they could recast talk of persons into terms accepted within their philosophical system, persons would have to refer in some form or another to existents. Yet, as Maimonides argued, there are certain theological and philosophical puzzles associated with ascribing any relation between God – the Necessary Existent – and creatures – possible existents.

Now it is not my intent to suggest that the figures whom I have considered are always representative of their religions' conception of divine love. Still, I do believe that they have posed pressing philosophical and theological concerns about divine love, a personal relation with God, and divine hiddenness. In fact, one may even go so far as to say that the problem of divine hiddenness (if there is a problem) would have been hidden from many medieval Muslim (and Jewish) intellectuals. For the very idea of a "personal relation" with God would have struck some of these thinkers as odd, ill-conceived, and even perhaps blasphemous, just as would have the analogy between God and a loving human, which motivates some of the contemporary versions of the argument. Having said that, neither would I want my comments to suggest that a personal relation with God is indefensible. I certainly hope it is not. Instead, I hope to have highlighted certain (arguably) Christian elements or presuppositions in Schellenberg's argument against theism from divine hiddenness, elements that are certainly worthy of further philosophical analysis. Ironically, then, the atheist who appeals to the argument from divine hiddenness might best be thought of as a "Christian atheist" in as much as he or she apparently agrees more with modern Christians about God than with theists historically and more generally.

10   The hidden God of the Jews: Hegel, Reb Nachman, and the *aqedah*

Jerome Gellman

Famously, Georg Hegel judged Judaism badly for worshipping a God hidden for eternity in God's utter transcendence.[1] In his early writings, especially in "The Spirit of Christianity and its Fate," and in the 1821 version of *Lectures on Philosophy of Religion*, Hegel was wholly negative about Judaism. Later, Hegel was willing at least to see Judaism, with its inherent defects, as a necessary stage to something higher – Christianity. Hegel discredited Judaism for believing in what Hegel defines in his *Science of Logic* as a "bad" or "spurious" infinity, namely an infinity "posited over *against* the finite." This is in contrast to an infinity that "finitizes" itself, one that self-differentiates to make manifest a world that is included within its own self.[2] The key to understanding Judaism, for Hegel, is its teaching of creation from nothing by a "wholly other" God who stands altogether *above* and has power *over* the natural order. With any of God's doings with the world, always God remains infinitely *disconnected* from it. Thus, Hegel calls Judaism a religion "*of* sublimity," which believes in a God who is "sublime," but not, by any means, what we might call a "sublime religion."

Because of the transcendent otherness of God for her, the Jew in her finiteness is alienated from God. But that is not all, for since the Jew's true essence is included in the Divine, yet the Jew believes the divine is forever hidden away from her, the Jew is alienated from her own true essence. God is an infinite negativity accompanied by human self-negation. The Jew must perceive herself as infinitely worthless.

Judaism becomes a religion striving for reconciliation with the hidden God. The defining concept of Judaism, then, is *dependence upon God*, and its operational principle is "command," externally imposed by a powerful master upon the slave, who must obey. The Jew, in obeying the commandments, shapes a relationship of *fear* with God from whom she is alienated. For Hegel, a hidden God can be approached only with fear. Thus, the Jews perform useless, meaningless acts without end, in an attempt to do God's will, as slaves, and thereby

---

[1] My understanding of Hegel on Judaism has benefitted from Yovel (1976).
[2] See Hegel (1984, vol. I, 302–8).

aim to achieve reconciliation.[3] For Hegel, alas, no amount of obedience to the Divine master or even compensatory self-affirmation as a "chosen people" can succeed in overcoming the essential ontological divide Judaism posits between transcendent creator and finite creature. The unfortunate Jews believe in "an infinite power set over against themselves [that] they could never conquer."[4]

The result is a persistent pain and unhappiness at the very heart of Jewish religious practice, a pain of frustration and alienation. But the obstinate Jews refuse to acknowledge the true source of their estrangement: their mistaken belief in an eternally hidden God. Judaism survives, according to Hegel, only by Jews self-deceptively blaming the absence of reconciliation on their sinfulness, a sinfulness never to be overcome, rather than on their underdeveloped concept of God.

A God who, in Hegel's words, "validates the moment of finitude within itself" is a "good" or "genuine" infinity. Hegel came to see Protestant Christianity as the absolute religion, a breakthrough from the Jewish God to a genuinely infinite God. Protestant Christianity presents in a pictorial way what Hegel's own philosophy of the Spirit and the genuinely infinite presents in a conceptual way. Christianity is the *consummate* religion because it teaches that the infinite enters into human finitude in the incarnation and suffers death, the ultimate mark of finitude. This synthesis is then sealed with the resurrection, signifying for Hegel the presence of the Divine within the community. Thus does Christianity portray the *genuine* infinite achieving self-consciousness within the finite. And this recognition constitutes, finally, true reconciliation between the person and God. The God of Christianity renders the divine–human incommensurability commensurate. Thus in Christianity fall away the minutiae of Jewish law and come love and the joy of self-reconciliation within the divine substance of reality.

Various Jewish thinkers have been concerned to defend Judaism from Hegel's attacks. These replies have been almost exclusively of two sorts. Some, such as Emile Fackenheim (1918–2003), deny the alleged Hegelian depraved consequences of believing in the Jewish God. So, Fackenheim derided Hegel for presenting a "caricature" of Judaism, for ignoring the massive postbiblical, rabbinic sources in Judaism, and for Hegel's arbitrary use of biblical sources to make the Jewish religion look bad.[5] Others met Hegel on his own turf, outflanking Hegel's metaphysics. So, Nachman Krochmal (1785–1840), an early Jewish Hegelian, trying to beat Hegel at his own game, denies ex nihilo creation to be a dogma of Judaism. Krochmal makes much of the biblical commentary of Abraham Ibn Ezra (1089–1164), who Krochmal interprets as understanding creation being from preexistent matter. Krochmal proclaims

---

[3] See Hegel (1948a, 68).   [4] Hegel (1948b, 199).
[5] Fackenheim (1973, 79–169).

there is no reality other than God and that all is derived from God's essence.[6] Furthermore, Krochmal rejects Hegel's denouncing the particularity of the Jews, a particularity, Hegel averred, emanating from their defective God concept. The Jews (yes!) are the true carriers of absolute universality. The other nations are the real particularistic ones![7]

Another metaphysical view that stands in contrast to Hegel is the panentheistic theology of Rabbi Abraham Isaac Kook (1865–1935). R. Kook rejected the God who is an object over against the world in favor of a God who has two facets, one a static perfection, and one a dynamic perfection. The static perfection is beyond the world, while the world itself exists *within* God, and its evolving to perfection is God's own dynamic "perfectioning." Thus is Hegel's attribution to Judaism of a wholly, transcendent, hidden God undercut.[8]

Reb Nachman of Breslov

One Jewish figure who openly and consciously embraced an inaccessible, hidden God of the sort Hegel ascribed to Judaism was Rabbi Nachman of Breslov (1772–1810), or simply, "Reb Nachman." A contemporary of Hegel who most likely never heard of him, and certainly never read Hegel, Reb Nachman was a great-grandson of the founder of the Hasidic movement, Rabbi Israel Baal-Shem Tov (1698–1760), and gained a Hasidic following that continues until this day. Reb Nachman was a charismatic teacher whose teachings were uniquely intriguing and novel. Reb Nachman taught explicitly that God was utterly and irrevocably hidden. But rather than react to this in fear and self-deception, as Hegel would have it, Reb Nachman's religious consciousness focuses on *yearning* for God, a yearning Sisyphean in its hopelessness of ever having that for which it yearns.

The hiddenness of God comes to the fore in Reb Nachman's writings,[9] particularly in a story he once told, "The Humble King and the Wise Man." The story begins as follows:

Once there was a king who had a wise man. The king said to the wise man: "There is a certain king who designates himself 'a mighty hero,' 'a man of truth,' and 'a humble person.' As to his might, I know that he is mighty … But why he designates himself 'a man of truth' and 'a humble person,'" this I do not know. And I want you to fetch me the portrait of that king."

---

[6] For Krochmal on Hegel and the Jews, see Harris (1991).

[7] See Avineri (1984, 60).

[8] For R. Kook see Mirsky (2014). R. Kook does not present his panentheism as a retort to Hegel, but there is reason to believe that he had Hegel, among others, in mind in his metaphysical writings.

[9] All the writings we have of Reb Nachman were recorded by his students and followers. "Reb Nachman" refers to those teachings written down in his name.

Ordinarily, the king in Reb Nachman's stories is God. So, the king who sends the wise man is God. But then we must suppose that the king to whom the wise man is sent is also God. So, it must be God who sends the wise man to discover the true nature of God.

The story continues:

Among all countries there is one country that includes all countries, and in that country there is one city that includes all cities of the whole country that includes all countries. In that city is a house that includes all the houses of the city that includes all the cities of the country that includes all countries. And there is a man who includes everybody from the house, etc. And there is someone there who performs all the jests and jokes of the country.

What is this mysterious place to which the wise man is sent? In a gloss to our story we are told that the place to which the wise man is sent is Zion. A disciple of Reb Nachman explains this as follows:

Perhaps this is what is meant in the story: That there is a country containing all countries; this is the encompassing holiness of the Land of Israel. And in that country there is a city that contains all cities in that country, and that is Zion and Jerusalem. And in that city there is a house that contains all houses in the city, and that is the Holy Temple.

We will return to this curious reference. The story now continues:

[The wise man] understood through the jokes that the country was full of lies from beginning to end because he saw how they were making fun, how they deceived and misled people in commerce, and how, when he turned for justice to the magistrate, everyone there lied and accepted bribery. He went to the higher court, and there, too, everything was a lie and in jest they faked all those things.

The wise man understood through that laughter that the whole country was full of lies and deceit, and there was no truth in it. He went and traded in the country and he let himself be cheated in commerce. He went to trial in court and he saw that they were all full of lies and bribery. On this day he bribed them, and on the next they did not recognize him. He went to the higher court, and there, too, everything was a lie, until he reached the senate and they, too, were full of lies and bribery. Finally he came to the king himself.

When he came to the king he stated: "Over whom are you king? For the country is full of lies, all of it, from beginning to end, and there is no truth in it!" He started telling all the lies of the country. The king bent his ears toward the curtain to hear his words, because he was amazed that there was a man who knew all the lies of the country ...

That wise man concluded: "And one could say that the king, too, is like them, that he loves deceit like the country. But from this I see how you are 'a man of truth.' You are far from them, since you cannot stand the lies of the country." He started praising the king very much. The king was very humble, and his greatness lay in his humility. And this is the way of the humble person: The more one praises and exalts him, the smaller, and humbler he becomes. Because of the greatness of the praise with which the wise man praised and exalted the king, the king became very humble and small, till he became nothing at all.

At this point, when the king had become nothing at all, the moment arrives when the wise man could "see" the king and fulfill his mission:

And the king could not restrain himself, but cast away the curtain, to see the wise man: "Who is it who knows and understands all this?" And his face was revealed. The wise man saw him and painted his portrait and he brought it to his king.[10]

The wise man accomplished his mission. He has discovered that the king is "a man of truth." This was on account of the king's utter *remoteness* from the corrupt, lying country.

The wise man also discovered the king's "humility." The more the wise man praised the king, the "smaller" and "humbler" the king became. This seems to signify a unique interpretation by R. Nachman of the Talmudic saying of Rabbi Yochanan, that wherever we find a reference to God's mightiness, we find as well a reference to God's humility (Babylonian Talmud, Megillah, 31a). In the Talmud, the sign of God's humility is that God cares personally for the downtrodden, the widows, the orphans, and the defeated, despite his mighty, exalted position. Here, the king is far from the burning world and all of its evil. For Reb Nachman, the "humility" of the king starts in the fact that our praise of his greatness does not begin to come even close to what God is. So, in thinking our praise appropriate, we make God small. The more a person praises God, the more a person must be made to realize that all of that praise does not even begin to apply to God. No amount of our praising God can bring us any closer to God than we were previously. The more the wise man praised the king, the more "wholly other" was the king, until the king became "nothing at all." It was then that the wise man was truly able to "see" the king for what he was. The portrait that the wise man brought back to the king was an *empty* portrait.

As we noted, the king has sent the wise man to Jerusalem to the Holy Temple. According to the Talmud, the entire world was created from the site of the Temple in Jerusalem (Yomah 54b). So, every place in the world is included in the Temple site. And Midrash Tanchumah tells us that: "The Land of Israel sits in the center of the world, Jerusalem in the center of the Land of Israel, and the Temple in the center of Jerusalem" (Kedoshim, 10; all translations from rabbinic literature are mine). Thus, the Holy Temple is the place to where the wise man goes. So, the jokester must be the High Priest. Can there be any comedy in the solemn service of sacrificing animals on the altar of the Lord? The Reb Nachman scholar Zvi Mark interprets the intended comedy at the Holy Temple as follows:

In the Temple, people give presents to the sublime Infinite God, atone before Him with a meal offering of fine flour, see in the smell of the incense the smell of His being pleased, and the Levites sing to Him to make his time pass pleasantly. Is there a greater comedy

---

[10] This translation can be found in Band (1978).

than that? … The divine comedy describes God, the "Infinite," as changing his mind because of the bribe of a calf!

The comedy played out in the Holy Temple signifies for Reb Nachman at its most intense the futility of *all* religious practice to an eternally hidden God. And so Reb Nachman writes elsewhere:

I do not know who can say that he serves God, because of God's greatness. Someone who knows even a little of His greatness I don't know how he can say that he serves God. However, the important thing is the will, that one's will be strong and unrelenting always to come close to God … The main thing is the will and yearning, that he shall always yearn for Him. And in this way to pray, study, and perform the commandments. And in truth, according to His greatness all of these services are nothing, but everything is "as though," for it is all just a joke, compared to His greatness.

God is so hidden in His greatness that nothing we do could possibly count as "serving God." As Hegel has told the Jews, the gap between God and us is so vast that to suppose we can bridge the gap between God and us is absurd. And so, for Reb Nachman, the important thing is to yearn for this God, a yearning that we know will never be fulfilled, because God is too hidden for that. So the yearning becomes the sole authentic means of our *living* God's hiddenness.

One of Reb Nachman's disciples wrote this about his master:

Our teacher said that the main thing is the will, to yearn always with a craving and a strong desire to fulfill His commandments. And thereby we study [Torah] *as though* we were studying, and pray *as though* we were praying, and perform the commandments *as though* we were performing the commandments.

The main thing for Reb Nachman is the yearning, the craving for God; to perform the commandments with utter devotion while aware that this has no power to bring us closer to God is *the only way to do justice both to our yearning and to God's utter transcendence.*

The more seriously one performs the ritual, knowing it is futile, the more one attests to the eternal hiddenness of God. This is because one thereby proclaims that no matter *how* seriously and meticulously one performs the minute details of the ritual, *it is all futile!* And that just shows the infinite inaccessibility of God.

We yearn, mind you, not to *show* God how great God is. We yearn for God, because we yearn for God. And, when one's focus is entirely on one's yearning for God with a purity of heart, there is no place and time for self-reflection, and, so, no place and time to observe one's self as without worth. For Reb Nachman, yearning comes in place of Hegel's self-negation.

Reb Nachman yearns for the hidden God knowing well that his yearning can never find realization. Reb Nachman yearns for the impossible over and over again, knowing it is impossible, and so, like Sisyphus, is doomed to never progress. But, again like Sisyphus, progress is not the point. Here, the point is to yearn for God, over and over again.

It is instructive to compare and contrast this impossible yearning to the formation of belief in the Absolute Paradox – the absurd belief that God became man – in the writings of Søren Kierkegaard. Kierkegaard, the Christian, does not believe in the essential hiddenness of God, and also believes that in a Leap of Faith human beings can come to believe that the infinite God became finite. On the one hand, for Kierkegaard the Leap of Faith involves a "passionate decision" of will, a decision made in individual freedom. On the other hand, "Faith is not an act of the will."[11] Faith is a gift of God. Kierkegaard scholars have struggled over how it is that for Kierkegaard it is true *both* that a person gets faith by his decision *and* that it is God who grants that belief in divine grace. How can these two contradictory requirements go together? I have argued elsewhere that understanding the Leap of Faith depends on the distinction between *achievement* and *task* verbs.[12] In using an *achievement* verb one asserts that an appropriate, desired outcome is caused to occur, over and above the undertaken task denoted by the verb. Achievement verbs are for this reason also called "success verbs." Examples of achievement verbs are "cure," "win," "cheat," "prove," and "conceal." Contrasted with achievement or success verbs are task verbs. With a *task* verb there is no implication of success in any aim of the task, only reference to performance of the task denoted by the verb. An example of a task verb is "hunt." When I hunt, my purpose is to succeed in capturing or killing an animal. Whether or not I succeed in doing that, I will have "hunted" in any case.

Some verbs can be used both as achievement verbs and task verbs. Take the sentence, "At 8:00 I went to work." "Went to" here can have an achievement sense, in which it will imply not only that I left my home at 8:00, but that I succeeded in arriving to work after leaving home. Such would be the case in a sentence like, "At 8:00 I went to work, and at 6:00 I came home." "Went to," however, also can carry a task sense, as when I say, "At 8:00 I went to work, but I never made it to the office because I fell sick on the way and instead went to the doctor." "I went to work," here, refers to nothing more than the going in the direction of where I work, not to having gotten to work. In both cases, it is true that I "went to" work at the mentioned time, but the meaning of the verb in each case is different.

My proposal is that for Kierkegaard, without the person willing faith *into existence*, faith would not come into existence. Yet, the existence of faith is entirely due to an act of grace. There is no contradiction between these, because of the two senses, achievement and task senses, possible in the statement, "S wills faith into existence." In the success sense, "I will faith into existence" implies that I execute an act of will, which act succeeds to bring my faith into

---

[11] Kierkegaard (1972, 77).
[12] See Gellman (2013). For the distinction between achievement and task verbs, see Ryle (1963).

existence. Faith comes into existence, and does so a result of my willing causing it to exist. In the task sense, on the other hand, "I will faith into existence"
implies only that I perform the task in question. For my part I do the willing,
but this time without implying success in actually bringing faith into existence.
In this sense, my willing faith into existence (not merely my *wanting* to have
faith, which is a different matter entirely) is a task term. "I will faith into existence" is like "At 8:00 I went to work," in "At 8:00 I went to work, but never
made it to the office." I can will faith into existence, in the task sense, but will
never succeed in having Faith come into existence as a result. Nobody can get
faith by willing it into existence.

I propose that for Kierkegaard for faith to come into existence, *I must will
it into existence.* However, Kierkegaard *knows* that this is impossible, since
nobody can succeed in bringing faith into existence by simply willing it into
existence. So in what sense must I "will faith into existence"? In the *task* sense
only. I perform the task of willing faith into existence, knowing that nobody
could possibly succeed in thereby bringing faith to be. The task itself is absurd,
because doomed to failure. Nevertheless, I do it in the only way such an absurd
act can be done: with great passion.

I do this knowing that my willing will achieve success only if God's grace
will bring its success. In willing faith, my hope is that God will acknowledge
my absurd willing and because of it will grant me faith as a gift. When the
Leap transpires, it is the person who has *willed* it ("taskly") into existence but
it is God who has made it to be. This is how it is possible for the Leap of Faith
to include human willing it to be, while it is God who brings faith to be by a
miracle of divine grace. I take Kierkegaard to be summarizing this position in
the following journal entry of 1849: "Thus the absurd, or acting by virtue of
the absurd, is acting in faith, trusting in God .... I ... turn to God in prayer saying: 'This is what I am doing; bless it, then; I cannot do otherwise.' "[13]

Reb Nachman and Kierkegaard, respectively, perform tasks that each
knows in principle can never be successful. Reb Nachman yearns for a God
he acknowledges to be forever inaccessible, and Kierkegaard wills faith into
existence, knowing that nobody can make faith come into existence by willing
it to be. To each, their absurd task lies at the very heart of their religious life.
Each says – "I cannot do otherwise."

Yet, there is a deep difference dividing these two. While Kierkegaard hopes
that God will complete his task, Reb Nachman has no such hope. The vivid
difference between Kierkegaard and Reb Nachman is that Kierkegaard recognizes the possibility of God completing the task, while for Reb Nachman
the hidden God will never satisfy the yearning. The leap of Reb Nachman to
God – or of God to Reb Nachman – will never take place.

---

[13] Cappelørn et al. (2011, 250).

Reb Nachman and the *aqedah*

Reb Nachman's stories have allegorical import, especially pointing to the patri-archs. I believe that our story, perhaps among other themes, is signaling Reb Nachman's understanding of Abraham at the *aqedah* (the binding of Isaac). The wise man is Abraham, and it is to the *aqedah* that Abraham is being sent. Abraham will be the first person in history to learn of the emptiness of the divine portrait; the *aqedah* turns out to be that very moment when it becomes manifest that God is forever a hidden God.

If I am right, then the interpretation I am about to give of the *aqedah* stands out from a background of Jewish and Christian commentaries that endeavor to style the God of the *aqedah* as transparent, rather than hidden, understandable rather than inexplicable. For on the interpretation I am going to present from Reb Nachman, the very purpose of the *aqedah* was to make known the irre-trievable hiddenness of God.

God can hide in two ways. One way for God to hide is for God to be inac-cessible. God is nowhere to be found. A second way for God to hide is for God to appear right before my eyes, to speak to me, yet be so inscrutable, so indecipherable, that God remains achingly hidden. In the first, I might (contra Reb Nachman) hold out hope that I might yet find God. This hiddenness is a "hiding of the Face," as in Isaiah 8:17, "I will wait for the LORD, who is hiding his face from the house of Jacob, and I will hope in him." In the sec-ond kind of hiddenness, however, my hope is shattered. For there, after having shown His face, God remains so incomprehensible, so shrouded in obscurity, that God might as well have remained hidden. God's appearing was for naught. It's almost as though God is mocking the very idea of my *ever* having seen or ever *going* to see beyond God's stone face. God appears alright, but what I see is only "Clouds and thick darkness" (Psalms 97:2).

The *aqedah*, on its face, threatens a profound hiddenness of God, of the second type. God, who has promised Abraham that a great nation will proceed from Isaac, now tells Abraham to sacrifice Isaac. God is here painfully unfath-omable, His appearance eclipsed by His own words. Can God ever be trusted to be revealing His true self?

In face of such hopeless hiddenness, several Jewish commentators have tried to turn the God of the *aqedah* into a transparent God, a God whose command to Abraham to kill Isaac is comprehensible, understandable, and even reason-able, even moral. God comes out of hiding with these commentators to bring back hope.

The Babylonian Talmud, Sanhedrin 89b (see also Genesis Rabbah, ch. 55), has Satan come to God and complain: "After Isaac was born Abraham did not bring even a bird for a sacrifice. Abraham does everything for his son and nothing for God." God answers "This is not so, and to prove it if I tell him to sacrifice his son, you will see that he will do it."

In *Seder Eliyahu Rabbah* (ch. 7) the angels come to God complaining that Abraham made a covenant with Abimelech. Abraham is not faithful to the divine promise. He does not believe in God's promise for the land. So he is making deals with human kings. God says to them, "I gave him a son at 100 years. If he will sacrifice him, then I will know that he trusts my promises and you are not right."

In each of these, we are made to understand why God tested Abraham, in such a way that God comes out of hiding. God becomes transparent. In the Middle Ages, Maimonides brings God out of hiding by showing the need of the *aqedah* in teaching truths for the ages, again in ways that uncover God's hiding place.

One of these notions consists in our being informed of the limit of *love* for God, may He be exalted, *and fear* of Him – that is, up to what limit they must reach. In this story Abraham was ordered to do something that bears no comparison either with sacrifice of property or with sacrifice of life. In truth it is the most extraordinary thing that could happen in the world.

The second notion consists in making known to us the fact that the prophets consider as true that which comes to them from God in a prophetic revelation ... Accordingly [scripture] wished to make it known to us that all that is seen by a prophet in *a vision of prophecy* is, in the opinion of the prophet, a certain truth, that the prophet has no doubts in any way concerning anything in it.[14]

In Christianity, the construal of the *aqedah* as a prefiguration of the crucifixion makes of the *aqedah* a stage on the way to God *coming out of hiding*. The *aqedah* was a *halted* version of the Christ event, preparing the way for God manifest on earth. Whereas Abraham was only *willing* to sacrifice his son, God really *did* sacrifice his son, on the cross. Among other apparent allusions in the New Testament to the *aqedah* as prefiguration, Jesus is God's "beloved son" (Mark 1:11, Matt. 3:17, Luke 3:22, 2 Peter 1:17). The Greek term for "beloved" is the same word the Septuagint uses in Genesis 22 to refer to Isaac.[15] And John portrays Jesus as "bound" during the Passion (John 18: 12, 24), just as Isaac was bound at his sacrifice.[16]

A second theme in the New Testament is of Isaac as a prefiguration of the resurrection of Jesus. The clearest instance of this is Hebrews 11:17–19: "By faith Abraham, when he was tried, offered up Isaac: and he that had received the promises offered up his only begotten son, Of whom it was said, That in Isaac shall thy seed be called: Accounting that God was able to raise him up, even from the dead; from whence also he received him in a figure." Here, Abraham's faith is his belief that God will bring Isaac back to life after Abraham has

[14] Maimonides (1963, 2:24, pp. 500–1).
[15] See Levenson (1993, 200).
[16] For these and further allusions in the NT to the *aqedah* as a prefiguration of the crucifixion, see Wood (1968) and Vermes (1973).

committed the sacrifice, just as God was to bring Jesus to life after the crucifixion. The "resurrection" of Isaac is to be realized in Jesus. In the words "in
a figure," we might see a reference to Isaac as portending the resurrection of
Jesus. In these traditional Christian themes, in retrospect, at the *aqedah* God
was starting to come out of hiding, into the light of day. God's hiddenness in
incomprehensibility was a mere facade of the true revealing of God in Jesus.

Eleonore Stump draws God out of hiddenness, once more, at the *aqedah* in her extraordinary book on biblical narratives and suffering.[17] There,
Stump presents an interpretation of the *aqedah* she describes as "an apparently similar interpretation" to Hebrews 11:17–19, involving Abraham's conviction that although he goes through with the deed, God will give him Isaac
back. Distinctively, Stump understands the *aqedah* in the context of its setting
within Genesis. In particular, Stump sees a close, integral connection between
the *aqedah* and Abraham's previous expulsion of Ishmael to the desert from
Abraham's home. The crucial verses for the *aqedah* for Stump in the Ishmael
story are when Sarah asks Abraham to expel Hagar and Ishmael because of
Ishmael's bad influence on Isaac. Abraham does not like the idea, until God
tells Abraham that he should heed Sarah and not worry for Ishmael, because
God will save Ishmael and make of him a nation in his own right, just like
Isaac. Abraham listens to God and expels Hagar and Ishmael into the desert.

Stump astutely asks what Abraham's motivation might have been when
sending out Ishmael. There were two possibilities. One was that Abraham himself did not want to do this. However, he was trusting in God when God said
Ishmael would survive and be the progenitor of an entire nation. So he did the
deed in full faith in God's word. Then Abraham would have had a holy motivation. The other possibility was that Abraham, given God's command, now
had a chance to get rid of a bad kid, as Sarah had sized Ishmael up. Abraham
could tell himself that, after all, God had told him to do this. On this alternative
Abraham would be using God's command and promise as a cover for less than
noble motives.

For Stump, the Ishmael story is the first *aqedah* for Abraham. Here too
Abraham is to act so that his child would die, given the natural conditions in the
desert. And here too Abraham is to trust in God's promise that the son would
live to be the father of an entire nation. The second *aqedah*, then, for Stump,
is God's way of having Abraham disambiguate the feelings and motivations
he had at the Ishmael *aqedah*. In the first *aqedah*, there was no clash between
God's command to expel Ishmael and Abraham heeding Sarah's desire to get
rid of the kid. Only at the second *aqedah* must Abraham choose between his
love and his desire for Isaac, and the divine command to do away with Isaac.
Abraham must come to the point where his choice reveals his true motive in

---

[17] Stump (2010, ch. 11, "The Story of Abraham: The Desires of the Heart," pp. 258–307).

acting. In going through with the act, Abraham reveals his trust in God's promises, and in stopping the act God reveals that God keeps His promises.

So understanding the *aqedah*, God comes out of hiding. We now have a reasonable, good reason why God should command such a thing, and God ends up being revealed, with no remainder.

In contrast with this tradition on the *aqedah*, for Reb Nachman the teaching of the *aqedah* is precisely that God is forever hidden. While Reb Nachman's interpretation does give a transparent reason for the *aqedah*, namely to convey God's utter hiddenness, this transparency gets swallowed up by the lesson of intrinsic, forever, divine hiddenness.

Here, now, are my reasons for thinking Abraham to be the wise man of our story, and for the story to be implicating the *aqedah*:

(1) Reb Nachman's stories have allegorical import, especially pointing to the patriarchs. Like the wise man sent by the king, Abraham is the patriarch sent to a different land, by God. ("Now the Lord said to Abram, 'Go from your country and your kindred and your father's house to the land that I will show you.'" Genesis 12:1.) Unlike Abraham, our wise man must return to the "king." But since God is everywhere, this does not imply Abraham having actually to go back to where he had set out.

(2) Jewish tradition speaks of Abraham as a wise man. A rabbinic Midrash comments on Proverbs 10:18, "The Wise in heart will accept commands," by saying that this refers to Abraham, who accepted God's commands (*Genesis Rabbah*, 52:3). More to the point here, another Midrash, commenting on Ecclesiastes 7:19, "Wisdom makes one wise," says that God commanded Abraham to go to the land of Canaan *because* he was a wise man (*Genesis Rabbah*, 39:4). Reb Nachman himself refers to Abraham as a wise man (Likutei Moharan I:30.) As far as I can tell, he does not so refer to any of the other patriarchs.

(3) A rabbinic Midrash says: "When a king and his beloved are together in a room with a curtain between them, when the king wishes to speak with his beloved, he folds the curtain and speaks with his beloved" (*Genesis Rabbah*, 74:7). In our story, the king is behind a curtain, and when the king wants to see the beloved, he folds the curtain away. Consistently in Jewish tradition, as in Isaiah 41:8, it is Abraham, among the patriarchs, who is called God's "beloved."

(4) A Midrash reads as follows: "And God said to Abram: Get thee out of thy country" (Genesis 12:1). Rabbi Isaac said: It is like a parable of a person who was wandering from place to place, and saw a mansion *doleket*. He said, "Can it be that the mansion has no master?" So the master of the mansion then peeked out on him, and said to him, "I am the master of the mansion." Similarly, Abraham said, "Can the world not have a master?"

So the Holy Blessed One looked out on him and said, "I am the master of the world" (*Genesis Rabbah*, 39:1).

The word *doleket* in the Midrash can have two meanings. On one, Abraham would have seen the world as a mansion that was "lit up." This might refer to the wondrous provision of sun, moon, and stars in the sky, providing light by day and guidance by night. Then Abraham would have been making a kind of inference from design, that there must be a designer of all of this.[18] The wondrous light of the world leads Abraham to tell himself there must be a "master" of this world. This interpretation, though, fails to account for the idea that Abraham was wandering from place to place, and does not explain why God must look out at Abraham to reveal that He is the master of the world. Abraham was figuring that out himself.

Another interpretation given for *doleket*, and certainly what Reb Nachman had in mind, is that when going from place to place Abraham sees the world "burning." The world is "on fire." In the words of one commentator, Abraham sees that "the wicked rule the world, and, seeing that, Abraham wondered – Can it be that the world has no master? – God looked out on him to reveal Himself."[19] Abraham goes from place to place and sees the world "on fire," a world of corruption and deceit. In bewilderment, Abraham cries out: "Is there no master to this forlorn world?" God then looks out "*on* him," not "*at* him." God looks out to see who it is that understands the world is ablaze with lies and corruption.

In Reb Nachman's story, the wise man has gone from place to place and found corruption up to the highest levels. He is at first displeased that God is nowhere to be seen in all of this. The king is impressed that there is someone who knows that everything is so corrupt and is bothered by it. The king peeks out *on* the wise man, to see who it is who knows the world is utterly ablaze. The wise man is Abraham, and Abraham learns of God's utter "otherness" to the world, being far from the fires of human finitude, corruption, lying, and evil. In our story, the king's speech to Abraham is the only kind that God can "speak" to Abraham: "I, the master of the world, am hidden from you forever."

(5) The wise man, we have noted, was sent to the Holy Temple. When God commanded Abraham to sacrifice Isaac, God sent him to the land of Moriah: And He said: "Take now thy son, your only son, whom you love, Isaac, and go to the land of Moriah" (Genesis 22:2). In Jewish tradition, Moriah is to be the location of the Temple. Jewish tradition also sees the command to Abraham to sacrifice his son as the culmination of God's earlier command to him to go to Canaan, as though the final purpose of

[18] This is the way Rashi, the medieval commentator, understands *doleket*.
[19] David Lurie (1798–1855) so writes about *doleket*.

sending Abraham to Canaan was that he reaches this place. Just so, our wise man: He finds what he was sent to find only when entering the private chambers of the king.

(6) At the end of the episode of the *aqedah*, we read in Genesis 22:14: And Abraham called the name of that place *A-donai-yireh*; as it is said to this day: "In the mount where *A-donai yera-eh*." The first term, *A-donai-yireh*, means literally that God *sees*, while the second, *A-donai yera-eh*, means that God *is* seen. Recall that at the end of Reb Nachman's story, the king both sees the wise man and is seen by him. If the story is about Abraham, then we have here a pointer to the double, mutual seeing contained in this verse, a double seeing that takes place only at the *aqedah*. God sees ("Now I know," says God at the *aqedah*) and is seen. For the first time, Abraham understands, seeing what can be captured only in an empty portrait.

Based on the identification of Abraham with the wise man, including elements of the *aqedah*, I suggest our story, in part, at least, allegorizes the *aqedah* story. I now provide a Reb Nachmanesque interpretation of the *aqedah* – where Abraham discovers that God is an eternally hidden God.

And it came to pass after these things, that God tested Abraham, and said to him: "Abraham"; and he said: "Here am I." And He said: "Take now your son, your only son, whom you love, Isaac, and go to the land of Moriah; and offer him there for a burnt-offering upon one of the mountains which I will tell you." (Genesis 22:1–2)

God had sent Abraham to Canaan, and Abraham obeyed God in righteousness and faithfulness. In all of these, Abraham believed he was coming ever closer to God. For that very reason, Abraham does not truly *know* who God is. For as Hegel has told us, there is no reconciliation between Abraham and the Jewish God. Now, the time has come for Abraham to see God face to face.

And so, God commands Abraham to sacrifice, not a fleecy lamb or a bleating goat, but the most beloved to him of all, his son, his only son, Isaac. In the words of Maimonides:

In this story [Abraham] was ordered to do something that bears no comparison either with sacrifice of property or with sacrifice of life. In truth it is the most extraordinary thing that could happen in the world, such a thing that one would not imagine that human nature was capable of. Here is a sterile man having an exceeding desire for a son ... and having the wish that his progeny should become a religious community. When a son comes to him after his having lost hope, how great will be his attachment to him and love for him! Because of his fear of God and because of his love to carry out His command, he holds this beloved son as little, gives up all his hopes regarding him, and hastens to slaughter him after a journey of days. (*The Guide of the Perplexed*, 3:24)

And Abraham rose early in the morning, and saddled his ass, and took two of his young men with him, and Isaac his son; and he cleaved the wood for the burnt-offering, and rose up, and went unto the place of which God had told him. (Genesis 22:3)

As Abraham travels to Mt. Moriah, with son in hand, excited thoughts run through his head: "I am on my way to perform the greatest act anybody could possibly do for God, sacrificing my own son! Isaac! Can you imagine? I am giving up that which is most dear to me, for God's sake. I am about to carry out an act that finally will bring reconciliation between God and me. I will be God's beloved! I will be God's Single One! I will be God's Knight of Faith!"

Abraham arrives at the glorious moment. He binds Isaac with supreme seriousness, and raises the knife for the greater glory of God. Abraham's heart pounds with awareness of the remarkable significance of this act. But then:

And the angel of the LORD called unto him out of heaven, and said: "Abraham, Abraham." And he said: "Here am I." And he said: "Lay not your hand upon the lad, neither do any thing to him ... (Genesis 22:11–12)

Just then an angel calls out: "Abraham! Abraham! Stop! Don't lower the knife to his throat!" Notice that it is not God Himself who tells him to stop. God is nowhere to be seen, only an angel. At this fateful moment Abraham is meant to grasp that even the most courageous sacrifice to the sublime Infinite is for naught! God is the infinite, forever hidden Other, with whom reconciliation is never possible! Yes, even sacrificing your beloved son will not achieve the desired result.

Alas, Abraham does not get it. A Midrash has the following conversation ensuing between the angel and Abraham:

The angel said: "Do not bring the knife down on the boy." [Abraham] said, "O.K., so I'll choke him." So the [angel] said, "Do nothing to him." So, Abraham replied, "I'll take a drop of blood from him." To which the angel answered, "Don't do to him anything [meumah]," meaning, "Don't make him a wound [mum]." (Genesis Rabbah, 56:6)

Abraham simply must be made to understand that no manner of harm he can do to his beloved son can possibly make him any closer to God. How much more so, no *lesser* act of obeying God can bring reconciliation. The angel continues,

"For now I know that you are a God-fearing man, for you have not withheld your son, your only son, from Me." (Genesis 22:12)

The angel is saying: "Dear Abraham, O.K. You have shown me you are a *fearer* of God, because you did not hold back your son. But you are *no more than* a fearer of God." "Fearers" of God, as Hegel has told us, are those who mistakenly think they can serve the *sublime* Infinite with their actions. Abraham, the would-be sacrificer of Isaac, has proved himself a supreme "fearer" of God, because he believed that sacrificing his son would be the ultimate service of God. Now, Abraham must internalize the fact that God did not allow the sacrifice. If sacrificing Isaac was not able to effect reconciliation, then nothing can.

And now, Abraham is about to become one who *loves* God, no longer a fearer of God, but one who yearns for the God who is beyond yearning. At the *aqedah*, Abraham has come up empty, with an empty portrait of God. And now Abraham returns that portrait to God, in the form of another sacrifice:

And Abraham lifted up his eyes, and looked, and behold behind him a ram caught in the thicket by his horns. And Abraham went and took the ram, and offered him up for a burnt-offering in place of his son. (Genesis 22:13)

Abraham now proceeds to "return the empty portrait to God." Abraham finally realizes that his having bound Isaac with purity of heart, yearning for God, with *no* sacrifice, was as "good" as sacrificing him with purity of heart, which means worth *only* the purity of heart. So, Abraham sacrifices a ram, doing so *in place of his son.* The key here is that in Abraham's mind, the ram is in place of Isaac. *The ram signifies absolutely no loss of anything to Abraham* – after all, he found the ram on the spot and simply took it and sacrificed it. Abraham thereby declares that *no* loss is the same as a *supreme* loss, no more – since God is unreachable in either case – and no less – since the purity of heart in yearning for God is what is of worth in both cases. So, Abraham sacrifices the ram, acknowledging God's unfathomable hiddenness. Abraham sacrifices the ram to God "as though" he were sacrificing the ram to God. Just as, for Reb Nachman, we are to pray as though we are praying, and do the commandments as though we were doing the commandments.

And Abraham called the name of that place A-donai-yireh; as it is said to this day: "In the mount where A-donai yera-eh." (Genesis 22:14)

Abraham then calls the place: "God sees and is seen." God has looked out on Abraham, the one who now knows how utterly "other God is from the world," and Abraham has seen God to be the king of the empty portrait.

And the angel of the LORD called unto Abraham a second time out of heaven, and said: "By Myself have I sworn, says the LORD, because you have done this thing, and have not withheld your son, your only son, for I will bless you." (Genesis 22:15–16)

The angel did not bestow the blessing on Abraham immediately after the halting of the sacrifice of Isaac. Abraham receives the blessings only after having sacrificed the ram *in place of* Isaac. The blessings are not given to Abraham until after Abraham has done "this thing," the "thing" here being the sacrifice of the ram! And now, and only now, can he be blessed for having been willing to sacrifice Isaac. For retroactively, Abraham understands the proper way to have bound Isaac. Abraham is truly blessed to have learned that there is no way to bring God out of hiding, that all he can do is yearn for God, who he will never reach.

So, Abraham returned unto his young men, and they rose up and went together to Beersheba; and Abraham dwelt at Beersheba. (Genesis 22:19)

According to Jewish tradition, "Abraham was tested with ten trials, and passed all of them" (*Mishnah, Avot* 5:3). Abraham endured and passed ten tests. The episode of the near sacrifice of Isaac was the final test. Abraham now comes back down the mountain and goes home, never needing to be tested again.

11   The hidden divinity and what it reveals

N. N. Trakakis

Hiddenness is revelatory. That is the thesis of this paper, in a nutshell. Revelatory of what? Of God. More precisely, of the nature of God. This is not easily or clearly seen, however, and is regularly resisted. Hiddenness is more commonly regarded as an objection to God, one more argument or piece of evidence against God's existence, as if the daily horrors of the world were not enough. But hiddenness, I will argue, helps us to see matters differently, *especially if we turn East*. The Eastern traditions I have in mind are not only the religions of the East, such as Hinduism and Buddhism, but also Eastern forms of Christianity, particularly the early and medieval patristic witness of the Eastern Orthodox church. Bringing these seemingly disparate religious perspectives in conversation with one another, while relating them also to classical Western expressions of theism, will enable a way of thinking about God, and God's relationship to the self and the world, that will help resolve the problem of divine hiddenness. Starting points are crucial, and in this instance it is a matter of understanding well what is meant by "God"; only after an attempt has been made in this direction can we turn to the question of God's hiddenness and what it reveals, and in particular whether it supports or warrants the rejection of belief in God.

1   From West to East

In turning to the aforementioned Eastern sources, however, my point of departure will be a quintessentially Western philosopher and theologian, Thomas Aquinas. Or, more precisely, one of his contemporary exponents, the Dominican Brian Davies. The question of how to think about God is addressed in an insightful "letter" Davies wrote and published as part of a special issue of *New Blackfriars* dedicated to his deceased fellow Dominican, Gareth Moore.[1] Davies, who has a teaching post at Fordham University in New York, had often

---

Work on this paper was supported by a William Paton Visiting Fellowship in Global Philosophy of Religion, at the John Hick Centre for Philosophy of Religion, University of Birmingham.

[1] Davies (2003). For a contrary Thomistic account of God, see Stump (2012).

been asked by Moore what American philosophers have to say about God. Moore at this time was Prior of a Dominican house in Belgium, and in 2001 he returned to Oxford to teach philosophy, but in June 2002 he was diagnosed with kidney cancer and died less than six months later. After Moore's death, Davies realized that he never provided Moore with an answer, and so his article was written as a belated letter in response to Moore's question.[2] But before directly addressing Moore's query, Davies emphasizes the familiar Thomist theme that "in speaking of God we must be careful not to attribute to him anything which is essentially creaturely."[3] In Davies's view, following Thomas, God is reduced to creaturely proportions if he is categorized as an "individual" or an "object," or if he is considered to be part of the world of space and time, or if he is viewed as subject to the limitations and changes that affect things that are spatial and temporal in nature.

Davies then poses the question: "How has God fared at the hands of American philosophers?"[4] He notes, first, that there are many recent American philosophers who "talk excellent sense about God," largely because they respect the distinction between creature and Creator and they are sensitive to the incomprehensibility of God (examples given include Norman Malcolm, Herbert McCabe, D. Z. Phillips, and David Burrell). But, Davies adds, there has also emerged a group of American philosophers who take a very different approach, an approach that ends up treating God as a mere creature. On this view, God, far from being incomprehensible, is

something very familiar. He is a person. And he has properties in common with other persons. He changes, learns, and is acted on. He also has beliefs, which alter with the changes in the objects of his beliefs. And he is by no means the source of all that is real in the universe. He is not, for example, the cause of my free actions. These come from me, not from God. He permits them, but they stand to him as an observed item stands to its observer. He is not their maker. He is only their enabler.[5]

Davies identifies Plantinga as the prime culprit of this approach. On Plantinga's view, God is a person, where this means that God is "a conscious individual in the same class as you and I."[6] Thus, like us, God has do deal with an external source or environment that often frustrates his purposes – for example, the (libertarian) free choices of others. Davies also points to similar views upheld by "open theists" and "process theists": the former, such as William Hasker, hold that God does not know in any comprehensive way how the future will turn out (the future is "open," even for God), thus rendering his creation of the

[2] Davies's "letter" has had quite an impact: it prompted D. Z. Phillips, for example, to organize a conference in 2005 around the themes it discusses, with the proceedings later published as *Whose God? Which Tradition? The Nature of Belief in God* (2008).
[3] Davies (2003, 375).   [4] Davies (2003, 377).
[5] Davies (2003, 377).   [6] Davies (2003, 379).

world a somewhat risky endeavor; and the latter, led by Charles Hartshorne, think of God as struggling and suffering, as continually improving and getting better.[7] But these ways of conceiving God, Davies states, are profoundly out of step with the classical theistic tradition, as represented by Jewish thinkers such as Maimonides, Islamic thinkers such as Avicenna (Ibn Sina), and the medieval and patristic Christian tradition.[8]

A similar view is expressed by another Dominican, Fergus Kerr.[9] Kerr notes that, "Historically, Thomas Aquinas was passionately concerned to stop Christians from thinking of God as one more item in the world, as a substance with properties, like a creature."[10] Kerr also seeks to avert a slide into anthropomorphism and to preserve the Creator/creature distinction. The resources for doing so, according to Kerr, can be found in Thomas's dynamic conception of divinity, a conception that explodes the myth of Thomas's God as a static and "religiously unavailable" deity. For Thomas, "there never was being which was not always already becoming: acting on others, interacting, has always been the ultimate perfection of any thing."[11] Thomas, in other words, thinks of being and substance in dynamic and relational terms, rather than in inert or static terms, as is often supposed. This becomes particularly clear in Thomas's account of God as *ipsum esse subsistens*, the subsistent act to-be itself, and *actus purus*, pure actuality and activity. On this view, God is not an individual entity, but the unrestricted act of existence, or pure act or activity, for in God being and doing completely coincide. As Kerr puts it,

God is not a substance with accidents, a subject with properties, and an agent capable of activities that occasionally express but never totally realise himself. That is what creatures are like; agents never completely and transparently *doing* our being, so to speak. In God, being, knowing, loving and creating are identical (the doctrine of divine simplicity); and this is, simply, being which is always already *doing*.[12]

In short, Thomas's God, according to Kerr, far from being a static entity, is more like a radically dynamic event, more like a verb than a noun.

This strikes me as a promising move toward a more adequate conception of God, one that avoids the anthropomorphic tendencies of perfect being theology (where God is made to look very much like a human being, albeit one inflated into infinite proportions: a "super-duper superman"[13]), preserving instead the Creator/creature distinction by taking seriously such ideas

---

[7] Helm (2008) discusses the anthropomorphic approaches of Swinburne and Wolterstorff, and shows how they stand in stark contrast to traditional Protestant views of God as found in, for example, John Calvin, Francis Turretin, Jonathan Edwards, and Herman Bavinck.

[8] David Burrell also highlights how this non-anthropomorphic conception of divinity is an "intercultural, interfaith achievement" across all three Abrahamic faiths. See Burrell (2008).

[9] Kerr (2004).   [10] Kerr (2004, 65–6).

[11] Kerr (2004, 65).   [12] Kerr (2004, 69, emphases in the original).

[13] I owe the nomenclature to Andrew Gleeson.

as divine simplicity and the ineffability and incomprehensibility of God. These three notions – simplicity, ineffability, and incomprehensibility – are of course closely intertwined, and have a long lineage in classical theism, as indicated by Augustine's remark, "Si comprehendis, non est Deus."[14] To be sure, the notion of "incomprehensibility" at play here needs to be carefully explicated. For it is not simply a matter of our expressive resources falling short in capturing our experience of God. The emphasis, rather, is on the wondrous and awe-inspiring mystery of God himself, something that is easily forgotten or occluded in our everyday and philosophical discourse about God.[15] That which is the very source of our existence and of the entire universe, that which is beyond space and time, is infinite, incorporeal, all-powerful, and all-knowing, can in our prosaic or technical language quickly begin to look like the person next door who can be singled out, comprehended, (psycho) analyzed, and judged.

Against this, the classical tradition holds that there is an important sense in which, when we speak of God, we literally do not know what we are talking about. This is perhaps what Thomas was indicating when speaking of God as *actus purus* and *ipsum esse subsistens*.[16] In talking about God in this way Thomas was not attempting to bring his readers closer to a knowledge of God, but to bring them to a knowledge of God's unknowability. As Denys Turner explains, Thomas's statements about God were

intended to mark out with maximum clarity and precision the *locus* of the divine incomprehensibility, the *ratio Dei*, the most fundamental of the "formal features" of God, to use Burrell's terminology. Since it is far from being the case that describing God as "pure act" gives us some firm purchase on the divine nature, one may go so far as to say that talking about God thus is a kind of "babble."[17]

But, Turner quickly adds, such theological speech is not *mere* babble, for it delineates the logic of the concept of "God" and thus shows what can and what cannot intelligibly be said and inferred about God. "To that extent," Turner states,

---

[14] Augustine, *Sermon* 52, 16; PL 38: 360. The full passage reads: "So what are we to say, brothers, about God? For if you have fully grasped what you want to say, it isn't God. If you have been able to comprehend it, you have comprehended something else instead of God. If you think you have been able to comprehend, your thoughts have deceived you" (Augustine, 1991, 57).

[15] As Denys Turner points out, "Philosophers seem happy enough to say, after Aristotle, that philosophy begins in wonder. Alas, all too often their philosophy ends in its elimination" (Turner, 2002, 332).

[16] However, even though Aquinas thinks we cannot possess "knowledge" (in the sense of *scientia*) of what God is, he would not deny that we can make many true propositions about God and we can be said to know that they are true. (I thank Brian Davies for reminding me of this.)

[17] Turner (2004, 142). The David Burrell reference is to Burrell (1987, 77).

theological talk has a grammar. It is a language. But that said, it is the grammar of a mystery, of language which breaks down according to determinable rules of breakdown. Theological speech is subject to a sort of *programmed* obsolescence. To be "theological" you have to get language to self-destruct.[18]

But this is not to reduce the theologian to silence. If anything, the very opposite is the case. The acknowledgement of the incomprehensibility of God does not erase speech, but rather liberates it so that we can now think and speak about God in a multitude of ways, always aware however that whatever we say will inevitably fail to contain the divine mystery. As Herbert McCabe nicely put it, God "is always dressed verbally in second-hand clothes that don't fit him very well."[19] But, to play on this metaphor, it is the size, color, and even eccentricity of God's wardrobe that underwrites his incomprehensibility. In other words, what defeats us in the end, or what defeats our cognitive capacity to understand and conceptualize God, is not the paucity of names and descriptions, but the dizzying *excess* of words and images. As Turner states, "God is beyond our comprehension not because we cannot say anything about God, but because we are compelled to say too much," and to illustrate his point he quotes Pseudo-Dionysius' dictum, "There is no kind of thing which God is, *and there is no kind of thing which God is not.*"[20] "That is why," Turner concludes, "we cannot comprehend God: the 'darkness' of God is the simple excess of light."[21]

The inescapable incomprehensibility of God may go some way toward accounting for God's hiddenness. But there is further way to travel. And a road less traveled, at least amongst analytic philosophers of religion (as well as some Thomists, such as Davies), is the one that veers towards the East. For directions we do well to look to David Bentley Hart's recent volume, *The Experience of God: Being, Consciousness, Bliss*, one of the most compelling contributions of late to philosophical discussions on the nature of divinity.[22] Much of what Hart engages in here could be considered a variety of conceptual analysis or clarification (Hart himself calls it "a kind of lexicographical exercise"[23]), rendering as clear and precise as possible the meaning of "God." As Hart states on the very first page:

My intention is simply to offer a definition of the word "God," or of its equivalents in other tongues, and to do so in fairly slavish obedience to the classical definitions of the divine found in the theological and philosophical schools of most of the major religious traditions.[24]

---

[18] Turner (2004, 143, emphasis in the original).

[19] McCabe (2002, 3).

[20] Turner (2004, 144, emphasis in the original). The Pseudo-Dionysius quote is from *Divine Names* 817D.

[21] Turner (2004, 145).   [22] Hart (2013).

[23] Hart (2013, 2).   [24] Hart (2013, 1).

He then explains his motivation for doing so:

> My reason for wanting to do this is that I have come to the conclusion that, while there has been a great deal of public debate about belief in God in recent years (much of it a little petulant, much of it positively ferocious), the concept of God around which the arguments have run their seemingly interminable courses has remained strangely obscure the whole time. The more scrutiny one accords these debates, moreover, the more evident it becomes that often the contending parties are not even talking about the same thing; and I would go so far as to say that on most occasions none of them is talking about God in any coherent sense at all.[25]

A situation of this sort, unfortunately, also holds with much of the contemporary philosophical debate around divine hiddenness, as I will go on to argue in the following section of this chapter.

But in the meantime I wish to briefly say something about Hart's strategy. As the subtitle of his book suggests, Hart is seeking to enrich the standard philosophical view of God, or the ultimate divine reality, by *globalizing* it – and in particular by drawing not only from Western accounts of divinity found in the classical sources of the Abrahamic faiths (Hart defers to, among others, Aquinas, Gregory of Nyssa, Maimonides, and the Sufi mystics), but also from complementary accounts found in many Eastern religious traditions. After all, *sat* (being, reality), *chit* (pure consciousness), and *ananda* (serene beatitude, or bliss) are the three characteristics traditionally ascribed to Brahman, regarded as the supreme reality within Hinduism. As Hart observes, "the three terms taken together constitute a particularly venerable Indian definition of the Godhead, with roots that reach back into the metaphysics of the *Upanishads*."[26] But these three "transcendentals" (as Hart calls them, borrowing from the schoolmen[27]) have global resonance, as "they provide a particularly elegant summary of many of the most ancient metaphysical definitions of the divine nature found in a number of traditions."[28] These traditions encompass both East and West, and within the East both non-Christian traditions (including forms of Hinduism, Buddhism, Sikhism, and Baha'i) as well as Eastern Orthodox Christian sources.[29] Hart, himself an Eastern Orthodox Christian, illustrates this by reference to one of his favorites, the fourth-century Cappadocian

---

[25] Hart (2013, 1).   [26] Hart (2013, 42).

[27] Hart (2013, 45; cf. 242–3). Hart is careful to point out: "Precise scholastic enumerations and definitions of the various transcendentals, however, do not concern me here. What interests me is the simple but crucial insight that our experience of reality does in fact have a transcendental structure" (p. 243).

[28] Hart (2013, 42).

[29] However, Hart's determination to single out a "classical theistic core" amongst many of the world religions – for example, when he states that "my approach is largely in keeping with the understanding of God found in the great theistic and metaphysical traditions of East and West" (Hart, 2013, 288) – opens him to the objection of overlooking the distinctiveness of religious communities, even those that are theistic.

Father, Gregory of Nyssa, who "describes the divine life as an eternal act of knowledge and love, in which the God who is infinite being is also an infinite act of consciousness, knowing himself as the infinitely good, and so is also an infinite love, at once desiring all and receiving all in himself."[30]

Hart's book is largely an analysis of the three elements that go to make up *satchitananda*, showing how individually they resist naturalist reduction and how as a group they illumine the nature of God. With respect to the latter, the trajectory of Hart's analysis generally steers him toward the notion of *the infinity of God* – an allusion, of course, to Gregory of Nyssa, described in another work of Hart's as "the first systematic thinker of divine infinity."[31] This is a peculiar sort of infinity (as most kinds of infinity are), implying both distance and intimacy. With reference to the dimension of distance, Hart notes:

One of the most provocatively counterintuitive ways of expressing the difference between God and every contingent reality is to say that God, as the source of all being, is, properly speaking, not himself *a* being – or, if one prefer, not a being among other beings.[32]

In opposition to the overly anthropomorphic and hence idolatrous notion of God existing as "some discrete object, essentially distinct from all others," an object that "possesses a certain determinate number of attributes, a certain quantity of potentialities, a certain degree of actuality, and so on, and is at once both intrinsically composite and extrinsically enumerable,"[33] Hart recalls Nyssen's conception of God as infinite:

He [i.e., God] is instead the infinite to which nothing can add and from which nothing can subtract, and he himself is not some object in addition to other objects. He is the source and fullness of all being, the actuality in which all things hold together; and so he is also the reality that is present in all things as the very act of their existence. God, in short, is not a being but is at once "beyond being" (in the sense that he transcends the totality of existing things) and also absolute "Being itself" (in the sense that he is the source and ground of all things).[34]

Brian Davies has expressed similar misgivings about the prevalent tendency to treat God as a specific thing, individual, or item in the universe, regarding this as an inadvertent reduction of God to creaturely proportions. According to Davies, it is

wrong to assert that God is an individual – in the familiar sense of "individual" where to call something an individual is to think of it as a member of a class of which there could be more than one member, as something with a nature shared by others but different

[30] Hart (2013, 42–3).   [31] Hart (2003, 29).
[32] Hart (2013, 107, emphasis in original).
[33] Hart (2013, 108–9).   [34] Hart (2013, 109).

from that of things sharing natures of another kind, things with different ways of working, things with different characteristic activities and effects.[35]

For any two individuals, Davies explains, a distinction can be drawn between "who they are" and "what they are." John and Mary share a common human nature, but neither John nor Mary constitutes human nature itself. What they are (beings belonging to the same species) cannot be equated with who they are (individual persons, with their own ways of thinking and working). But God cannot be one of a kind, for this would introduce a distinction between God's existence and God's nature, as when we distinguish the existence of John from his human nature. And so, "who God is and what God is are not distinguishable. We cannot get a purchase on the notion of a class of Gods or on the notion of God in a class."[36] It might make sense, then, to think of John and Mary as individuals that exist alongside other things, but it would be a mistake to think this of the very source of the being of everything, of the reality which lies beyond the world and makes it to be as it is, of the reason why there is something rather than nothing. It would indeed be a category mistake, analogous in Davies's words to "a mistake of the kind which we would be making if we took 'salt' or 'beef' to be the names of things we might buy two of in a shop."[37] Herbert McCabe similarly writes that

If God is whatever answers our question, how come everything? then evidently he is not to be included amongst everything. God cannot be a thing, an existent among others. It is not possible that God and the universe should add up to make two.[38]

Like Davies, Hart contends that "many Anglophone theistic philosophers," committed as they are to "theistic personalism" (Davies's term), "have effectively broken with classical theistic tradition altogether,"[39] which he takes to be epitomized by the common repudiation nowadays of divine simplicity as incoherent. For Hart, as for Davies, simplicity is non-negotiable: "the idea is not open to dispute if one believes that God stands at the end of reason's journey toward the truth of all things; it seems obvious to me that a denial of divine simplicity is tantamount to atheism."[40]

It follows that God, as infinite and indivisible, absolute and unconditioned, cannot be placed in the same ontological order as ordinary beings and objects. As Aquinas put it, the idea of God as the ultimate source of the universe means that "the divine will must be understood as existing outside of the order of beings, as a cause producing the whole of being and all its differences."[41]

---

[35] Davies (2003, 376).   [36] Davies (2003, 376).
[37] Davies (1998, 181).   [38] McCabe (2005, 6).
[39] Hart (2013, 127).   [40] Hart (2013, 128).
[41] Aquinas, *Commentary on Aristotle's "On Interpretation,"* I, XIV, 22. Davies is fond of quoting this passage, though it is a view that is by no means unique to Aquinas within the Christian patristic and medieval tradition.

However, the infinity of God, as I mentioned earlier, has a dual aspect, carrying a connotation of height and distance (God as "beyond being"), while at the same time pointing to the dimension of depth and intimacy (God as "Being itself," or as Sufis say: *al-Haqq*, "Reality as such"). Hart expresses this in well-known Augustinian terminology: "God is not only *superior summo meo* – beyond my utmost heights – but also *interior intimo meo* – more inward to me than my inmost depths."[42] This of course is a prominent theme in monist traditions such as the Advaita Vedanta school of Hinduism, founded by Shankara (or Sankaracarya ["Samkara the Teacher"], early eighth century; traditionally 788–820 CE), which rejects all duality and upholds the fundamental identity between Brahman and our true, unchanging self or *atman* (which is not to be conflated with our "empirical self"). However, as Hart's reference to Augustine indicates, something similar can be said in Christian terms about the relation between the human person and God. I have found this developed particularly well in the innovative work of Sara Grant (1922–2000), a Scotswoman who became a prominent figure in Indian Christian theological and contemplative circles. A constant preoccupation in her life and writings, she states, were "the implications of the Hindu experience of non-duality for Christian theological reflection."[43] One such implication is an enriched understanding of the human person, formulated by means of the Hindu concept of *kosas*, or "depths of interiority," "to speak of a new and progressively developing capacity for awareness of Atman-Brahman, or God, as the Self of my own self, the prompter from within of every thought, word, and deed, without prejudice to the autonomy and freedom of the person."[44] The non-dual Advaita saying beloved by Grant – "in every 'I' which I attempt to utter, his 'I' is already glowing"[45] – is therefore something that the Christian too may affirm. As Meister Eckhart recognized, it is erroneous to think of God and the human soul as two entirely separate things, the one standing over against the other: "One should not apprehend God nor consider Him outside oneself, but as our own and as what is in ourselves."[46]

This way of thinking about God and self naturally lends itself to the metaphysics of monism and idealism. It is no surprise, then, that Hart (like many of the figures he names in his book as fellow travelers) occasionally speaks

---

[42] Hart (2013, 10). Hart is referring to Augustine's famous description of his futile search for God in the outer world, when he failed to see that (as it is sometimes put) God is closer to us that we are to ourselves: "Yet you were deeper than my inmost understanding and higher than the topmost height that I could reach" (Augustine, 1961, book 3, §6, p. 62). And later on, in another well-known passage, Augustine states: "I have learnt to love you late! You were within me, and I was in the world outside myself. I searched for you outside myself and, disfigured as I was, I fell upon the lovely things of your creation. You were with me, but I was not with you" (book 10, §27, p. 231).

[43] Grant (2002, 1).   [44] Grant (2002, 79–80).

[45] Grant (2002, 63, 95).   [46] Eckhart (1957, 189).

of this metaphysics as the only viable framework within which the notions of being, consciousness, and bliss can be properly accommodated.[47] This also, as mentioned earlier, is the perspective of Advaita Vedanta, where the relation between the *atman* and Brahman is understood in outright non-dualist terms. Indeed, non-duality (as indicated by the Sanskrit term *a-dvaita*, which means "non-dual") is adopted as the fundamental metaphysical principle, so that (in line with monism) there are ultimately no discrete or separate things, for reality is essentially one or a unified whole. On this view, all plurality, including the world of material objects, is founded on illusion and ignorance, preventing us from recognizing the underlying unity of reality. This is conjoined with a variety of absolute idealism: the most basic or fundamental reality is the "Absolute" (in this case, "Brahman"), that which has an unconditioned existence (not conditioned by, or dependent upon, anything else), and is regarded as mental or spiritual in nature, so that matter or the physical world is only an appearance to or expression of mind. Brahman, on the Advaita view, is the ultimate ground of all being, and is described as an eternal and undifferentiated consciousness that transcends all qualities and distinctions (such as subject and object, personal and impersonal).

Although in Anglophone philosophy idealism has not survived the hostile turn taken early in the twentieth century against metaphysics, previously idealism consistently played a significant part in the history of Western philosophy. One could point, for instance, to the idealist movement of the late eighteenth and early nineteenth centuries in German philosophy led by Fichte, Schelling, Schopenhauer, and above all Hegel. An important though neglected successor of this German movement was the British form of idealism that held sway in the nineteenth and early twentieth centuries, and included such philosophers as F. H. Bradley, T. H. Green, Edward Caird, J. M. E. McTaggart, and Bernard Bosanquet. Turning away from the naturalism, utilitarianism, and empiricism characteristic of British philosophy (e.g., Hume), the British idealists held that physical objects and the subjective points of view of conscious individuals stand in a system of "internal relations" called the "Absolute." Bradley provided one of the most influential defenses of this view in his 1893 magnum opus, *Appearance and Reality*. In this work Bradley sought to show that the Absolute, or reality as it truly is as opposed to how it appears to us to be, is an all-embracing and harmonious Whole, the totality of all things (without being a mere aggregate of them), which consists in a single, seamless, timeless, and inconceivably rich "experience" (in a broad sense of the term, so as to encompass feeling, thought, and volition). This is a version of *monism* (all is one, or in Bradley's case: a one-in-many) as well as of *idealism* (reality is mind-like), and specifically of *absolute* idealism (given that reality is not construed in

---

[47] See, for example, Hart's comments (2013, 225–34).

terms of the contents of the human mind, as in "subjective" idealism, but in terms of a non- or supra-personal consciousness). As with Hart's conception of divinity and the Advaita notion of *brahman nirguna* (Brahman without attributes, Brahman-in-itself), the Absolute for Bradley is infinite, always outstripping discursive thought, and thus it is a reality that is ultimately ineffable or transcategorical (beyond the range of human categories of thought).

As strange as these ideas might strike modern, even modern Christian, ears, they have a venerable pedigree not only in Eastern traditions such as Advaita Vedanta but also in the Abrahamic faiths. Sara Grant, for example, makes a compelling case for the essential metaphysical complementarily between Shankara and Aquinas, an "extraordinary agreement between the two men, deep calling to deep across the centuries."[48] For Grant, it is the notion of "relation" that binds the two thinkers together, specifically the view that the relation between creation and the ultimate Source of all being is a *non-reciprocal dependence relation* – that is, a relation in which a subsistent effect (or "relative absolute") is dependent on its cause for its very existence as a subsistent entity, whereas the cause is in no way dependent on the effect for its subsistence.[49] As Grant writes:

Both [Shankara and Aquinas] were non-dualists, understanding the relation of the universe, including individual selves, to uncreated Being in terms of a non-reciprocal relation of dependence which, far from diminishing the uniqueness and lawful autonomy of a created being within its own sphere, was their necessary Ground and condition, while apart from that relation of total dependence no created being would *be* at all.[50]

This asymmetric relation, or distance and difference, between the Creator and the created world was expressed in the Christian East by Gregory of Nyssa in terms of *diastema*, the fundamental ontological divide between the infinite creator and the finite creation. This is a divide that no created being can ever bridge, and this explains why it is the notion of *diastema* that largely motivates the apophatic character of Greek patristic theology. At the same time, however, it is a divide that can be traversed by God, who has done so through the incarnation, but also by giving himself to be known or experienced through scripture and creation. This, in turn, lends itself to the rejection of any strict demarcation between the spiritual and the material: as in idealist thought, "the universe is spirit-woven, God is immanent in it, and every meanest object is in its way 'filled full of magical music, as they freight a star with light.' "[51] Indeed, the patristic tradition, like much ancient and late antique philosophy, was developed within a broadly idealist metaphysics. As Hart points out, Christian

---

[48] (Grant, 2002, 54).   [49] (Grant, 2002, 40).

[50] (Grant, 2002, 52, emphasis in original).

[51] This is a quote from the British idealist Henry Jones (1905, 20). Jones is quoting from Robert Browning's 1835 poem "Paracelsus" (Part V, 114–16).

thinkers of this period, in many ways following the lead of the Platonists and Aristotelians, "understood spirit as being more substantial, more actual, more 'supereminently' real than matter, and as in fact being the pervasive reality in which matter had to participate in order to be anything at all."[52] The Cappadocians, for example, were just as committed as the pagan Neoplatonists to the view that the source and basis of reality is only to be found in the One (or the one-in-three, in the Cappadocians' case), an infinite reality that is absolutely simple, singular, and spiritual.

Returning to Gregory of Nyssa, Hart has elsewhere characterized Gregory's theology in Berkeleyan terms:

Gregory, like Basil before him, in various places denies that the world possesses any material substrate apart from the intelligible acts that constitute its perceptible qualities: the world of bodies is a confluence of "thoughts," "bare concepts," "words," noetic "potentialities," proceeding from the divine nature; its *esse*, one might almost say, is *percipi*.[53]

Hart goes on to describe Gregory's God as a "speculative God," not in the sense of a conceptual abstraction, but in the sense that God creates and bestows being only by "speculating" or reflecting his own light and delight. Creation, too, in this play of mirrors is a "specular economy" as it is "constituted as simply another inflection of an infinite light … Creation *is* only as the answer of light to light."[54] Idealist themes of this kind abound in the history of Western philosophy, where it is not uncommon to find a theistic worldview couched in the language (or in one of the many languages) of idealist metaphysics – consider, for example, the monadism of Leibniz, the subjective idealism of Berkeley, the philosophy of the Absolute developed by German and British idealists, and in more recent times the work of Timothy Sprigge and Keith Ward. This makes perfect sense once the deep affinities of theism and idealism are recognized, as both take the ultimate reality to be spiritual or mind-like, thus rendering all other aspects of reality (including the material world) in some sense contingent upon, or an expression or creation of, the Supreme Mind.

2   Implications for the problem of divine hiddenness

If God is understood in one of the foregoing ways, then what becomes of the problem of divine hiddenness? A fairly standard formulation of this problem is provided in a recent paper by Michael Rea,[55] who points out that anti-theistic

[52] Hart (2013, 167).   [53] Hart (2002, 548).
[54] Hart (2002, 548, emphasis in original). On Gregory of Nyssa's idealism, see Cherniss (1971, esp. 35, 62); and Sorabji (1983, ch. 18). But see also Hibbs (2005).
[55] Rea (2009).

arguments from hiddenness typically seek to show that theism is committed to the following inconsistent set of premises:

P1. God has allowed himself to remain hidden from many people.

P2. It would be bad for an omnipotent, omniscient God to remain hidden from anyone.

P3. God, being perfectly good, cannot do anything that is bad.[56]

Given the internal inconsistency of this triad, the theist must give up at least one of the premises in order to continue rationally upholding theistic belief. But it seems difficult to give up any of these premises: they are all intuitively plausible, and hence the *problem* of God's hiddenness, which Rea regards as "next to the problem of evil, the most important objection to belief in God."[57]

One popular strategy, mimicking the construction of theodicies in response to the problem of evil, is to attempt to delineate some plausible reasons as to why God might go into hiding, so to speak; these reasons, then, would function as "moral justifications" for divine hiddenness, in much the same way that theodical reasons (such as free will, soul-making, a lawlike natural order) are thought to serve as morally sufficient reasons for God's permission of suffering. Hiddenness, on this view, might be intrinsically bad, but it is necessary for the realization of a greater good, or at least the prevention of a state of affairs that is equally bad or worse; in which case, P2 is shown to be false: hiddenness is overall good, even though bad in itself.

Rea also follows the mainstream theistic response in rejecting P2, but he does so in an innovative way that does not implicate him in the theodical project. To begin with P1, however, Rea notes that this premise tends to be supported by appeal to one or the other (or both) of the following considerations:

IE (Inconclusive Evidence): For many people, the available *a priori* and empirical evidence in support of God's existence is inconclusive: one can be fully aware of it and at the same time rationally believe that God does not exist.

AE (Absence of Religious Experience): Many people – believers and unbelievers alike – have never had an experience that seems to them to be a direct experience or awareness of the love or presence of God; and those who do have such experiences have them rarely.[58]

Rea regards IE and AE as giving rise to *divine silence*, rather than divine hiddenness, the difference (in Rea's eyes) being that the notion of hiddenness, but not silence, carries with it the implication that what is hidden "has been deliberately concealed or that it has been concealed (deliberately or not) to such a degree that those from whom it is hidden can't reasonably be expected to find it."[59]

---

[56] Rea (2009, 76).   [57] Rea (2009, 76).
[58] Rea (2009, 76).   [59] Rea (2009, 80).

Hiddenness in this sense stands in need of justification: God must have good reason for concealing his presence in this way; moreover, it is often thought, whatever reason God has must be "sufferer-centered," in that it has to be of benefit to those from whom God is hidden, thus demonstrating that God desires their well-being after all. But if IE and AE are the product of a sort of willful blindness on our part, then it would be more accurate to say that we are hiding from God, rather than God from us, in which case there is no onus on the theist to identify any "sufferer-centered" goods to excuse God's seeming absence. Rea, then, is led to think of IE and AE as providing grounds not for regarding God as hidden but for viewing him as silent, and silent in the specific sense that "God hasn't made a special effort to ensure that most of his rational creatures detect (as such) whatever signs of his existence there might be or whatever messages he might be sending us."[60]

Rea goes on to argue that divine silence, and by extension IE and AE, are compatible with the idea of "divine concern," this being the idea that "God strongly desires to promote the well-being of all of his creatures, both now and in the afterlife."[61] And this is so because God has provided at least two readily and widely accessible ways for us to find him and experience his presence, in the midst of his silence: scripture and liturgy.[62] These ways, Rea points out, are "mediated," in that they afford not direct or first-hand experience of God, but an encounter with God mediated by something else, whether it be biblical narratives or liturgical acts. Rea therefore concludes, in the very last lines of his paper:

> Suffering human beings longing for the presence of God can go to the scriptures and the liturgy and find it – in small and mediated ways to be sure, but nevertheless in ways that provide them with the resources to see themselves not as lost and abandoned by God but rather as living daily in the presence of a loving but silent God.[63]

If the presence of God can be mediated in this way, then divine silence is no longer a problem. Returning to the schematic form of the argument given earlier, Rea can be seen as endorsing P1 (suitably reinterpreted by way of the notion of "silence") and the grounds usually adduced for P1: IE and AE. What he is contesting is P2, but he does so not in the typical fashion of providing a theodicy or justification for God's hiddenness, but by seeking to show – in a way analogous to Marilyn McCord Adams's delineation of defeating strategies in response to the problem of evil – how God can remain good to human creatures (or in Rea's terminology, caring and concernful toward human creatures) despite his silence.

In some respects, this is to provide an explanation for silence, albeit not a theodical explanation. If Rea is right, then divine silence can be explained or

---

[60] Rea (2009, 80).   [61] Rea (2009, 77).
[62] See Rea (2009, 88–93).   [63] Rea (2009, 93).

accounted for in part by appealing to our failure to take advantage of the mediatory possibilities God has afforded us in scripture and liturgy (though many more could be listed: e.g., the contemplation of natural beauty, art and poetry, the embrace of a loved one). It might be objected that many people who search the scriptures and participate in religious rituals nevertheless come away empty handed. This is a common phenomenon even amongst devout theists: taking part in the celebration of the eucharist may only reinforce, rather than overcome, the sense of divine absence and silence. A significant lesson may lie here, and in the deeply sacramental tradition of Eastern Orthodoxy the liturgy is seen not only as a way of coming to an awareness and knowledge of God, but even more so as a way of "unknowing" God, experiencing the absence and unknowability of God – what Jean-Luc Marion calls a "counter-experience," as it runs counter to the conditions for the possibility of experiencing an object. In this sense, what is given to experience is "nothing," at least nothing that can pass as an object, or be grasped by an objectifying gaze. And when one's participation in and reception of the eucharist are processed and internalized in the same way that, say, dinner is digested or a table is perceived, then the inevitable outcome is disappointment and frustration.[64]

Often overlooked in this context, as Rea points out, is the ineradicability of *hermeneutics*: actions, like texts, always stand in need of interpretation. A person's silence, for example, can receive any number of interpretations:

A senior member of your department doesn't greet you in the hallway. Is he offended by you? Does he think you're beneath him? Is he depressed and having a bad day? Or is that *just him*, a little preoccupied and not really noticing his surroundings?[65]

I clearly require quite a bit of background information about the other person in this scenario (his history, character, etc.) before I could justifiably take his silence as a gesture of rejection or indifference. In fact, as Rea intimates, the problem might lie with me – that is to say, if I do interpret the other's silence as rejection or indifference, that may only be because I suffer from some immaturity, or a dysfunctional attitude or way of relating to others, or certain epistemic or moral vices. The same, of course, might apply to our response to, or interpretation of, God's silence:

… it might be that our suffering in the face of divine silence is unreasonable, due more to our own immaturity or dysfunction than to any lack of kindness on God's part. Perhaps it results from our own untrusting, uncharitable interpretations of divine silence, or from an inappropriate refusal to accept God for who God is and to accept God's preferences about when and in what ways to communicate with us.[66]

[64] On the notion of "counter-experience," see Marion (2002, 215–16; 2007).
[65] Rea (2009, 82, emphasis in original).
[66] Rea (2009, 84–5).

But if we take seriously the approach to God discussed in section 1, there arises another way of interpreting divine silence not explicitly countenanced by Rea, and one that might make better sense of the seeming intransigence of God in the midst of our pleas that he reveal himself more clearly and more often to us. Earlier I indicated how contemporary thinkers such as Brian Davies and David Bentley Hart have turned to classical theistic sources, from Aquinas to Shankara, in order to retrieve a way of conceiving God that avoids misleading anthropomorphisms and is faithful to the traditional notion of "the infinity of being, consciousness, and bliss that is God," as Hart puts it.[67]

In various places in his paper, even if inadvertently, Rea gives the impression of being beholden to the very ideas and imagery of God that the likes of Davies and Hart are trying to dislodge. This is evident in Rea's references to God as a "divine person" (despite the fact that in the Christian tradition God is never spoken of as a "person"), one whose behavior can be compared to that of human persons.[68] It is even more evident in Rea's proposal that we take seriously the idea that "God might have a genuine, robust personality, and that it might be *deeply good* for God to live out his own personality."[69] Rea goes on to suggest that God, like human persons, might have "a highly complex personality and motivational structure," and that it is a good thing (for God, as it is for human persons) to "live out" the personality he has, presumably by means of his deliberations and actions, or by putting into practice his preferences. If that is so, Rea argues, then it might be good for God (even if it is not good for us) not to clearly reveal himself to us: "it might be good for God to be who God is," that is, a God who is silent.[70]

Perhaps there is a way of translating such language about God into an idiom that is free of any crude anthropomorphisms. But at first glance, at least, it seems that ascribing a personality or subjectivity to God, replete with an unexpressed interiority or motivational structure that has to be lived out in relation to, if not in competition with, the deliberations and dispositions of external realities (in this case, human persons), is to ascribe the kind of dependent finitude to God that the classical traditions of East and West have consistently sought to avoid. The complexity Rea introduces into God, and the way in which God's interests are depicted as competing with human well-being, stands in contrast to the classical conception of an absolutely simple God who infinitely transcends the kind of personhood we possess. This is not to say that God is not personal in any sense, but only to say that even those "person-making" properties that could intelligibly be ascribed to God (e.g., knowing, willing, caring) can only be applied to God in an extended or diluted sense, and even then they do not tell us anything about who

---

[67] Hart (2013, 83).   [68] Rea (2009, 82–3).
[69] Rea (2009, 86, emphasis in original).
[70] Rea (2009, 86).

God is in himself or in essence, apart from his relation to the created world. God, therefore, is better conceived as "supra-personal," in much the same way that the ultimate reality in Advaita Vedanta or Absolute Idealism is thought to transcend the dichotomy between the personal and the impersonal.[71]

This qualitative difference between our creaturely and personal mode of being and God's mysterious supra-personal existence has often been pressed by Rowan Williams, in a manner much like that of Davies and Hart. For example, in the course of expounding Wittgenstein's comment that the existence of God is analogous to the existence of color in the visual field, Williams writes that talk of God "is structurally more like talking about some 'grid' for the under-standing of particular objects than talking about particular objects in them-selves."[72] Elsewhere, in a discussion on the problem of evil, Williams notes the anthropomorphic tendency prevalent amongst theodicists to think that God

...is (like us) an agent in an environment, who must "negotiate" purposes and desires in relation to other agencies and presences. But God is not an item in any environment, and God's action has been held, in orthodox Christian thought, to be identical with God's being – that is, what God does is nothing other than God's being actively real. Nothing could add to or diminish this, because God does not belong in an environment where the divine life could be modified by anything else.[73]

Williams is making use here of the doctrine of divine simplicity, and if (as Hart maintains) "any denial of divine simplicity is equivalent to a denial of God's reality,"[74] then the appearance of hiddenness and silence may bespeak a failure to come to grips with the nature and otherness of the reality of God.

This has something in common with Rea's own proposal of positing "wide-spread cognitive or emotional dysfunction" in explanation (though not nec-essarily theodical justification) of the human suffering occasioned by divine silence.[75] Like Rea, I am interpreting divine silence as a sign that, possibly, our way of relating to God (and to others, including the natural world) is deeply amiss, so that we all-too-easily and quickly infer God's indifference or non-existence from his silence. Rea, however, does not trace the "dysfunction" back to what I'm presuming to be its ultimate source; he only remarks, for instance, that it may lie in a kind of spiritual immaturity, where the requisite training to sharpen the "spiritual senses" has not been undertaken.[76] But if, as I have been suggesting, what hiddenness reveals is that our understand-ing of God is incorrigibly confused or defective – perhaps because (following Hart) we have became so enthralled by a mechanistic picture of reality that we

[71] I am indebted here to Keith Ward's excellent paper "Is God a Person?" (Ward, 1992).
[72] Williams (2007, 242–3).   [73] Williams (1996, 143).
[74] Hart (2013, 134).   [75] Rea (2009, 87).
[76] Rea (2009, 92–3).

cannot envision God's relationship to nature in any other way than as a demi-urge, a watchmaker, one being amongst others rather than Being itself – then the reasonable response to hiddenness is indeed atheism of some sort, but one that "purifies" our preconceptions, enabling a more adequate understanding to emerge.

A further consequence follows, rarely recognized in the contemporary debate over divine hiddenness. If what we are talking about is not some finite or limited reality, but God as Absolute Being – where God is, as Hart states, "not just some especially resplendent object among all the objects illuminated by the light of being, or any kind of object at all, but is himself the light of being"[77] – then to properly understand that this is what "God" means and yet to reject belief in God would amount to rejecting the legitimacy or intelligi-bility of the age-old, though admittedly odd, metaphysical question: Why is there something rather than nothing? It would be to dispense with the ultimate source of contingent reality, the Absolute, and to accept a naturalistic view of the world as a pure contingency, a brute fact – it's "just there, and that's all," as Russell once replied to Copleston.[78] Given that, as the current philosophical landscape suggests, naturalism constitutes the sole or major alternative to the classical theistic worldview, it appears then that the choice we are faced with is a faith consistent with reason and a seemingly rational outlook based upon an absurdist faith. This is not the place for a defense of this position, though Hart goes a long way toward showing up the inadequacies of naturalism in coming to grips with his tripartite object of study: being, consciousness, and bliss (the last comprising the good and the beautiful). But if indeed these three funda-mental givens of human life cannot be understood by naturalism as anything other than eliminable or inexplicable data, then as Hart states, compared with such naturalism,

[t]heism has nothing so magnificently wild and rhapsodically anarchic to offer; the faith it supports depends at some point upon a consistent set of logical intuitions, and so lacks the sheer intellectual brio of that sort of madly, romantically adventurous absurdism.[79]

Ironically, this is the very reverse of the relationship between religion and rationality that often passes as the obvious truth of the matter today. In that case, nonbelief in the midst of divine silence or hiddenness is not non-culpable, at least for "intellectually sophisticated adult nontheists in our culture" (adopt-ing Philip Quinn's phrase). It evinces, rather, a strange refusal or incapacity to see what it is that hiddenness reveals.

---

[77] Hart (2013, 143).   [78] Russell and Copleston (1964, 175).
[79] Hart (2013, 150).

12 Hiddenness and transcendence

Michael C. Rea

For over two decades, the philosophical literature on divine hiddenness has been concerned with just one problem about divine hiddenness that arises out of one very particular concept of God. The problem – I'll call it *the Schellenberg problem* – has J. L. Schellenberg as both its inventor and its most ardent defender. The concept of God in question construes God as a *perfect heavenly parent*, and seems to be the product of perfect being theology deployed within constraints imposed by modern ideals of parenthood. The idea that God is our heavenly Father is traditional within Christian theology (which shall be my focus in this paper, as it is the tradition that I know best), and the method of perfect being theology has enjoyed an important place in that tradition as well. Nevertheless, one might reasonably wonder to what extent it makes sense to allow modern ideals about parenthood to drive our theological reflections in the ways that it has done in the contemporary hiddenness literature.

Within the Christian tradition, theologians have typically allowed their views about the fatherhood of God to be shaped in light of their views about divine holiness and transcendence rather than the other way around. The same is true for the theology of divine motherhood that developed in monastic circles in the high Middle Ages. This is not to say that ideals about parenthood have been irrelevant to the theology of divine motherhood and fatherhood; far from it. But I think that it is fairly safe to say that, for the most part throughout the tradition, such ideals have rarely, if ever, played the sort of primary, driving role in theological reflection that they have done in the literature on the Schellenberg problem. Upon attending to this fact, one *might* conclude that Schellenberg and those who have embraced his method of theological reflection are simply taking Christian theology in a new and better direction. Alternatively, one might

For helpful comments on earlier drafts, I am grateful to Rebecca Chan, Helen DeCruz, Adam Green, Carl Mosser, Sam Newlands, Eleonore Stump, and the members of audiences at the weekly discussion group of the University of Notre Dame Center for Philosophy of Religion and at the 2014 annual meetings of the American Academy of Religion and the Evangelical Theological Society. Work on this paper was supported by The Experience Project, funded by The John Templeton Foundation in partnership with the University of Notre Dame and the University of North Carolina, Chapel Hill.

start to wonder whether the Schellenberg problem is in fact not a problem for traditional Christian theism at all, but rather an attack inadvertently mounted against a straw deity.

In this paper, I argue that the Schellenberg problem *is* an attack on a straw deity. More specifically, I argue that Schellenberg's argument against the existence of God depends on certain theological claims that are not *commitments* of traditional Christian theology and that would, furthermore, be repudiated by many of the most important and influential theologians in the Christian tradition. I close with some very brief remarks about the implications of this conclusion for what I take to be the real import of the Schellenberg problem.

1

Let me begin by stating the Schellenberg problem, with an eye to highlighting its most important underlying theological assumptions. The problem takes the form of an argument for the conclusion that God does not exist. In *Divine Hiddenness and Human Reason*, Schellenberg formulates the argument as follows:[1]

S1. If there is a God, God is perfectly loving.
S2. If a perfectly loving God exists, reasonable nonbelief does not occur.[2]
S3. Reasonable nonbelief occurs.
S4. Therefore: No perfectly loving God exists.
S5. Therefore: there is no God.

Theists will not dispute S1; and, although S3 has been the subject of much dispute, it presupposes no substantive theological claims, nor are any such claims required for its defense. Accordingly, for the remainder of this paper I shall focus on S2.

Let me begin with some brief remarks about which God, exactly, Schellenberg has in view. Even Schellenberg acknowledges that not every conception of God is one on which S2 is plausible. For example, as we shall see in more detail at the beginning of section 2, he seems happy to concede that those who regard God as absolutely incomprehensible might find S2 unacceptable. But if so, then whose God, exactly, is in view with this argument? Schellenberg's answer to

---

[1] Schellenberg has expressed the argument in several slightly different ways over the years (including in his contribution to the present volume). But the differences among these formulations do not make a difference to the arguments that follow; for, as readers can easily verify, they are all predicated on the same basic theological assumptions (T1–T3 below). (See, e.g., chapter 1 of the present volume.)

[2] In discussing S2, Schellenberg has made it clear that by "reasonable nonbelief" he means "inculpable nonbelief," and that when he says that such belief "does not occur" he means that it *never* occurs. So S2 should be understood as equivalent to the thesis that, if a perfectly loving God exists, inculpable nonbelief never occurs. (Cf. Schellenberg, 1993, 25–9 and Schellenberg, 2005a, 201, 203.)

this question is quite explicit: the argument targets belief in "the personal God of traditional theism" (2005a, 209). But what God is that? Theism itself is not a religious tradition in its own right; and the various religions that are paradigmatically theistic – Judaism, Christianity, Islam, and a few of their offshoots – embrace very different conceptions of God, very different views about how God is to be worshipped, and very different views on a wide range of other theological topics. Granted, all three of these religious traditions share *some* common views about God. Indeed, they have traditionally overlapped on a small family of theological claims that together comprise the philosophical-theological position known as *classical theism*. But there is no such thing as *theistic* orthodoxy to which one could appeal for support for S2; and, given the wide diversity of views about divine love and personality that have been developed within and across these various religious traditions, it is singularly implausible to suppose that there is any conception of either divine love or divine personality that could be considered a commitment of theism as such and that would be robust enough to lend support to S2.

In light of this, it is perhaps unsurprising that Schellenberg's own defenses of S2 tend to appeal to very general considerations (e.g., analogies with human love, or alleged conceptual truths) rather than to particular theological doctrines. Moreover, when he does appeal to particular theological doctrines, he seems to draw only on small portions of the Christian tradition rather than either considering that tradition writ large or examining views about divine love and personality that are common to all three of the theistic traditions.[3] The result of this methodology has been a rather remarkable detachment of his defense of S2 from virtually all of the theological work on divine love and personality that has been done in any of the major theistic traditions. This is noteworthy; for one would expect that if each of the theistic religions is committed to S2, then the easiest and most straightforward way to defend that claim would be to cite a variety of theologians in each tradition who more or less explicitly endorse it. Likewise, showing that many of the most influential theologians in any one of these traditions are *not* committed to S2 would suffice to undermine the claim that S2 is a commitment of theism in general, or of that tradition in particular.

I am in no position to comment on the contours of Jewish or Islamic theology; but I think that one would be hard pressed to draw much unqualified support for S2 from the work of Christian theologians writing before the twentieth century (or even *during* the twentieth century, apart from the work of American evangelical protestants). Be that as it may, in section 2 I shall argue that many of the most influential theologians in the Christian tradition are, at any rate, not committed to S2. If that is correct, then the Schellenberg problem fails as

---

[3] Cf. p. 223 below.

an argument against the existence of the God of traditional Christianity, and a fortiori, it also fails as an argument against the God of theism in general.

Before turning to that argument, however, let us examine in a bit more detail Schellenberg's reasons for thinking that theists *are* committed to S2. Although Schellenberg has had a lot to say in support of S2 over the years, so far as I can tell, there is no final, master argument for that premise to be found in any one article or book chapter. Instead, what we find is an extended defense of S2 in *Divine Hiddenness and Human Reason*, followed by a variety of clarifications and supplementary remarks in subsequent articles written mostly in response to critics. Nevertheless, thanks to the steadfastness and internal coherence of Schellenberg's views about the nature of divine love over the years, it is not difficult to reconstruct a master argument on his behalf.[4] In doing so, we can also highlight some important underlying theological assumptions.

The crucial premise in Schellenberg's defense of S2 is the following claim:

S6. Perfect love toward another person includes a strong disposition to seek *personal relationship* with him or her.

According to Schellenberg, a *personal relationship* is to be understood as an *explicit, reciprocally interactive* relationship. Given this, S6 implies the following two theological claims:

T1. One has a personal relationship with God only if one is involved in an explicit, reciprocally interactive relationship with God.

T2. Divine love manifests a bias toward explicit, reciprocally interactive relationship with human beings.

Schellenberg, does not define what he means by "explicit, reciprocally interactive relationship," but he does give some illustrative examples. On God's side, such a relationship with a human person would involve such things as giving guidance, support, forgiveness, and consolation; on the human side, it would involve such things as worship and obedience; and the relationship would count as *reciprocally* interactive at least in part because what God gives in the relationship is relevantly connected to what the human being gives, and vice versa (Schellenberg, 1993, 18–21). This suggests that what he has in mind is (at least) a relationship in which each participant is aware of the other as a person, and there is some kind of communicative interaction between the two such that each party to the relationship is evidentially in a position both to believe reasonably that the other person is intentionally communicating something to him or her and to understand the specific content of what is being communicated.

---

[4] In doing this, I draw on what I take to be his most important extended discussions of S2 (specifically, Schellenberg, 1993, 2003, and 2005a).

The route from S6 to S2 is fairly simple. Given S6 and T2, it follows that if God is perfectly loving toward *everyone*, God will be strongly disposed to seek explicit, reciprocally interactive relationship with everyone. God will, in other words, manifest a strong bias toward explicit, reciprocally interactive relationship with human beings. But manifesting such a bias, he thinks, will involve *at a minimum* supplying every nonresistant person with enough evidence to form rational belief in God. As he puts it, a perfectly loving God "would, as it were, have to be *convinced* that there was reason to deprive us of the evidence for belief which an opportunity to enter into personal relationship with God requires" (Schellenberg, 2005b, 288; emphasis in original). So, if God is perfectly loving, reasonable nonbelief does not occur – which is just to say that S2 is true. I note in passing that, on Schellenberg's view, *divine hiddenness* – a term that surprisingly appears nowhere in the summary formulation of his *argument* from divine hiddenness – is just the fact that God has *not* provided evidence sufficient to form belief in God to every human being capable of a personal relationship with God. Given this terminology, Schellenberg's argument from S6 to S2 boils down to this: a perfectly loving being will be biased toward explicit, reciprocally interactive relationship with everyone who is not resisting such relationship, and therefore such a being will be hidden from nobody except those who are resisting. I will not here contest this argument (except to challenge its starting point, S6). I present it simply in order to highlight the importance of S6 to the case for S2. Rejecting S6 undermines the argument, and it is hard to see how S2 could be defended without appeal to something like S6.

So S6 is important. Why think it is true? Schellenberg has offered several different reasons. In *Divine Hiddenness and Human Reason*, he defends it by appeal to the following two claims: (i) divine love, insofar as it is analogous to the *best human love*, would seek to maximize the well-being of God's beloved, and (ii) participating in a personal relationship with God would greatly enhance the well-being of any human person. Elsewhere, he takes a more direct route, defending S6 by saying that divine love would be analogous to *parental love*. Ideal parental love has been variously conceived across times and cultures; but in our time and culture, at any rate, ideal parental love is widely understood to include an overwhelming disposition to seek ongoing explicit and reciprocally interactive relationship with one's child. Thus, taking modern ideals of parenthood for granted, the parent analogy seems to lend a great deal of support to S6 (Schellenberg, 2003, 32–5). In a later article, he claims that S2 is a conceptual truth about divine love; and part of his basis for saying this seems to be the thought that S6 is a conceptual truth (Schellenberg, 2005a, 212–13).

By invoking the parent analogy, Schellenberg presupposes a further theological claim:

T3: The fact that normal human parental love manifests a strong bias toward explicit reciprocally interactive relationship with one's child is weighty evidence in support of the truth of T2.

Moreover, each of the other two lines of defense seems to depend on it as well. If T3 were false, it would be implausible to suggest that S6 is a conceptual truth about divine love (cf. again Schellenberg, 2005a, 212–13); and it would likewise be untenable to rest a case for S6 on an analogy with the *best human love*, given that parental love has strong claim to being among the best forms of human love.

So Schellenberg's case for S2 depends importantly on all three of the theological assumptions just highlighted. However, in the next section I will argue that each of these claims is an uneasy fit with the broad theological framework endorsed by many of the most important and influential theologians in the Christian tradition and that, as a result, neither they nor S6 nor S2 can sensibly be thought to be commitments of traditional Christian theology.

2

In his own discussions of the implications of divine transcendence for the Schellenberg problem, Schellenberg has focused exclusively on the question whether and to what extent a transcendent God could act so as to render theistic belief reasonable. He grants that a strong theology of divine transcendence – one according to which God is *absolutely incomprehensible*, such that human concepts do not even analogically apply to God – makes it hard to see either how theistic belief could be evidentially supported or how one could meaningfully say that God has acted so as to provide evidence of God's existence (1993, 46). But he says that *only* a doctrine of absolute incomprehensibility would have this result. So long as familiar predicates like "is just" or "is loving" at least analogically apply to God, God *can* supply us with evidence for theistic belief and, furthermore, divine love would *require* that God do so. Moreover, he insists that, in the context of the Schellenberg problem,

reference is being made not to an incomprehensible God, but to the personal God of traditional theism, whose love and justice, and so on, are conceived as sharing properties with their human counterparts, though of course they are thought of as perfected in various ways, and the *manner* of their instantiation or exercise might well be incomprehensible to us. (2005a, 209, emphasis in original)

On the strength of these considerations, and particularly in light of the alleged contrast between an incomprehensible God and the God of "traditional theism,"

Schellenberg seems to think that the doctrine of divine transcendence has no significant bearing on the premises of the Schellenberg problem.

I am with Schellenberg in thinking that many human predicates apply to God at least analogically. I am also with Schellenberg in thinking that the method of perfect being theology, properly construed and implemented, is a route to genuine, even if only partial, understanding of the divine nature. Despite these points of agreement, however, I think that Schellenberg is mistaken both in his views about the importance of divine transcendence generally in the Christian tradition and in his understanding of the potential bearing of even a modest doctrine of transcendence for the premises of his argument.

Note again the unqualified contrast between an incomprehensible deity on the one hand and "the personal God of traditional theism" on the other. Divine incomprehensibility and divine transcendence go hand in hand as divine attributes. Often enough the terms "transcendence," "incomprehensibility," and "hiddenness" are used interchangeably. But the claim that God is *both* transcendent and personal enjoys overwhelming support from the Christian tradition, and is a crucial part of the theological framework endorsed by theologians as diverse as Gregory of Nyssa, Pseudo-Dionysius, Thomas Aquinas, Jonathan Edwards, Karl Barth, and many others.[5] In short, the personal God of traditional Christianity *is* a transcendent, incomprehensible deity. Indeed, many theologians would say that the personal God of traditional Christianity is *absolutely* transcendent.

Witness, for example, the opening remarks of Elizabeth Johnson's "The Incomprehensibility of God and the Image of God as Male and Female":

The holiness and utter transcendence of God over all of creation has always been an absolutely central affirmation of the Judeo-Christian tradition. God as God – source, redeemer, and goal of all – is illimitable mystery who, while immanently present, cannot be measured or controlled. The doctrine of divine incomprehensibility is a corollary of this divine transcendence. In essence, God's unlikeness to the corporal and spiritual finite world is total; hence we simply cannot understand God. No human concept, word, or image, all of which originate in experience of created reality, can circumscribe the divine reality, nor can any human construct express with any measure of adequacy the mystery of God, who is ineffable. (1984, 441)

Johnson's gloss on (absolute) divine transcendence is controversial. But that is neither here nor there as far as the present point is concerned. Her understanding of the *tradition* is entirely typical,[6] whereas Schellenberg is committed to the first three sentences of the quoted paragraph being fundamentally mistaken. His unqualified contrast between the personal God of the

[5] Cf. N. N. Trakakis's contribution to the present volume (chapter 11) and references therein.
[6] For a detailed, and extremely useful, survey of the doctrine of divine incomprehensibility from the patristic period on through the Reformation, see Bavinck (2004, 36–41).

tradition and an incomprehensible deity presupposes the following broad theological claim:

T4. The Christian tradition as such is committed to an understanding of God's personal attributes (love, justice, etc.) that straightforwardly conflicts with the claim that God is absolutely transcendent.

T4 might indeed be true, but, at best, it will be extremely controversial. This is due partly to the fact that there are diverse understandings of "absolutely transcendent" in the tradition, not all of which are identical to Schellenberg's (or Johnson's, for that matter). But it is also due to the fact that there are diverse understandings within the tradition of the nature of divine love, justice, and other personal attributes. Thus, T4 cannot simply be taken for granted in an argument that relies heavily on a particular understanding of God's personal attributes en route to the conclusion that the God of traditional Christianity does not exist.

Schellenberg might insist that even if T4 is false on some precisifications, at least the following claim (which replaces the term "absolutely transcendent" with Schellenberg's own particular understanding of absolute transcendence) is true:

T5. The Christian tradition as such is committed to an understanding of God's personal attributes that straightforwardly conflicts with the claim that familiar predicates like "is just" and "is loving" neither univocally nor analogically apply to God.

But T5 will also be extremely controversial. For many theologians will want to distinguish between analogy and metaphor, and will want to say that claims like "God is loving" and "God is just" are true or apt metaphors rather than univocal or analogical truths. Thus, again, insofar as Schellenberg's target is the God of traditional Christianity, T4 and T5 cannot simply be taken for granted; they stand in need of substantial defense.

But suppose we grant the truth of T5. Suppose we furthermore allow, as I think we must in order for Elizabeth Johnson's understanding of the tradition to be genuinely uncontroversial, that the claim that God is *utterly* or *absolutely* transcendent admits of interpretations that are fully consistent with the claim that familiar predicates like "is loving" apply analogically or even univocally to God. Let us also insist, as Schellenberg must, given the way in which he defends his premises, on the legitimacy of the method of perfect being theology as a way of discovering truths about God. Should we then agree that, despite the centrality of divine transcendence to the Christian tradition, the doctrine has no bearing on the premises of the Schellenberg problem? I think that we should not, and this largely for methodological reasons. In the remainder of this section I explain why.

Commitment to the method of perfect being theology is, first and foremost, commitment both to the thesis that God is a perfect being and to the viability of relying on at least some of our intuitions about perfection – for example, about what it would take for a being to be perfectly loving, or perfectly knowledge-able – as a means for arriving at further true claims about God. Importantly, it is no part of perfect being theology to suppose that this method is perfectly reliable, or that intuitions about perfection are evidentially superior to or even on a par with the claims of scripture as evidence about what God is like. Nor is it any part of perfect being theology to suppose that the thesis that *God is perfect* (or any other claim about God) can be known independently of divine revelation. One can, I believe, deploy the method of perfect being theology even within Barthian constraints, affirming that God is known, independently of revelation, only by God, that unaided human cognitive activity is inadequate to the task of arriving at substantive theological truths, and that "[n]o one has ever said, or can say, of himself ... what God is; God is inexpressible ... He is, therefore, visible only to faith and can be attested only by faith" (Barth, 1957, 190; cf. the distinction between ontotheology and "theo-ontology" in Vanhoozer, 2010, 104).

The import of all of this is as follows. One *can*, as a perfect being theolo-gian, start with the thesis that God is perfectly loving or that God is a perfect parent and rely on one's intuitions about love in general or about parental love in particular to arrive at conclusions like T1–T3. In doing so, one would then very naturally attenuate one's understanding of divine transcendence (or other divine attributes) in light of one's understanding of divine love or divine par-enthood. But that is just *one way* of deploying the method. Alternatively, one might start with the thesis that God is transcendent (or with other theses that lead via the method of perfect being theology to the conclusion that God is transcendent) and allow one's understanding of divine transcendence to shape one's understanding of divine love and divine parenthood. Moreover, in tak-ing this alternative approach, one need not abandon the idea that divine love is analogous to human love in general or to parental love in particular; but one might well endorse very different views from Schellenberg about the *extent* to which these loves are analogous, or about which features of human love or human parenthood are most salient for understanding the nature and attributes of God.

The alternative approach just described is not merely hypothetical; it, or something very much like it, has dominated the Christian tradition. The per-sonal God of *traditional* Christianity has, for many of the most important and influential theologians throughout history, been the transcendent, sim-ple, immutable, and *a se* God of classical theism. The idea that these are non-negotiable divine attributes has traditionally been seen to be one of the results of the method of perfect being theology, and it has exerted enormous

influence both on the conceptions of divine love that are to be found in the
tradition and also on the conceptions of what it might look like to enter into
unitive, loving relationship with God.

In the work of theologians who lay emphasis on transcendence as a divine
attribute, divine love toward creatures is commonly understood not as the
homey yearning of a human parent for an explicitly communicative and mutually reassuring relationship with her child, but rather simply as God's *goodness*
toward creation, God's *willing* the good for particular creatures, God's use of
creation for good purposes, God's grounding and illuminating creaturely goodness, or some combination of these.[7] Some of these theologians seem to eschew
talk of divine desire as a component of divine love altogether.[8] Others identify
the desire(s) involved in divine love either as a desire for the good of human
creatures (or creation generally), or as a desire for union with human creatures,
or both. But even those who identify the desire for union as a component of
divine love typically do not envision such union as something that God longs
to have with every human being under just any conditions whatsoever, nor do
they envision it as something that requires rationally supported belief in God.
Instead, union with God is typically seen as something that God brings about in
a person only after she has directed her *will and desire* toward God, apparently
wholly independently of the degree or epistemic status of her belief in God.[9]

In the writings of the apophatic mystics – among the most important works
in the Christian tradition on the subject of just how human beings might
achieve union with God – the concept of contemplative union seems to stand
in for the notion of a personal relationship with God. But the idea that this
might regularly, reliably, or essentially involve anything like *explicit, reciprocal interaction* is largely foreign to that tradition. Instead, achieving contemplative union is commonly construed as mainly a matter of bringing one's will
into conformity with the will of God. To be sure, most of these authors envision
the process of attaining contemplative union as one in which God sometimes
causes within a person intense and vivid religious experiences and provides

---

[7] See, for example, Pseudo-Dionysius (1987, 79–84); Augustine, *On Christian Doctrine* 1.31.34;
Aquinas, *Summa Theologica* 1.20; and the discussion of divine love in the work of John of the
Cross in Williams (2014). See also Bavinck (2004, 215–16), and Peckham (2015, esp. ch. 2).
Cf. also Anselm's treatment of divine mercy (*Proslogion* 8), according to which God counts as
merciful simply by virtue of the fact that God *acts* as merciful people do rather than by virtue of
possessing any of the characteristic emotions or desires of mercy. Similar things have been said,
mutatis mutandis, about divine love throughout the history of Christianity. (Thanks to Jordan
Wessling for this last point. Thanks also to Jordan Wessling and Peter Martens for the references
to Augustine and Aquinas.)

[8] Cf. Augustine, *On Christian Doctrine* 1.31.34; Peckham (2015, 66, 74).

[9] Cf. Aquinas, *Summa Theologica* 1.20; Pseudo-Dionysius (1987, 81–2); Anonymous (1981, sec.
34); Teresa of Avila, *The Interior Castle* IV.1.7 (Rodriguez and Kavanaugh, 1980, 319) and John
of the Cross, *The Ascent of Mount Carmel*, Bk 2, ch. 5.3 (Kavanaugh, 1988, 89). See also Muller
(2003, 561–9, esp. 564–5, 567).

various "consolations" in prayer. But the experiences in question are generally not seen as the ultimate goal of our quest for union with God, nor are they even typically seen as favors that ought to be explicitly sought for their own sake.[10]

Broadly speaking, then, in the work of those theologians who lay heavy emphasis on God's transcendence, aseity, simplicity, and immutability, we find no substantial support for the idea that God might have anything like a bias toward mutual reciprocal interaction, or that a relationship with God would have to be what Schellenberg would think of as mutually reciprocally interactive, or that empirical and a priori evidence for the existence of God might be a necessary condition for such a relationship.[11] Not only this, but when we look to the details of what these theologians have had to say about divine love and union with God, Schellenberg's ideas about the nature of divine love and about the nature of "personal relationship" with God are, at best, an uneasy fit.[12] This is not to say that such authors *never* speak of God as relating to human beings in a mode of explicit, mutually reciprocal interaction. Aquinas, for example, seems to think that the indwelling of the Holy Spirit involves (or can involve) something like relationship in that mode.[13] Similarly, John of the Cross seems to think that the highest mode of divine presence to believers involves at least what Schellenberg would call *explicit* relationship.[14] Rather, my point is that, in contrast to Schellenberg, none of these authors seems to think that God counts as perfectly loving only if God has a *bias* toward this sort of relationship and brings it about that everyone can have this sort of relationship with God just by willing it. The indwelling of the Holy Spirit is available only to believers; and it was surely as obvious to Aquinas as it is to us that not even every believer has what Schellenberg would call an explicit, mutually interactive relationship with God. Similarly, the highest mode of divine presence is, according to John of the Cross, available only to those who have devoted a lot of effort toward progressing along the route to contemplative union; but there is no indication in his works that God counts as less than perfectly loving to those who do not – and, in their present state, *cannot*, even if they desire it – enjoy that mode of presence with God.

[10] See, for example, Teresa of Avila, *The Interior Castle*, IV.2.9 (Rodriguez and Kavanaugh, 1980, 326), and John of the Cross, *The Dark Night of the Soul* 1.5 (Kavanaugh, 1988, 173–5). For John of the Cross, such consolations seem to be little more than an impediment and distraction that one must hope to overcome in pursuing union with God.
[11] See Peckham (2015, esp. chs. 2–3), for a brief survey of different conceptions of divine love in the history of Christian theology and for detailed discussion of what he calls the "transcendent-voluntarist model," which develops a conception of divine love within constraints imposed by an emphasis on divine transcendence.
[12] In discussing Augustine's conception of divine love, for example, John Peckham writes: "Augustine's ontology ... prohibits a dynamic, reciprocal relationship between God and creatures" (2015, 66).
[13] On this, see Stump (2011b, 36–9).
[14] Cf. Payne (1990, 53–4).

But what about the force of the parent analogy in its own right? The idea that God is our heavenly Father is a scriptural and creedal mainstay of the Christian tradition; and if God is perfect and a Father, then God is a perfect Father. Thus, if we are prepared to grant (as I think that many of us would) that *perfect parental love* is much like what Schellenberg takes it to be, one might very well wonder what would justify leaving that analogy and our intuitions about parental love in the dust as we theologize about the nature of divine love.[15] The answer, in short, is that, although the claim that God is our heavenly Father is entrenched in the tradition, and although the claim that God is our Mother also has a surprisingly important place in the tradition, these claims have not nearly always been seen as telling us anything important about divine biases toward relationship with human beings in general.

According to Peter Widdicombe, for example, in the writings of Athansius, Origen, and other patristic authors, the fatherhood of the first person of the Trinity is understood in terms of his being "the unoriginate first principle," the creator of all things, an "inherently generative" deity, and "the fount of the Godhead." Moreover, he writes:

It is notable that Origen and Athanasius, and the other Fathers discussed in this study, did not support their picture of God as Father either by drawing on the biological or on the psychological and sociological dimensions of human fatherhood. Contemporary ideas about the family and about adoption play no role in their discussions of the divine being or of the Father's relation to us. (1994, 255)

Widdicombe makes this remark at the beginning of a discussion of how the views of Origen, Athanasius, and other church Fathers about the Fatherhood of God might be brought to bear on contemporary controversies about the *patriarchal* assumptions that might be involved in calling God "Father" rather than "Mother" or "Parent" or something else entirely. But what he says here bears just as much on the question whether biblical, creedal, or historical theological affirmations of the fatherhood of God presuppose anything about the distinctively parental nature of divine love. They do not, at least not in the writings of the patristics.[16]

---

[15] One interesting answer, which I will not pursue in detail here, is that the force of the parent analogy needs to be understood, and perhaps somewhat mitigated, in light of other scriptural imagery apparently aimed at illuminating the nature of divine love for creatures. For example, God is portrayed (e.g., in the divine speeches of the book of Job) as showing loving concern for non-human animals; but presumably God's love toward those creatures would not have to involve a quest for personal relationship as Schellenberg perceives it. Likewise, God's concern for human beings is communicated in the New Testament not only via parent analogies but also via shepherd analogies, which themselves lend no support whatsoever to the idea that divine love for humans would involve a bias toward explicit, reciprocally interactive relationship. (Thanks to Helen DeCruz and Rebecca Chan for suggestions along these lines.)

[16] But not just the patristics. Bavinck, for example, seems to reduce God's fatherhood to his unbegottenness (2004, 306) and says explicitly that the name of "Father" is "not a metaphor derived

It is also worth noting that even when scriptural affirmations of divine fatherhood do seem to tell us something about the nature of God's love for human beings, it is almost always God's love for *believers*, or for *Israel*, or for others who already believe in and in some sense worship God (e.g., "those who fear him" in Psalm 103:13) that is in view in these verses. There is little, if any, scriptural support for the claim that God is a father to *everyone*; thus, even if perfect parental love were as Schellenberg envisions it, one would be hard pressed to find support from scriptural affirmations of divine fatherhood for anything as strong as T1 or S6.

In light of all this, I am inclined to think that anyone looking to support general claims about traditional Christianity's understanding of divine love by appeal to parental imagery found in the tradition would do better to draw on the theology of divine *motherhood* that developed and flourished in the high Middle Ages. Unlike paternal imagery for God, maternal imagery in theological writings has often been used in a way that is clearly designed to exploit for theological use human understandings of parental love. Still, such imagery seems not to have been employed to convey anything like the idea that divine love manifests a bias toward explicit, reciprocal interaction. Rather, its most central uses were to convey by way of maternal metaphors facts about how God nourishes us through scripture and the teachings of the church, facts about divine compassion, and facts about human dependence upon God (Bynum 1982, 146–69).

My point is *not* that there is no precedent at all in the Christian tradition for thinking that the fact that God is our Father (or Mother) tells us something about the nature of God's love for human beings. Rather, my point is simply that certain very prominent and influential understandings of the significance of paternal and maternal imagery as applied to God lend no support whatsoever to T1–T3. Likewise, the main point of my earlier discussion about divine love and unitive knowledge of God was not to say that the Christian tradition speaks unequivocally against T1–T3, but rather that the tradition neither unequivocally *endorses* them nor even relegates their denials to the outer fringes.

Let me be clear, then, about how the response to the Schellenberg problem offered in this paper differs from other responses in the literature. Most responses to the Schellenberg problem – at least those that focus on S2 rather than other premises of the argument – have operated with a specific conception of God (usually Schellenberg's) and have tried to find some reason that might justify God thus conceived in permitting the occurrence of reasonable nonbelief. What I have done instead is to argue that the whole problem is predicated

from the earth and attributed to God. Exactly the opposite is true: fatherhood on earth is but a distant and vague reflection of the fatherhood of God" (p. 307). He cites Eph. 3:14–15 in support of this claim.

on a theology that is not part of traditional Christianity and is, furthermore, an uneasy fit with commitment to one of the historically major tenets of traditional Christianity – namely, the view that God is transcendent. In short, the theological credentials of T1–T3 are shaky at best. Although they are not outright denied by the Christian tradition, they can hardly be regarded as commitments of traditional Christian theology. Insofar as S2 and S6 depend on them, the same is true for those theses as well.

As I mentioned earlier, Schellenberg himself shows some concern for the theological credentials of S2. But he treats the topic only briefly and, interestingly, the theological case he offers rests not on insights about divine love that are common to the theistic religions, but rather more on claims about the nature of Christian salvation. He says that his case for the conclusion that theologians as such are committed to S2 is summed up "nicely" by the following quotation from Grace Jantzen:

Salvation is not (or at least not primarily) about our future destiny but about our relationship to God and the gradual transforming effect of that relationship in our lives ... If religious experience is centrally the sense of the loving presence of God, gradually helping people to reorient and integrate their lives in accordance with their love for him, is this not precisely what salvation is? Salvation must, surely, be religious experience if anything ever is: not in the sense of being a single climactic experience ... but in the sense of a gradual opening of all life, all of experience to the wholemaking love of God. (Jantzen, 1987, 128–9, quoted in Schellenberg, 1993, 29)

Schellenberg follows this quotation immediately with the remark, "Hence theologians, too, seem committed to the affirmation of [S2]" (p. 29). But, of course, that is true (of the Christian tradition, anyway) only if the Christian tradition generally is on board with the claim that salvation is religious experience, and that the religious experience that salvation consists in is something that God's love would lead God to provide for everyone at every moment of his or her life. Not even Jantzen seems to affirm the latter of these two claims; and, as is readily seen from my earlier discussion of what the apophatic mystics have to say about unitive knowledge of God, the conjunction of these two claims is neither an unequivocal affirmation of the Christian tradition nor even a clear majority view.

3

I noted earlier that Schellenberg regards S2 as a *conceptual truth* about divine love. Although he does not say it explicitly, he pretty clearly also takes S6 and T2 to be conceptual truths as well. If he is right, then all that I have said in section 2 might seem irrelevant to the Schellenberg problem, for the Christian tradition would then be committed to S2 and S6 *regardless* of what anyone has had to say about the nature of divine love or about what it might be like to enter into a unitive relationship with God.

But here again the centrality of divine transcendence to the Christian tradition is vitally important. For one very plausible consequence of even a very modest doctrine of divine transcendence is that we have no revelation-independent concept of divine love. There may well be purely conceptual truths about creaturely love, and about perfected creaturely love; but insofar as God is transcendent, there is good reason to think that it will always be at least partly an exegetical or systematic theological question (rather than a matter of mere conceptual analysis) to what extent divine love would resemble a hypothetically perfected creaturely love.

Karl Barth, toward the beginning of his discussion of the perfections of divine freedom, makes roughly the same point in a very general way. Having already asserted that divine hiddenness (which, for him, is equivalent to divine incomprehensibility) is "the first word of the knowledge of God instituted by God himself" (1957, 183), Barth writes:

> The recognition of divine attributes cannot be taken to mean that for us God is subsumed under general notions, under the loftiest ideas of our knowledge of creaturely reality, and that He participates in its perfections. It is not that we recognize and acknowledge the infinity, justice, wisdom, etc. of God because we already know from other sources what all this means and we apply it to God in an eminent sense, thus fashioning for ourselves an image of God after the pattern of our image of the world, i.e., in the last analysis after our own image ... God is subordinate to no idea in which He can be conceived as rooted or by which He can be properly measured. There are not first of all power, goodness, knowledge, will, etc. in general, and then in particular God also as one of the subjects to whom all these things accrue as a predicate. (Barth, 1957, 333–4)

The idea here and in the surrounding context is that our knowledge of attributes like wisdom, power, goodness, *and love* is subordinate to what we learn by way of revelation, rather than the other way around. This has not been a minority view in the tradition; nor is it a minority view among contemporary theologians. But, if it is correct, it has as a straightforward consequence the claim that we have no revelation-independent concept of divine love; and if *that* is correct, then S2 and S6 are conceptual truths about divine love only if the concept of divine love that they presuppose is one that is somehow grounded in divine revelation. I have no argument for the conclusion that this is *not* the case; but neither has Schellenberg done the exegetical or systematic theological work that would be required to show that it *is* the case.

Suppose I am right about all of this. What conclusions should we draw about the significance of the Schellenberg problem? Even if the Schellenberg problem fails as an argument against the existence of the God of theism in general, or as an argument against the existence of the God of traditional Christian theism in particular, it still poses a threat to belief in a God about whom Schellenberg's theological assumptions are true. Many theists do accept those assumptions; so, although it is an attack on a straw deity if the

God whose existence it targets is supposed to be the God of theism or of traditional Christianity, the Schellenberg problem can easily be reframed as an argument with a real, definite target. I suspect that Schellenberg's God has some claim to being the God of certain strands of contemporary American evangelicalism. Thus, in light of the arguments of the present paper, one might reasonably see the Schellenberg problem as a referendum on *that* concept of God, and as a general challenge to rethink the biblical and systematic theological warrants for thinking about divine love and about personal relationship with God in a way that privileges parent analogies understood in light of contemporary (probably also predominantly American) ideals of parenthood. For the most part, respondents to the Schellenberg problem have tacitly agreed with Schellenberg in thinking that the salient questions about the nature of divine love and personal relationship can mostly be settled a priori rather than by taking a more systematic or historical theological approach. The arguments of the present paper are meant primarily to pose a challenge to that way of thinking.

Part VI

God's Hiddenness: Suffering and Union
with God

13   Divine hiddenness or dark intimacy? How John of the Cross dissolves a contemporary philosophical dilemma

Sarah Coakley

Introduction: what *is* the problem of "divine hiddenness"?

Close to the beginning of his celebrated spiritual treatise *The Dark Night* the sixteenth-century Carmelite friar John of the Cross makes the following revealing statement: "beginners desire to feel God and to taste him as if he were comprehensible and accessible. This desire is a serious imperfection and, because it involves impurity of faith, is opposed to God's way."[1] In fact, as John avers in this context, it represents one of the prime errors of what he terms "spiritual gluttony," that is, the false requirement that God make Godself manifestly and satisfyingly available to those who seek Him. For in contrast, "God very rightly and discreetly *and lovingly* denies this satisfaction to these beginners. If he did not, they would fall into innumerable evils ... This is why it is important for these beginners to enter the dark night and be purged of this childishness."[2]

Who is to say what John of the Cross would have made of the long-running debate in contemporary analytic philosophy of religion on the "problem" of "divine hiddenness"? Would he have dismissed it entirely as a manifestation of spiritual "childishness"? The inevitable charge of anachronism will hover over my attempt in what follows to co-opt him into this discussion, given the seemingly profound difference of basic concerns in the modern debate; for how could an avowedly Christian sixteenth-century mystic be in a position to diagnose a contemporary atheist's dilemma? However, my hope is that I shall be able, en passant, both to acknowledge the difference of context and presumptions with which John of the Cross writes, and to justify my claim that his insights are nonetheless surprisingly apposite.[3] In fact, John has already been

This essay has been written during a period of research leave generously funded by the Leverhulme Foundation. I would like to express my gratitude to the Foundation, and also to Eleonore Stump and Adam Green for their patience and critical insights as editors.

[1] John of the Cross (1981, 372 (*Ascent* I, 6. 5)).

[2] John of the Cross (1981, 373 (*Ascent* I, 6. 6)).

[3] It has often been pointed out that the "problem of divine hiddenness" may be construed in two rather different ways: 1. As an aporetic philosophical problem of theodicy or "defense," closely linked to the "problem of evil"; or 2. as an intra-Christian theological riddle about the reasons

appealed to with some effect once before in this context of debate,[4] although not yet – as I shall suggest below – with sufficient attention to the fundamental ways in which his thought forms question the starting assumptions of almost all of the contemporary contestants involved.

Thus in what follows I shall attempt, with the aid of John's distinctive insights, to explore afresh the reasons a creator God might have for seemingly "hiding" Godself from creaturely beings, whilst – paradoxically – actually making Godself completely and uniquely available to them all along. Crucial to this explication will be the fullest recognition (sometimes neglected or forgotten in contemporary analytic discussion) of the qualitative ontological uniqueness of a creator and cosmic sustainer God such as is acknowledged and worshipped in "classical theism." The fundamental paradox to be explored here is that what *appears* to be divine "hiding" is actually a unique form of divine self-disclosure for the purposes of redemption; but the recognition of this redemptive undertaking involves a transformative process of human response that is both subtle and enormously demanding. Without it, the true ontological state of affairs cannot be discerned.

By means of this approach I hope then to advance the contemporary philosophical discussion of divine "hiddenness" in this essay in at least two distinct ways.

The first contribution is to argue that, from the sanjuanist theological perspective that I shall here propound, the appearance of divine "hiddenness" is the effect of a human *epistemological* and *moral* condition,[5] not an ontological state of affairs that bespeaks any divine failure to communicate or self-disclose, let alone to effect an intentional withdrawal or abandonment.[6]

---

for divine obscurity or ineffability. Whilst the construction of the first problem could be called essentially modern (or at least post-Leibnizian) in its assumptions – it puts God in the dock, so to speak – a rich response to the second question may, by back-formation, nonetheless throw light on the first, albeit by calling its underlying presumptions into question. That is the strategy that will be pursued in this essay.

[4] See Garcia (2002), who does an excellent preliminary job of explaining why John of the Cross would not expect God to make Himself "very obvious to every person" (p. 95) according to the logic of the "dark nights." However, Garcia does not explore the further dimensions of John's position that I emphasize in this essay, in particular, 1. John's insistence that, despite appearances, God never actively and intentionally "hides" from us; and 2. the prime transformative epistemic significance for John of the entrance of the soul into the state of "infused contemplation."

[5] We shall need to ramify and distinguish, below, more than one reason why God may *appear* "hidden" (or "dark," in John's preferred language). These reasons are (variously) ontological, noetic, and moral.

[6] Here is my main divergence from Garcia's presumptions, and those of most commentators in the contemporary debate, who unsurprisingly focus on strands in the biblical tradition that precisely posit forms of "divine hiding," mostly associated with divine wrath (see, e.g., Deut. 31:17–18; 32:20; Isaiah 8:17; 54:8; 64:7; Ezekiel 39:23, 24; Micah 3:4; Job 13:24; 34:29; and numerous instances in the Psalms). One interesting exception to the contemporary presumptions about the problem of divine "hiddenness," qua literal, is Rea (2011), who makes a case for the supposition that "silence is nothing more or [sic] less than God's preferred mode of interactions with creatures like us" (p. 266).

On the contrary: as John insists, the idea that God has intentionally hidden Himself or rejected His creatures is an existentially understandable, but in fact quite erroneous, interpretation of the true state of affairs.[7] For God is all along lovingly protecting His creatures from a too sudden or naked encounter with Him.[8] But in order to explain how one might gain this seemingly paradoxical perspective on "divine hiddenness," a particular account of *practised* noetic loss of control to the divine ("contemplation," in John's parlance) has to be given, which is deeply antithetical to most contemporary philosophical assumptions about the self and its agency. An analysis of this complicating epistemological factor (without which the particular insights that John enjoins on us would be rendered void) will form the central point of discussion in section I. And as we shall see, this factor will turn out to have as many moral as epistemological implications. It will also have an unexpected bearing on the contemporary "atheistic" problem, given its account of the particular epistemic conditions in which God may best be understood as present to the contemplative practitioner.

The second contribution offered here (section II) goes on to explore what may be called the *incarnational* dimensions of this paradoxical perspective, something that is importantly correlative to the first point. As John of the Cross sees it, it is not just the mind that must undergo transformation in order to enjoy full intimacy with the divine, but the whole self: body and spirit.[9] At a deep level, this is the necessary implication of belief in a specifically incarnational God (a principle that John for the most part assumes rather than argues[10]). It

---

[7] This paradox is discussed with particular existential sympathy and insight in John of the Cross (1981, 395–497 (*Night*, II, in toto)). It is here, in the (second) "night" (of spirit) that *feelings* of abandonment or assault by God (and of course biblical precedents for those feelings – Jonah, Lamentations, etc., feature large in the text) are most pronounced, but analyzed by John as false renditions of an ongoing "purgation" en route to union. So John is deliberately correcting a literal rendition of such biblical accounts as divine "hiding." For more on this theme see section II.

[8] The biblical mandate for this idea is of course Exodus 33:17–23: Moses thus sees only the "backside" of God.

[9] Some clarification of John's preferred terminology of the self is important here. Drawing broadly on a Thomistic theory of the faculties, but reaching back to Augustine for a renewed emphasis on "memory" alongside "understanding" and "will," John will regularly distinguish "sense/spirit" in a mode equivalent to "body/mind" (the former however includes both outer and inner sensuality [including imagination], the latter the three faculties of memory, understanding, and will). "Soul," in contrast, is regularly used as shorthand for the *whole self* before God. It should also be mentioned that "desire" plays a special role in John's theory of ascent as a generic conative propulsion of the self that persists even when the will (to which it is closely related) is being "emptied" in the purgation of the second "night."

[10] It is often remarked how *implicit* is John's Christology throughout the *Ascent* and *Night*, and this is precisely because he is describing states that are "dark" both sensually and spiritually, just as Jesus's own human temptations and agony were dark. But since the whole point of the ascent to God is ultimately to enjoy inner-trinitarian union (as described in the *Flame*: John of the Cross, 1981, 638–731), we may take it that the reappearance of Christ as the Bridegroom in the *Spiritual Canticle* (John of the Cross, 1981, 469–630) is the result of the soul's preparatory purification, both bodily and spiritual, for such union with Him. In *Night* II, 11.4 (John of the

follows that the "dark" processes involved in moving toward union with this God are purificatory not just of the kind of intellectual responses normally associated with conscious philosophical thinking, but of what John calls the lower, "sensual" dimensions of the self. Indeed, in John's schema the purification of the mind/spirit cannot even begin until the sensual has *first* been transformed in a preparatory fashion: hence the charge of gustatory imperfection (the "spiritual gluttony" of "beginners," as mentioned above), in riposte to a particular way of stating the "problem of divine hiddenness." In order to get at this problem in any sort of appropriate way, John implies, one must start with attention to the life of the senses, and only move from there to the life of the spirit: this marks the necessary unfolding logic of any response that integrates every aspect of the self. But this transition, too, involves an existential paradox: while the senses are being purged from false attachment, it may *seem* that they are being negated or even rejected altogether in favor of the life of the spirit; indeed, John's own rhetoric often suggests that. But in fact the opposite is the case, as becomes clear only much higher up "Mount Carmel" when one can look back at the lower slopes and discern the true trajectory.[11]

Now even to outline the way this essay is set to develop is of course to invite an immediate scream of protest from our modern atheistical discussion partners – let us, in jocular shorthand, call these interlocutors the "Schellenbergers."[12] The central objection may be obvious: If the concept of God assumed in the "problem of divine hiddenness" has to be so paradoxically reconfigured in order to answer the problem, and the epistemology of religious belief equally so complexified, does not the proposed "solution" already seem to be "dying the death of a thousand qualifications"?[13] The answer to this obvious riposte

Cross, 1981, 420) John provides the implicitly incarnational rationale for the necessary transference of energy from (purged) sense to (purged) spirit in the ascent to union: "God gathers together all the strength, faculties, and appetites of the soul, spiritual and sensory alike, so the energy and power of this whole harmonious composite may be employed in ... love."

[11] See John's remarkable drawing, "the sketch of Mount Carmel" (John of the Cross, 1981, 110–11), in which he charts the principles of the ascent, by which all desires must be purged en route to union: "To come to enjoy what you have not, you must go by a way in which you know not," etc. The hinge importance of the principle of "Nada, nada" in this sketch is often misunderstood as a *rejection* of body and feelings, whereas in fact John intends that all facets of selfhood (in their purged and purified form) are ultimately taken up at the height of the mountain where "Only the honor and glory of God dwells."

[12] I hope my friend John Schellenberg will forgive this "umbrella" descriptor for a varied set of *different* arguments which have been brought against the existence of God from the seeming facts of God's "hiddenness." Indeed Schellenberg has himself offered more than one version of this argument: compare Schellenberg (1993), Schellenberg (2002), and Schellenberg (2010): the last of these braids together two different versions of the argument and so claims to strengthen it.

[13] Recall Antony Flew's classic parable (Flew, 1955) of the invisible gardener who resisted all attempts to entrap or trace him and thus to demonstrate his reality: this well-known phrase is at p. 95.

can of course only emerge in the telling. But one very significant pointer may be laid down at the outset. As John of the Cross puts it, if we are truly to understand the nature of God's *love* for His creation, and especially for the sentient and intellectual nature of humans "made in His image," we must at least allow the possibility that He desires from us something more intellectually profound, more personally and affectively pervasive, and indeed more morally demanding, than a speedy and reassuring demonstration of His mere existence. But note that for John this response does not represent a simple "soul-making" argument such as is common in the contemporary "hiddenness" and problem of evil literatures in response to atheistical critique.[14] Rather it involves an extra new theodicy twist of its own: God could *only* Himself save us from "innumerable ills," argues John, if the journey toward true knowledge and love of Him, in His ineffable intimacy, proceeded in this particular way.

We shall of course certainly want to know from John *why* this is the "only" way, according to him, for us to enjoy perfect peace and intimacy with God. Given that the route up Mt. Carmel involves so much suffering, both affective and intellectual, a new moral problem presses here, demanding an explanation that justifies this much pain for the sake of an admittedly greater good. As we shall see, John has important arguments up his sleeve on this front, and they must be weighed carefully.

But what then *is* the "problem of divine hiddenness," given this new complexity of factors for consideration? It is this that we shall now examine afresh through the lens of John's spiritual programme. As I shall argue, the ultimate effect of his approach is to dissolve the "problem" in its contemporary form, but to reconstruct it in a different, richly diachronic, and invitatory one. Nothing less than the promise of final intimacy with God is at stake.

I   Hiddenness, darkness, and epistemic asceticism: the entry into "contemplation"

John of the Cross's account of the journey of the Christian self from the state of "beginners" to that of actual "betrothal" or "union" with God involves various stages of development, which he discourses on both from the point of view of "active" human agency and from the "passive" perspective of divine grace operative on the soul. This distinction between "active" and "passive," though providing the rhetorical means of dividing the primary focus of two of his great works (*The Ascent of Mount Carmel* and *The Dark Night of the Soul*,

---

[14] See Hick (1966) for a now classic "soul-making" defense in relation to the problem of evil, with "eschatological verification" as a crucial *additum*. For a recent response specifically to the problem of "hiddenness" à la Schellenberg along such a "soul-making" trajectory, see Murray (2002).

respectively), actually breaks down in practice in John's writing, since operative and cooperative grace – to use a distinction from Thomas Aquinas with
which John was well familiar – are two sides of one coin, together drawing the
soul into progressively deeper participation in the divine. But one of the more
important features of the *heuristic* distinction between "active" and "passive,"
at any rate, is that John needs to explain to his readers at every turn the paradoxical difference between the disconcerting human feelings that accompany
these stages (ones that often seem to erode effective human agency as normally
understood) and the graced actions of God that are actually propelling the journey.[15] It is of course because John claims to write as one who has himself
traversed the territory, that he is able to distinguish between what is actually
going on in these stages and what seems to be awry.

In this light, perhaps the most important transition in the spiritual journey,
according to John, is what he terms the "entry into contemplation," the moment
when God secretly begins to infuse divine contemplation directly into the "passive intellect"[16] in order to begin the profound purgations (of sense, and then
of spirit) that may ultimately lead to union. John discourses on this transition
in three places in his oeuvre, with subtle differences in each account,[17] and he
is particularly exercised here with inept spiritual directors who may not rightly
read the signs. But the crucial matter at stake for him in each discussion is
much the same: the key importance of this transition is easy to miss, precisely
because it *feels* so disconcerting and lacking in any sort of affective or intellectual satisfaction. Prayer becomes dry, restless yet seemingly "time-wasting,"
because God is now infusing Himself directly, albeit "obscurely," into the *passive* intellect, without giving the active intellect anything specific to do:

> God conducts the soul along so different a path, and so puts it in this state, that a desire
> to work with the faculties would hinder rather than help his work; whereas in the begin-
> ning of the spiritual life everything was quite the contrary ... He therefore binds the
> interior faculties and leaves no support in the intellect, nor satisfaction in the will, nor
> remembrance in the memory. At this time a person's own efforts are of no avail, but are
> an obstacle to the interior peace and work God is producing in the spirit through the
> dryness of sense.[18]

---

[15] The contrary may also hold: seemingly positive locutions or visions may actually be the work
of the devil: see John of the Cross (1981, 178–89 (*Ascent* II, 10–12)).

[16] Note that John follows Thomas Aquinas in locating contemplation (as done by *God*) in the passive *intellect*, rather than – as in the medieval "affective Dionysians" such as Thomas Gallus
and *The Cloud of Unknowing* – in the (active) will. Bare "faith," according to John, propels the
ascent when all three mental faculties are in a state of disorientation and purification during the
second "night": see John of the Cross (1981, 177–8 (*Ascent* II, 9)).

[17] John of the Cross (1981, 189–97 (*Ascent* II, 13–15); 377–82 (*Night* I, 9–10); 685–98 (*Flame*,
3.31–62)). In the last of these discussions John is chiefly concerned to excoriate spiritual directors who do not rightly discern these signs in their directees and therefore inadvertently cause
great damage.

[18] John of the Cross (1981, 379 (*Night* I, 9.7)).

In other words, the apparent absence ("hiddenness") of God at this crucial juncture is actually His most intimate and secret presence; yet the gustatory desire for sensual satisfaction goes unrelieved, the memory and will appear lost or restless, and the intellectual desire for conscious knowledge of God (such as would be appropriate to the world of created objects) remains completely unsatisfied.[19]

And yet, John insists, the purest "knowledge" of God *is* being infused by grace in the unique way completely appropriate to the divine being: that is why he speaks of contemplation's knowledge as "general" – in the very strange sense of appearing weirdly contentless or pointless, yet simultaneously all-pervasive. But this, John teaches, is precisely the sign of its authenticity: it is a matter of learning to know God by "unknowing" – by allowing the active analytical dimensions of the intellect to be switched off during the time of prayer so that a simple "loving attention" can respond inchoately to the divine presence at work.[20] What *appears* to be all wrong in this state, then, is in fact completely right: God is now leading the soul directly, albeit secretly, into a purification first of sense and then of spirit, in preparation for full and direct union with Him, whether in this life or beyond.

It seems worth pausing at this point to reflect on the epistemological significance of this particular contemplative crux for the contemporary philosophical "hiddenness" debates.

Recall first that the chief objection of those who regard divine hiddenness as an argument *against* God's existence (regardless of whether they see this problem as merely a form of the "problem of evil" or as a problem distinct from it) is that there is no manifest appearance of God to many of those who might be interested in rationally considering His existence.[21] This assumption in fact dominates both the minimalist, aporetic, form of the problem and the more ramified, intra-traditional, version of it. But by now it may be clear that John of the Cross would almost certainly find modern empiricist anxieties about the proper conditions of assent to God's existence inapposite to the task he himself has in hand.[22] In contrast, the novel epistemic point he suggests

---

[19] This is where John's analysis of "turning inwards" is nuanced differently from Augustine's famous account in the *Confessions*, although the fundamental point is the same: God has been there all along, but we look for Him in the wrong places, running around outside ourselves.

[20] John often cites Pseudo-Dionysius in support of this position; we recall also Thomas Aquinas, *Summa Theologiae* Ia.3: "we cannot know what God is, but only what he is not," a sentiment equally influenced by the Dionysian tradition. Wynn (2013, 181–7) provides a brief but astute analysis of John of the Cross's indebtedness to Aquinas on this theme, but it should be stressed that John's direct reading of Dionysius is even more important for him.

[21] In fact this problem can be posed in various different ways: see Poston and Dougherty (2007) for a particularly astute analysis of the alternatives.

[22] And this is not just because he never seriously considers "atheism" in the modern sense (this of course makes his perspective disconcerting, or possibly just not at all *au point*, for the "Schellenberger" complainant); the more important point is that he construes the cognitive

for our own consideration is this: the ongoing purgation in contemplation requires a particular, and *practised*, undoing of the noetic instinct for autonomous human "control," and thus – at least during the time of prayer – an acknowledged *loss* of the sort of epistemic comprehension and clarity appropriate to our knowing of creaturely entities (or, for that matter, appropriate to incisive philosophical reasoning about *any particular proposition* about such entities, including the issue of whether "God exists"). Moreover, John's claim is that these are the conditions, indeed the only relevant epistemic conditions, under which a profound, albeit "obscure," new sensibility of an all-sustaining and loving *presence* of God can manifest itself. This is because John regards our epistemic apparatus as inadequate to the task of such a response until directly worked upon afresh by God. What follows, however, is that the very idea that God was previously "hiding" will now come under question: we now see that God has been there all along, lovingly sustaining us in being. These contemplative conditions, John further insists, are also the only ones under which a certain progressive transformation of the mental faculties can begin to occur en route to personal union with the divine; in other words, the "problem of divine hiddenness" will now transmute into an invitation to a *practised* epistemic transformation in response to divine grace, a practised ascetic detachment from anything *other than* God.

It follows that the purification of sensuality will be inextricably tied up with the development of virtue as well as with its own special kind of epistemic honing: as illusions and false attachments fall away,[23] so do the virtues progressively develop, climaxing in the crowning theological virtues of faith, hope, and love. The more attuned we become to the disconcertingly direct and abiding presence of God to us in infused contemplation, the more effectively we avoid idolatrous instincts and the more truly we become ourselves as God intends us to be – "free" in the paradoxical sense of having our choices strangely conformed to the divine will.

By now we have illustrated how John of the Cross complexifies and enriches the epistemological question of the perception of God's presence through his account of infused contemplation. So what exactly, then, does divine "darkness" mean for him in this ramified understanding of bodily and spiritual transformation though the contemplative path, if it does not mean "hiddenness" in the sense of our contemporary philosophical debates? John's answer to this key

conditions of the "successful" apprehension of God very differently from most contemporary traditions of analytic philosophy of religion, whether theist or atheist.

[23] For John, "false attachments" mean any investment of significance in creaturely matters at a level of priority and intensity that should be reserved solely for God. That does not mean, for instance, that anything beautiful and virtuous in the creaturely realm should not be celebrated and enjoyed *in God*; the problem comes in insidiously substituting anything creaturely, however good, for God in Godself.

question is also complex and multi-faceted. To respond to it properly we need to look in a little more detail at his account of the *two* "nights" through which the soul must pass – the night of sense and the night of spirit. At the same time we shall examine how this ("incarnational") progression from sense to spirit implicitly builds further inherent resistances to asking the wrong kind of philosophical questions about God's "hiddenness."

II "Darkness" in the night of sense and the night of spirit

One of the aspects of John's account of the entry into the "nights" that often creates confusion is his announcement, at the start of the *Ascent*, that *all* "attachments" to sense must be obliterated if the soul is to advance to a state of "proficiency."[24] This can easily be read as a straightforward rejection of the body and sensuality, just as the equivalent "Nada, nada" ("not this, not that") as applied to spiritual goals may also strike the reader as *literally* "annihilating" of selfhood at its core. But John's disjunctive rhetoric here is hyperbolic for a reason: he wishes above all to underscore the necessary and radical nature of the uprooting of *falsely directed* desires, precisely in order to preserve *dispossessed* desire as the true and animating force of the ascent to union. The scheme of the successive nights, therefore, is to purge sensuality, first, of false outward attachments in order to transfer the gains of that purification to the inner realm of spirit. Here, and secondly, takes place a rarer and more terrible purgation, as the inner spirit too is darkened and emptied of all familiar content: "This is precisely what the divine ray of contemplation does. In striking the soul with its divine light, it surpasses the natural light and thereby darkens and deprives the soul of all natural affections and apprehensions it perceived by means of its natural light."[25] The reason for this (apparently tortuous) procedure is the necessary habituation of the soul to this new intimacy with the transcendent God, and the necessary purification of it from its habitual sins. But the final goal of these various purgations is the full and triumphant return of sensuality and spirit in new and transformed guise: the soul will now be ready to meet the Bridegroom Christ, and to be knit completely into the trinitarian life of the Godhead.[26]

Taken together, then, the two nights slowly effect a painful erasure not only of the noetic, but also the moral, effects of the Fall. The night of spirit, in

[24] See esp. John of the Cross (1981, 127–30, 147–50 (*Ascent* 1.5 and 1.13)).
[25] John of the Cross (1981, 411 (*Night* II, 8.4)); the hyperbolic language of "annihilation" is repeatedly used here: see for example (1981, 410 (*Night* II, 8.3)).
[26] It is in the *Spiritual Canticle* that Christ is mainly characterized as the bridegroom: see esp., at the climax of the ascent, John of the Cross (1981, 628–30 (*Canticle*, Stanza 40)). The most explicit description of union in inner-trinitarian terms is to be found in John of the Cross (1981, 622–8 (*Canticle*, 39) and 715 (*Flame*, 4.17)).

particular, penetrates deep into the hidden faults of the memory, the understanding, and the will in order to burn them, spitting, out of the wood and
into the flame of divine love.[27] Yet John remains insistent, throughout his close
description of the terrible trials of the second night, that what is *felt* as divine
"abandonment" or divine "affliction" is actually nothing less than the light,
caressing touch of divine love: it only feels the way it does on account of the
still imperfect form of its reception.[28] When the infusion of divine grace has
finally worn away all resistance, the soul may participate truly in the love that
is eternally shared between Father and Son by the Spirit, breathing in and out
that same "breath" between them.[29]

We are now in a better position to clarify the different senses in which John
has to speak of God as "dark" to us (or "hidden," if taken metaphorically,
as John would construe it). Fortunately John himself explicitly distinguishes
between the two most important understandings of divine "darkness" he
espouses: one, we may say, is ontological, and the other epistemic and moral.
And this represents John's own particular blend of different strands from both
Eastern and Western Christian traditions about "darkness." Thus, when describing the afflictions of the second night of spirit, he remarks: "there are two reasons why ... divine wisdom is not only night and darkness for the soul, but
also affliction and torment. First, because of the height of the divine wisdom
which exceeds the capacity of the soul. Second, because of the soul's baseness
and impurity; and on this account it is painful, afflictive, and also dark for the
soul."[30] In other words, the primary reason for "darkness" is the intrinsic ontological "otherness" and ineffability of the divine: to speak in the language of
the psalmist, this is the God who "makes darkness his secret place" (Ps. 18:11),
or, in Aquinas's terms (as cited above), the One of whom we can only, strictly
speaking, say what he is not. Here John recapitulates and extends the tradition
of Philo, Nyssen, and Pseudo-Dionysius on the ineffable nature of the divine
being, as already received into the Western scholastic tradition, and gives it
his own particular flavor. But the secondary reason for "darkness," according
to John, is no less important, and it is the direct effect of the seriousness of the
Fall as construed by Augustine: both the noetic and moral implications of sin
mean that – for us – divine love is mistakenly *felt* as judgment and affliction
until the full purgation of sense and spirit is complete. Indeed, the higher we
ascend in the second "night" (of spirit) the more painfully do we become aware
of our own depravity. Mercifully, therefore, and almost by inversion, there is

---

[27] John of the Cross (1981, 416–18 (*Night* II, 10)).
[28] See John of the Cross (1981, 403 (*Night* II, 6.7)).
[29] John of the Cross (1981, 622–3 (*Canticle*, 39. 3)).
[30] John of the Cross (1981, 401 (*Night* II, 5.2)). There is an illuminating discussion of the patristic
      sources of John's thought here, and the extent to which his rendition is novel, in Louth (1981,
      ch. 9).

also one final reason for "darkness" in relation to God, according to John: this is God's loving protection of us from the full force of His direct presence, until the time for union is right. Thus, toward the end of the *Living Flame of Love* John reminds us: "It should be known that God dwells secretly in all souls and is hidden in their substance, for otherwise they would not last."[31] So the problem then is not that God has ever gone away or is deliberately unavailable to us, but that there are only certain conditions under which his unfailing but secret presence is progressively made manifest to His creatures. Admittedly, not all will respond with equal solicitude or speed to the demands of those conditions.[32] But John is insistent that what undergirds these differences is the loving concern and protection of God Himself. Since it is a "fearful thing to fall into the hands of the living God" (Hebrews 10:31), God never distresses us by too sudden or stark a revelation of Himself, but "rightly, discreetly, and lovingly" prepares the ground first. This too is part of what we may (mistakenly) perceive as "the problem of divine hiddenness." Far from being a problem, this last factor is a blessing.

In sum, there are at least these three forms of "darkness" in John's unique account of the divine presence to us: the darkness intrinsic to our inherent human incapacity to grasp transcendent divine otherness; the darkness caused by fallen human inadequacy and depravity, both noetic and moral; and the protective darkness with which God intentionally and lovingly shields the unready soul until the time has come to meet Him face to face. *None* of these factors, we note again in closing, equates precisely to the particular modern concern about "hiddenness" with which our investigation began. The task now remains to draw some conclusions for that debate from John of the Cross's insights.

Conclusions: "rightly and discreetly and lovingly"

The central argument of this paper, as stated at the outset, is that the effect of John of the Cross's approach to divine darkness, if judged cogent and convincing, is to "dissolve the [problem of divine hiddenness] in its contemporary form, but to reconstruct it in a different, richly diachronic, and invitatory one." This general ploy in countering some of John Schellenberger's earlier statements of the problem is not of course new. Others have suggested that the problem is not cogently parsed in the first place;[33] or that it assumes things about the "God" (which it does not believe in) that are fundamentally open to question.[34]

---

[31] John of the Cross (1981, 713 (*Flame*, 4.14)).

[32] John of the Cross (1981, 713 (*Flame*, 4.14)).

[33] Kvanvig (2002, 162) argues that the "evidential value of hiddenness" cannot do "any epistemic work" because it is "merely epiphenomenal."

[34] See Rea (2011), who counters the supposition that a loving God would necessarily want to communicate with us in some explicit and obvious way.

Others too, have riposted with alternative narratives or scenarios that complexify and transform the question in ways somewhat parallel to John's account: by focussing on God's protection of human libertarian freedom;[35] by insisting on the necessity of a narrative of diachronic journeying;[36] by stressing the importance of an affective as well as a noetic response to God;[37] and by alerting us to the ever-present dangers of idolatry in such a philosophical debate.[38] Where John's account goes beyond these existing defenses, as I trust this essay has demonstrated, is both in its insistence that the characteristic atheist anxiety over divine absence is ultimately illusory, and also in its promise that there is a clear, *practised* pathway for responding to the apparent crisis of "hiddenness." The rich detail John brings to this narrative response, as we have seen, is no less significant: his is a God who is "dark" to us for several, discrete, and very profound theological reasons, but who also wants us *whole* – body and spirit – as He remolds us by degrees into the likeness of his Son, knitting us finally into the very life of the Trinity. Finally, key to an understanding of John's perspective is the crucial epistemological complication engendered by the divine infusion of contemplation. Our epistemic capacities are themselves in transit under grace, according to John – themselves *in via* as we struggle toward the divine goal. It follows that the "rational" considerations we bring to this debate will subtly shift as the journey continues.

But what on earth, we must press in closing, would an avowed atheist such as Schellenberg make of such a complex alternative metanarrative of grace such as John of the Cross supplies?[39] Does it not simply resummon the old problems of Flew's evasive gardener God, as mentioned at the outset, whose

[35] See Murray (2002, 63–6) on the importance of "morally significant [human] freedom" as a defense against the divine hiddenness critique; though it should be noted that John's account of freedom, as already mentioned, differs markedly from that of a modern incompatibilist.

[36] Again, see Murray (2002) for a detailed response to Schellenberg along the lines of a necessarily diachronic "soul-making" trajectory, and Garcia (2002), who provides a preliminary account of John of the Cross's narrative of "ascent."

[37] See Moser (2002, esp. 140), on the importance of divine love in converting the soul, rather than merely "drawing inferences."

[38] Moser (2002, esp. 135–7) also stresses the problem of "cognitive idolatry" in the "hiddenness" debates as defined by Schellenberg. Schellenberg has replied to a good number of the critiques mentioned here in Schellenberg (2005a and 2005b).

[39] In fact Schellenberg has several times in his writing briefly mentioned the issue of the "the dark night of the soul" (see, e.g., Schellenberg, 1993, 203–4; 2005b, 299–301; 2007, 217–18; chapter 1, this volume); but his claim is that appeals to it do not touch his own argument against God because they merely *assume* God's existence as given, prior to His apparent withdrawal from our "experience." My own riposte here is that that very response again begs the question: A general, restless concern about God's apparent non-existence (and Schellenberg has surely written enough on this topic to exhibit such a restless concern!) might well indicate, from John of the Cross's perspective, a challenge to change the terms and conditions of the questioning to a posture of receptive waiting. Note that this response to Schellenberg is subtly different from the argument from the cognitive benefit of doubts, to which Schellenberg has responded in Schellenberg (2005a and 2005b).

"presence" constantly slipped through all attempts to capture Him by ever more evasive manoeuvers and re-descriptions? If so, are we perhaps consigned to an inevitable impasse between believers and nonbelievers on the topic of "hiddenness" such as evoked by Richard Hare in his own latterday response to Flew: is it, as Hare suggested there, an irreducible matter of *blik* whether we see the world as suffused with the glory of God, whether we "mind" in this sense about whether there is a God or not, and so are moved to consider His existence with something other than mere skeptical aloofness?[40]

My suggestion is that there do remain several possible avenues of fruitful exploration with the atheist detractor in the light of John of the Cross's particular insights, ones which might at least open up new arenas of discussion rather than leaving the contestants in irresolvable *blik* conflict; and these are therefore worth enumerating briefly in closing. Of course, if the arguments from the atheist side remain *dogmatic*, that is, resistant in principle to changing the presumptions or principles of the debate, then there is unlikely to be any worthwhile exchange. But let us proceed on the presumption that the atheist in question is at least broad-minded enough to entertain such possibilities of change. If so, these are the questions that might at least intrigue him, since they constitute the heart of John of the Cross's "invitatory" reconstruction of the modern "hiddenness" problem. (Note that the *force* of these considerations are for now precisely as John of the Cross would want them: invitatory rather than rationally conclusive.)

Thus I now propose three considerations for final reflection.

First, as many others have remarked before me, the "hiddenness" problem as posed in its initial form by Schellenberg was open to critique as to the unclarified meaning of some of its key terms. Recall the original formulation in its barest outline:

(1) If there is a God, He is perfectly loving.
(2) If a perfectly loving God exists, reasonable nonbelief does not occur.
(3) Reasonable nonbelief does occur. Thus,
(4) No perfectly loving God exists. So,
(5) There is no God.[41]

But this original statement of the aporia begs particular questions about its second premise, as many have commented: we need to know with some precision what "reasonable nonbelief" *is* in order to assess the force of the argument. But why, in any case, *need* the mere the existence of "nonbelief" always and necessarily be incompatible with the will of a perfectly loving God? (Answer: it

---

[40] See Hare (1955) and note Basil Mitchell's comment (1955, 105): "of course, you can't have reasons for *bliks*."

[41] See Schellenberg (1993, 83; also 7).

will depend vitally what "story" is being told about this God and His ways with humans.) It has also been noted that the relation of the second to the third premise can be similarly problematic, again depending on the rendition of "reasonable nonbelief." As Poston and Dougherty argue, "In order for (2) to be true the reading of 'reasonable nonbelief' would have to be so strong that we have no reason to believe the reinterpreted (3)."[42] On either of these scenarios, then, the key matter at stake is the parsing of "reasonable nonbelief." And in order to get to the bottom of what this might mean (on various renditions), *some* kind of "story" of relationship with a putative God is already necessarily in play. Thus what seems initially like a mere logical puzzle inexorably opens out into a debate about one sort of theological narrative or another. As Adam Green has well put it: "I find it plausible to suppose that the issue of hiddenness *only really arises* when we posit the existence of a personal God who is interested in us."[43]

Now, as we have already noted, Schellenberg has himself conceded in the past that one such story of relationship between God and humans that *might* be told is that of "the dark night of the soul." So in order to disambiguate his key premises, he at least owes it to his interlocutor to consider the possible virtues of a rich ontological and epistemological story such as John of the Cross's.[44] Further, it is not reasonable to rule it out simply because it is a *complex* story. Occam's razor notwithstanding, this particular story still might in principle provide the most richly convincing rendition of the crucial variables in the original problem ("a perfectly loving God," and a "reasonable nonbelief"), such that the dilemma could be resolved. So the sanjuanist account is at least worthy of careful consideration.

Secondly, as we have stressed throughout this paper, a key component in John of the Cross's story is one of spiritual *practice*, specifically the practice of prayer in the form of contemplation. It is here that things get a little more tricky (and simultaneously more interesting). What impact, if any, on the contemporary debate on "hiddenness" should insights gained from particular *practices* have? Recall (see section I) that for John himself the entry into "contemplation" provides the crucial epistemological hinge from which his other judgments about "darkness" (sensual, spiritual) follow. Yet for him the "infused" practice of contemplation is first and foremost an act of divine grace, not a human skill that one may choose to explore to expand one's range of (say) leisure pursuits or relaxation techniques. So in what way, if at all, could

---

[42] Poston and Dougherty (2007, 184).

[43] Green (chapter 8, this volume, my emphasis).

[44] In principle, Schellenberg acknowledges this (see, e.g., Schellenberg, 2005b, 299); but he insists that John's account is not to the point because it already "requires" that "God's existence is beyond reasonable non-belief." It is just this claim of Schellenberg's that I am querying.

the atheist reasonably allow that his "hiddenness" argument be affected by the purported insights of contemplative practice such as this?

There is, I suggest, one possible answer to this dilemma, but it involves departing somewhat from John of the Cross's own account of contemplation as essentially (and solely) "infused." Both in earlier, medieval traditions of "mystical theology" (such as the *Cloud of Unknowing*), and in later modifications of John's teaching (such as in the teaching of the Welsh Benedictine Augustine Baker), practices of so-called "acquired contemplation" have been developed for beginners in which the human will itself activates a preliminary practice of "naked" loving attention to God, as far as possible devoid of any active intellectual engagement. In most ways the *epistemic* effects of such contemplation, long-term, are closely akin to what John of the Cross describes at a higher stage of spiritual advance. That is, a sensibility is gradually developed of knowing by unknowing in which the strange epistemic blankness of the undertaking is nonetheless perceived as revelatory of an obscure but enduring divine sustenance.[45] Whilst this is not clearly a discrete "religious experience" in any of the senses regularly invoked in the literature of analytic philosophy of religion, it is arguable that it nonetheless deserves to be treated with similar respect for its potential veridical force.[46]

To a skeptical atheist such as Schellenberg, of course, such a practice might seem merely to reinforce beliefs already acquired elsewhere, in short to be obviously and viciously circular. But in fact the testimony of those engaged in such practice is more commonly that – over time, or even quite quickly – they are destabilitzed out of fixed or dogmatic patterns of thinking, forced to reconsider in considerable depth the nature and reality of what it is that they claim to believe, and drawn to reconceive their very notion of an "experience" of God.[47] Moreover, the practice here described as "acquired contemplation" is in principle open to those with various religious beliefs or none: sometimes, for instance, it may be packaged as a secular form of "mindfulness" or "relaxation response," or an opportunity to replenish the mind by a re-engagement with the creative "right brain" hemisphere. Therefore, one might well issue the

---

[45] The contemporary American Cistercian Thomas Keating, one of the founders of the Centering Prayer movement, gives accurate and clear teaching on this phenomenon, drawing on the *Cloud of Unknowing*, John of the Cross, and several of John's twentieth-century interpreters, especially the Benedictine John Chapman: see Keating (1995, esp. chs. 8, 9).

[46] I have argued this point in some detail (though in relation to the work of John's senior Carmelite friend and advisee Teresa of Ávila) in Coakley (2009), where I bring Teresa into conversation with the later religious epistemology of William P. Alston. The criterion of "spiritual fruits" is crucial for Teresa as a justificatory tool, just as it is also for John.

[47] These features of contemplative practice are described with considerable philosophical sophistication in Foster (2015, esp. chs. 1, 4). Foster's analysis is particularly apropos to the discussion in this paper given that Foster faces squarely the difficulty *phenomenologically* of distinguishing the epistemic oddity of contemplative experience from a presumption of atheism.

invitation to one such as Schellenberg: "Taste and see." The point here is that a particular *practice* may yield interesting epistemic rewards in a way unavailable to standard active, analytic thought. To be sure, even such an undertaking as "acquired contemplation" takes considerable application of time and commitment, and the upheavals of self-knowledge that it tends to bring in its wake are not easy to interpret without pre-assuming (or re-choosing) one set of hermeneutical tools or another – whether psychoanalytic, or religious, or both. Nonetheless, that such a practice as this does bring about significant epistemic change (new levels of unified attention, new awareness of unconscious motivation, new capacities of intuitive insight, at the very least) is widely attested to by those both inside and outside the Christian fold. In short, the very idea of "knowing by unknowing," so crucial to understanding John of the Cross's distinctive inversion of the usual "problem" of divine "hiddenness" is in principle open to preliminary investigation by spiritual "beginners," even by those who are intrinsically skeptical about the existence of the very God who is under question. The invitation to such a practice, then, is rather like one offered to someone who in adulthood has never learned to swim: to stop arguing about the counterintuitive evidence for whether the water will hold one up, and give it a try. For if John of the Cross's narrative is to be believed even in outline, the potential thereby for radically changing the way that divine "darkness"/"hiddenness" and the problem of God's existence *should* be construed is inestimable. At the very least there is epistemic territory to be explored here.[48]

Finally, and thirdly, I offer the "Schellenberger" a kind of peace trophy, a doubtless unexpected bonus from the investigation we have here pursued. It is sometimes suggested that the various waves of modern secular atheism in the nineteenth and twentieth centuries themselves effected a kind of religious and cultural "purgation" somewhat akin to the searing effects of John of the Cross's "dark nights."[49] The God that John of the Cross does not believe in (the idolatrous God finally left behind in the successive detachments of the "Nada, nada") is perhaps closely, and ironically, akin to the God whom Schellenberg also rejects, whose failure to eradicate rational human doubts about His existence supposedly demonstrates His very non-existence. There is, therefore, a final irony in these "hiddenness" debates that perhaps the perspective of

---

[48] Of course, a "Schellenberger" might take up such a practice in a secular frame, and – on encountering certain intuitions of a sustaining unitary ground in the practice – nonetheless choose to explain this in neurophysiological or psychoanalytic terms, or perhaps in nontheistic Buddhist terms. Still, a bridge of communication would at least have opened up here for a further hermeneutical discussion of such states and their epistemological significance. What is "obscurely" sensed in such practice is not so much "hidden" as regrettably ignored until relevant states of attention are entered into voluntarily.

[49] See Buckley (1979), a remarkable essay which deserves to be more widely known.

John of the Cross alone detects; for from his position the skeptical atheist of Schellenberg's stripe might seem already some way along the true path of sensual purgation and detachment. Thus, although he seemingly asks, with the "spiritual gluttony" of a "beginner," for manifest signs of God's presence (see above), his response to dissatisfaction in this area arguably manifests an instinct "not far from the kingdom." In short, the God that Schellenberg does not believe in is certainly one that John of the Cross would not believe in either. In this sense, Schellenberg's debate has cleared space precisely for a possible adventure into dark intimacy to which John, "rightly, discreetly, and lovingly" continues to invite us.

14 Silence, evil, and Shusaku Endo

Yujin Nagasawa

1 Introduction

Philosophers of religion have discussed divine hiddenness intensively in recent decades. They have focused their debate primarily on God's apparent hiddenness from nonresistant nonbelievers (Howard-Snyder and Moser, 2002; Schellenberg, 1993).[1] My interest in this chapter, however, is on God's hiddenness from *devout believers*. I develop and discuss what I call the "problem of divine absence," which is a combination of the most intense form of the problem of divine hiddenness and the most intense form of the problem of evil. The problem of divine absence raises a challenge for belief in God through a scenario in which devout believers experience severe pain and suffering without understanding why God remains hidden and fails to respond to their desperate agony and pleas for help. I consider the problem of divine absence in light of historical events in seventeenth-century Japan, which are vividly described in Shusaku Endo's novel *Silence*. I argue that theodicies are of little use in solving the problem of divine absence because merely demonstrating the logical consistency of the existence of God with a state of affairs involving divine absence does not eliminate the experiential part of the problem. That is, the puzzlement and agony that arise in the experience of pain and suffering cannot be eliminated by logical reasoning. I propose a radically different way of approaching the problem. While the proposed approach does not *solve* the problem it does suggest how theists might be able to *respond* to it without giving up their faith.

This chapter has the following structure. In section 2, I describe the persecution of the Kakure Kirishitans, or Hidden Christians, in seventeenth-century Japan through Endo's *Silence*. I explain in detail how much pain and suffering the Kakure Kirishitans had to endure. In section 3, I explain the structure of

I presented an earlier version of this paper to the Faculty of Theology at the University of Uppsala. I would like to thank the audience, consisting of Mikael Stenmark, Ulf Zackariasson, and their students. I am particularly grateful to the editors of this volume, Adam Green and Eleonore Stump, for their helpful written comments.

[1] For recent works on divine hiddenness see Howard-Snyder and Moser (2002) and Schellenberg (1993).

the problem of divine absence and point out how it is exemplified in the cases involving the Kakure Kirishitans. In section 4, I address the persistence of the problem of divine absence. I distinguish between the intellectual and experiential problems of divine absence and argue that no theodicy can solve the experiential problem because that problem is not concerned with logical consistency between the existence of God and His absence. In section 5, I develop a response to the experiential problem, a response which diverges radically from the strategic approach entailed in theodicies. I base this response on Endo's unique way of understanding the nature of religion and the essence of religious faith. Section 6 concludes.[2]

2   Persecution of Kakure Kirishitans

In seventeenth-century Japan, Kakure Kirishitans, or Hidden Christians, were persecuted. In order to smoke out the underground Christians, security officials forced people to step on a *fumie*, a plate featuring iconography of Jesus or Mary, to prove that they were not Christians. Those who refused to do so were imprisoned and severely tortured.

In an early phase of this campaign of persecution, Kakure Kirishitans who refused to give up their faith were killed by decapitation, crucifixion, or execution by burning at the stake. However, the security officials came to believe that these methods of execution were too "easy" – they did not involve sufficient pain and suffering. Also, in some cases methods of martyrdom were visually impressive and encouraged other Kakure Kirishitans not to give up their faith. Hence, the officials introduced slower, more painful, and more dreadful methods of torturing Kakure Kirishitans.

For instance, they made sure that the process of burning the Kakure Kirishitans at the stake would go slowly. They kept a certain distance between the firewood and the victims' bodies or rotated their bodies while burning them to prolong their pain and suffering. It is reported that smoke rose from their mouths as their bodies burned internally. The officials also made the Kakure Kirishitans wear straw capes, which they set on fire while their victims were still alive. The Japanese authorities called this the "straw cape dance" because it caused the victims' bodies to shake as if they were dancing. They also amputated fingers, noses, and ears of the Kakure Kirishitans. They poured boiling water onto them from a sulphur spring at the Unzen Volcano in Nagasaki. The victims usually lost consciousness and were severely burnt, after which they were treated; and once they were healed they were tortured again in the same way. Some Kakure Kirishitans were soaked in frozen ponds and if they lost

---

[2] Apart from passages from William Johnson's translation of *Silence*, I translate all passages from the Japanese works cited in this chapter.

consciousness the security officials rescued them and warmed their bodies only to be soaked in the frozen water again. The methods of torture also included being stuffed into straw bags with their heads exposed, piled together, and whipped; being tied to pillars and having their necks slashed with knives; and having bamboo saws left next to them so that passers-by could saw their necks, making for a slow and painful death because bamboo saws are not as sharp as metal saws. Among the most "effective" methods of torture was *anazuri*, which involved hanging Kakure Kirishitans upside down in pits and punching holes through their ears so that they would bleed slowly and not die too quickly, succumbing as their heads became congested with blood. During this process the victims' bodies were bound tightly with ropes to prevent their organs from sagging within their bodies and the complete darkness of the pits added an extra measure of fear.

It is important to note that the aim of the security officials in applying such cruelly painful techniques was to make the Kakure Kirishitans renounce their faith rather than kill them in punishment. This feature and the fact that a large number of Christians were martyred in a relatively short period make these cases unique. Hirofumi Yamamoto remarks, "The martyrdoms in Japan are unique in history. Apart from the time when Christians were persecuted in the Roman Empire, there has hardly been any twenty-year period in history in which over 4,000 people were martyred." In the early seventeenth century, Japan's population was twenty million, among whom 450,000 were said to be Christians. It is difficult to estimate the exact number of Kakure Kirishitans who were martyred but 4,045 cases are reported in print. Some scholars estimate that as many as 40,000 Kakure Kirishitans were martyred (Miyazaki, 1995).

Endo's novel *Silence* (1980, originally 1969) – which was made into a movie in Japan in 1971 by the director Masahiro Shinoda and is currently being filmed in Hollywood by Martin Scorsese – vividly describes the agony of the Christians who were tortured.[3] One of the key characters in *Silence* is Cristóvão Ferreira, a historical figure who came to Japan from Portugal as a Jesuit missionary. He apostatized after being tortured by *anazuri* for five hours. Later he was given a Japanese name, Chuan Sawano, and married a Japanese woman. He published a book criticizing Christianity and contributed to the crackdown against the Kakure Kirishitans.

The main character of *Silence* is Ferreira's disciple, a Portuguese Jesuit named Sebastião Rodrigues. He is a fictional character but is modeled on the historical figure Giuseppe Chiara from Italy. Like Ferreira, Rodrigues is arrested and severely toured. He initially hopes to experience glorious

---

[3] Philip L. Quinn (1989) discusses Endo's *Silence*, but apart from that there are very few philosophical discussions of Endo's novels. This is surprising given the philosophical content of *Silence* and many other Endo novels.

martyrdom. However, he hears the groaning voices of Japanese Christian peasants being tortured. Rodrigues asks, "Why is God continually silent while those
groaning voices go on? ... Why do these people not apostatise?" The security
official laughs and answers, "They have already apostatised many times. But
as long as you don't apostatise these peasants cannot be saved" (pp. 168–9).
Throughout the novel the silence of God torments Rodrigues and makes him
question God's existence. Rodrigues wants God to break the silence and rescue the tortured. Failing that, Rodrigues wants Him at least to explain why He
cannot do it:

Why have you abandoned us so completely?, he prayed in a weak voice. Even the village was constructed for you; and have you abandoned it in its ashes? Even when the
people are cast out of their homes have you not given them courage? Have you just
remained silent like the darkness that surrounds me? Why? At least tell me why. We are
not strong men like Job who was afflicted with leprosy as a trial. There is a limit to our
endurance. Give us no more suffering. (Endo, 1980, 96)

Rodrigues's deep perplexity about God's silence increases as he witnesses a
seemingly endless series of Kakure Kirishitan deaths. He cannot bear it and
eventually decides to trample on *fumie* of Jesus to renounce his faith:

The priest raises his foot. In it he feels a dull, heavy pain. This is no mere formality. He
will now trample on what he has considered the most beautiful thing in his life, on what
he has believed most pure, on what is filled with the ideals and the dreams of man. How
his foot aches! ... The priest placed his foot on the *fumie*. Dawn broke. And far in the
distance the cock crew. (Endo, 1980, 171)

3   The problem of divine absence

I have focused on the cases of the Kakure Kirishitans described in *Silence*
because they vividly illustrate the problem of divine absence. Divine absence
is defined as a form of divine hiddenness from devout believers who suffer
from horrendous evil. I believe that the problem of divine absence constitutes
one of the greatest challenges for theists because it involves (i) horrendous
evil as opposed to ordinary evil; (ii) divine hiddenness from devout believers
as opposed to divine hiddenness from ordinary believers or nonbelievers; and
(iii) the simultaneous, intertwined occurrence of horrendous evil and divine
hiddenness from devout believers.

Let me explain how these three features are realized in the cases of the
Kakure Kirishitans.

(i) Horrendous evil, as opposed to ordinary evil, occurs

The problem of evil is often cited as the greatest challenge for theists.
However, the force of the problem varies substantially depending on which

type of evil is involved. The problem of evil is most forceful when it is formulated in terms of what Marilyn Adams calls "horrendous evil." Adams defines horrendous evil as a form of evil "the participation in which (that is, the doing or suffering of which) constitutes prima facie reason to doubt whether the participant's life could (given their inclusion in it) be a great good to him/her on the whole" (1999, p. 26). Adams's examples of horrendous evil include "the rape of a woman and axing off of her arms, psycho-physical torture whose ultimate goal is the disintegration of personality, betrayal of one's deepest loyalties, child abuse of the sort described by Ivan Karamazov, child pornography, parental incest, slow death by starvation, [and] the explosion of nuclear bombs over populated areas" (p. 26). While we might be comfortable believing that God allows a state of affairs to obtain that involves relatively minor mishaps (perhaps in order to instantiate greater goods), it is much more difficult to believe that God allows a state of affairs to obtain that involves utterly awful pain and suffering – so awful that it makes us doubt that a participant's (especially the victim's) life could be a great good to him or her on the whole. The problem of divine absence is so forceful because it involves horrendous evil as opposed to ordinary evil. As we saw in section 2, the Kakure Kirishitans underwent horrific tortures, such as being hanged in *amazuri* for hours, being burnt to death slowly, and being axed at the neck. These are instantiations of horrendous evil.

(ii) Divine hiddenness from devout believers, as opposed to divine hiddenness from ordinary believers or nonbelievers, occurs

As I mentioned earlier, the philosophical debate on divine hiddenness has focused primarily on God's hiddenness from *nonresistant nonbelievers* (Howard-Snyder and Moser, 2002; Schellenberg, 1993). This is because theists often claim that God is not hidden from believers and that God has reasons not to reveal himself to resistant nonbelievers. However, the problem of divine hiddenness is most forceful when it is formulated in terms of God's hiddenness from devout believers. Why God is hidden from nonresistant nonbelievers is certainly puzzling but why God is hidden even from many devout believers, some of whom are prepared to sacrifice their lives for God, is more puzzling. Hence, just as the problem of evil can be strengthened by formulating it in terms of horrendous evil rather than ordinary evil, so the problem of hiddenness can be strengthened by formulating it in terms of God's hiddenness from devout believers rather than ordinary believers or nonbelievers.

The focus of *Silence* is indeed on God's hiddenness from devout believers. What Rodrigues finds puzzling is that God remains hidden even from devout Kakure Kirishitans who are prepared to die for God:

What he [Rodrigues] could not understand was the stillness of the courtyard, the voice of the cicada, the whirling wings of the flies. A [Kakure Kirishitan] man had died. Yet the outside world went on as if nothing had happened. Could anything be more crazy? Was this martyrdom? Why are you silent? Here this one-eyed man has died – *and for you.* You ought to know. Why does this stillness continue? This noon-day stillness. The sound of the flies – this crazy thing, this cruel business. And you avert your face as though indifferent. This ... this I cannot bear... Do not abandon me in this mysterious way. (Endo, 1980, 119, emphasis added)

The one-eyed man, a devout believer, is executed with a sword for refusing to renounce his faith. As Rodrigues remarks, it is utterly puzzling why God remains completely hidden even when someone is willing to die *for Him.* God's hiddenness with respect to such a death is particularly difficult to understand.

(iii) Horrendous evil and divine hiddenness from devout believers are intertwined and occur simultaneously

Divine absence takes place when the above two features (i) and (ii) are intertwined and occur simultaneously. Devout believers in these cases suffer from horrendous evil without understanding why God remains silent despite their severe pain and suffering. The horrendous evil and the divine hiddenness enhance each other, creating great perplexities for believers. The presence of horrendous evil alone (despite the existence of God) is puzzling enough. God's hiddenness from devout believers alone is puzzling enough. God's hiddenness from devout believers despite their experience of horrendous evil is doubly puzzling.

Ferreira apostatized not because he could not bear the torture, the horrendous evil, or divine hiddenness in general. He apostatized because he could not bear God's hiddenness with respect to horrendous evil that devout believers, such as himself and his fellow Kakure Kirishitans, had to endure. In the novel, Ferreira explains to Rodrigues:

Listening to those groans all night I was no longer able to give praise to the Lord. I did not apostatise because I was suspended in the pit. For three days, I who stand before you was hung in a pit of foul excrement, but I did not say a single word that might betray my God ... The reason I apostatised ... are you ready? Listen! I was put in here and heard the voice of those people for whom God did nothing. God did not do a single thing. I prayed with all my strength; but God did nothing. (Endo, 1980, 167–8)

It is interesting to note that the simultaneous occurrence of divine hiddenness and evil (not necessarily horrendous evil) is described in the Bible as well. In fact, most examples of divine hiddenness found in the Bible involve the combination of divine hiddenness and evil, rather than divine hiddenness alone: "Why standest thou afar off, O Lord? why hidest thou thyself in times of trouble?" (Ps. 10:1); "Awake, why sleepest thou, O Lord? arise, cast us not off for ever. Wherefore hidest thou thy face, and forgettest our affliction and our oppression? For our soul is bowed down to the dust: our belly cleaveth unto the earth" (Ps. 44:23–5). These passages seem to agree that God's hiddenness is puzzling particularly for believers who are in "times of trouble," suffering "affliction" and "oppression."

4   The intellectual problem and the experiential problem

The problem of divine absence can be presented as two distinct problems: an intellectual problem and an experiential problem. The intellectual problem, as I call it, which is formulated from a third-person perspective, involves logical consistency between the existence of God and the occurrence of divine absence. It asks how it is logically possible that an omnipotent and morally perfect God remains silent when devout believers suffer from horrendous evil. (There is also a version of the intellectual problem that is concerned with whether or not divine absence constitutes good *evidence* against the existence of God. In what follows I focus, for the sake of simplicity, on logical consistency when I address the intellectual problem. My claims, however, apply equally to the question regarding evidence.) On the other hand, the experiential problem, which is formulated from a first-person perspective, involves emotional puzzlement and confusion about divine absence. It asks God why He remains silent and abandons devout believers who suffer from horrendous evil.

Over the years theists have developed many theodicies in response to the problem of evil. One might wonder if we can apply theodicies to the problem of divine absence as well. Consider, for example, the free will theodicy, which is arguably among the most popular. If the free will theodicy is applied to the problem of divine absence, it would say, roughly speaking, that free humans, rather than God, are morally responsible for horrendous evil and that God has to remain hidden from the victims of the horrendous evil because not doing so would undermine their free will. That is, horrendous evil is a consequence of human free will and divine absence is a necessary condition for maintaining human free will. To take another example, if the soul-making theodicy is applied to the problem of divine absence, it would say, roughly speaking, that God has to allow horrendous evil and remain hidden if humans are to grow spiritually. That is, both horrendous evil and divine hiddenness are necessary conditions for humans to cultivate their spirituality. However, these responses address only the intellectual aspect of divine absence, which is, again, concerned with logical consistency between the existence of God and the occurrence of divine absence. It does not answer the experiential problem, which goes beyond the question of logical consistency.

The question "Why is God silent in response to our pain and suffering?" – which Ferreira and Rodrigues pose in agony – should not be interpreted as equivalent to the consistency question: "How is it logically possible that God both exists and remains silent when we, devout believers, are in pain and suffering?" Ferreira and Rodrigues do not mean to raise a question for which someone can provide an intellectual answer from a third-person perspective. They raise a question *for God* who remains silent despite their pain and suffering. The above question should, therefore, be interpreted as a plea for help from a first-person perspective: "God, why are you silent? If you exist, you should not be. Help us or at least explain to us why you cannot help us. Present your existence to us."

Consider a parallel example. Suppose that a child is in trouble. She believes that her parents can easily help her and are willing to help her. However, her parents remain silent. The child asks, "Why are my parents silent in response to my suffering?" It is mistaken to construe this as a consistency question: "How could the existence of my parents and their absence be logically consistent?" This question should rather be construed as a plea for help from a first-person perspective: "Mum and Dad, why are you silent? You should not be. Help me or at least explain to me why you cannot help me." We can make a similar claim about the saying of Jesus on the cross: "Eli, Eli, lama sabachthani? that is to say, My God, my God, why hast thou forsaken me?" (Mark 15:34). Here, Jesus is not raising a consistency question; he is raising an experiential question. Philosophers seem to have assumed that the entirety of the problem of the co-occurrence of evil and hiddenness can in principle be reduced to the consistency problem, which can in principle be fully answered by a theodicy. Yet theodicies do not address the experiential aspects of the problems.

A relevant point was expressed in 2005 by Rowan Williams, then the Archbishop of Canterbury. He published an article entitled "Of Course This Makes Us Doubt God's Existence" when the catastrophic tsunami disaster took place in December 2004, killing approximately 280,000 people in Southeast Asia. In the article he contends that even if there were intellectual answers to the question "How can you believe in a God who permits suffering on this scale?" it would not make us feel any better because an experiential problem remains unanswered: "If some religious genius did come up with an explanation of exactly why all these deaths made sense, would we feel happier or safer or more confident in God?" (Williams, 2005). Williams's focus is on the problem of evil but the same point applies to the problem of divine absence.

One might think that I am advocating so-called "anti-theodicy" here. Proponents of anti-theodicy argue that theodicies always fail to respond to the problem of evil. Some of them go as far as saying that theodicies are immoral (Felderhof, 2004; Phillips, 2004) or even evil (Tilley, 1991) because they are attempts to *justify* horrific events. Williams makes a similar point: "[If someone did come up with a solution to the problem of evil] wouldn't we feel something of a chill at the prospect of a God who deliberately plans a programme that involves a certain level of casualties?" It is important to emphasize that I am not defending anti-theodicy here. I hold that theodicies can in principle be useful in solving the intellectual problem and might even offer believers limited consolation. I maintain, however, that theodicies do not eliminate the problem of divine absence altogether because they fail to answer the experiential problem, which concerns the pain and suffering of real people. We are mistaken if we think that theodicies can eliminate the experiential problem; that would perhaps be as absurd as thinking that we could eliminate a toothache with an intellectual argument. My focus in the rest of this chapter is on the experiential problem rather than the intellectual problem not only because that is what tormented Ferreira and Rodrigues but also because it poses a greater challenge to faith than the intellectual problem does.

A remarkable feature of the events described in *Silence* regarding the experiential problem is that the Japanese security officials, whether consciously or unconsciously, created an artificial mechanism to force the Kakure Kirishitans to *experience* the problem of divine absence. As I mentioned earlier, it is important to note that the goal of the security officials was not to kill the Kakure Kirishitans in punishment, nor even to torture them merely for the sake of causing suffering, but to make them renounce their faith. This goal could have in principle been accomplished by presenting to the Kakure Kirishitans the intellectual problem in an abstract manner. In fact, some attempts of this kind were made. For example, after committing apostasy Ferreira wrote a book entitled *Kengiroku* aimed at undermining Christianity by presenting intellectual arguments against it. In the book he writes, for example, "Since God is the creator of heaven and earth, the master of all there is and the source of wisdom, He must create everyone in the world in such a way that He knows everything about them. If God is the source of mercy why did He create the eight types of suffering for humans, the five decaying conditions for angels, and the three realms without any peace [the formless realm, the form realm, and the desire realm in Buddhist cosmology]?" (Ferreira, 1644). It is quite common even today for atheists to challenge believers by presenting similar intellectual arguments. Yet the officials concluded that it would be more effective to make the Kakure Kirishitans *experience* the problem of divine absence from a first-person perspective. This makes sense as most Kakure Kirishitans were poor peasants who were uneducated and illiterate. The security officials artificially created horrendous evil by torturing them brutally, which effectively made them acknowledge from a first-person perspective God's absence and failure to do anything for them. This forced them to face the experiential, rather than intellectual, problem of divine absence. While it is difficult to prove that the security officials adopted the strategy with this distinction in mind, their campaign to eradicate Christianity in this way was very successful. Today, less than 1 percent of the Japanese population is said to be Christians partly because of the persecution of Christianity in the seventeenth century.

Note again that Rodrigues renounced his faith not because he could not stand the physical pain. In fact, he had originally wished to experience the pain and achieve a glorious martyrdom. He renounced his faith because he could not stand the absence of God. He just could not accept that God would remain silent despite the pain and suffering he and other devout Christians experienced. Of course there were other Kakure Kirishitans who reacted differently to the persecution. For example, Hirofumi Yamamoto argues that many Kakure Kirishitans passionately *wished* to go through torture and die in martyrdom so that they could go to heaven. (Yamamoto, 2009, 42 and 251). There were also cases in which Kakure Kirishitans renounced their faith after being tortured but regained it later. The act of regaining faith is called *shinjin modoshi* in Japanese. There are reported cases of *shinjin modoshi* in which Kakure Kirishitans renounced their faith but regained it later and were martyred subsequently. However, cases like Ferreira's – in which Kakure Kirishitans permanently renounced their faith after experiencing the problem of divine absence and spent the rest of their lives supporting the persecution of Christians – were not uncommon. This suggests that at least in some of these cases it is not simply that Kakure Kirishitans renounced their faith because they could not endure the physical pain of being tortured, saying whatever they needed to say to stop the torture. They were experientially or intellectually persuaded that the problem of divine absence undermines their faith.

What would then be a satisfactory solution to the experiential problem? Recall that Ferreira apostatized because he "heard the voice of those people [being tortured] for whom God did nothing." He says, "God did not do a single thing. I prayed with all my strength; but God did nothing" (Endo, 1980, 167–8). Rodrigues also shouts to God, "Stop! Stop! Lord, it is now that you should break the silence. You must not remain silent. Prove that you are justice, that you are goodness, that you are love. You must say something to show the world that you are the august one" (Endo, 1980, 168). Rodrigues says that he cannot accept God's silence by appealing to His mysterious nature, either: "[Y]ou avert your face as though indifferent. This ... this I cannot bear... Do not abandon me in this mysterious way" (Endo, 1980, 119). He, like many other victims of horrendous evil, just cannot stand that God, who is meant to be omnipotent and morally perfect, remains completely silent. And he cannot accept that God leaves them in mystery as it is equivalent to abandonment. This suggests that the only situation that would fully satisfy such victims as Ferreira and Rodrigues who raise the experiential problem of divine absence is one in which God breaks His silence and eliminates their pain and suffering, or at least explains to them why He cannot do so. No other situation would satisfy them fully. Yet, clearly, no such situation is forthcoming – this is the very core of the experiential problem.

5   Responding to the experiential problem

How can we solve or address the experiential problem of divine absence if the only way to solve it fully satisfactorily is that God breaks His silence and eliminates the pain and suffering of the victims of horrendous evil or at least explains why He cannot help them? In this case no successful *solution* to the problem is available to us, because God does remain silent. Yet, I argue, there is a *response* to the problem which suggests how theists might try to live with the problem. In what follows, I develop a response by appealing to Shusaku Endo's religious insights into the nature of religion and the essence of religious faith.

Endo was a prolific author who published numerous essays as well as novels. In a book-length presentation of his religious views, *Watashi Ni Totte Kami Towa* (*What is God for Me*), which has not been translated into English, he writes as follows:

"Eli, Eli, lama sabachthani? that is to say, My God, my God, why hast thou forsaken me?" Without this, true religion does not even start. Imagine, for example, that a child is dying from leukemia. Her parents pray hard. Yet, the child dies. A New Age religion might say that the child won't die, but it's most likely that she will die. So there is no God, and there is no Buddha. That's the essence of "Eli, Eli, lama sabachthani?" But that is precisely where true religion starts. People start thinking seriously about what religion really is when they face the very situation that compels them to think that there is no God and no Buddha. (Endo, 1988b, 71–2)

Endo does not present the above view in response to the experiential problem of divine absence but we can expand on his thought and apply it to that problem.

Endo implies in the above passage that we should reverse how we look at the experiential problem of divine absence. Atheists start with divine absence, which is, again, the hiddenness of God from devout believers who suffer from horrendous evil, and conclude that God does not exist. This is a common pattern of reasoning through which people reject theism. In fact, this is the reasoning through which, in the novel, Ferreira and Rodrigues decide to renounce their faith. By this reasoning, divine absence is where one's religious faith ends. Yet is divine absence really the right place to end one's faith? Let us hark back to the origin of religion and consider why people need faith in the first place. It seems reasonable to say that people need faith precisely because there are horrendous situations that make them think there is no hope at all – so hopeless that no mercy from God or Buddha seems forthcoming. If, on the other hand, we had not faced such situations, or we had had found solutions to such situations by ourselves, we would not have needed faith in the first place. Indeed, it might not be an exaggeration to say that all the major religions of the world arose from human encounters with evil and suffering. So the existence of evil is not the end of religion but *the very start of true religion*, which takes seriously the most difficult situations in life. Endo writes:

I have gone through questions about religion that people commonly raise. Everyone wonders, "Why does this have to happen?" when they see, for example, innocent children dying in a war. I wonder too. That is why, I said to myself so many times, "I should give up my faith." But if faith does not go through such questions it is not true faith. It's not true religion. Conversely, believers who avoid these questions are not true believers. No matter how far we go it is unlikely that we can resolve all the problems. Yet our effort to always keep in mind these problems and tackle them represents true faith and true religion; an attempt to solve all of them easily and quickly does not. (Endo, 1988b, 200–1)

Faith does not offer easy or quick solutions to difficult problems. Avoiding the problem or pretending that it does not exist does not represent true religion. True religion faces the most significant challenges to faith directly, maintaining optimism and thereby sustaining faith. We would not need faith in the first place if there were easy or quick solutions. But the more seriously we consider these problems and the more deeply we grasp their persistence, the more seriously we take religion.

How can we understand faith in this framework? Endo expresses his sympathy with the view of the French author Georges Bernanos, according to which faith is 90 percent doubt and 10 percent hope (Endo, 1988b, 15–16). Endo says that faith is *not* 100 percent confidence. He says instead that it is mostly doubt but leaves a small space for hope and that space is crucial. Endo is not a philosopher, so he does not develop this idea as a philosophical view. We could nevertheless develop it as follows: If we focus on the problem of divine absence the world appears religiously negative, which means that the world appears more compatible with the non-existence of God rather than with the existence of God. However, people with faith can still try to keep a small portion of hope and hold onto "cosmic optimism," according to which ultimately all is good on a cosmic scale (Hick, 1989).

Philosophers of mind discuss "cognitive closure" and "epistemic boundedness." Proponents of these theses argue that given our cognitive and epistemic limitations it is reasonable to think that solutions to certain fundamental philosophical problems, such as the problem of consciousness and the problem free will, are beyond our ken.[4] In the same way that dogs are cognitively closed with respect to solutions to problems in physics and mathematics, they say, we are cognitively closed with respect to solutions to these philosophical problems. Whether or not their application of the theses to those specific philosophical problems is tenable, it seems undeniable, given the finitude of our brain functions, that our cognitive or epistemic capacity is limited and that there are many things beyond our comprehension. Our capacity seems particularly limited compared with the vast extent of God's power, knowledge, and love.

---

[4] See Chomsky (1975), Fodor (1983), and McGinn (1989).

Cosmic optimism is not epistemic confidence but an *attitude* that believers can choose to hold with respect to the place of humans in the universe. This is an attitude of hope that the gap in our cognitive and epistemic capacity corresponds to the puzzlement raised by divine absence. Cosmic optimists regard their encounters with divine absence not as the end of their faith but as an opportunity to embrace cognitive and epistemic humility. There is no definitive argument to establish that it is rational to adopt such an attitude but notice that (i) the focus of the problem of divine absence is on devout believers who are already committed to faith – so my proposal here is not directed to those with a weak commitment to faith or without faith; and (ii) we are not seeking a successful *solution* to the problem – we have concluded that there is no such thing. We seek instead a *response* to the problem which suggests how devout beliers can accept the problem yet try to live with it without giving up their faith.

It should be noted that what I am sketching here is related to but distinct from skeptical theism. Skeptical theism purports to solve the intellectual problem of evil by appealing to our limited knowledge, particularly of morality. Again, my intention here is not to address the intellectual problem or establish a solution that persuades everyone. I am only suggesting an attitude that people such as the Kakure Kirishitans, who are already committed to faith, can adopt in the face of the experiential problem.

In *Silence*, Rodrigues's old faith ends when he steps on *fumie* but doing so opens up a new phase of his religious life:

No doubt his fellow priests would condemn his act as sacrilege; but even if he was betraying them, he was not betraying his Lord. He loved him now in a different way from before. Everything that had taken place until now had been necessary to bring him to this love. "Even now I am the last priest in this land. But Our Lord was not silent. Even if he had been silent, my life until this day would have spoken of him." (Endo, 1980, 191)

Rodrigues's new faith takes divine absence seriously but does not undermine itself as it retains a small portion of optimism.

6   Conclusion

In this chapter, I have made three main points. First, I have argued that the problem of divine absence constitutes one of the most significant challenges for theists because it combines the most forceful form of the problem of divine hiddenness and the most forceful form of the problem of evil. I have addressed the cases of the Kakure Kirishitans in seventeenth-century Japan and Endo's novel to illustrate the force of the problem. Second, I have argued that theodicies cannot eliminate the experiential problem of divine absence because, unlike the intellectual problem, the experiential problem is not concerned with logical consistency between the existence of an omnipotent and morally perfect God on the one hand and divine absence on the other. It is concerned rather with the emotional puzzlement and confusion that devout believers who suffer from horrendous evil feel when they make a plea for help from God that is seemingly unanswered. Third, I have developed a response to the experiential problem by relying on Endo's insights into faith and religion. While such a response does not solve the problem it does suggest how believers can take divine absence as the starting point of true religion rather than the end. It reverses how we think about the relationship between the problem of divine absence and faith and motivates believers to embrace cosmic optimism.

Ian DeWeese-Boyd

"The world is chárged wíth the grándeur of God."[1] This line from one of Gerard
Manley Hopkins's most well-known poems captures his deep conviction that all
things course with the electrifying energy of God, not only the beautiful, irides-
cent flash of feather and wing, but also the horrifying crash of wave and lightning. In his recent biography of Hopkins, Paul Mariani suggests Hopkins spent
his life formulating "a theodicy and poetics which would articulate and sing what
his whole self – head and heart – felt."[2] But what sort of theodicy is it exactly
that Hopkins offers in his poems? And, how could poems answer what Hopkins
calls "the unshapeable shock night" anyway?[3] Many of his darkest poems complain of God's absence and attest to Hopkins's constant struggle to shape the
night of his experience. "[M]y lament," he writes in one of his so-called sonnets
of desolation, "Is cries countless, cries like dead letters sent / To dearest him
that lives alas! away."[4] As these lines suggest, the problem Hopkins's poems
express is not precisely the one philosophers have generally set themselves to
addressing, namely, whether God's apparent hiddenness from nonresistant nonbelievers is conceptually compatible with God's existence. Hopkins's problem
is more nearly what Yujin Nagasawa terms the "problem of divine absence," a
problem encountered by devout believers who experience God's hiddenness.
Hopkins's intense personal experience of divine abandonment in tandem with
his deep devotion to God renders his problem irreducibly existential. And this is
a problem that philosophers widely acknowledge to be untouched by even the
most sophisticated conceptual explanations of evil and hiddenness. So, to ask

I am grateful for encouraging feedback from the audience at The Hopkins Conference at Regis
Regis College in 2014; Jennie-Rebecca Falcetta who read and commented on the paper; and
especially Joaquin Kuhn, whose comments and correspondence about earlier instantiations of
this essay helped me avoid a number of errors. Finally, Margie DeWeese-Boyd for her support
throughout the process.

[1] "God's Grandeur," l. 1. All Hopkins poems are cited from the text in *Hopkins* (2010).
[2] Mariani (2008, 3). Mariani's poetic, meditative biography of Hopkins has been a constant
    companion in the construction of this essay, providing insight into Hopkins's life and spiritual
    journey.
[3] Hopkins, "The Wreck of the Deutschland," l. 227.
[4] Hopkins, "I wake and feel," ll. 6–8.

whether Hopkins's poems offer an answer to what philosophers call the problem of evil and the problem of hiddenness – a theodicy – seems like the wrong question, because it assumes Hopkins's problem is intellectual, not existential. But, even understanding his problem as existential, we may still wonder how the articulation of the pain of abandonment we find in his poems could be any kind of answer to it, much less a theodicy.

In this essay, I argue that Hopkins's poems themselves constitute a substantive response to the experience of existential suffering and hiddenness, and that his lyric theodicy fills a gap left by conceptual approaches to these problems precisely by giving voice to the existential crisis faced by those who feel the searing pain of the lightning and the numbing, leaden echo of silence. Hopkins's poems of existential suffering do not simply describe instances of intense suffering and stunning emptiness, they disclose it by bringing the reader into the experience that is their focus. While some of his poems might be understood as offering or assuming a theodicy of the traditional sort, I argue that the consolation they offer doesn't stem from these theological and philosophical constructions. Their consolation is the warm hand of a fellow sufferer reaching through the words. The darkest poems don't resolve, they know better, they shout in dereliction, thereby proving the faith they struggle to hold. The reader entering into these experiences, lifting up these laments, finds not only strength in the solidarity, but possibly hope in the darkness. The main aim of this essay, then, is to consider more precisely the way these Hopkins poems do this work, and how the approach they embody might contribute to the philosophical conversation about evil and hiddenness. The first section locates Hopkins's problem within the larger discussion of the problem of suffering and hiddenness. The second section argues that Hopkins's use of lyric enables his poems to speak into existential suffering in ways unavailable to traditional theodicies, ways akin to the lamentations of Job, Jeremiah, and Jesus. The final section contends that, when understood within Hopkins's view of the incarnation and Passion, his poems of existential suffering make it possible to identify with Christ in the experience of hiddenness, thereby bringing God's presence into the experience of absence.

I   Locating Hopkins's problem

From the very start, people working on the problem of suffering and hiddenness in the analytic tradition have recognized that there are aspects of suffering – the personal and existential – that this discourse does not address and for which it is signally unsuited to answer. This existential problem is raised for those for whom the experience of suffering and hiddenness, whether in the lives of others or their own, has made the problem undeniably concrete. My interest in this essay is specifically with the experience of suffering that is related to the existential problem of divine hiddenness, or what Nagasawa calls "the problem of divine absence."[5] This existential problem is raised for committed believers when they suffer and keenly feel the chill of God's absence. For such people suffering and seeing no sign of God poses a threat to the positive value of their lives, because in their suffering what they most long for is God's redemptive presence. Eleonore Stump argues that a person suffers in the sense relevant to this discussion when her experience "undermines (partly or entirely) her flourishing, or deprives her (in part or in whole) of the desires of her heart, or both."[6] Accordingly, those who experience divine absence feel their flourishing destroyed and hopes dashed, because they have identified their flourishing with God's presence and hoped that God would alleviate their suffering, or, at least, accompany them in it. Their question is not how suffering is conceptually compatible with a God of love, rather it is more in line with the cries of the psalmist, "Why hast thou forsaken me?" (Ps. 22:1) or "Why standest thou afar off, O Lord? why hidest thou thyself in times of trouble?" (Ps. 10:1). For those suffering in this way, no merely theoretical explanation will suffice. As Howard-Snyder and Moser note, answers to this existential problem "often seem lame, if not contrived," leading in some cases to "further frustration, and eventually to bitterness and despair."[7] Conceptual answers in such a situation are sand to the thirsty and stone to those who hunger for bread. Hopkins's darkest poems trace his striving in the face of this sort of existential suffering, despite his possession of conceptual answers, and, I argue, show both the need for and the way to an existential response.

It is perfectly possible to believe firmly that God exists and is loving and even that you will one day understand your suffering and God's silence, and nevertheless confront the existential problem I've described. Gerard Manley Hopkins seems to have experienced the existential problem in just this way.[8] On January 1,1889, just months before his death, Hopkins began his annual retreat, re-enacting Ignatius's *Spiritual Exercises*. His notes for the first day

[5] See Nagasawa's essay "Silence, evil and Shusaku Endo" (chapter 14, this volume). For Nagasawa the experiential "problem of divine absence" is raised when devout, as opposed to ordinary, believers or simple nonbelievers experience divine hiddenness when they suffer horrendous evil. Hopkins's suffering certainly creates serious self-loathing, but it probably doesn't rise to the level of horror as it is typically used in the discussion of the problem of evil. Otherwise, Hopkins's case fits Nagasawa's definition, since he is a devout believer and his experience of divine hiddenness from his existential suffering deepens that problem considerably.
[6] Stump (2010, 11).
[7] Howard-Snyder and Moser (2002, 3).
[8] I use the phrase "existential suffering" to cover both the experience of suffering and the experience of hiddenness. In Hopkins's case, hiddenness is a significant source of suffering, because he desires God's presence. God's being hidden undermines his flourishing, giving him prima facie reason to despair. In general, the experience of hiddenness is a source of suffering for one who believes and desires the loving presence of God. *Existential* hiddenness, then, is a distinctly religious problem and inevitably involves existential suffering.

record his assessment of his life up to that point. He expresses certainty about his vocation and his faith, and, at the same time, the deep conviction that his life has become loathsome to him. Here is how he concludes his notes for that day:

I was continuing this train of thought this evening when I began to enter on that course of loathing and hopelessness which I have often felt before, which made me fear madness and led me to give up the practice of meditation except, as now, in retreat and here it is again. I could therefore do no more than repeat *Justus es, Domine, et rectum judicium tuum* ... What is this wretched life? Five wasted years almost have passed in Ireland. I am ashamed of the little I have done, of my waste of time ... [W]hat is life without aim, without spur, without help? All my undertakings miscarry: I am like a straining eunuch. I wish then for death: yet if I died now I should die imperfect, no master of myself, and that is the worst failure of all. O my God, look down on me.[9]

Notice the way faith and suffering coexist for Hopkins. Repeating the prayer drawn from Psalm 119, "Thou art just, O Lord, and thy judgment is right," which continues, "deal with thy servant according to thy mercy: and teach me thy justifications," we can see Hopkins not only confessing but also calling out to God. Though he clearly believes – or wants to believe – God exists and is just, as his repetition of the prayer attests, he nevertheless feels as if his suffering is unseen and his cries unheard; God's silence and hiddenness serve only to make his suffering worse. The sonnet, "I wake and feel," penned at the beginning of his tenure in Ireland, highlights the role hiddenness plays in Hopkins's suffering:

> I wake and feel the fell of dark, not day.
> What hours, O what black hours we have spent
> This night! what sights you, heart, saw, ways you went!
> And more must, in yet longer light's delay.
>
> With witness I speak this. But where I say
> Hours I mean years, mean life. And my lament
> Is cries countless, cries like dead letters sent
> To dearest him that lives alas! away. (ll.1–8)

What these passages make clear is that a certain double-mindedness is at the center of Hopkins's struggle. This clash between his beliefs regarding God and his experience of suffering and absence is the core of his problem. As long as he is true to both, as long as he holds tightly to each, he experiences his suffering as a pressing problem. If he were to let go of belief in God's goodness, he would still suffer but he would not experience the *problem* of suffering; if he let go of his belief that God must not remain hidden, again he might suffer crushing loneliness, but not divine hiddenness.

[9] Hopkins (1959, 262).

Denis Sobolev contends that this tension between his theological and philosophical commitments and his existential experience runs through all of Hopkins's poetry. Hopkins's poems reflect his struggle to hold his faith and experience together. The result, in Sobolev's view, is that Hopkins often

refused to mediate the gap between the two, and no reconciliation between what he held to be true and what he experienced as a human being – in all the concreteness and historicity of his existence – was possible for him. Oscillating between the ecstasies of spiritual contemplation and the depth of unredeemed pain, his poetry thus dramatizes a split mode of perception, in which neither the life of the spirit nor the world of actual existence is denied, nor is one subordinated to the other.[10]

Whether we can conclude that no resolution was possible for him is unclear, but Sobolev is surely right that the poems themselves derive much of their power from their vivid expression of Hopkins's personal desolation and their resolute refusal to relieve the pressure that this put upon his faith. Hopkins's choice to speak from within the welter of existential suffering and not from some divine point of view marks a refusal to claim that perspective or authority. As Sobolev remarks, "The person who speaks about his hopes, his ruptures, and his pain is Gerard Manley Hopkins, in all the unauthoritative unreliability of his humanity."[11] His poems, accordingly, bring the reader into the heart of his confusion and despair. By eschewing dogmatic authority, focusing instead on the raw existential tension of the speaker's situation, these poems gain human authority even if they give no explanation.

In this way, Hopkins's poetry raises theodicean questions, but, offering no clear, discursive answer to them, implies that theodicy, if available at all, may well leave us stumbling in the night. This feature of his poetry reflects what Hopkins had said in an early sermon of October 25, 1880, namely, that "God's providence is dark and we cannot hope to know the why and the wherefore of all that is allowed to befall us."[12] As he comments in the 1889 retreat notes mentioned earlier, "It is as if one were dazzled by a spark or star in the dark, seeing it but not seeing by it: We want a light shed on our way and a happiness spread over our life."[13] Instead we stand in the darkness, seeing some hopeful star too small and distant to provide such light. For Hopkins, neither God nor his own flourishing can be seen from his existential location. The refusal of existential suffering to clear like some morning mist under the ray of theological truth and metaphysical commitment is Hopkins's *real* problem.

Hopkins's existential problem, then, is generated and sustained by his faith. In this sense, his version of the problem is uniquely Christian. With this we have located Hopkins's problem and seen that his response is not in any

[10] Sobolev (2011, 12).   [11] Sobolev (2011, 287).
[12] Hopkins (1959, 62).   [13] Hopkins (1959, 262).

straightforward sense a theodicy.[14] If anything, Hopkins consistently represents theodicy as either unattainable or impotent in the face of the suffering he experiences. In view of this contention, we may wonder whether there is any helpful way to respond to this problem.

Hopkins's poems themselves, the ones that most vividly express the existential problem, show us the way. Hopkins's contribution is that his poetry communicates faithful struggle and discloses a kind of knowledge that goes beyond the rational justification found in theodicy. As a consequence, unlike theodicy, his poetry has the potential to offer the consolation to others experiencing existential suffering that even if they are in the dark they are not alone.

II   Lyric, lamentation, and the problem of existential suffering

Why think Hopkins's darkest poems do anything more than express the problem of existential suffering – an achievement in its own right – why suppose they could be part of a helpful response to it? Poetry, particularly lyric of the sort Hopkins writes, creates solidarity by inviting the reader to enter the poetic space not only as a spectator or listener but also as the speaker. This intimate identification places the poet's words on our own tongues. If the words and the space are only nihilistic despair, dread, and deadly loneliness, however, they may do little to relieve our burdens, even if they help us see we are not alone. To be a robust response to existential suffering, these poems would have to be more than mere cries of despair, they would also need to be cries of faith and hope. Accordingly, we need some reason to think that entering into these words and taking up these lamentations might lift us from despair. In this section, I explore the nature of lyric – Hopkins's in particular – in the mode of biblical lamentation and argue that read along these lines Hopkins's poems do more than offer company in the darkness, they shed light by articulating a space to confront an absent God.

Lyric of intimate knowledge: weep with them that weep

Quoting the critic R. P. Blackmur, John Berryman's poem "Olympus" captures an essential feature of poetic discourse:

> "The art of poetry
> is amply distinguished from the manufacture of verse
> by the animating presence in the poetry
> of a fresh idiom: language

[14] I am not claiming that one couldn't extract a theodicy from Hopkins's prose and poetry (in fact, I think there is one and that Hopkins at some level trusted in it). Instead, I am arguing that whatever theodicy he may have articulated or accepted, his poems do not represent it as being existentially effective.

> so twisted & posed in a form
> that it not only expresses the matter at hand
> but adds to the available stock of reality."
> I was never altogether the same after *that*. (ll. 5–12)[15]

As a poet, Berryman is changed by the notion that his vocation might be the provision of language adequate to reality. Language that gives readers access to the world – whether the one right before her eyes or nearer still the world within her own mind – is, at least in Blackmur's view, what poets give and what both they and their readers at some level need. The poet Denise Levertov construes this vocation as a sort of bearing witness to one's life; poems are "testimonies of lived life."[16] When this testimony finds an audience, it has tapped into a need; it has provided a language that answers a longing in the reader, a longing not only for a way to word reality but also for companionship in it. The moment of recognition is a moment of solidarity. If Blackmur and Levertov are right, poems can function to put words to reality and thereby make it more bearable for writer and reader alike.

Lyric is "the most intimate of genres," according to Helen Vendler.[17] To read the lines of a lyric is to be invited "to own the words, to become for the moment the one speaking."[18] What lyric offers is nothing short of self-transformation by means of identification with the poem's speaker. In a letter to his brother, Hopkins wrote "the true nature of poetry" is as "the darling child of speech, of lips and *spoken* utterance: it must be *spoken*."[19] Hopkins insists that his poems be spoken, not simply read on the page, because they have their full force only when they are incarnated in the reader's own voice. The intimate identification of lyric helps to explain how poetry expands "the available stock of reality" and why the knowledge it confers is impossible to explain without remainder from a third-person, propositional perspective. By collapsing the distance between reader and speaker, lyric induces the experience of the speaker; it brings us inside. If it is the epiphanic experience Hopkins has when he sees the kestrel hunting one morning in the Welsh countryside, as in "The Windhover," the reader crouches in hiding too, spying the majestic flight and buckling fall of the bird. This is a first-person experience, "*I* caught this morning morning's minion" (l. 1, my emphasis). There is all the difference in the world between noting the fact that there was a kestrel about this morning, and actually seeing it, feeling the intensity of the sun break upon you, as the bird dives. When the reader identifies with the speaker in this way, she too turns with the speaker to regard this kestrel as at once Christ, on the hunt, buckling to capture her

---

[15] Berryman (1989, 179).   [16] Levertov (1992, 21).
[17] Vendler (2010, xl).   [18] Vendler (2010, xli).
[19] Hopkins (1980, 137).

crouching, hiding self.[20] What the reader understands from this position cannot be fully explained from the third-person perspective.[21]

In addition to this knowledge gained inside the poem – when we are the speaker, we also learn something when we stand outside the poetic space. When we reflect upon the speaker, taking up the position of a bystander, we understand the person of the speaker as other. From this position, the speaker's words become *testimony*. This is testimony of a special sort; since we have been privy to the experience that generated it, it can be *our* testimony.

What Vendler's comments on lyric help us to see is that poetry like Hopkins's communicates an intimate knowledge that no mere description can. When he asks "not to live this tormented mind / with this tormented mind tormenting yet" (ll. 3–4), we are brought inside this mind and learn from experience what it is to be in that dark place.[22] When this is a place we've been or are, the words expand the reality that is available and by articulating it enable us to share it. Stepping back, we can hear the "tormented mind" as a witness to the experience, and, because we have shared the experience, we can hear the testimony with sympathy. But, why suppose that sharing this experience is any sort of answer to the existential problem?

Lyric of lamentation: blessed are they that mourn

Sharing this experience by taking up the speaker's words might only have the effect of making the existential problem *more* real to us. And, the dismal testimony that we're not alone in our suffering might only sink us lower. As I suggested earlier, for lyric's intimate knowledge to lift us, it cannot be a song of despair alone, it must be one of faith as well. For the lyric of suffering to be a productive means of responding to the existential problem, we need some reason to think its expression of desolation doesn't merely make us desolate. We need a reason to think that it somehow alters the experience of the one who needed to express pain this way. Turning to scriptural forms of lamentation suggests a way that a lyric of existential suffering might not only express painful despair but also anguished hope.

The psalms are replete with complaint over existential suffering. Job and Jeremiah both face terror and create poetry that struggles to understand where

---

[20] For a fascinating article on the hawk imagery see Bouchard (1999).

[21] Eleonore Stump (2010) explores the way narrative discloses knowledge that is distinct from the third-person variety that is often the focus of philosophy in general and theodicy in particular. Her focus is on the way narrative communicates knowledge of persons – what she terms second-person knowledge. Her account complements what I am arguing here regarding lyric insofar as the experience of inhabiting the speaker's place inevitably discloses knowledge of that person.

[22] Hopkins, "My own heart let me more have pity on."

God could be in it, and like the psalmist, they plead, protest, complain, question, demand, lament, all in the hope that their cries will be heard. The inclusion of these poems and their liturgical use over the centuries suggests not only their power to express grief but also their power to relieve it. Given Hopkins's own familiarity with and liturgical use of scripture, these poets of existential suffering stand as relevant exemplars of the way lyric might address and transform such pain.[23] They give us reason to think the lyric of suffering may enable us to bear it.

In a series of meditations on suffering that grew out of his own battle with bone cancer, the poet Christian Wiman asks "[w]hat ... the difference [is] between the cry of pain that is also a cry of praise, and a cry of pain that is pure despair?" His own unsteady response is: "Faith? The cry of faith, even if it is a cry against God, moves toward God, has its meaning in God, as in the cries of Job."[24] The cry of suffering, then, is a not simply sorrow over suffering, but a *complaint* directed toward or, at least, before God, a complaint that makes sense only in the presence of God.[25] Complaint is active and directed outward. Like Jacob, those who cry out to or even against God pull God close, unwilling to let go, intent on receiving a blessing.

Paul Ricoeur highlights the significance of this mode of response, arguing that theoretical answers to the problem of suffering – theodicies and defenses – never completely overcome the suffering itself, because they require complainants – those experiencing existential suffering – to stand silent. The successful defense renders the charges illegitimate and further complaint inappropriate.[26] What is called for in his view is not a *solution* to the problem of suffering, but a response that renders it productive, a response that is a catharsis of the felt pain. To allow lament to "develop into a complaint against God," he suggests, is an expression of "the impatience of hope ... [that] has its origin in the cry of the Psalmist, "How long O Lord?"[27] This is a hope that can sound like hopelessness: "How long wilt thou forget me, O Lord? for ever? How long wilt thou hide thy face from me? How long shall I take counsel in my soul, having sorrow in my heart daily?" (Psalm 13:1–2). It is a faith that can sound like despair: "My God, my God, why hast thou forsaken me?" (Psalm 22). In such cries, there is the hope of being heard alongside the unmistakable sorrow, anger, and incomprehension at being abandoned. This response to suffering

---

[23] I am not claiming here that Hopkins consciously emulated these biblical laments (except where it is explicit, as in "Thou art indeed just"), only that they gave him practice for dealing with suffering that works its way into his poetry.
[24] Wiman (2013, 53).
[25] There is a significant literature dedicated to the form and rhetorical function of lament in biblical sources. I will not be using the term technically in what follows, though I will be making reference to some of this scholarship to highlight important features of biblical paradigms.
[26] Ricoeur (1995).   [27] Ricoeur (1995, 260).

rests upon the conviction that God, as the source of all goodness, must affirm the justice of the complaint. In Ricoeur's view, crying out in this way plays a role in the "catharsis of lament" and enables those experiencing existential suffering to "believe in God *in spite of* evil," that is, without an explanation.[28]

Ricoeur is not perfectly plain about what he means by "catharsis of lament," or how complaint accomplishes it, but he is clearly right to see that when personal suffering shifts from a wallowing self-enclosed lament to complaint that is open before the just and loving God of one's convictions, this suffering is imbued with a different light. The original insight Aristotle captured in his notion of catharsis is instructive here. Aristotle saw that in the rousing of pity and fear tragedy alters not only the emotions but also the beliefs that underwrite them. As Martha Nussbaum puts it, "pity and fear will be sources of illumination or clarification, as the agent, responding and attending to his or her responses, develops a richer self-understanding concerning the attachments and values that support the responses."[29] Perhaps the catharsis that Ricoeur has in mind consists of this sort of illumination. When the Psalmist cries out, "My God, my God why hast thou forsaken me?," the cry reveals to the Psalmist not only the felt dread of godforsakenness, but also the beliefs that prompt her to complain of it: her belief that God must not forsake her, her belief that God will hear her cry. It is true that the cry of complaint stems from doubt of these beliefs in the face of existential suffering and divine silence. But this doubt and its accusatory questioning reveal a stubborn love for God that is unwilling to cut off the relationship and to cease demanding God's presence and response.[30] Commenting on the pain of this doubt (he calls it "devotional doubt") Wiman notes that it

is active rather than passive, purifying rather than stultifying. Far beneath it, no matter how severe the drought, how thoroughly your skepticism seems to have salted the ground of your soul, faith, durable faith, is steadily taking root.[31]

I would argue that voicing pain in lyric form is a purifying act that may well denote life in even the driest roots and accomplish a "catharsis of lament" in the sense that it illuminates the unwillingness to let go of God even when God is nowhere to be seen, or, worse, is seen as the source of the suffering.

"Catharsis of lament" in this sense, then, is not simply a salve for wounded feelings. As theologian and biblical scholar Walter Brueggemann insists, biblical laments are "real prayers and not merely psychological acts of catharsis whereby the speaker 'feels better' by expressing need out loud."[32] Those who lament do not simply seek religious succor; they expect divine redress. As such

---

[28] Ricoeur (1995, 260).   [29] Nussbaum (1986, 388).
[30] I owe this image of stubborn love to C. Mandolfo's excellent treatment of lamentation (Mandolfo, 2007, 163).
[31] Wiman (2013, 76).   [32] Brueggemann (2002, 119).

these poetic utterances are "acts of hope" that hold God responsible and antici-
pate transformation. The inclusion of this form of prayer as a necessary expression of faith signals not only the legitimacy but also the obligation to raise
theodic questions.[33] The lyrical articulation of suffering along the lines of these
biblical models suggests the way lament, as practice, aims to effect change by
confronting God with the intolerable breaches of justice encountered individually and collectively. The one who laments is thereby bearing suffering; to cry
out to God is to hope for relief.[34]

Jesus's cry of dereliction exemplifies the sort of use of lyric I have in mind.
When he feels the dread of abandonment on the cross, he chooses to voice
his desolation in the lyric of Psalm 22. When he recites the opening lines, he
becomes the speaker of the lyric, and finds in it language adequate to the reality he is facing. In that moment, he not only finds solidarity with the Psalmist
but with all those others who have entered these words, and in this solidarity
the solace that he is not alone. Jesus reaches for these words, then, not just to
express despair but somehow to have the strength to bear it.

Hopkins's late poem "Thou art indeed just, Lord, if I contend," which
takes this first line from Jeremiah 12.1, operates in a similar manner. When
he translates the opening lines of Jeremiah's lament, Hopkins is reaching for
that poet's words to articulate his own struggle with God's justice and grounding his own speech in that tradition. Like Jeremiah, Hopkins simultaneously
affirms and disputes God's justice; he cries injustice in the hope for justice.
Whereas Jeremiah's primary focus is the unjust flourishing of the wicked,
Hopkins's is his own comparative languishing. "Why," he demands, "must /
Disappointment all I endeavour end?" (ll. 3–4). Not only the prospering sinners, but also the fecund world all about him serve to painfully reveal his own
sterility. This is the heart of his complaint. For years he has despaired over his
inability to produce scholarly and poetic work. As early as 1883, he complains
to Bridges "it kills me to be time's eunuch and never to beget."[35] In another
letter to Bridges, he says, "All impulse fails me: I can give myself no sufficient
reason for going on. Nothing comes: I am a eunuch."[36] And, just months before
this poem was written, he despondently writes, "All my undertakings miscarry: I am like a eunuch. I wish then for death."[37] The poem's sestet captures
this despair, forming it into a robust complaint against this God who claims
justice and friendship. The speaker insists on action reflective of these claims.

---

[33] Brueggemann (1995, 104, 107).

[34] See Brueggemann (1995). Brueggemann's discussion of Job 21 (Brueggemann, 1994) points
out that that complaint is not directed to God overtly. To rail against injustice is to appeal to
justice and to God for redress (cf. Brueggemann, 2002, 118f.).

[35] Hopkins (1955, 222).   [36] Hopkins (1955, 270).

[37] Hopkins (1959, 262).

... See, banks and brakes
Now leavèd how thick! lacèd they are again
With fretty chervil, look, and fresh wind shakes
Them; birds build – but not I build; no, but strain,
Time's eunuch, and not breed one work that wakes.
Mine, O thou lord of life, send my roots rain.

As the last line indicates, the speaker owns this inscrutable God in the very act of insisting on just and loving treatment. The final plea signifies that the speaker stands finally in anguished hope, not despair. We can imagine that for Hopkins, who persistently and painfully felt the sting of failure in the work he believed he was meant to do, this lament represents his commitment to hold on to God and his refusal to settle quietly in resigned acceptance of what seems a betrayal of friendship and justice. Mariani suggests this is Hopkins's "own version of Holy Saturday, with Jesus still in the tomb, helpless, waiting upon the Father, his one hope, to fill him with His own life."[38] Like Jesus's own use of lament, Hopkins's poem expresses the sense of betrayal and raises the theodic question, not in the hope of an explanation, but in the hope of redemptive action. It is a hope that the poem itself proves to be realized; indeed, this is a work that wakes.

In view of what I have argued above, this active voicing of feelings of god-forsakenness and betrayal may be understood as cathartic in the substantive not merely psychological sense. In calling God to account, the speaker reveals a stubborn love that will not let go of God or silently accept suffering. This active, rather than passive, response to feelings of abandonment and despair alters them and makes them "productive," as Ricoeur would say. It transforms them into acts of hope and faith that the work of mourning, complaining, even despairing can bring God close. Ultimately, those who voice their woe express faith that those who mourn will find blessing and comfort. Earlier I suggested that for lyric to speak into existential suffering in a positive way, it cannot simply be a hopeless expression of pain. In this section, I have argued that the expression of doubt, desolation, and the like can be expressions of faith and as such "productive" responses to existential suffering. Though these poems do not remove uncertainty or provide theodicy, they do articulate a space for those who suffer to meet God, even if it is only to contend. And yet, it isn't obvious that this contentious space, where one's sense of God's fidelity and love is blotted out by the darkness of one's existential experience, is, in any substantive sense, redemptive. Seemingly, God remains absent and divine action still only a far off hope. To understand why Hopkins's poems might add substance to this hope and be, in fact, redemptive, it is necessary to consider the role the incarnation plays in his poetry.

---

[38] Mariani (2008, 415).

III   The incarnate Word: touching God in the darkness, touching God in suffering

Hopkins's poems of existential suffering are rooted, like the rest of his poems, in the incarnation – the great "outstress" of God into the world.[39] The world, he says, is none other than "God's utterance of himself ... outside himself" and "its end, its purpose, its purport, its meaning, is God and its life or work to name and praise him."[40] For Hopkins, incarnation is *the* context for all things striving to realize their nature. Hopkins's notion of the incarnation is complex, embracing far more than the historical incarnation of God in the person of Jesus, and treating it in detail is beyond the scope of this essay.[41] Focus on the human incarnation of God in Jesus will suffice to shed light on the way Hopkins's poems of existential suffering make it possible to find solidarity with God even in the darkness of God's absence. By tapping into the struggle, pain, and turmoil involved in the human experience that incarnating Christ entails, these poems allow sufferers to touch the hidden God in the one who emptied himself of God to be with them. To appreciate this aspect of Hopkins's poems, then, we need to consider what he took the incarnation to mean for Christ and how he understood Christ's incarnation to connect to his own spiritual journey.

For Hopkins, incarnation and kenosis go hand in hand. Entering matter and taking human form requires an unimaginable emptying on God's part. As he put it in one poem, "God's infinity / dwindled to infancy."[42] When Hopkins asks why the son of God goes forth from the Father, the answer he gives is this: "To give God glory and that by sacrifice, sacrifice offered in the barren wilderness outside of God."[43] To become incarnate requires the son to somehow go outside of God into the wilderness; this is what is meant by kenosis: God empty of God; God outside of God; God hidden from God. Hopkins relates his understanding of what Christ's self-emptying involves and means for his followers in a letter to his friend, the poet Robert Bridges:

[Christ] finding, as in the first instant of his incarnation he did, his human nature informed by the godhead ... thought it nevertheless no snatching matter ... to be equal with God, but annihilated himself, taking on the form of a servant ... he emptied and exhausted himself so far as that was possible, of godhead and behaved only as God's slave, as his creature, as man, which also he was, and then being in the guise of man humbled himself to death, the death of the cross. It is this holding of himself back, and not snatching at the truest and highest good, the good that was his right ... his own

---

[39] Hopkins (1959, 197).   [40] Hopkins (1959, 129).
[41] Lichtmann (1991) admirably lays out some of the details.
[42] Hopkins, "The Blessed Virgin compared to the Air we Breathe," line 19.
[43] Hopkins (1959, 197).

being and self, which seems to me the root of all his holiness and the imitation of this the root of all moral good in other men.[44]

As the last line indicates, this giving up is the paradigm of all human goodness, and its imitation the goal for all would-be followers of Christ. That Hopkins took this goal to heart is evident throughout his writings. He understands God's grace as the action by which God "carries a creature to the end of its being, which is its self-sacrifice and salvation."[45] In his own case, he recognized his desire for grace amounted to a desire "to be lifted on a higher cross."[46] He saw his desire for union with God through the lens of the Passion and the crucifixion. Paradoxically, he found the greatest union with God in the incarnational moment of the greatest emptiness and suffering. To be one with God, he implies, requires that one follow Christ to the cross and there enter into the suffering of divine absence.[47]

As a Jesuit, Hopkins annually re-enacted Ignatius's *Spiritual Exercises*. This afforded him the opportunity to contemplate key moments of Christ's journey to the cross. Entering into these moments enabled him to see that in this God empty of God, he could find solidarity and strength. For instance, when he considers the hidden life of Jesus – those years from twelve to thirty about which we hear nothing in the Gospels – he writes: "the hidden life at Nazareth is the great help to faith for us who must live more or less an obscure, constrained, and unsuccessful life ... And sacrificing all to obedience his very obedience was unknown. But the pleasingness of Christ's life there in God's eyes is recorded in the words spoken when he had just left it: 'this is my beloved Son' etc."[48] His letters and journal entries suggest that he felt himself to be living an "obscure, constrained, unsuccessful life" in Dublin. His energy wasted on setting and grading examinations for all Irishmen seeking a degree in classics; his own projects scattered, unfinished, and those finished, rejected, or misunderstood. As the comment suggests, he could see that Christ had stood precisely where he was standing and that his submission to such a life could be pleasing to God. In a letter to his friend Richard Dixon dated July 3, 1886, he makes a similar observation, but this time noting the psychological toll this self-emptying must have taken on Christ:

Above all Christ our Lord: his career was cut short, and whereas he would have wished to succeed by success – for it is insane to lay yourself out for failure ... nevertheless

---

[44] Hopkins (1955, 175).   [45] Hopkins (1959, 154).
[46] Hopkins (1959, 254).
[47] For example, Hopkins (1959, 255). Hopkins directs himself to "see Christ's body nailed, consider the attachment of his will to God's will. Wish to be as bound to God's will in all things, in the attachment of your mind and attention to prayer and the duty in hand; the attachment of your affections to Christ our Lord and his wounds instead of any earthly objects."
[48] Hopkins (1959, 176). Here, he is recalling Father Whitty's remarks on this moment in the *Spiritual Exercises*.

he was doomed to succeed by failure; his plans were baffled, his hopes dashed, and his work was done by being broken off undone. However much he understood all this he found it an intolerable grief to submit to it. He left the example: it is very strengthening, but except in that sense it is not consoling.[49]

Though the comments are aimed at consoling Dixon for not being elected to Oxford's Chair of Poetry, it's hard not to hear the dark sonnets' "baffling ban," "ruins of wrecked past purposes," and "lonely began" behind these lines, which were written just a year later.[50] Hopkins's comments to Dixon show how he might have found strength to endure those difficult years when consolation and comfort eluded his grasp and his cries felt unheard. Hopkins sees that strength can be drawn from solidarity with Christ, specifically, in his experience of grief. His understanding of kenosis also implies that though Christ must have at some level understood why he suffered – that is, he possessed a theodicy – God was so hidden to him that he nevertheless found it an intolerable grief to submit to this suffering. This is the grief felt in Gethsemane and expressed from the cross. It is precisely this grief of Jesus that grounds his solidarity with human beings and legitimates complaint, instead of docile, detached, submission. For Hopkins, Jesus's experience of this human grief connects him to those who feel divine neglect in the face of the jarring blows of failure and injustice that threaten the positive value of their lives. He points to this aspect of the incarnation, then, because it is *the* meeting place for all who experience the bewildering anguish of God's absence in circumstances of suffering.

Hopkins's reflections on the sorrows of Christ, again using Ignatius's *Exercises*, further indicate the depth and the significance of Christ's kenosis for those experiencing suffering. In one exercise, Ignatius asks the exercitant to consider the sufferings of Christ at the time of the Passion not simply as a bystander but as Christ himself felt them. As David Flemming's commentary on this meditation makes explicit, the exercitant should "pay special attention to how the divinity hides itself so that Jesus seems so utterly human and helpless [and] should make every effort to get inside the Passion, not just staying with external sufferings, but entering the loneliness, the interior pain of rejection and feeling hated, the anguish within Jesus."[51] This exercise prompts reflection on what Christ's kenosis and sacrifice entailed, in particular, what it felt like for Jesus to experience the hiddenness of God at the moment of his greatest suffering. Hopkins describes this "withdrawal and hiding of the Godhead" as a "deep severance between it and the [Jesus] manhood."[52] While neither Hopkins nor Ignatius aim to question the hypostatic union, they do

[49] Abbott (1955, 136–8).
[50] The lines are from "To seem a stranger seems my lot, my life" and "Patience" respectively.
[51] Fleming (1996, 149–51).
[52] Hopkins (1959, 191), from notes for a planned commentary on *The Exercises*.

want to emphasize that in this great sacrifice Jesus genuinely felt forsaken. As Hopkins notes elsewhere, "Christ our Lord … feels and understands what pain and fear and desolation are – all … that you can ever feel on earth."[53] This observation is offered to those who, having worked through Ignatius's meditation on hell, find themselves terror-stricken. "Turn," he says in his most pastoral tone, "Turn to Christ our Lord," because he has known pain, fear, and desolation.

What this sampling of Hopkins's thoughts on the incarnation suggests is that when he considers the reality of Christ's kenosis, he recognizes that Christ didn't walk impervious through the wilderness, but experienced sorrow and grief and desolation like all human beings. What this implies is that in his poems of existential suffering we might touch more than suffering – we might touch God's suffering. This incarnational context combined with the intense subjectivity of these poems' speaker and the immediacy of the experiences related enable them to reach into the lives of those who suffer, not with an explanation, but with the possibility of God's companionship.

"Carrion Comfort" offers an example of the way Hopkins's poems, understood along these lines, might offer this strength to the suffering.[54] This poem points to the way that entering into the kenotic space Jesus occupied raises the theodic question in a form that radically reorients the speaker's relation both to God and suffering. This poem, especially the second quatrain, is a prayer, more specifically, a prayer in the tradition of biblical laments. Hopkins's insistent questions:

> But ah, but O thou terrible, why wouldst thou rude on me
> Thy wring-world right foot rock? lay a lionlimb against me? scan
> With darksome devouring eyes my bruisèd bones? and fan
> O in turns of tempest, me heaped there; me frantic to avoid thee and flee?

brings to mind Job's complaint: "I am full of confusion; therefore see thou mine affliction; for it increaseth. Thou huntest me as a fierce lion: and again thou shewest thyself marvellous upon me" (Job 10:15).[55] Like Job, the speaker of this poem feels hunted and confused, battered and bruised, and yet, like Job, he does not simply feed on his despair; instead, he confronts this "terrible" one, piling question on question. Robert Alter says, "Job will not let the terror of God confound him or silence him. He still wishes to voice his protest, not

---

[53] Hopkins (1959, 244).

[54] I am not arguing that Hopkins explicitly sought to express these moments in Christ's experience in his poems of existential suffering or that he explicitly structured them on Ignatian meditation, only that given this background Hopkins seems to recognize that these places of darkness are not utterly empty of God.

[55] See also, Lamentations 3:10: "He was unto me as a bear lying in wait, and as a lion in secret places."

succumbing to fear."[56] So, too, the speaker in Hopkins's poem, though he is "frantic to avoid and flee," will not be silenced by his fearsome adversary.

The volta begins by reiterating the question at the heart of the existential problem, and at the heart of the tumbled and tossed questions of the second quatrain, "Why?" The question isn't blandly, why does God allow suffering?, but accusingly, why do you, God, inflict suffering on me? The theodic answer, "That my chaff might fly, my grain might lie, sheer and clear" is answered "Nay," not because it is untrue, but because the answer is both more complex and more personal. The speaker is coming to see in an almost giddy realization that the rod that wrecked him is also the hand that holds his heart, the rod that seemed to beat him down is the one the shepherd holds that protects and comforts. Feeling joy such as would cheer and make his heart laugh, he wonders:

> Cheer whom though? the hero whose heaven-handling flung me, fóot trod
> Me? or me that fought him? O which one? is it each one? That night, that year
> Of now done darkness I wretch lay wrestling with (my God!) my God.
>   (ll. 12–14)

These last lines reference Jacob's wrestling with God at Peniel.[57] Jacob, who would not let the stranger go until he was blessed, is said to have contended with God and prevailed; he found victory in holding on. Jacob, of course, had already received a promise, already met God and survived, but in both of his encounters with God, Jacob is shocked – "Surely the Lord is in this place, and I knew it not" (Gen. 28:16) – and confused – "Tell me ... thy name" (Gen. 32:27). Only in retrospect does he realize, "I have seen God face to face and my life is preserved" (Gen. 32:30). In Hopkins's poem, this Jacobean struggle culminates with the speaker voicing the words of Psalm 22, joining both the Psalmist and Christ on the cross in their confused cry of abandonment, and at the same time infusing it with a new light. Unlike Jacob who is staggered to find as the day breaks that he grapples with God, the speaker, who knew this at some level, is staggered to find he is not alone in this struggle. Christ too suffered before God, felt shame and abandonment, and cried out. The insight here is not that God uses suffering to purify us – the theodic answer immediately given – the insight is something both more intimate and apocalyptic.[58] The speaker finds that even in that "now done darkness" he was not alone, Christ was with him, more joltingly, *was* him. As he says in "That Nature is a Heraclitean Fire," "I am all at once what Christ is, since

---

[56] Alter (2010, 46), note on Job 9:35.

[57] Cf. Sobolev (2011, 191–6). My approach owes much to Sobolev's spectacular exposition of this poem, but where he sees the function of the last line as disclosing to Hopkins that he wrestles with God and that this God is his God, I suggest that the echo of Jesus' lament places him in much more intimate relation to God.

[58] Goss (2011). Goss's larger argument is that the body itself is what enables us to persist through this displacement.

he was what I am" (l. 22). Christ occupied his position when he cried out from the cross. What Hopkins's speaker sees is that God is where he least expected: God is *in* his suffering. Not only does his cry in the poem register the positive action of lamentation, it suggests that the lamentation is not simply spoken to God, it is spoken by God. In this way, Hopkins's poem suggests that we can touch God in our suffering. And, yet, to touch God in this way does not explain our suffering or God's justice; instead it legitimizes lamentation as an authentic moment in the struggle to love God by showing it to be a moment in God's own life.

This essay began with the observation that theodicy of the standard philosophical sort has little to say to those experiencing existential suffering and hiddenness. As Mariani observes, Hopkins spent his life developing a theodicy and poetics that would be true not only to his mind but also his heart. I have argued that this "theodicy," if that is the right title for it, is not the sort philosophers have commonly sought to articulate, and as a consequence might prove to be a more productive response to the existential problem. Hopkins's is a practical theodicy lyrically expressed. One that speaks out of and therefore into the intensity of existential suffering without attempting to explain it away. Like the prophets and poets of the scripture, he renders the problem in the form of lamentation. I have argued that Hopkins's poems of existential suffering, such as "Thou art indeed just" and "Carrion Comfort," effect identification with the speaker that has the potential to yield solidarity and strength by bringing readers into the suffering speaker's position to cry out against God. When Jesus's own experience of existential suffering is considered, the cry against God may be understood to be uttered by God, effecting a union in such suffering that is potentially redemptive.[59] The poems redeem, I think, in the same way Christ is said to redeem, by entering into and acknowledging the horror and confusion that are perhaps ineradicable elements of the human condition.[60] To enter and acknowledge this condition, however, is not to explain it away or to justify it. Lyric, specifically, lyric of Hopkins's sort, informed by the biblical tradition of lament and incarnation, then, offers a means of encountering the inscrutable face of God even in the darkness of God's appalling absence.

[59] Sobolev rejects the possibility of a redemptive reading of Hopkins's dark sonnets, arguing instead that they contain an irreducible tension between orthodox and heterodox elements (cf. 2011, 263–76). As I suggest, the very tension Sobolev rightly identifies is what gives these poems redemptive potential. Acknowledging the vertiginous position of one who experiences suffering, the poems make space for this experience within the struggle to find and follow God.
[60] Marilyn McCord Adams's notion of horror captures this aspect of the human condition and its implications for Christology and the problem of evil; see Adams (2006).

References

Abbott, C. C., ed. 1955. *The Correspondence of Gerard Manley Hopkins and Richard Watson Dixon*, rev. edn. (Oxford University Press).

Acar, R. 2004. "Reconsidering Avicenna's Position on God's Knowledge of Particulars," in J. McGinnis (ed.), *Interpreting Avicenna: Science and Philosophy in Medieval Islam* (Leiden: Brill), 142–56.

Adams, Marilyn. 1999. *Horrendous Evils and the Goodness of God* (Ithaca: Cornell University Press).

2006. *Christ of Horrors* (New York: Cambridge University Press).

Adams, Robert M. 1987. *The Virtue of Faith* (New York: Oxford University Press).

Adamson, P. 2005. "On Knowledge of Particulars," *Proceedings of the Aristotelian Society*, 105, 273–94.

Aijaz, I. 2008. "Belief, Providence and Eschatology: Some Philosophical Problems in Islamic Theism," *Philosophy Compass*, 3/1, 231–53.

Ainsworth, M. 1979. "Infant–Mother Attachment," *American Psychologist*, 34, 932–7.

Al-Fārābī. 1964. *al-Siyāsa l-madaniyya l-mulaqqab bi-mabādi᾽ al-mawjūdāt*, ed. F. Najjār (Beirut: Imprimerie Catholique); translated in McGinnis and Reisman, 81–104.

1985. *On the Perfect State (Mabādi᾽ ār᾽ā ahl al-madīnat al-fāḍilah)*, ed. and trans. R. Walzer (Oxford University Press; reprinted KAZI Publications).

Al-Ghazālī. 1992.*The Ninety-Nine Beautiful Names of God*, trans. D. Burrell and N. Daher (Cambridge: The Islamic Text Society).

2000. *The Incoherence of the Philosophers*, trans. M. E. Marmura, 2nd edn. (Provo, UT: Brigham Young University Press).

Al-Sijistānī. 1974. "On the Proper Perfection of the Human Species," in ῾A. R. Badawī (ed.), *Muntakhab Ṣiwān al-ḥikma* (Tehran: Bunyād-yi Farhang-yi Īran); translated in McGinnis and Reisman, 139–45.

Alston, William P. 1989. "Referring to God," in *Divine Nature and Human Language: Essays in Philosophical Theology* (Ithaca: Cornell University Press), 103–17.

1991. *Perceiving God: The Epistemology of Religious Experience* (Ithaca, NY: Cornell University Press).

Alter, Robert. 2010. *The Wisdom Books* (New York: W. W. Norton).

Anonymous. 1981. *The Cloud of Unknowing*, trans. James Walsh (New York: Paulist Press).

Augustine, Saint. 1961. *Confessions*, trans. R. S. Pine-Coffin (London: Penguin).

1991. *Sermons III (51–94) on the New Testament*, ed. John E. Rotelle, trans. Edmund Hill (Brooklyn, NY: New City Press).

1997. *On Christian Teaching* (Oxford University Press).

Averroes. 2001. *Decisive Treatise & Epistle Dedicatory*, ed. and trans. C. E. Butterworth (Provo, UT: Brigham Young University Press).

Avicenna. 1894. "Risāla fī l-ʿishq," in M. A. F. Mehren (ed.), *Traités mystiques* (Leiden: Brill), 3rd fascicle, pp. 1–28; English trans. in Fackenheim; French translation in Sabri.

1959. *Avicenna's De Anima (Arabic Text), Being the Psychological Part of Kitāb al-Shifāʾ* (Oxford University Press); relevant passages translated in McGinnis and Reisman, 175–209.

1963. *Kitāb al-ḥudūd (Book of Definitions)*, ed. and trans. A.-M. Goichon in *Livre des définitions* (Cairo: Publications de l'Institute Français d'Archéologie Orientale de Caire); English trans. in K. Kennedy-Day, *Books of Definition in Islamic Philosophy* (London and New York: RoutledgeCurzon, 2003).

1964. "Risāla fī l-ʿišq," in M. Soreth, "Text- und quellenkritische Bemerkungen zu Ibn Sīnā's Risāla fī l-ʿišq," *Oriens*, 17, 118–31.

1985. *al-Najāt*, ed. M. Dānishpāzhūh (Tehran: Dānishgāh-yi Tihrān).

2005. *The Metaphysics of The Healing*, ed. and trans. M. E. Marmura, Islamic Translation Series (Provo, UT: Brigham Young University Press).

2009. *The Physics of The Cure*, ed. Jon McGinnis, 2 vols. (Provo, UT: Brigham Young Press).

2013. *al-Taʿlīqāt*, ed. S. H. Mousavian (Tehran: Iranian Institute of Philosophy).

Avineri, Shlomo. 1984. "Fossil and Phoenix: Hegel and Krochmal," in Robert Perkins (ed.), *History and System: Hegel's Philosophy of History* (New York: SUNY Press), 47–64.

Azadegan, E. 2013. "Ibn ʿArabī on the Problem of Divine Hidenness," *Journal of the Muhyiddin Ibn ʿArabi Society*, 53, 49–67.

Babb, L. A. 1981. "Glancing: Visual Interaction in Hinduism," *Journal of Anthropological Research*, 37, 387–401.

Band, Arnold J. 1978. *The Tales* (Mahwah, NJ: Paulist Press).

Barber, C. 2011. "On Connectedness: Spirituality on the Autistic Spectrum," *Practical Theology*, 4, 201–11.

Baron-Cohen, S., Bolton, P., Wheelwright, S., Scahill, V., Short, L., Mead, G., and Smith, A. 1998. "Autism Occurs More Often in Families of Physicists, Engineers, and Mathematicians," *Autism*, 2, 296–301.

Barrett, Justin L. 2004. *Why Would Anyone Believe in God?* (New York: Altamira Press).

2012. *Born Believers: The Science of Children's Religious Beliefs* (New York: Free Press).

Barth, Karl. 1957. *Church Dogmatics*, vol. II, part 1: *The Doctrine of God*, ed. G. W. Bromiley and T. F. Torrance, trans. T. H. L. Parker and J. L. M. Haire (London: T&T Clark).

Bavinck, Hermann. 2004. *Reformed Dogmatics, vol. II: God and Creation* (Grand Rapids, MI: Baker Academic).

Belo, C. 2007. *Chance and Determinism in Avicenna and Averroes* (Leiden: Brill).

Bergmann, Michael. 2001. "Skeptical Theism and Rowe's New Evidential Argument from Evil," *Noûs* 35 (2), 278–96.

Bering, J. M. 2006. "The Folk Psychology of Souls," *Behavioral and Brain Sciences*, 29, 453–62.

Berryman, John. 1989. *John Berryman: Collected Poems 1937–1971*, ed. Charles Thornbury (New York: Farrar Strauss and Giroux).

Bloom, P. 2007. "Religion Is Natural," *Developmental Science*, 10, 147–51.

Bouchard, Gary. 1999. "The Curious Case of Robert Southwell, Gerard Hopkins and a Princely Spanish Hawk," *Renascence* 51 (3): 181–9.

Bourget, David and Chalmers, David J. 2013. "What Do Philosophers Believe?," *Philosophical Studies*, 168, 1–36.

Bowlby, J. 1969. *Attachment and Loss*, vol. I (New York: Basic Books).

Bradley, Ian. 1995. *The Power of Sacrifice* (London: Darton, Longman, and Todd).

Brueggemann, Walter. 1994. "Theodicy in a Social Dimension," in P. D. Miller (ed.), *A Social Reading of the Old Testament* (Minneapolis: Fortress Press), 174–96.

　1995. "The Costly Loss of Lament," in P. D. Miller (ed.), *The Psalms and the Life of Faith* (Minneapolis: Fortress Press), 98–111.

　2002. *Theological Reverberations of Faith* (Louisville: Westminster/John Knox Press).

Buckley, Michael, S. J. 1979. "Atheism and Contemplation," *Theological Studies*, 40, 680–99.

Burrell, David. 1987. "On Distinguishing God from the World," in Brian Davies (ed.), *Language, Meaning and God: Essays in Honour of Herbert McCabe OP* (London: Geoffrey Chapman), 75–91.

　2008. "Anthropomorphism in Catholic Contexts," in D. Z. Phillips (ed.), *Whose God? Which Tradition? The Nature of Belief in God* (Aldershot: Ashgate), 129–36.

Bynum, Caroline Walker. 1982. "Jesus as Mother and Abbot as Mother: Some Themes in Twelfth-Century Cistercian Writing," in *Jesus as Mother: Studies in the Spirituality of the High Middle Ages* (Berkeley: University of California Press), 110–69.

Calvin, J. 1559 [1960]. *Institutes of the Christian Religion, trans.* F. L. Battles (Philadelphia: Westminster Press).

Cappelørn, Niels Jørgen, et al. 2011 *Kierkegaard's Journals and Notebooks*, vol. V: *Journals NB6–NB10* (Princeton and Oxford: Princeton University Press).

Cassidy, J. 1994. "Emotion Regulation: Influences of Attachment Relationships," *Monographs of the Society for Research in Child Development*, 59, 228–49.

Cherniss, Harold Fredrik. 1971 [1930]. *The Platonism of Gregory of Nyssa* (New York: Burt Franklin).

Chittick, W. C. 2005. *Ibn 'Arabī: Heir to the Prophets* (Oxford: Oneworld Publications).

Chomsky, Noam. 1975. *Reflections on Language* (New York: Pantheon Books).

Coakley, Sarah. 2009. "Dark Contemplation and Epistemic Transformation: The Analytic Theologian Re-Meets Teresa of Ávila," in Oliver D. Crisp and Michael C. Rea (eds.), *Analytic Theology: New Essays in the Philosophy of Theology* (Oxford University Press), 280–312.

　2013. "Beyond 'Belief': Liturgy and the Cognitive Apprehension of God," in T. Greggs, R. Muers, and S. Zahl (eds.), *The Vocation of Theology Today: A Festschrift for David Ford* (Eugene, OR: Wipf and Stock), 131–45.

Code, L. 1991. *What Can She Know? Feminist Theory and the Construction of Knowledge* (Ithaca: Cornell University Press).

Cohen, E. 2007. *The Mind Possessed: The Cognition of Spirit Possession in an Afro-Brazilian Religious Tradition* (New York: Oxford University Press).

Cohen, L. Jonathan. 1992. *An Essay on Belief and Acceptance* (Oxford: Clarendon Press).

Craig, Edward. 1990. *Knowledge and the State of Nature: An Essay in Conceptual Synthesis* (Oxford University Press).

Daly, Robert J. 2009. *Sacrifice Unveiled: The True Meaning of Christian Sacrifice* (London: T&T Clark).

Davidson, H. 1992. *Alfarabi, Avicenna, and Averroes, on Intellect* (Oxford University Press).

Davies, Brian. 1998. "The Problem of Evil," in B. Davies (ed.), *Philosophy of Religion: A Guide to the Subject* (London: Cassell), 163–201.

2003. "Letter from America," *New Blackfriars*, 84, 371–84.

Dawes, Gregory W. 2013. "Belief is not the Issue: A Defense of Inference to the Best Explanation," *Ratio*, 26, 62–78.

De Cruz, H., and De Smedt, J. 2013a. "Mathematical Symbols as Epistemic Actions," *Synthese*, 190, 3–19.

2013b. "Reformed and Evolutionary Epistemology and the Noetic Effects of Sin," *International Journal for Philosophy of Religion*, 74, 49–66.

Dennett, Daniel. 2006. *Breaking the Spell: Religion as a Natural Phenomenon* (New York: Viking).

Diodorus Siculus. 1939. *Bibliotheca historica*, vol. III, trans. C. H. Oldfather (Cambridge, MA: Harvard University Press).

Donnellan, Keith S. 1966. "Reference and Definite Descriptions," *The Philosophical Review*, 77, 281–304.

Dostoyevsky, Fyodor. 1950 [1890]. *The Brothers Karamazov*, trans. Constance Garnett (New York: Random House/The Modern Library).

Dougherty, Trent. 2012. *New Essays on Skeptical Theism* (Oxford University Press).

Drange, T. M. 1993. "The Argument from Non-Belief," *Religious Studies*, 29, 417–32.

Draper, Paul. 2002. "Seeking But Not Believing: Confessions of a Practicing Agnostic," in Daniel Howard-Snyder and Paul Moser (eds.), *Divine Hiddenness*, 197–214.

Eckhart, Meister. 1957. *An Introduction to the Study of his Works with an Anthology of his Sermons*, trans. James M. Clark (London: Thomas Nelson & Sons).

Eilan, Naomi, Hoerl, Christoph, McCormack, Teresa, and Roessler, Johannes. 2005. *Joint Attention: Communication and Other Minds* (New York: Oxford University Press).

Eisen, R. 1995. *Gersonides on Providence, Covenant, and the Chosen People* (Albany: State University of New York Press).

Endo, Shusaku. 1980 [1966]. *Silence* (Marlboro, NJ: Taplinger).

1988a [1976]. *Watashi No Iesu (My Jesus)* (Tokyo: Kobunsha).

1988b [1983]. *Watashi Ni Totte Kami Towa (What is God for Me)* (Tokyo: Kobunsha).

Erdman, Phyllis, and Kok-Mun, Ng 2010. *Attachment: Expanding the Cultural Connections* (New York: Routledge).

Evans, C. Stephen. 2010.*Natural Signs and Knowledge of God: A New Look at Theistic Arguments* (Oxford University Press).

Evans, Gareth. 1973. "The Causal Theory of Names," *Proceedings of the Aristotelian Society: Supplementary Volume* 47, 187–208.

Fackenheim, Emile. 1973. *Encounters Between Judaism and Modern Philosophy* (New York: Basic Books).

1945. "A Treatise on Love by Ibn Sina," *Medieval Studies*, 7, 208–28.

Fales, Evan. 2005. "The Road to Damascus," *Faith and Philosophy*, 22, 442–59.

2010. *Divine Intervention: Metaphysical and Epistemological Puzzles* (New York: Routledge).

Fantl, Jeremy, and McGrath, Matthew. 2009. *Knowledge in an Uncertain World* (Oxford University Press).

Farroni, T., Johnson, M. H., Menon, E., Zulian, L., Faraguna, D., and Csibra, G. 2005. "Newborns' Preference for Face-Relevant Stimuli: Effects of Contrast Polarity," *Proceedings of the National Academy of Sciences USA*, 102, 17,245–50.

Felderhof, Marius C. 2004. "Evil: Theodicy or Resistance?," *Scottish Journal of Theology*, 57, 397–412.

Ferreira, Cristóvão (Chuan Sawano). 1644. *Kengiroku*.

Fleming, David. 1996. *Draw Me into Your Friendship* (Saint Louis: The Institute for Jesuit Sources).

Flew, Antony. 1955. "Theology and Falsification. A.," in Antony Flew and Alasdair MacIntyre (eds.), *New Essays in Philosophical Theology* (London: S.C.M. Press), 96–9.

Fodor, Jerry. 1983. *The Modularity of Mind* (Cambridge, MA: MIT Press).

Foster, Dom David. 2015. *Contemplative Prayer: A New Framework* (London: Bloomsbury).

Freud, S. 1927. *Die Zukunft einer Illusion* (Leipzig, Vienna, and Zürich: Internationaler Psychoanalytischer Verlag).

Gallagher, Winifred. 2002. *Spiritual Genius: The Mastery of Life's Meaning* (New York: Random House).

Gaon, Saadia. 1880. *Al-Amānāt wa-l-Iʿtiqādāt*, ed. Samuel Landauer (Leiden: Brill).

1948. *The Book of Beliefs and Opinions*, trans. S. Rosenblatt, Yale Judaica Series, vol. I (New Haven, CT: Yale University Press).

Garcia, L. 2002. "St. John of the Cross and the Necessity of Divine Hiddenness," in D. Howard-Snyder and P. K. Moser (eds.), *Divine Hiddenness: New Essays*, 83–98.

Gellman, Jerome. 2013. "Constancy of Faith? Symmetry and Asymmetry in the Kierkegaardian Leap of Faith," in Tamar Aylat-Yaguri and Jon Stewart (eds.), *The Authenticity of Faith in Kierkegaard's Philosophy* (Newcastle: Cambridge Scholars Publishing), 49–60.

Gimaret, D. 1990. *La doctrine d'al-Ashʿari* (Paris: Les Éditions du Cerf).

Goldberg, Sanford. 2007. *Anti-Individualism: Mind and Language, Knowledge and Justification* (Cambridge University Press).

Goss, Erin M. 2011. "'Almost Unmade': Hopkins and the Body Apocalyptic," *Victorian Poetry*, 49/1 (Spring), 83–103.

Gottlieb, A. 2014. "Is it Time to Detach from Attachment Theory? Perspectives from the West African Rain Forest," in H. Otto and H. Keller (eds.), *Different Faces of Attachment: Cultural Variations on a Universal Human Need* (Cambridge University Press), 187–214.

Graham, Peter. In press. "Epistemic Normativity and Social Norms," in John Greco and
    David Henderson (eds.), *Epistemic Evaluation* (Oxford University Press).
Grant, Sara. 2002 [1991]. *Toward an Alternative Theology: Confessions of a Non-Dualist
    Christian* (Notre Dame, IN: University of Notre Dame Press).
Greco, John. 2008. "Friendly Theism," in James Kraft (ed.), *Religious Tolerance
    through Epistemic Humility* (Burlington, VT: Ashgate), 51–60.
    In press. "Testimonial Knowledge and the Flow of Information," in John Greco and
    David Henderson (eds.), *Epistemic Evaluation* (Oxford University Press).
Green, Adam. 2009. "Reading the Mind of God (without Hebrew Lessons): Alston,
    Shared Attention, and Mystical Experience," *Religious Studies*, 45 (4), 455–70.
    2012. "Perceiving Persons," *Journal of Consciousness Studies*, 19, 49–64.
Griffith, S. H. 2013. *The Bible in Arabic, The Scriptures of the "People of the Book" in
    the Language of Islam* (Princeton University Press).
Guthrie, S. E. 1993. *Faces in the Clouds: A New Theory of Religion* (New York and
    Oxford: Oxford University Press).
Hare, R. M. 1955. "Theology and Falsification. B.," in Antony Flew and Alasdair
    MacIntyre (eds.), *New Essays in Philosophical Theology* (London: S.C.M. Press),
    99–103.
Harris, Jay M. 1991. *Nachman Krochmal, Guiding the Perplexed of the Modern Age*
    (New York University Press).
Harris, Paul L., and Koenig, Melissa A. 2007. "The Basis of Epistemic Trust: Reliable
    Testimony or Reliable Sources?," *Episteme*, 4 (3), 264–84.
Hart, David Bentley. 2002. "The Mirror of the Infinite: Gregory of Nyssa on the Vestigia
    Trinitatis," *Modern Theology*, 18, 541–61.
    2003. *The Beauty of the Infinite: The Aesthetics of Christian Truth* (Grand Rapids,
    MI: William B. Eerdmans Publishing Company).
    2013. *The Experience of God: Being, Consciousness, Bliss* (New Haven: Yale
    University Press).
Hawthorne, John. 2004. *Knowledge and Lotteries* (Oxford University Press).
Hector, Kevin. 2011. *Theology without Metaphysics: God, Language and the Spirit of
    Recognition* (Cambridge University Press).
Hegel, G. W. F. 1948a. "The Positivity of the Christian Religion," in *Early Theological
    Writings*, trans. T. M. Knox (Chicago: Harper & Brothers), 67–180.
    1948b. "The Spirit of Christianity," in *Early Theological Writings*, trans. T. M. Knox
    (Chicago: Harper & Brothers), 182–300.
    1984. *Lectures on the Philosophy of Religion*, ed. Peter Hodgson (Oakland: University
    of California Press).
Helm, Paul. 2008. "Anthropomorphism Protestant Style," in D. Z. Phillips (ed.), *Whose
    God? Which Tradition? The Nature of Belief in God* (Aldershot: Ashgate), 137–57.
Heschel, Abraham. 1962. *The Prophets* (New York: Jewish Publication Society).
Hibbs, Darren. 2005. "Was Gregory of Nyssa a Berkeleyan Idealist?," *British Journal
    for the History of Philosophy*, 13, 425–35.
Hick, John. 1966. *Evil and the God of Love*, reissued with new introduction, 2010
    (London: Palgrave Macmillan).
    1982. *God Has Many Names* (Philadelphia: Westminster Press).
    1989. *An Interpretation of Religion: Human Responses to the Transcendent*
    (Basingstoke: Palgrave Macmillan).

2009. "Religious Pluralism and Salvation," in Kevin Timpe (ed.), *Arguing About Religion* (London: Routledge), 57–66.

Hopkins, Gerard Manley. 1955. *The Letters of Gerard Manley Hopkins to Robert Bridges*, ed. C. C. Abbott (Oxford University Press).

1959. *The Sermons and Devotional Writings of Gerard Manley Hopkins*, ed. Christopher Devlin, S.J. (London: Oxford University Press).

1980. *Gerard Manley Hopkins: Selected Prose*, ed. Gerald Roberts (Oxford University Press).

2010. *Gerard Manley Hopkins: The Major Works*, ed. Catherine Philips (New York: Oxford University Press).

Howard-Snyder, Daniel. 1996a. "The Argument from Divine Hiddenness," *Canadian Journal of Philosophy*, 26, 433–53.

1996b. *The Evidential Argument from Evil* (Indiana University Press).

Howard-Snyder, D. and Moser, P. K. (eds.). 2002. *Divine Hiddenness: New Essays* (Cambridge University Press).

Hume, D. 1757 [2007]. "The Natural History of Religion," in T. L. Beauchamp (ed.), *A Dissertation on the Passions: The Natural History of Religion. A Critical Edition* (Oxford: Clarendon Press), 30–87.

Iuculano, T., Rosenberg-Lee, M., Supekar, K., Lynch, C. J., Khouzam, A., Phillips, J., Uddin, L. Q., and Menon, V. 2014. "Brain Organization Underlying Superior Mathematical Abilities in Children with Autism," *Biological Psychiatry*, 75, 223–30.

Jaarsma, P., and Welin, S. 2012. "Autism as a Natural Human Variation: Reflections on the Claims of the Neurodiversity Movement," *Health Care Analysis*, 20, 20–30.

James, William. 1896. "The Will to Believe," *The New World*, 5, 327–47.

Jantzen, Grace. 1987. "Conspicuous Sanctity and Religious Belief," in William J. Abraham and Steven W Holtzer (eds.), *The Rationality of Religious Belief: Essays in Honour of Basil Mitchell* (New York: Clarendon Press), 121–40.

John of the Cross. 1981. *The Collected Works of John of the Cross*, revised edn. trans. Kieran Kavanaugh and Otilio Rodriguez (Washington, D.C.: Institute of Carmelite Publications).

Johnson, Elizabeth A. 1984. "The Incomprehensibility of God and the Image of God as Male and Female," *Theological Studies*, 45 (3),http://search.proquest.com .proxy.library.nd.edu/docview/1297019083/675B1F0BA6EC49A0PQ/4?accoun tid=12874.

Johnston, Mark. 2009. *Saving God: Religion After Idolatry* (Princeton University Press).

Jones, Henry. 1905. *The Immortality of the Soul in the Poems of Tennyson and Browning* (London: Philip Green).

Kavanaugh, Kieran (ed.). 1988. *John of the Cross: Selected Writings*, new edn. (New York: Paulist Press).

Keating, S. T. 2006. *Defending the "People of Truth" in the Early Islamic Period: The Christian Apologies of Abū Rā'iṭah* (Leiden: Brill).

Keating, Thomas. 1995. *Intimacy with God* (New York: Crossroad).

Kelemen, D. 2004. "Are Children 'Intuitive Theists'? Reasoning about Purpose and Design in Nature," *Psychological Science*, 15, 295–301.

Kennedy, G. E. 2005. "From the Ape's Dilemma to the Weanling's Dilemma: Early Weaning and its Evolutionary Context," *Journal of Human Evolution*, 48, 123–45.

Kerr, Fergus. 2004. "God in the Summa Theologiae: Entity or Event?," in Jeremiah Hackett and Jerald Wallulis (eds.), *Philosophy of Religion for a New Century: Essays in Honor of Eugene Thomas Long* (Dordrecht: Kluwer Academic), 63–79.

Kierkegaard, Soren. 1972. *Philosophical Fragments* (Princeton University Press).

Kirkpatrick, L. A. 1999. "Toward an Evolutionary Psychology of Religion and Personality," *Journal of Personality*, 67, 921–52.

  2005. *Attachment, Evolution, and the Psychology of Religion* (New York: Guilford Press).

Kirkpatrick, L. A., and Shaver, P. R. 1990. "Attachment Theory and Religion: Childhood Attachments, Religious Beliefs, and Conversion," *Journal for the Scientific Study of Religion*, 29, 315–34.

Konvalinka, I., Xygalatas, D., Bulbulia, J., Schjødt, U., Jegindø, E.-M., Wallot, S., Van Orden, G., and Roepstorff, A. 2011. "Synchronized Arousal between Performers and Related Spectators in a Fire-Walking Ritual," *Proceedings of the National Academy of Sciences USA*, 108, 8,514–19.

Kripke, Saul. 1977. "Speaker's Reference and Semantic Reference," *Midwest Studies in Philosophy*, 255–76.

  1980. *Naming and Necessity* (Cambridge: Harvard University Press).

Kvanvig, Jonathan L. 2002. "Divine Hiddenness: What is the Problem?," in Daniel Howard-Snyder and Paul K. Moser (eds.), *Divine Hiddenness: New Essays*, 149–63.

Lane, E. W. 1985. *Arabic–English Lexicon* (New Delhi: Asian Educational Services).

Levenson, Jon D. 1993. *The Death and Resurrection of the Beloved Son, the Transformation of Child Sacrifice in Judaism and Christianity* (New Haven and London: Yale University Press).

Levertov, Denise. 1992. *New and Selected Essays* (New York: New Directions).

Lewis, David. 1984. "Putnam's Paradox," *Australasian Journal of Philosophy*, 62 (3), 221–36.

  1999. "New Work for a Theory of Universals," in *Papers in Metaphysics and Epistemology* (Cambridge University Press), 8–55.

Lichtmann, Maria. 1991. "The Incarnational Aesthetic of Gerard Manley Hopkins," *Religion & Literature*, 23 (1), 37–50.

Lobel, D. 2000. *Between Mysticism and Philosophy: Sufi Language of Religious Experience in Judah Ha-Levi's Kuzari* (Albany, NY: State University of New York).

Louth, Andrew. 1981. *The Origins of the Christian Mystical Tradition: From Plato to Denys* (Oxford: Clarendon Press).

McCabe, Herbert. 2002. *God Still Matters*, ed. Brian Davies (London: Continuum).

  2005. *God Matters* (London: Continuum).

McCauley, R. N. 2011. *Why Religion is Natural and Science is not* (Oxford University Press).

McGinn, Colin. 1989. "Can We Solve the Mind–Body Problem?," *Mind*, 98, 349–66.

McGinnis, J. 2010. *Avicenna*, Great Medieval Thinkers Series (Oxford University Press).

McGinnis, J., and Reisman, D. C. 2007. *Classical Arabic Philosophy* (Indianapolis and Cambridge: Hackett Publishing Company, Inc.).

Mackie, J. L. 1955. "Evil and Omnipotence," *Mind*, 64 (254), 200–12.

Mackintosh, H. R. 1912. *The Doctrine of the Person of Jesus Christ* (Edinburgh: T&T Clark).

Maimonides. 1980. *Dalālat al-ḥā'irīn* (*Guide for the Perplexed*), ed. H. Ātāy (Cairo: Maktabat al-Thaqāfa al-Dīnīya).

    1963. *The Guide of the Perplexed*, trans. S. Pines, 2 vols. (University of Chicago Press).

Maitzen, Stephen. 2006. "Divine Hiddenness and the Demographics of Theism," *Religious Studies*, 42(2), 177–91.

Malhotra, D. 2010. "'Sunday Effect' on Pro-Social Behavior," *Judgment and Decision Making*, 5, 138–43.

Mandolfo, C. 2007. "Psalm 88 and the Holocaust: Lament in Search of a Divine Response," *Biblical Interpretation*, 15, 151–70.

Mariani, Paul. 2008. *Hopkins: A Life* (New York: Viking).

Marion, Jean-Luc. 2002. *Being Given: Toward a Phenomenology of Givenness*, trans. Jeffrey L. Kosky (Stanford University Press).

    2007. "The Banality of Saturation," trans. Jeffrey L. Kosky, in Kevin Hart (ed.), *Counter-Experiences: Reading Jean-Luc Marion* (University of Notre Dame Press), 383–418.

Markov, S. 2012. "Theodor 'Abū Qurra als Nachfolger des Johannes von Damaskus," in A. Speer and P. Steinkrüger (eds.), *Knotenpunkt Byzanz: Wissensformen und kulturelle Wechselbeziehungen* (Berlin: De Gruyter), 111–22.

Marmura, M. E. 1962. "Some Aspects of Avicenna's Theory of God's Knowledge of Particulars," *Journal of the American Oriental Society*, 82, 299–312.

    1975. "Avicenna's Chapter 'On the Relative,' in the *Metaphysics* of the *Shifā'*," in G. F. Hourani (ed.), *Essays on Islamic Philosophy and Science* (Albany: State University of New York Press), 83–99.

Matsuzawa, T. 2009. "The Chimpanzee Mind: In Search of the Evolutionary Roots of the Human Mind," *Animal Cognition*, 12, 1–9.

Matthews, W. R. 1936. "Who is God?," *The Modern Churchman*, 26, 176–82.

Mikulincer, Mario, and Shaver, Philip. 2007. *Attachment in Adulthood* (New York: Guilford Press).

Mirsky, Yehuda. 2014. *Rav Kook: Mystic in a Time of Revolution* (New Haven: Yale University Press).

Mitchell, Basil. 1955. "Theology and Falsification. C.," in Antony Flew and Alasdair MacIntyre (eds.), *New Essays in Philosophical Theology* (London: S.C.M. Press), 103–5.

Miyazaki, Kentaro. 1995. "*Kirishitan No Dan Atsu To Junkyo (Persecutions of Kirishitans and Martyrdom)*," *Nihon Kiristutokyo Souran* (*Handbook of Japanese Christianity*) (Tokyo: Shinjinbutsu Ouraisha).

Mizuno, Y., Takeshita, H., and Matsuzawa, T. 2006. "Behavior of Infant Chimpanzees during the Night in the First 4 Months of Life: Smiling and Suckling in Relation to Behavioral State," *Infancy*, 9, 221–40.

Moltmann, Jürgen. 1981. *The Trinity and the Kingdom* (San Francisco: Harper and Row).

2008. *The Elusive God: Reorienting Religious Epistemology* (New York: Cambridge University Press).

Moser, Paul K. 2002. "Cognitive Idolatry and Divine Hiding," in Daniel Howard-Snyder and Paul K. Moser (eds.), *Divine Hiddenness: New Essays*, 120–48.

2008. *The Elusive God: Reorienting Religious Epistemology* (Cambridge University Press).

2010. *The Evidence for God: Religious Knowledge Reexamined* (Cambridge University Press).

2013a. *The Severity of God* (Cambridge University Press).

2013b. "God and Evidence: A Cooperative Approach," *European Journal for the Philosophy of Religion*, 5, 47–61.

Mother Teresa. 2007. *Come Be My Light: The Private Writings of the Saint of Calcutta*, ed. B. Kolodiejchuk (New York: Doubleday).

Muller, Richard A. 2003. *Post-Reformation Reformed Dogmatics: The Rise and Development of Reformed Orthodoxy, ca. 1520 to ca. 1725*, 2nd edn, vol. III (Grand Rapids, MI: Baker Academic).

Murray, Lynne, and Trevarthan, Colwyn. 1985. "Emotional Regulation of Interactions Between Two-month-olds and Their Mothers," in Tiffany Field and Nathan Fox (eds.), *Social Perception in Infants* (Norwood, NJ: Ablex), 177–97.

Murray, Michael J. 2002. "Deus Absconditus," in D. Howard-Snyder and P. K. Moser (eds.), *Divine Hiddenness: New Essays*, 62–82.

Nagel, Thomas. 1997. *The Last Word* (New York: Oxford University Press).

Nettle, D., Nott, K., and Bateson, M. 2012. "'Cycle Thieves, We Are Watching You': Impact of a Simple Signage Intervention against Bicycle Theft," *PloS One*, 7, e51738.

Noffke, Jacqueline, and Hall, Todd. 2007. "Attachment Psychotherapy and God Image," in Glendon Moriarty and Louis Hoffman (eds.), *God Image Handbook for Spiritual Counseling and Psychotherapy* (Philadelphia, PA: Haworth Press).

Norenzayan, A. 2013. *Big Gods: How Religion Transformed Cooperation and Conflict* (Princeton University Press).

Norenzayan, A., and Gervais, W. M. 2013. "The Origins of Religious Disbelief," *Trends in Cognitive Sciences*, 17, 20–5.

Norenzayan, A., Gervais, W. M., and Trzesniewski, K.H. 2012. "Mentalizing Deficits Constrain Belief in a Personal God," *PLoS One*, 7, e36880.

Nowak, M. A. 2006. "Five Rules for the Evolution of Cooperation," *Science*, 314, 1560–3.

Nussbaum, Martha. 1986. *The Fragility of Goodness* (New York: Cambridge University Press).

Payne, S. 1990. *John of the Cross and the Cognitive Value of Mysticism: An Analysis of Sanjuanist Teaching and its Philosophical Implications for Contemporary Discussions of Mystical Experience* (Dordrecht: Kluwer).

Peckham, John. 2015. *The Concept of Divine Love in the Context of the God–World Relationship* (New York: Peter Lang).

Phillips, D. Z. 2004. *Problem of Evil and the Problem of God* (London: SCM Press).

2008. *Whose God? Which Tradition? The Nature of Belief in God* (Aldershot: Ashgate).

Plantinga, Alvin. 1974. *God, Freedom, and Evil* (Grand Rapids, MI: Eerdmans).

2000. *Warranted Christian Belief* (Oxford University Press).

Poston, Ted, and Dougherty, Trent. 2007. "Divine Hiddenness and the Nature of Belief," *Religious Studies*, 43, 183–98.

Pseudo-Dionysius. 1987. *Pseudo-Dionysius: The Complete Works*, trans. Colm Luibheid (New York: Paulist Press).

Purzycki, B. G. 2013. "The Minds of Gods: A Comparative Study of Supernatural Agency," *Cognition*, 129, 163–79.

Quinn, Philip L. 1989. "Tragic Dilemmas, Suffering Love, and Christian Life," *Journal of Religious Ethics*, 17, 151–83.

Randolph-Seng, B., and Nielsen, M. E. 2007. "Honesty: One Effect of Primed Religious Representations," *International Journal for the Psychology of Religion*, 17, 303–15.

Rea, Michael. 2009. "Narrative, Liturgy, and the Hiddenness of God," in K. Timpe (ed.), *Metaphysics and God: Essays in honor of Eleonore Stump* (New York: Routledge), 76–96.

  2011. "Divine Hiddenness, Divine Silence," In Louis Pojman and Michael Rea (eds.), *The Philosophy of Religion: An Anthology*, 6th edn. (Boston: Wadsworth/ Cengage), 266–75.

Reddy, Vasudevi. 2003. "On Being the Object of Attention: Implications for Self–Other Consciousness," *Trends in Cognitive Sciences*, 7, 397–402.

  2008. *How Infants Know Minds* (Cambridge, MA: Harvard University Press).

Rezendes, Michael, Caroll, Matt, and Pfeiffer, Sacha. 2002. "Clergy Sex Abuse Crisis," *The Boston Globe*, January 6. Available at http://www.bostonglobe.com/metro/ specials/clergy.

Richardson, Alan. 1958. *An Introduction to the Theology of the New Testament* (London: SCM Press).

Ricoeur, Paul. 1995. *Figuring the Sacred: Religion, Narrative and Imagination*, trans. David Pellauer, ed. Mark I. Wallace (Minneapolis: Fortress Press).

Robinson, H. Wheeler. 1942. *Redemption and Revelation* (London: Nisbet).

Rodriguez, Otilio, and Kavanaugh, Kieran (trans.). 1980. *Collected Works of St. Teresa of Avila*, vol. II, 1st edn. (Washington, D.C.: ICS Publications).

Roes, F. L., and Raymond, M. 2003. "Belief in Moralizing Gods," *Evolution and Human Behavior*, 24, 126–35.

Rossano, M. J. 2010. *Supernatural Selection: How Religion Evolved* (Oxford University Press).

Rowe, William L. 1979. "The Problem of Evil and Some Varieties of Atheism," *American Philosophical Quarterly*, 16 (4), 335–41.

Rufus, A. and McGinnis, J. 2015. "Willful Understanding: Avicenna's Philosophy of Action and Theory of the Will," *Archiv für Geschichte der Philosophie*, 97, 160–95.

Russell, Bertrand. 1903. "A Free Man's Worship," in *Mysticism and Logic* (New York: Doubleday), 46–57.

Russell, Bertrand and Copleston, F. C. 1964. "A Debate on the Existence of God," in John Hick (ed.), *The Existence of God* (New York: Macmillan), 167–91.

Ryle, Gilbert. 1963. *The Concept of Mind* (Harmondsworth: Penguin).

Sabri, T. 1993/4. "Risāla fi l-ʿišq, Le traité sur l'amour d'Avicenne," *Revue des études islamiques*, 61/2, 175–220.

Sanderson, S. K., and Roberts, W. W. 2008. "The Evolutionary Forms of the Religious Life: A Cross-Cultural, Quantitative Analysis," *American Anthropologist*, 110, 454–66.

Sargant, William. 1974. *The Mind Possessed: A Physiology of Possession, Mysticism, and Faith Healing* (Philadelphia, PA: J. B. Lippincott).

Schellenberg, J. L. 1993. *Divine Hiddenness and Human Reason* (Ithaca, NY: Cornell University Press).

1996. "Response to Howard-Snyder," *Canadian Journal of Philosophy*, 26, 455–62.

2002. "What the Hiddenness of God Reveals: A Collaborative Discussion," in Daniel Howard-Snyder and Paul K. Moser (eds.), *Divine Hiddenness: New Essays*, 33–61.

2004. "Divine Hiddenness Justifies Atheism," in Michael J. Peterson and Raymond J. Vanarragon (eds.), *Contemporary Debates in Philosophy of Religion* (Oxford and Cambridge, MA: Blackwell), 30–41.

2005a. "The Hiddenness Argument Revisited (I)," *Religious Studies*, 41, 201–15.

2005b. "The Hiddenness Argument Revisited (II)," *Religious Studies*, 41, 287–303.

2005c. *Prolegomena to a Philosophy of Religion* (Ithaca, NY: Cornell University Press).

2006. *Divine Hiddenness and Human Reason, with new preface*, Cornell Studies in the Philosophy of Religion (Ithaca, NY: Cornell University Press).

2007. *The Wisdom to Doubt: A Justification of Religious Skepticism* (Ithaca, NY: Cornell University Press).

2010. "The Hiddenness Problem and the Problem of Evil," *Faith and Philosophy*, 27, 41–57.

In press. "Evil, Hiddenness, and Atheism," in Paul Moser and Chad Meister (eds.), *The Cambridge Companion to the Problem of Evil (Cambridge University Press)*.

Schjoedt, U., Stødkilde-Jørgensen, H., Geertz, A. W., and Roepstorff, A. 2009. "Highly Religious Participants Recruit Areas of Social Cognition in Personal Prayer," *Social Cognitive and Affective Neuroscience*, 4, 199–207.

Searle, John R. 1958. "Proper Names," *Mind*, 67, 166–73.

Seemann, Axel. 2011. *Joint Attention: New Developments in Psychology, Philosophy of Mind, and Social Neuroscience* (Cambridge, MA: MIT Press).

Shariff, A. F., and Norenzayan, A. 2007. "God is Watching: Priming God Concepts Increases Prosocial Behavior in an Anonymous Economic Game," *Psychological Science*, 18, 803–9.

2011. "Mean Gods Make Good People: Different Views of God Predict Cheating Behavior," *International Journal for the Psychology of Religion*, 21, 85–96.

Shariff, A. F., Norenzayan, A., and Henrich, J. 2010. "The Birth of High Gods: How the Cultural Evolution of Supernatural Policing Influenced the Emergence of Complex, Cooperative Human Societies, Paving the Way for Civilization," in M. Schaller, A. Norenzayan, S. J. Heine, T. Yamagishi, and T. Kameda (eds.), *Evolution, Culture, and the Human Mind* (New York and London: Psychology Press), 179–95.

Shariff, A. F., and Rhemtulla, M. 2012. "Divergent Effects of Beliefs in Heaven and Hell on National Crime Rates," *PloS One*, 7, e39048.

Sider, Theodore. 2011. *Writing the Book of the World* (Oxford University Press).

Sijistānī. 1974. *Muntakhab ṣiwān al-ḥikma*, ed. ʿAbd al-Raḥman Badawī (Tehran: Bunyād-yi Farhang-i Īran).

Sobolev, D. 2011. *The Split World of Gerard Manley Hopkins* (Washington, D.C.: Catholic University Press).

Sorabji, Richard. 1983. *Time, Creation and the Continuum: Theories in Antiquity and the Early Middle Ages* (London: Duckworth).

Spikins, P. 2009. "Autism, the Integrations of 'Difference' and the Origins of Modern Human Behaviour," *Cambridge Archaeological Journal*, 19, 179–201.

Staal, H. 1983–4. *Mt. Sinai Arabic Codex 151, Scriptores Arabici*, vols. XL–XLIII, Corpus Scriptorum Christianorum Orientalium, vols. CCCCLII–CCCCLIII, CCCCLXII–CCCCLXIII (Louvain: Peeters).

Stanley, Jason. 2005. *Knowledge and Practical Interests* (Oxford University Press).

Strawson, Peter F. 1952. "Dissolving the Problem of Induction," in *Introduction to Logical Theory* (London: Methuen and Company), ch. 9.

2010. *Wandering in Darkness: Narrative and the Problem of Suffering* (Oxford University Press).

Stump, Eleonore. 1979. "Petitionary Prayer," *American Philosophical Quarterly*, 16, 81–91.

2010. *Wandering in Darkness: Narrative and the Problem of Suffering* (Oxford: Clarendon Press).

2011a. "Eternity, Simplicity, and Presence," in Gregory T. Doolan (ed.), *The Science of Being as Being: Metaphysical Investigations* (Washington, DC: Catholic University of America Press), 243–63.

2011b. "The Non-Aristotelian Character of Aquinas's Ethics: Aquinas on the Passions," *Faith and Philosophy*, 28, 29–43.

2012. "God's Simplicity," in Brian Davies and Eleonore Stump (eds.), *The Oxford Handbook of Aquinas* (Oxford University Press), 135–46.

Sullivan, Meghan. 2012. "Semantics for Blasphemy," *Oxford Studies in Philosophy of Religion*, 4, 159–73.

2014. "Uneasy Grace," *First Things*, 47–51.

Swinburne, Richard. 1979. *The Existence of God* (Oxford: Clarendon Press).

1998. *Providence and the Problem of Evil* (Oxford: Clarendon Press).

Taylor, John V. 1992. *The Christlike God* (London: SCM Press).

Taylor, Vincent. 1937. *Jesus and his Sacrifice* (London: Macmillan).

Thielicke, Helmut. 1961. *How the World Began*, trans. J. W. Doberstein (Philadelphia: Muhlenberg).

1962. *Out of the Depths*, trans. G. W. Bromiley (Grand Rapids: Eerdmans).

Tilley, Terence W. 1991. *The Evils of Theodicy* (Washington, D.C.: Georgetown University Press).

Tomonaga, M., Tanaka, M., Matsuzawa, T., Myowa-Yamakoshi, M., Kosugi, D., Mizuno, Y., Okamoto, S., Yamaguchi, M. K., and Bard, K. A. 2004. "Development of Social Cognition in Infant Chimpanzees (*Pan troglodytes*): Face Recognition, Smiling, Gaze, and the Lack of Triadic Interactions," *Japanese Psychological Research*, 46, 227–35.

Turner, Denys. 2002. "How To Be An Atheist," *New Blackfriars*, 83, 317–35.

2004. "On Denying the Right God: Aquinas on Atheism and Idolatry," in Jim Fodor and Frederick Christian Bauerschmidt (eds.), *Aquinas in Dialogue: Thomas for the Twenty-First Century* (Malden, MA: Blackwell), 137–58.

Vallicella, W. F. 2006. "Divine Simplicity," *Stanford Encyclopedia of Philosophy* (first published March 20, 2006; substantive revision July 2, 2010), http://plato.stanford .edu/entries/divine-simplicity/.

Vanhoozer, Kevin. 2010. *Remythologizing Theology: Divine Action, Passion, and Authorship* (Cambridge University Press).

Van Ijzendoorn, M. H., and Kroonenberg, P.M. 1988. "Cross-Cultural Patterns of Attachment: A Meta-Analysis of the Strange Situation," *Child Development*, 59, 147–56.

van Inwagen, Peter. 2002. "What is the Problem of the Hiddenness of God," in Daniel Howard-Snyder and Paul Moser (eds.), *Divine Hiddenness*, 24–32.

2006. *The Problem of Evil* (Oxford University Press).

Vendler, Helen. 2010. *Poems, Poets, Poetry: An Introduction and Anthology*, 3rd edn. (Boston: St. Martins).

Vermes, G., 1973. "Redemption and Genesis XXII," in *Scripture and Tradition in Judaism: Haggadic Studies* (Leiden: E. J. Brill), 193–227.

Ward, Keith. 1992. "Is God a Person?," in Gijsbert van den Brink, Luco J. van den Brom, and Marcel Sarot (eds.), *Christian Faith and Philosophical Theology: Essays in Honour of Vincent Brümmer* (Kampen, The Netherlands: Kok Pharos), 258–66.

Weber, C. 2011. *Surprised by Oxford: A Memoir* (Nashville: Thomas Nelson).

Widdicombe, Peter. 1994. *The Fatherhood of God from Origen to Athanasius* (New York: Clarendon Press).

Wiesel, Elie. 1976. "Job: Our Contemporary," in *Messengers of God: Biblical Portraits and Legends*, trans. Marion Wiesel (New York: Summit Books), 211–36.

Williams, A. N. 2014. "The Doctrine of God in San Juan de La Cruz," *Modern Theology*, 30 (October), 500–24.

Williams, Rowan. 1996. "Redeeming Sorrows," in D. Z. Phillips (ed.), *Religion and Morality* (London: Macmillan), 132–48.

2005. "Of Course This Makes Us Doubt God's Existence," *The Telegraph*, January 2.

2007. " 'Religious Realism': On Not Quite Agreeing with Don Cupitt," in Mike Higton (ed.), *Wrestling with Angels: Conversations in Modern Theology* (Grand Rapids: William B. Eerdmans Publishing Company), 3–24.

Williamson, Timothy. 2000. *Knowledge and its Limits* (Oxford University Press).

Wiman, Christian. 2013. *My Bright Abyss* (New York: Farrar, Strauss, and Giroux).

Wolterstorff, Nicholas. 2009. "How Philosophical Theology Became Possible within the Analytic Tradition of Philosophy," in Oliver D. Crisp and Michael C. Rea (eds.), *Analytic Theology: New Essays in the Philosophy of Theology* (Oxford University Press), 155–69.

2015. "Would You Stomp on a Picture of Your Mother? Would You Kiss an Icon?," *Faith and Philosophy*, 32, 3–24.

Wood, Edwin J. 1968. "Isaac Typology in the New Testament," *New Testament Studies*, 14, 583–9.

Wynn, Mark R. 2013. *Renewing the Senses: A Study of the Philosophy and Theology of the Spiritual Life* (Oxford University Press).

Yamamoto, Hirofumi. 2009. *Junkyo: Nihonjin Wa Nani Wo Shinkou Shita Ka (Martyrdom: What did the Japanese Believed?)* (Tokyo: Kobunsha).

Yovel, Yirmiyahu. 1976. "Hegel's Concept of Religion and Judaism as the Religion of Sublimity" (Hebrew), *Tarbiz*, 45, 303–26.

Zuckerman, Philip. 2007. "Atheism: Contemporary Numbers and Patterns," in M. Martin (ed.), *The Cambridge Companion to Atheism* (Cambridge University Press), 47–65.

2009. "Atheism, Secularity, and Well-Being: How the Findings of Social Science Counter Negative Stereotypes and Assumptions," *Sociology Compass*, 3 (6), 949–71, 10.1111/j.1751-9020.2009.00247.x.

2012. "Contrasting Irreligious Orientation: Atheism and Secularity in the USA and Scandinavia," *Approaching Religion*, 2, 8–20.

Index

CPSIA information can be obtained
at www.ICGtesting.com
Printed in the USA
LVOW13s2009070318

569004LV00012B/177/P